CRITICAL SURVEY OF POETRY

Poets of Jewish Culture

Editor

Rosemary M. Canfield Reisman
Charleston Southern University

SALEM PRESS
A Division of EBSCO Publishing, Ipswich, Massachusetts

Cover photo:
Allen Ginsberg (© Lynn Goldsmith/Corbis)

ISBN: 978-1-42983-663-0

CONTENTS

CONTRIBUTORS

Lowell A. Bangerter
University of Wyoming

David Barratt
Montreat College

Franz G. Blaha
*University of Nebraska-
Lincoln*

Steven Brown
*University of Rhode Island,
Kingston*

Mary Hanford Bruce
Monmouth College

Edward Butscher
Briarwood, New York

Anita Price Davis
Converse College

Desiree Dreeuws
Sunland, California

Doris Earnshaw
*University of California,
Davis*

Thomas L. Erskine
Salisbury University

Jack Ewing
Boise, Idaho

Kenneth E. Gadomski
University of Delaware

Michael Heller
Stuyvesant Station, New York

Sarah Hilbert
Pasadena, California

Jeffrey D. Hoeper
Arkansas State University

Tracy Irons-Georges
Glendale, California

Maura Ives
Texas A&M University

Philip K. Jason
*United States Naval
Academy*

Jeffry Jensen
Pasadena, California

Sheila Golburgh Johnson
Santa Barbara, California

Leslie Ellen Jones
Pasadena, California

Rebecca Kuzins
Pasadena, California

Leon Lewis
*Appalachian State
University*

Michael Paul Novak
Saint Mary College

Norman Prinsky
Augusta State University

David Rigsbee
Virginia Tech

Helene M. Kastinger Riley
Clemson University

Kathy Rugoff
*University of North
Carolina-Wilmington*

Jay Ruud
Northern State University

Stephanie Sandler
Amherst College

Steven P. Schultz
*Loyola University of
Chicago*

R. Baird Shuman
*University of Illinois at
Urbana-Champaign*

Linda Simon
Atlanta, Georgia

Karen F. Stein
University of Rhode Island

POETRY OF JEWISH WORLD CULTURE

Ancient Hebrew literature speaks to a long history of hardship and the desire to settle in a Jewish homeland. Over the centuries, Jewish poets have found themselves wandering far and wide, both literally and metaphorically. Poems written for the liturgy in ancient Palestine would later help to nurture the flowering of medieval poetry. During the Middle Ages, there was an extraordinary rekindling of Hebrew poetry, and thousands of the poems written during the medieval period found their way into the Jewish liturgy. This was possible because there already was a tradition established for the kind of poem that fit into the religious realm. Such a tradition did not exist when it came to writing for the secular world.

Taking inspiration from the Bible and Arabic literature, Hebrew poetry eventually expanded into more popular themes of love and wine. Hebrew poets of the Middle Ages were also influenced by European forms of poetry such as the sonnet. Meter and rhyme schemes became more sophisticated in the hands of these newly emboldened poets. Some of this new, livelier verse was composed in Spain and Italy, where it became common for the same poet to write both doggerel and deeply philosophical verse, a poetic dexterity that was not as evident in the northern areas of Europe. The poets Samuel ha-Nagid and Solomon ibn Gabirol wrote extraordinary secular and religious poetry during the eleventh century in Spain. Of all the Hebrew poets from Spain, the one who stands out as the greatest is Judah ha-Levi. He wrote with deep intensity about the things of God as well as the things of man. He believed in rejoicing and being a positive force.

POETRY OF CONVICTION

The Jewish Enlightenment, known in Hebrew as the Haskalah, evolved as a movement during the eighteenth and nineteenth centuries. It encouraged European Jews to broaden their interests in the secular world while also increasing their studies of Hebrew literature. Some of the poets who were most active in this movement are Judah Leib Gordon, Isaac Baer Levinsohn, and Constantin Shapiro.

Born in Prussia at the end of the eighteenth century, Heinrich Heine would become a great German lyric poet. In 1827, he published one of his most riveting collections, *Buch der Lieder* (*Book of Songs*, 1856). Because of Prussian anti-Semitism, Heine moved to Paris in the early 1830's, where he died in 1856.

One of the most important Russian poets of the twentieth century is Osip Mandelstam, born in Warsaw, Poland, and educated in St. Petersburg, Russia. His first collection, *Kamen* (*Stone*, 1981), was published in 1913. In 1922, he published the startling collection *Tristia* (English translation, 1973), in which he writes eloquently about the purpose of life itself. Living in Russia during great turmoil and the rise of Joseph Stalin, Mandelstam was faced with issues of personal integrity. He was even so bold as to write a poem that was critical of Stalin. At the end of the poem, known as "Poem no. 286 (on Stalin)," the poet bluntly states:

> He forges decrees like horseshoes—decrees and decrees:
> This one gets it in the balls, that one in the forehead, him right between the eyes.
> Whenever he's got a victim, he glows like a broadchested
> Georgian munching a raspberry.

For this act, Mandelstam was arrested and sent into exile. He suffered from terrible episodes of deep depression but still continued to write. In 1938, he was sentenced to five years in a labor camp. He died in a transit camp near Vladivostok, most likely on December 27, 1938.

Tristan Tzara (born Samuel Rosenstock) and Hugo Ball were two of the principal founders of Dadaism in 1916. This artistic and literary movement rejected everything about traditional bourgeois society, which Tzara held responsible for World War I. He recognized that his Jewishness set him apart, but he was determined to place all of his faith in his own poetic imagination.

Two of the greatest World War I poets were the English poets Isaac Rosenberg and Siegfried Sassoon. Rosenberg's parents had been forced to leave Lithuania by the increasingly common violence against Jews. Both Rosenberg and Sassoon would write haunting poetry about the terrifying nature of trench warfare. Sassoon survived the war, but Rosenberg was killed in 1918.

The poet Karl Kraus, born in Bohemia and educated in Vienna, would go on to satirize much of the liberal intelligentsia of Austria. He had left Judaism by the end of the nineteenth century and went so far as to believe that Jews were in some way responsible for anti-Semitism. He joined the Catholic Church, but in 1922 would turn away from that organization as well. Klaus was known for being a wonderful German stylist, and his lyric poetry was published as *Worte in Versen* in nine volumes between 1916 and 1930.

POETRY AS SHELTER FROM EVERY STORM

In order to escape Romanian anti-Semitism, Irving Layton's Jewish parents moved his family to Canada in 1913. Born Israel Pincu Lazarovitch, the young Layton would grow up poor in Montreal. Unfortunately, anti-Semitism was also a problem in French Canada. Layton published his first volume of poetry in 1945. A prolific poet, he was very forthright about his views on religion, politics, and cultural matters. He had been schooled in the Old Testament and believed in the struggle to make life better, to make it whole.

Itzik Manger was born in 1901 in Czernowitz, then part of the Austro-Hungarian Empire. He began writing Yiddish poetry when he was still a teenager, and also wrote drama, long fiction, and nonfiction. Manger was a master at modernizing biblical stories. Anti-Semitism forced him to leave his home in Warsaw, while his father and younger brother died in concentration camps. He lived in Paris, England, and the United States before finally settling in Israel in 1958. At the time of his death in 1969, Manger was considered to be Israel's national poet.

Another Jewish poet born in Romania and forced to leave his birth country was Paul Celan, born Paul Antschel in 1920. He suffered from anti-Semitism at the Romanian state school that he attended. Celan worked as a field surgeon in a psychiatric unit during World War II, while his parents perished in a concentration camp. Throughout the rest of his life, he felt great guilt for having survived the war, and he drowned in the Seine River in 1970 in what is believed to have been a suicide. Celan's poetry, inspired by the work of the French Symbolists and the German expressionists, is difficult to penetrate. After all that he had endured, language became the only refuge that he had left, and he exhibits this love of language in such collections as *Von Schwelle zu Schwelle* (1955; *From Threshold to Threshold*, 1988), *Sprachgitter* (1959; *Speech-Grille and Other Poems*, 1971; also as *Language Mesh*, 1988), and *Die Niemandsrose* (1963; *The No-one's Rose*, 1988).

Yehuda Amichai was born in Germany in 1924. His Orthodox Jewish family moved to Palestine when he was twelve years old. Amichai published his first Hebrew poetry in the 1950's. Writing in Hebrew provided his poetry a footing in both the ancient biblical tradition and the more modern secular world. Another important Israeli poet is the Romanian-born Holocaust survivor Dan Pagis, who endured the horrors of a Ukrainian concentration camp and went on to write harrowing poetry about the unspeakable experiences of his youth.

Jewish poets have had to endure hatred from the outside world as well as within their own hearts. Whether schooled in Hebrew, Yiddish, or some other European tongue, they have tried to exist as the sum of many parts. Through it all, these poets have taken refuge in the power of words and worked to construct a future on their own terms.

Jeffry Jensen

BIBLIOGRAPHY

Bradshaw, Ross. "Different Passengers: Jews and Poetry." *European Judaism* 37, no. 2 (Autumn, 2004): 68-77. An examination of the diversity that exists among Jewish poets.

Gubar, Susan. *Poetry After Auschwitz: Remembering What One Never Knew.* Bloomington: Indiana University Press, 2003. Explores how poets can be witnesses to great horror without becoming overly grotesque or maudlin.

Kerbel, Sorrel, ed. *Jewish Writers of the Twentieth Century.* New York: Fitzroy Dearborn, 2003. Includes many entries on Jewish writers, plus some overviews of the different Jewish literatures of the twentieth century.

Lawson, Peter. *Anglo-Jewish Poetry from Isaac Rosenberg to Elaine Feinstein.* Lon-

don: Vallentine Mitchell, 2006. A study into the experience of being a Jewish poet in
    Great Britain.
Wirth-Nesher, Hana, ed. *What Is Jewish Literature?* Philadelphia: Jewish Publication
    Society, 1994. A discussion of how to define Jewish literature.
Yudkin, Leon Israel. *Jewish Writing and Identity in the Twentieth Century.* New York:
    St. Martin's Press, 1982. A critical study of the many identities that simultaneously
    exist in Jewish writing.

POETRY OF JEWISH AMERICAN CULTURE

Historically, immigrant Jewish American poets have combined a deep and abiding devotion to their new home in America with a strong connection to the culture that they brought with them. Coming from Europe in order to escape persecution and to work for a better future in a new land, these poets still remained connected to their faith and heritage. Out of their hardship was shaped a unique Jewish literary tradition, one that respects learning, language, mythology, and family. A rich poetry has emerged from this long tradition.

While Jewish tales, novels, and nonfiction are generally given a favorable reading by scholars and the public alike, the same cannot be said of poetry. It has been said that poetry is a marginal literary form at best, one that does not always present itself as "user friendly." Poetry can be puzzling, provocative, and downright irritating. The scholar Maeera Shrieber has bluntly surmised that poetry is simply too explosive for its own good. The American Language poet Charles Bernstein states that poetry is "an agent of turbulent thought." Jewish American poets have not been deterred, however. They have been active participants in the American dream since their arrival on North American shores, although the first Jewish immigrants were originally unfamiliar or uncomfortable with the English language; they came to America with the sacred language of Hebrew in their hearts and the Yiddish language on their tongues. While new immigrants produced prayers in Hebrew and social commentary in Yiddish, it would take time before the new Jewish American writers could successfully create in their adopted language.

While a Jewish literary tradition can be traced as far back as colonial America, Jewish poetry has a far shorter history. At the time of the American Revolution, less than three thousand Jews were living in the colonies. The great migration of Jews from Europe took place during the late nineteenth and early twentieth centuries. Historical records indicate that Penina Mo{iuml}se's *Fancy's Sketch Book* (1833) is probably the first poetry collection by a Jewish American to be published in the United States. It is Emma Lazarus, however, who must be considered the most important Jewish American poet of the nineteenth century. Her poetry has a richness of spirit and social purpose and serves as a link to the poetry that would be written by Jewish American poets during the coming century.

TIME FOR A NEW LANGUAGE

By the early twentieth century, Jewish American poets had made the English language their own. Charles Reznikoff published his first collection, *Rhythms*, in 1918. It was obvious from this first collection that Reznikoff did not wish to perpetuate the poetic norms of the nineteenth century. His work contained a matter-of-fact realism that was more akin to prose writing than to traditional poetry, and he incorporated much from the immigrant experience into his verse, blending the Bible and immigrant traditions with what he experienced growing up in New York City. He has been grouped with the Objectivists of the 1930's, along with George Oppen, Carl Rakosi, and Louis Zukofsky. For them, everything they wrote about had to be presented as objectively as possible. Even the poem itself became an object.

During the years of the Great Depression, a young Delmore Schwartz wrote with passionate intensity about the gloom that seemed to pervade the times. In his 1938 collection *In Dreams Begin Responsibilities*, he speaks of dreams being dashed by circumstances beyond a person's control. The themes of exile and alienation have been common in much of Jewish American literature, and it is no different for Schwartz. He was born in Brooklyn in 1913 and grew up trying to find his place in America. His parents, immigrants from Eastern Europe, had trouble with the English language. Although he proved his brilliance at an early age, he struggled with personal demons, and tragically died in 1966 after suffering a heart attack. In such poems as "The Heavy Bear Who Goes with Me" and "A Dog Named Ego," the poet speaks of the gap that exists between the spirit and the flesh. For Schwartz, it seems as though the better self inevitably is defeated by the weaker, grotesque self.

While Stanley Kunitz, two-time United States poet laureate, understood that tragedy is an integral part of life, he never fell prey to it or became a victim. As a poet, Kunitz always presented the face of survival. In his examinations of the human experience, he stood firm in his belief that the creative act does make a difference. In one of his most recognized poems, "Father and Son," Kunitz speaks to what maturity really means.

TIME FOR SOMETHING BOLD

Since the 1950's, American poetry has been in the throes of reinventing itself. As one of the leading Beat movement poets, Allen Ginsberg dramatically changed the poetic landscape with the publication of his poem "Howl" in 1956. The poem concerns itself with friends, family, America, the Old Testament, and much more. Ginsberg recognized that he was an outcast in society not only for being a provocative poet but also for being Jewish and gay. In the poem "Kaddish," he examines the reality of his own mother as well as the mythology of the Jewish mother. Other Jewish American poets who have contributed greatly to American poetry include Karl Shapiro, John Hollander, Charles Bernstein, Albert Goldbarth, Anthony Hecht, Howard Nemerov, Philip Levine, Robert Pinsky, and countless others. Each of these poets found their own profound way to incorporate their heritage, their history, and their mythology into the poetry that they have written.

Some of the most inventive and perceptive American poetry has been written by Jewish women. One of the most unique and bold female poets is Gertrude Stein. Ever the experimenter, in art as well as in life, Stein relished the endless possibilities that language provided her. In addition to Stein, several other Jewish American women poets have charted an independent course for themselves, including Muriel Rukeyser, Marilyn Hacker, Denise Levertov, Alicia Suskin Ostriker, Marge Piercy, and Adrienne Rich. Taking inspiration from Allen Ginsberg's poetry of self-exploration, these women have expanded the scope of where poetry can go. For Rich, being Jewish, a feminist, and a lesbian are all part of her poetic mix. It is important for her and other female activist poets to build a language that incorporates all these parts and more. Her 1973 collection *Diving into the Wreck* won the 1974 National Book Award for Poetry. In this volume, Rich alters Western civilization's heroic myth in order to demonstrate that women can be strong and accomplish much on their own.

Jewish American poets continue to probe their past and question how best to use poetry in order to communicate with the larger community. The desire to have poetry connect in a relevant way to as many people as possible across America is what drives most poets. As Philip Levine said after he was named the United States Poet Laureate in 2011, "I want to bring poetry to people who have no idea how relevant poetry is to their lives." This is the American dream for poets who do not believe that alienation is forever.

Jeffry Jensen

BIBLIOGRAPHY

Barron, Jonathan N., and Eric Murphy Selinger, eds. *Jewish American Poetry: Poems, Commentary, and Reflections.* Hanover, N.H.: University Press of New England, 2000. A collection that includes poetry, essays, and the poets' own commentaries and reflections on their work.

Chametzky, Jules, John Felstiner, Hilene Flanzbaum, and Kathryn Hellerstein, eds. *Jewish American Literature: A Norton Anthology.* New York: W. W. Norton, 2001. A compilation of Jewish American literature, featuring several introductions that put the history of this literary tradition into perspective.

Finkelstein, Norman. *Not One of Them in Place: Modern Poetry and Jewish American Identity.* Albany: State University of New York Press, 2001. A concise critical study of the importance of Jewish poets in the development of American poetry.

Pacernick, Gary. *Meaning and Memory: Interviews with Fourteen Jewish Poets.* Columbus: Ohio University Press, 2001. Interviews that get to the heart of what drives these poets.

Shreiber, Maeera Y. *Singing in a Strange Land: A Jewish American Poetics.* Stanford, Calif.: Stanford University Press, 2007. A look at the achievements of Jewish American poets.

Wirth-Nesher, Hana, and Michael P. Kramer, eds. *The Cambridge Companion to Jewish American Literature.* Cambridge, England: Cambridge University Press, 2003. An essay collection that covers several issues crucial to Jewish American literature.

MARVIN BELL

Born: New York, New York; August 3, 1937

PRINCIPAL POETRY

Things We Dreamt We Died For, 1966
A Probable Volume of Dreams, 1969
Escape into You, 1971
Residue of Song, 1974
Stars Which See, Stars Which Do Not See, 1977
These Green-Going-to-Yellow, 1981
Drawn by Stones, by Earth, by Things That Have Been in the Fire, 1984
New and Selected Poems, 1987
Iris of Creation, 1990
The Book of the Dead Man, 1994
A Marvin Bell Reader: Selected Poetry and Poems, 1994
Ardor: The Book of the Dead Man, Volume 2, 1997
Rampant, 2004
Mars Being Red, 2007
Seven Poets, Four Days, One Book, 2009 (with others)

OTHER LITERARY FORMS

Although Marvin Bell published mainly poetry, he wrote essays about poetry in *Old Snow Just Melting: Essays and Interviews* (1983). Bell also collaborated with poet William Stafford on two books, *Segues: A Correspondence in Poetry* (1983) and *Annie-Over* (1988). He also made a sound recording of *The Self and the Mulberry Tree* (1977) for the Watershed Foundation. His poetry has appeared in many anthologies, and in 1998, he published some of his collected poems in *Wednesday: Selected Poems, 1966-1997* in Ireland.

Bell has extensive editing experience, first with *Statements* (1959-1964), which he founded, and later as poetry editor for the *North American Review* (1964-1969) and the *Iowa Review* (1969-1971). Partly because of his long association with the *Iowa Review* and the University of Iowa, he was twice interviewed at length by the editors of the *Iowa Review*: in the winter edition of 1981 and in the fall issue of 2000.

ACHIEVEMENTS

Marvin Bell has steadily acquired critical acclaim. He won the James Laughlin Award from the Academy of American Poets for *A Probable Volume of Dreams* and the Bess Hokin Award from *Poetry* magazine, both in 1969; the Emily Clark Balch Prize from the *Virginia Quarterly Review* in 1970; and the prestigious Literature Award from the American Academy of Arts and Letters in 1994. He was also the recipient of a Guggenheim Fellowship (1976) and National Endowment for the Arts Fellowships (1978 and 1984). He has twice held Senior Fulbright Scholarships (Yugoslavia, 1983; Australia, 1986) and has served as visiting professor at several universities. In 1986, his alma mater, Alfred University, awarded him the Lh.D., and in 2000, he was named the first poet laureate in Iowa; he served two terms.

BIOGRAPHY

Marvin Hartley Bell was born in New York City but spent his childhood in Center Moriches, a small Long Island town sixty miles from Manhattan. His parents, Saul Bell and Belle Bell, were the children of Russian Jews who had emigrated to escape persecution. In his boyhood, Bell played on soccer, baseball, and basketball teams, became a ham radio operator, and played the trumpet in a jazz group. His early writing experience consisted of writing a column about school events for the local weekly newspaper.

After high school, Bell attended Alfred University in upstate New York. There he continued with his trumpet playing in the university orchestra; worked for the yearbook and *Fiat Lux*, the weekly newspaper, which he edited his senior year; and became interested in ceramics and photography. Bell was initially more attracted to journalism than to literature, and when he found appropriate political causes (discriminatory clauses in sororities and fraternities, for example), he wrote and mimeographed an underground newsletter. After graduation from Alfred, Bell enrolled in the graduate journalism school at Syracuse University, where he met Al Sampson, who became a lifelong friend, and Mary (Mickey) Mammosser, who became his first wife. The couple then moved to Rochester, where they founded *Statements*, a journal that enabled them to include both literature and photography.

At the urging of Sampson, who was now studying literature at the University of Chicago, the Bells moved to Chicago in 1958. Bell enrolled in the M.A. program in English at the University of Chicago, continued to publish *Statements* (five issues ultimately appeared), wrote poems, and did still photography. His marriage to Mickey ended after the birth of their son Nathan, who stayed with Bell. He later married Dorothy Murphy, with whom he had another son, Jason, in 1966. Bell comments, "My story since 1960 is forever woven together with the stories of Dorothy, Nathan, and Jason." The three often appear in Bell's poems.

While in Chicago, Bell took a writing seminar with John Logan, who had encouraged Bell to contribute an article and a photograph to *Choice*, which Logan had just founded. When Logan recommended the Writers' Workshop in Iowa, Bell applied for the doctoral program at the University of Iowa and was accepted. Studying with Donald Justice and Paul Engel, Bell writes, "In the midst of a swirl of literary fellowship, I still felt that I was following my own road." Bell, however, left Iowa to go on active duty with the U.S. Army (he had been in the Reserve Officers' Training Corps program at Alfred) in 1965. After his military tour of duty, Bell returned to Iowa City, where he taught with Justice and George Starbuck in the Writers' Workshop. After 1966, when his first volume of poems appeared, Bell published a poetry volume about every three years, while also serving as poetry editor for the *North American Review* (1964-1969) and the *Iowa Review* (1969-1971). He continued to teach at Iowa until 2005, but he also taught abroad and at other universities in the United States. After 1985, he divided his time between Iowa and Port Townsend, Washington, where he bought a house. In the 1990's, a series of fellowships took him to several universities and colleges, including the University of Redlands (1991-1993), St. Mary's College of California (1994-1995), Nebraska-Wesleyan University (1996-1997), and Pacific University (1996-1997) in Oregon, where he also taught in the M.F.A. graduate program. He frequently acts as judge for various writing competitions. He was named the first poet laureate of Iowa in 2000 and served two terms.

ANALYSIS

The dominant themes and motivations of Marvin Bell's poetry perhaps can be best understood by hearing him speak of his own work. Discussing his personal aesthetic, he told Wayne Dodd and Stanley Plumly in an *Ohio Review* interview,

> I would like to write poetry which finds salvation in the physical world and the here and now and which defines the soul, if you will, in terms of emotional depth, and that emotional depth in terms of the physical world and the world of human relationships.

Indeed, Bell is a poet of the family and the relationships within. He writes of his father, his wives, his sons, and himself in a dynamic interaction of love and loss, accomplishment, and fear of alienation. These are subjects that demand maturity and constant evaluation. Bell's oeuvre highlights his ability to understand the durability of the human heart. As a son of a Jew who immigrated from Ukraine, Bell writes of distance and reconciliation between people, often touching on his complex relationship to his heritage.

While concern with the self and its relationships provides a focal point in Bell's early poetry, many of his poems have crystallized around a reflection on the self in relation to nature, evident in collections such as *Stars Which See, Stars Which Do Not See*. Growing up among farmers, Bell has always felt nature to be an integral part of his life. The rural life that so fascinated other writers during the 1960's back-to-nature movement was not Bell's inspiration. Rather, nature forms a critical backdrop for events and relationships in his life, and in that sense, he says, "I *am* interested in allowing nature to have the place in my poems that it always had in my life."

Bell further notes that

contemporary American poetry has been tiresome in its discovery of the individual self, over and over and over, and its discovery of emotions that, indeed, we all have: loneliness, fear, despair, ennui. . . . I think it can get tiresome when the discovery of such emotions is more or less all the content there is to a poem. I think, as I may not always have thought, that the only way out of the self is to concentrate on others and on things outside the self.

Thus, Bell has evolved his ability to perceive and praise small wonders in a quiet and reserved fashion and, as one critic noted, "has found within his *own* voice that American voice, and with it the ability to write convincingly about the smallest details of a personal history."

A PROBABLE VOLUME OF DREAMS

"An Afterword to My Father," which ironically begins *A Probable Volume of Dreams*, is a fairly typical early Bell poem. The "probable" part of the book's title and the placement of an "afterword" at the beginning of a poem reflect Bell's characteristic ambiguity and uncertainty.

> Not so much "enough,"
> there is more to be done,
> yes, and to be done with.
>
> You were the sun and moon.
> Now darkness loves me;
> the lights come on.

Here Bell uses cliches, an allusion ("done") to Donne, and metaphors (father as sun and moon). What remains to be "done" must also be "done with," moved beyond. The father, a recurrent image in Bell's poems, was the poet's source of light; the darkness that follows the father's death now provides light, but what is illumined is not stated, nor is it necessarily positive.

ESCAPE INTO YOU

Escape into You chronicles the breaking up of a marriage and a poet's gradual coming to terms not only with a wife and sons but also with himself. As Arthur Oberg puts it, the poems describe "a poetic self that is still learning to bury the dead and to walk among the living." "Homage to the Runner," also the title of a column Bell wrote, is about running, one of Bell's athletic outlets, but also about poetry and how poetry affects others. Running and poetry both involve "pain," and "the love of form is a black occasion/ through which some light must show/ in a hundred years of commitment." While there is "some light," the occasion is "black." The runner and poet "ache" to end the race and poem, which begin in darkness, but there "is no finish; you can stop [running or writing] for no one," not even family, as much as you care for them.

RESIDUE OF SONG

Residue of Song contains thirteen poems to Bell's father and concerns loneliness. "Residue of Song" begins with "you were writing a long poem, yes,/ about marriage, called 'On Loneliness.'" Like the "probable" in his *A Probable Volume of Dreams*, the "residue" also undercuts its subject matter. In fact, in "Residue of Dreams" "you" decide not to write the poem. In Bell's poem it is the speaker who is the lonely one as he describes a woman's egotism and violence and his callous responses to her; but, as is usually the case with Bell, the poem ends in bittersweet acceptance of the "residue" in a relationship:

> Your cries,
> for ecstatic madness, are not sadder than some things.
> From the residue of song, I have barely said my love again,
> as if for the last time, believing that you will leave me.

The use of "barely" and "as if" is part of Bell's tendency to qualify, to undercut, and to leave meaning implied but not defined.

STARS WHICH SEE, STARS WHICH DO NOT SEE

Stars Which See, Stars Which Do Not See contains poems about Dorothy, Bell's wife, but also includes several poems about poetry. In his "To a Solitary Reader," an allusion to William Wordsworth's poem about the solitary reaper, Bell discusses the development of his poetry: "If once he slept with Donne/ (happily) now he sleeps/ with Williams/ the old Williams." Bell thereby indicates his movement from John Donne's metaphysical style to William Carlos Williams's stress on a poem being, rather than meaning. The remainder of the poem distinguishes between "memory," which is what we "are" in the sense that "they/ think they know us," and what our "being" is, that which is inexplicable, without meaning. The poem concludes, "Time's determinant./ Once I knew you." Bell leaves behind certainty and memory and instead embraces the idea that nothing can be "known."

THESE GREEN-GOING-TO-YELLOW

In the title poem of *These Green-Going-to Yellow* the poet states, "I'm raising the emotional ante" by attempting to align himself with nature, particularly the leaves of a gingko tree someone planted in New York City. The poem concerns people's perspectives on life and asks if they really see beauty. Of course, the answer is "no." People look down "not to look up" and "look at the middles of things." Comfortable with mediocrity, like the seasons, people go from green to yellow, age like autumn, and lose their creative powers. Bell declares that people's perspective would be different "if we truly thought that we were gods." This line denies people even an erroneous presumption about their place in the universe, but in his acceptance of the situation Bell somehow remains "green." He has said, "I started out green and I intended to remain so."

THE BOOK OF THE DEAD MAN AND ARDOR

In the Dead Man poems in *The Book of the Dead Man* and *Ardor*, Bell moves in a new direction, adopting a persona or mask that he often denies but on at least one occasion accepts: "He was my particular and my universal./ I leave it to the future to say why." The Dead Man has enabled Bell to erase distinctions such as the one between life and death. In "About the Dead Man" the poet writes, "He [the Dead Man] thinks himself alive because he has no future." Statements like this, especially when they are preceded by and followed by other seemingly unrelated statements, would appear to be incredibly complicated, but Bell asserts that they are complex, rather than complicated. Complexity, for him, is "the fabric of life and the character of emotion." In his poetry things "connect," even if the connections are not always apparent to the reader.

The "Baby Hamlet" poem in this section embodies Bell's ideas about complexity, which requires "a fusion of many elements, some of them seemingly disparate, even contradictory." Hamlet's indecision is fused with the world's indecision, its "hopeless pacifism" and the "Platonic ideal carried to its logical inconclusion." According to Bell, "It doesn't seem a stretch to me to parallel Hamlet's indecision with the world's reluctance to act early and decisively against the Nazis." After all, "events occur while waiting for the news./ Or stuck in moral neutral."

OTHER MAJOR WORKS

NONFICTION: *Old Snow Just Melting: Essays and Interviews*, 1983.

MISCELLANEOUS: *Segues: A Correspondence in Poetry*, 1983 (with William Stafford); *Annie-Over*, 1988 (with Stafford).

BIBLIOGRAPHY

Bell, Marvin. "An Interview with Marvin Bell." Interview by David Hamilton. *Iowa Review* 30 (Fall, 2000): 3-22. Because Bell was the first poetry editor for the *Iowa Review*, which interviewed him in 1981, this review provides an excellent overview of Bell's writing career. Hamilton discusses the development of the Dead Man poems, beginning with *Iris of Creation* with later appearances in *A Marvin Bell Reader* (1994). These lead to *The Book of the Dead Man* and *Ardor*. The Resurrected Dead Man first appeared in *Wednesday* (1997), published in Ireland. Hamilton describes the Dead Man as "an archetypal figure with sacramental dimensions." Bell distinguishes between the two figures by stating that a Dead Man poem is a field, but a Resurrected Dead Man poem is a path: "I go first. If you want to follow me, you have to stay on the path."

_____. "My Twenties in Chicago: A Memoir." *TriQuarterly* 60 (Spring/Summer, 1984): 118-126. Bell's vivid account of the years 1958 to 1961, which he spent in the artistic neighborhood of Hyde Park in Chicago. Bell describes the "activist" nature of the neighborhood, his growing involvement with photography, his master's writing classes at the University of Chicago, and his many colleagues, friends, and teachers. John Logan, poet and professor, is discussed at length. Of special interest is his discussion of the Chicago artistic and literary scene, including the work of several prominent Beat poets such as Jack Kerouac, Allen Ginsberg, and Gregory Corso.

Harp, Jerry. "Inexactly Dead: On Marvin Bell's *Mars Being Red*." *Pleiades* 28, no. 2 (2008): 177-183. A thorough review of Bell's 2007 poetry collection *Mars Being Red*. Examines how many of the poems in this book are "extended meditation[s] on multiple senses of time, as well as on the times."

Jackson, Richard. "Containing the Other: Marvin Bell's Recent Poetry." *North American Poetry Review* 280 (January/February, 1995): 45-48. Jackson focuses on *The Book of the Dead Man*, which he finds rich in complexity. For Jackson, Bell extends his emphasis on inclusiveness and counterpointing in the Dead Man poems. The book begins with poems about feeling and sensing, moves to dreams and the psychic life, and concludes "with two poems about our relation to the cosmos." Jackson finds in Bell's poetry the joy of life.

Kitchen, Judith. "'I Gotta Use Words. . . .'" *Georgia Review* 51 (Winter, 1997): 756. Kitchen believes that in the Dead Man poems, Bell has found "a liberating spirit, someone who could serve his poetic innovation." She finds *Ardor*, not surprisingly, more passionate than *The Book of the Dead Man* and sees Bell moving from a forward look at death to a backward look at life. As a result, she claims, the poems in the later book to be a cohesive whole, to be able to create a contextual world and then provide a "take" on that world. For her, Bell is sending poetry into new and original territory.

Thomas L. Erskine
Updated by Sarah Hilbert

PAUL CELAN
Paul Antschel

Born: Czernowitz, Romania (now Chernivtsi, Ukraine); November 23, 1920
Died: Paris, France; April, 1970
Also known as: Paul Ancel

OTHER LITERARY FORMS

The literary reputation of Paul Celan (TSEHL-on) rests exclusively on his poetry. His only piece of prose fiction, if indeed it can be so described, is "Gespräch im Gebirg" (1959), a very short autobiographical story with a religious theme. Celan also wrote an introductory essay for a book containing works by the painter Edgar Jené; this essay, en-titled *Edgar Jené und der Traum vom Traume*, (1948; *Edgar Jené and the Dream About the Dream*, 1986), is an important early statement of Celan's aesthetic theory. Another, more oblique, statement of Celan's poetic theory is contained in his famous speech, "Der Meridian" (1960), given on his acceptance of the prestigious Georg Büchner Prize. (An English translation of this speech, "The Meridian," was published in the Winter, 1978, issue of *Chicago Review*.)

ACHIEVEMENTS

Paul Celan is considered an "inaccessible" poet by many critics and readers. This judgment, prompted by the difficulties Celan's poetry poses for would-be interpreters seeking traditional exegesis, is reinforced by the fact that Celan occupies an isolated position in modern German poetry. Sometimes aligned with Nelly Sachs, Ernst Meister, and the German Surrealists, Celan's work nevertheless stands apart from that of his contemporaries. A Jew whose outlook was shaped by his early experiences in Nazi-occupied Romania, Celan grew up virtually trilingual. The horror of his realization that he was, in spite of his childhood experiences and his later residence in France, a German poet was surely responsible in part for his almost obsessive concern with the possibilities and the limits of his poetic language. Celan's literary ancestors are Friedrich Hölderlin, Arthur Rimbaud, Stéphane Mallarmé, Rainer Maria Rilke, and the German expressionists, but even in his early poems his position as an outsider is manifest. Celan's poems, called Hermetic by some critics because of their resistance to traditional interpretation, can be viewed sometimes as intense and cryptic accounts of personal experience, sometimes as religious-philosophical discussions of Judaism, its tradition and its relation to Christianity. Many of his poems concern themselves with linguistic and poetic theory to the point where they cease to be poems in the traditional sense, losing all contact with the world of physical phenomena and turning into pure language, existing only for themselves. Such "pure" poems, increasingly frequent in Celan's later works, are largely responsible for the charge of inaccessibility that has been laid against him. Here the reader is faced with having to leave the dimension of conventional language use, where the poet uses language to communicate with his audience about subjects such as death or nature, and is forced to enter the dimension of metalanguage, as Harald Weinrich calls it, where language is used to discuss only language—that is, the *word* "death," and not death itself. Such poems are accessible only to readers who share with the poet the basic premises of an essentially linguistic poetic theory.

In spite of all this, much of Celan's poetry can be made accessible to the reader through focus on the personal elements in some poems, the Judaic themes in others, and by pointing out the biblical and literary references in yet another group.

BIOGRAPHY

Paul Celan was born Paul Ancel, or Antschel, the only child of Jewish parents, in Czernowitz, Romania (now Chernivtsi, Ukraine), in Bukovina, situated in the foothills of the Carpathian Mountains. This region had been under Austrian rule and thus contained a sizable German-speaking minority along with a mix of other nationalities and ethnic groups. In 1918, just two years before Celan's birth, following the collapse of the Austro-Hungarian Empire, Bukovina became part of Romania. Thus, Celan was reared in a region of great cultural and linguistic diversity, the tensions of which energized his poetry.

Little is known of Celan's early childhood, but he appears to have had a very close relationship with his mother and a less satisfying relationship with his father. Positive references to his mother abound in his poems, whereas his father is hardly mentioned. After receiving his high school diploma, the young Celan went to study medicine in France in 1938, but the war forced his return in the following year to Czernowitz, where he turned to the study of Romance languages and literature at the local university. In 1940, his hometown was annexed by the Soviet Union but was soon occupied by the Germans and their allies, who began to persecute and deport the Jewish population. Celan's parents were taken to a concentration camp, where they both died, while the young man remained hidden for some time and finally ended up in a forced-labor camp. These events left a permanent scar on Celan's memory, and it appears that he had strong feelings of guilt for having survived when his parents and so many of his friends and relatives were murdered. After Soviet troops reoccupied his hometown, he returned there for a short time and then moved to Bucharest, where he found work as an editor and a translator. In 1947, his first poems were published in a Romanian journal under the anagrammatic pen name Paul Celan. In the same year, he moved to Vienna, where he remained until 1948, when his first collection of poetry, *Der Sand aus den Urnen*, was published.

After moving to Paris in the same year, Celan began to frequent avant-garde circles and was received particularly well by the poet Yvan Goll and his wife. Unfortunately, this friendship soured after Goll's death in 1950, when Goll's wife, Claire, apparently jealous of Celan's growing reputation as a poet, accused him of having plagiarized from her husband. A bitter feud resulted, with many of the leading poets and critics in France and Germany taking sides. During this period, Celan also began his work as a literary translator, which was to be a major source of both income and poetic inspiration for the rest of his life. He translated from the French—notably the writings of Rimbaud, Paul Valéry, and Guillaume Apollinaire—as well as the poetry of William Shakespeare, Emily Dickinson, and Marianne Moore from the English and the works of Aleksandr Blok, Sergei Esenin, and Osip Mandelstam from the Russian.

In the following years, Celan married a French graphic artist, Gisèle Lestrange, and published his second volume of poetry, *Mohn und Gedächtnis* (poppy and memory), containing many poems from his first collection, *Der Sand aus den Urnen*, which he had withdrawn from circulation because of the large number of printing mistakes and editorial inaccuracies it contained. *Mohn und Gedächtnis* established his reputation as a poet, and most of his subsequent collections were awarded prestigious literary prizes.

Celan remained in Paris for the rest of his life, infrequently traveling to Germany. During his later years, he appears to have undergone many crises both in his personal and in his creative life (his feud with Claire Goll is only one such incident), and his friends agree that he became quarrelsome and felt persecuted by neo-Nazis, hostile publishers, and critics. His death in April of 1970, apparently by suicide—he drowned in the Seine—was the consequence of his having arrived, in his own judgment, at a personal and artistic dead end, although many critics have seen in his collections *Lightduress*, *Snow Part*, and *Zeitgehöft*, published post humously, the potential beginning of a new creative period.

ANALYSIS

Paul Celan's poetry can be viewed as an expressive attempt to cope with the past—his personal past as well as that of the Jewish people. Close friends of the poet state that Celan was unable to forget anything and that trivial incidents and cataclysmic events of the past for him had the same order of importance. Many of his poems contain references to the death camps, to his dead parents (particularly his mother), and to his changing attitude toward the Jewish religion and toward God. In his early collections, these themes are shaped into traditional poetic form—long, often rhymed lines, genitive metaphors, sensuous images—and the individual poems are accessible to conventional methods of interpretation. In his later collections, Celan employs increasingly sparse poetic means, such as one-word lines, neologisms, and images that resist traditional interpretive sense; their significance can often be intuited only by considering Celan's complete poetic opus, a fact that has persuaded many critics and readers that Celan's poems are nonsense, pure games with language rather than codified expressions of thoughts and feelings that can be deciphered by applying the appropriate key.

MOHN UND GEDÄCHTNIS

Mohn und Gedächtnis, Celan's first collection of poetry (discounting the withdrawn *Der Sand aus den Urnen*), was in many ways an attempt to break with the past. The title of the collection is an indication of the dominant theme of these poems, which stress the dichotomy of forgetting—one of the symbolic connotations of the poppy flower—and remembering, by which Celan expresses his wish to forget the past, both his own personal past and that of the Jewish race, and his painful inability to erase these experiences from his memory. Living in Paris, Celan believed that only by forgetting could he begin a new life—in a new country, with a non-Jewish French wife, and by a rejection of his past poetic efforts, as indicated by the withdrawal of his first collection.

Mohn und Gedächtnis is divided into four parts and contains a total of fifty-six poems. In the first part, "Der Sand aus den Urnen" ("Sand from the Urns"), Celan establishes the central theme of the collection: The poet "fills the urns of the past in the moldy-green house of oblivion" and is reminded by the white foliage of an aspen tree that his mother's hair was not allowed to turn white. Mixed with these reflections on personal losses are memories of sorrows and defeats inflicted on the Jewish people; references to the conquest of Judea by the Romans are meant to remind the reader of more recent atrocities committed by foreign conquerors.

The second part of *Mohn und Gedächtnis* is a single poem, "Todesfuge" ("Death Fugue"), Celan's most widely anthologized poem, responsible in no small part for establishing his reputation as one of the leading con temporary German poets. "Death Fugue" is a monologue by the victims of a concentration camp, evoking in vivid images the various atrocities associated with these camps. From the opening line, "Black milk of daybreak we drink it at sundown . . ."—one of the lines that Claire Goll suggested Celan had plagiarized from her husband—the poem passes on to descriptions of the cruel camp commander who plays with serpent-like whips, makes the inmates shovel their own graves, and sets his pack of dogs on them. From the resignation of the first lines, the poem builds to an emotional climax in the last stanza in which the horror of the cremation chambers is indicated by images such as "he grants us a grave in the air" and "death is a master from Germany." Although most critics have praised the poem, some have condemned Celan for what they interpret as an attempt at reconciliation between Germans and Jews in the last two lines of the poem. Others, however, notably Theodor Adorno, have attacked "Death Fugue" on the basis that it is "barbaric" to write beautiful poetry after, and particularly about, Auschwitz. A close reading of this long poem refutes the notion that Celan was inclined toward reconciliation with the Germans—his later work bears this out—and it is hard to imagine that any reader should feel anything but horror and pity for the anonymous speakers of the poem. The beautifully phrased images serve to increase the intensity of this horror rather than attempting to gloss it over. "Death Fugue" is both a great poem and one of the most impressive and lasting documents of the plight of the Jews.

"Auf Reisen" ("Travel"), the first poem of the third part of the collection, again indicates Celan's wish to leave the past behind and to start all over again in his "house in Paris." In other poems he makes reference to his wife, asking to be forgiven for having broken with his heritage and married a Gentile. As the title of the collection suggests, the poppy of oblivion is not strong enough to erase the memory of his dead mother, of his personal past, and of his racial heritage. In poems such as "Der Reisekamerad" ("The Traveling Companion") and "Zähle die Mandeln" ("Count the Almonds"), the optimistic view of "Travel" is retracted; in the former, the dead mother is evoked as the poet's constant travel companion, while in the latter, he acknowledges that he must always be counted among the "almonds." The almonds (*Mandeln*) represent the Jewish people and are an indirect reference also to the Russian Jewish poet Osip Mandelstam, whose work Celan had translated. The irreconcilable tension between the wish to forget and the inability to do so completely is further shown in "Corona," a poem referring to Rainer

Maria Rilke's "Herbsttag" ("Autumn Day"). Whereas the speaker of Rilke's poem resigns himself to the approaching hardships of winter, Celan converts Rilke's "Lord: it is time" into the rebellious "it is time that the stone condescended to bloom."

The poems in *Mohn und Gedächtnis* are not, for the most part, innovative in form or imagery, although the long dactylic lines and the flowery images of the first half begin to give way to greater economy of scope and metaphor in the later poems. There is a constant dialogue with a fictional "you" and repeated references to "night," "dream," "sleep," "wine," and "time," in keeping with the central theme of these poems. Celan's next collections show his continued attempts to break with the past, to move his life and his poetry to new levels.

Von Schwelle zu Schwelle

In *Von Schwelle zu Schwelle* (threshold to threshold), Celan abandoned his frequent references to the past; it is as if the poet—as the title, taken from a poem in *Mohn und Gedächtnis*, suggests—intended to cross over a threshold into a new realm. Images referring to his mother, to the persecution of the Jews, to his personal attitude toward God, and to his Jewish heritage are less frequent in this volume. Many German critics, reluctant to concentrate on Celan's treatment of the Holocaust, have remarked with some relief his turning away from this subject toward the problem of creativity, the possibilities of communication, and the limits of language. Indeed, if one follows most German critics, *Von Schwelle zu Schwelle* was the first step in the poet's development toward "metapoetry"—that is, poetry that no longer deals with traditional *materia poetica* but only with poetry itself. This new direction is demonstrated by the preponderance of terms such as "word" and "stone" (a symbol of speechlessness), replacing "dream," "autumn," and "time." For Celan, *Von Schwelle zu Schwelle* constituted a more radical attempt to start anew by no longer writing about—therefore no longer having to think about—experiences and memories that he had been unable to come to grips with in his earlier poems.

Speech-Grille

Speech-Grille is, as the title suggests, predominantly concerned with language. The thirty-three poems in this volume are among Celan's finest, as the enthusiastic critical reception confirmed. They are characterized by a remarkable discipline of expression, leading in many cases to a reduction of poetry to the bare essentials. Indeed, it is possible to see these poems as leading in the direction of complete silence. "Engführung" ("Stretto"), perhaps the finest poem in the collection and one of Celan's best, exemplifies this tendency even by its title, which is taken from musical theory and refers to the final section of a fugue. A long poem that alludes to "Death Fugue," it is stripped of the descriptive metaphors that characterized that masterpiece, such as the "grave in the air" and "the black milk of daybreak"; instead, experience is reduced to lines such as "Came,

came./ Came a word, came/ came through the night,/ wanted to shine, wanted to shine/ Ash./ Ash, ash./ Night."

DIE NIEMANDSROSE

Celan's attempt to leave the past behind in *Speech-Grille* was not completely successful; on the contrary, several poems in this collection express sorrow at the poet's detachment from his Jewish past and from his religion. It is therefore not surprising that Celan's next collection, *Die Niemandsrose* (the no-one's rose), was dedicated to Mandelstam, a victim of Joseph Stalin's persecutions in the 1930's. One of the first poems in this collection makes mention of the victims of the concentration camps: "There was earth inside them, and/they dug." Rather than concentrating on the horrors of camp existence, the poem discusses the possibility of believing in an omnipotent, benevolent God in the face of these atrocities; this theme is picked up again in "Zürich, zum Storchen" ("Zurich, the Stork Inn"), in which Celan reports on his meeting with the Jewish poet Nelly Sachs: "the talk was of your God, I spoke/ against him." Other poems contain references to his earlier work; the "house in Paris" is mentioned again, and autumn imagery, suggesting the memory of his mother, is used more frequently. Several other poems express Celan's renewed and final acceptance of his Jewish heritage but indicate his rejection of God, culminating in the blasphemous "Psalm," with its bitter tribute: "Praised be your name, no one."

LATER YEARS

Celan's poetry after *Die Niemandsrose* became almost inaccessible to the average reader. As the title *Breathturn* indicates, Celan wanted to go in entirely new directions. Most of the poems in Celan's last collections are very short; references to language and writing become more frequent, and striking, often grotesque, portmanteau words and other neologisms mix with images from his earlier poems. There are still references to Judaism, to an absent or cruel God, and—in a cryptic form—to personal experiences. In the posthumously published *Snow Part*, the reader can even detect allusions to the turbulent political events of 1968. The dominant feature of these last poems, however, is the almost obsessive attempt to make the language of poetry perform new, hitherto unimagined feats, to coerce words to yield truth that traditional poetic diction could not previously force through its "speech-grille." It appears that Celan finally despaired of ever being able to reach this new poetic dimension. The tone of his last poems was increasingly pessimistic, and his hopes, expressed in earlier poems, of finding "that ounce of truth deep inside delusion," gave way to silence in the face of the "obstructive tomorrow." It is the evidence of these last poems, more than any police reports, which make it a certainty that his drowning in the Seine in 1970 was not simply the result of an accident.

Celan's poetry can be understood only by grasping his existential dilemma after

World War II as a Jewish poet who had to create his poetry in the German language. Desperate to leave behind everything which would remind him of his own and his people's plight, he nevertheless discovered that the very use of the German language inevitably led him back to his past and made a new beginning impossible. Finally, the only escape he saw still open to him was to attempt to abandon completely the conventions of German lyric poetry and its language, to try to make his poetry express his innermost feelings and convictions without having to resort to traditional poetic diction and form. Weinrich suggests that Celan, like Mallarmé before him, was searching for the "absolute poem," a poem that the poet creates only as a rough sketch and that the reader then completes, using private experiences and ideas, possibly remembered pieces of other poems. If this is true, Celan must have ultimately considered his efforts a failure, both in terms of his poetic intentions and in his desire to come to terms with his personal and his Jewish past.

OTHER MAJOR WORKS

SHORT FICTION: "Gespräch im Gebirg," 1959.

NONFICTION: *Edgar Jené und der Traum vom Traume*, 1948 (*Edgar Jené and the Dream About the Dream*, 1986); *Collected Prose*, 1986.

TRANSLATIONS: *Der goldene Vorhang*, 1949 (of Jean Cocteau); *Bateau ivre/Das trunkene Schiff*, 1958 (of Arthur Rimbaud); *Gedichte*, 1959 (of Osip Mandelstam); *Die junge Parzel/La jeune Parque*, 1964 (of Paul Valéry); *Einundzwanzig Sonette*, 1967 (of William Shakespeare).

MISCELLANEOUS: *Prose Writings and Selected Poems*, 1977; *Selected Poems and Prose of Paul Celan*, 2001.

BIBLIOGRAPHY

Baer, Ulrich. *Remnants of Song: Trauma and the Experience of Modernity in Charles Baudelaire and Paul Celan*. Stanford, Calif.: Stanford University Press, 2000. Baer sees a basis for comparison of the nineteenth and the twentieth century poets. Bibliographical references, index.

Bernstein, Michael André. *Five Portraits: Modernity and the Imagination in Twentieth-Century German Writing*. Evanston, Ill.: Northwestern University Press, 2000. Compared with Celan are four other German poets and philosophers: Rainer Maria Rilke, Robert Musil, Martin Heidegger, and Walter Benjamin. Includes bibliographical references, index.

Chalfen, Israel. *Paul Celan*. New York: Persea Books, 1991. A biography of Celan's youth and early career. Includes bibliographical references.

Colin, Amy D. *Paul Celan: Holograms of Darkness*. Bloomington: Indiana University Press, 1991. An overview of Celan's cultural background as well as postmodernist textual analysis.

Del Caro, Adrian. *The Early Poetry of Paul Celan: In the Beginning Was the Word.* Baton Rouge: Louisiana State University Press, 1997. A detailed treatment of the early volumes *Mohn und Gedächtnis* (1952) and *Von Schwelle zu Schwelle* (1955).

Felstiner, John. *Paul Celan: Poet, Survivor, Jew.* 1995. Reprint. New Haven, Conn.: Yale University Press, 2001. Illuminates the rich biographical meaning behind much of Celan's spare, enigmatic verse. Includes bibliographical references, illustrations, map, index.

Hillard, Derek. *Poetry as Individuality: The Discourse of Observation in Paul Celan.* Lewisburg, Pa.: Bucknell University Press, 2009. An examination of individuality in the writings of Celan. Touches on philosophy and the psychology of knowledge.

Rosenthal, Bianca. *Pathways to Paul Celan.* New York: Peter Lang, 1995. An overview of the varied and often contradictory critical responses to the poet. Illustrated; includes bibliographical references, index.

Tobias, Rochelle. *The Discourse of Nature in the Poetry of Paul Celan: The Unnatural World.* Baltimore: The Johns Hopkins University Press, 2006. Provides critical analysis of Celan's poetry in terms of its relationship to the natural world.

Wolosky, Shira. *Language and Mysticism: The Negative Way of Language in Eliot, Beckett, and Celan.* Stanford, Calif.: Stanford University Press, 1995. A useful comparative study that helps to place Celan in context. Bibliographical references, index.

Franz G. Blaha

ALLEN GINSBERG

Born: Newark, New Jersey; June 3, 1926
Died: New York, New York; April 5, 1997

PRINCIPAL POETRY
Howl, and Other Poems, 1956, 1996
Empty Mirror: Early Poems, 1961
Kaddish, and Other Poems, 1958-1960, 1961
The Change, 1963
Reality Sandwiches, 1963
Kral Majales, 1965
Wichita Vortex Sutra, 1966
T.V. Baby Poems, 1967
Airplane Dreams: Compositions from Journals, 1968
Ankor Wat, 1968
Planet News, 1961-1967, 1968
The Moments Return, 1970
Ginsberg's Improvised Poetics, 1971
Bixby Canyon Ocean Path Word Breeze, 1972
The Fall of America: Poems of These States, 1965-1971, 1972
The Gates of Wrath: Rhymed Poems, 1948-1952, 1972
Iron Horse, 1972
Open Head, 1972
First Blues: Rags, Ballads, and Harmonium Songs, 1971-1974, 1975
Sad Dust Glories: Poems During Work Summer in Woods, 1975
Mind Breaths: Poems, 1972-1977, 1977
Mostly Sitting Haiku, 1978
Poems All over the Place: Mostly Seventies, 1978
Plutonian Ode: Poems, 1977-1980, 1982
Collected Poems, 1947-1980, 1984
White Shroud: Poems, 1980-1985, 1986
Hydrogen Jukebox, 1990 (music by Philip Glass)
Collected Poems, 1992
Cosmopolitan Greetings: Poems, 1986-1992, 1994
Making It Up: Poetry Composed at St. Marks Church on May 9, 1979, 1994 (with
    Kenneth Koch)
Selected Poems, 1947-1995, 1996
Death and Fame: Poems, 1993-1997, 1999
Collected Poems, 1947-1997, 2006

OTHER LITERARY FORMS

Allen Ginsberg recognized early in his career that he would have to explain his intentions, because most critics and reviewers of the time did not have the interest or experience to understand what he was trying to accomplish. Consequently, he published books that include interviews, lectures, essays, photographs, and letters to friends as means of conveying his theories about composition and poetics.

ACHIEVEMENTS

The publication of "Howl" in 1956 drew such enthusiastic comments from Allen Ginsberg's supporters, and such vituperative condemnation from conservative cultural commentators, that a rift of immense proportions developed, which has made a balanced critical assessment very difficult. Nevertheless, partisan response has gradually given way to an acknowledgment by most critics that Ginsberg's work is significant, if not always entirely successful by familiar standards of literary excellence. Such recognition was underscored in 1974, when *The Fall of America* shared the National Book Award in Poetry. Ginsberg was awarded a Los Angeles Times Book Prize (1982) and the Frost Medal by the Poetry Society of America (1986). Included among the many honors he garnered during his lifetime were an Academy Award in Literature from the American Academy of Arts and Letters in 1969, the Woodbury Poetry Prize, Guggenheim fellowships, the National Arts Club Medal of Honor, the Before Columbus Foundation award for lifetime achievement, the University of Chicago's Harriet Monroe Poetry Award, an American Academy of Arts and Sciences fellowship, and the Medal of Chevalier de l'Ordre des Arts et Letters.

The voice Ginsberg employed in "Howl" not only has influenced the style of several generations of poets, but also has combined the rhythms and language of common speech with some of the deepest, most enduring traditions in American literature. In both his life and his work, Ginsberg set an example of moral seriousness, artistic commitment, and humane decency that made him one of the most popular figures in American culture. The best of his visionary and innovative creations earned for him recognition as one of the major figures of the twentieth century.

BIOGRAPHY

Allen Ginsberg was born Irwin Allen Ginsberg, the second son of Naomi Levy Ginsberg, a Russian-born political activist and communist sympathizer, and Louis Ginsberg, a traditional lyric poet and high school English teacher. He attended primary school in the middle-class town of Paterson, New Jersey. He grew up in a conventional and uneventful household, with the exception of his mother's repeated hospitalizations for mental stress. He entered Columbia University in 1943, intending to pursue a career in labor law, but the influence of such well-known literary scholars as Lionel Trilling and Mark Van Doren, combined with the excitement of the Columbia community, which included fellow student Jack Kerouac and such singular people as William Burroughs and Neal Cassady, led him toward literature as a vocation. He was temporarily suspended from Columbia in 1945 and worked as a welder and apprentice seaman before finishing his degree in 1948. Living a "subterranean" life (to use Kerouac's term) that incorporated drug use, a bohemian lifestyle, and occasional antisocial acts of youthful ebullience, Ginsberg was counseled to commit himself for several months to Columbia Presbyterian Psychiatric Institute to avoid criminal charges associated with the possession of stolen goods; there, in 1949, he met Carl W. Solomon, to whom "Howl" is dedicated. During the early 1950's, he began a correspondence with William Carlos Williams, who guided and encouraged his early writing, and Ginsberg traveled in Mexico and Europe.

In 1954, Ginsberg moved to San Francisco to be at the center of the burgeoning Beat movement. He was living there when he wrote "Howl," and he read the poem for the first time at a landmark Six Gallery performance that included Gary Snyder, Philip Whalen, and Michael McClure. His mother died in 1956, the year *Howl, and Other Poems* was published, and he spent the next few years traveling, defending *Howl* against charges of obscenity, working on "Kaddish"—his celebration of his mother's life, based on a Hebrew prayer for the dead—and reading on college campuses and in Beatnik venues on both coasts.

The growing notoriety of the Beat generation drew Ginsberg into the media spotlight in the early 1960's, and he was active in the promotion of work by his friends. He continued to travel extensively, visiting Europe, India, and Japan; he read in bars and coffeehouses, and published widely in many of the prominent literary journals of the counterculture. His involvement with various hallucinatory substances led to the formation of LeMar (Organization to Legalize Marijuana) in 1964 with the poet, songwriter, and publisher Ed Sanders, and his continuing disaffection with governmental policies took him toward active political protest. In 1965, he was invited to Cuba and Czechoslovakia by Communist officials, who mistakenly assumed that his criticism of American society would make him sympathetic to their regimes, but Ginsberg's outspoken criticism of all forms of tyranny and suppression led to his expulsion from both countries.

His political activism—particularly in reaction to the Vietnam War—and close association with the counterculture continued throughout the 1960's and 1970's. During the 1960's, he invented the nonviolent concept of "flower power" in an attempt to neutralize martial aggression. In 1967, he was one of the organizers of the first "Human Be-In." The following year, he was arrested in Chicago at the Democratic National Convention with many other demonstrators, and in 1969, he testified at the Chicago Seven trials; that same year, he was at the center of a semi-serious effort to exorcise the Pentagon. In the early 1970's, he spent some time on a farm in rural New York, formally accepted the teachings of Buddhism from Chögyam Trungpa, who initiated him with the name "Lion of Dharma," and afterward cofounded, with Anne Waldman, a school of literary inquiry, the Jack Kerouac School of Disembodied Poetics at the Naropa Institute in Colorado. He was inducted into the American Institute of Arts and Letters in 1974, an indication of recognition as an artist in the mainstream of American culture, and he further confirmed this status by traveling with Bob Dylan's Rolling Thunder Review as a "poet-percussionist" in 1975. Continuing to combine artistic endeavor with a commitment to social justice, Ginsberg took part—with longtime lover Peter Orlovsky—in protests at the Rocky Flats Nuclear Facility in 1978 and wrote the "Plutonium Ode," which expressed his concern about the destructive forces humans had unleashed.

During the 1980's, Ginsberg continued to travel, teach, write, and perform his work. The publication of his *Collected Poems, 1947-1980* in 1984 was received with wide attention and respect, and he was appointed distinguished professor at Brooklyn College in 1986, the year he published *White Shroud*, which includes an epilogue to "Kaddish" along with other poems from the 1980's. His ability as a teacher was clearly demonstrated in his appearance on the Public Broadcasting Service series *Voices and Visions* in 1987. As the decade drew to a close, he was involved in collaboration with composer Philip Glass on a chamber opera called *Hydrogen Jukebox* (a phrase from "Howl"), which was performed in 1990. Continuing to write with energy while teaching a graduate-level course on the Beats at the City University of New York Graduate Center, Ginsberg described his goals in the 1990's, in a poem called "Personals Ad," as similar to the ones he had always pursued: "help inspire mankind conquer world anger & guilt." It was an appropriate task for a "poet professor in his autumn years." Afflicted with diabetes, hepatitis, and liver cancer, he died at age seventy following a stroke on April 5, 1997, in New York City.

ANALYSIS

"Howl," the poem that carried Allen Ginsberg into public consciousness as a symbol of the avant-garde artist and as the designer of a verse style for a postwar generation seeking its own voice, was initially regarded as primarily a social document. As Ginsberg's notes make clear, however, it was also the latest specimen in a continuing experiment in form and structure. Several factors in Ginsberg's life were particularly important in this breakthrough poem, written as the poet was approaching thirty and still drifting through a series of jobs, countries, and social occasions. Ginsberg's father had exerted more influence than was immediately apparent. Louis Ginsberg's very traditional, metrical verse was of little use to his son, but his father's interest in literary history was part of Ginsberg's solid grounding in prosody. Then, a succession of other mentors—including Williams, whose use of the American vernacular and local material had inspired him, and great scholars such as art historian Meyer Shapiro at Columbia, who had introduced him to the tenets of modernism from an analytic perspective—had enabled the young poet to form a substantial intellectual foundation.

In addition, Ginsberg was dramatically affected by his friendships with Kerouac, Cassady, Burroughs, Herbert Hunke, and other noteworthy denizens of a vibrant underground community of dropouts, revolutionaries, drug addicts, jazz musicians, and serious but unconventional artists of all sorts. Ginsberg felt an immediate kinship with these "angelheaded hipsters," who accepted and celebrated eccentricity and regarded Ginsberg's homosexuality as an attribute, not a blemish. Although Ginsberg enthusiastically entered into the drug culture that was a flourishing part of this community, he was not nearly as routed toward self-destruction as Burroughs or Hunke; he was more interested in the possibilities of visionary experience. His oft-noted "illuminative audition of William Blake's voice simultaneous with Eternity-vision" in 1948 was his first ecstatic experience of transcendence, and he continued to pursue spiritual insight through serious studies of various religions—including Judaism and Buddhism—as well as through chemical experimentation.

His experiments with mind-altering agents (including marijuana, peyote, amphetamines, mescaline, and lysergic acid diethylamide, or LSD) and his casual friendship with some quasi-criminals led to his eight-month stay in a psychiatric institute. He had already experienced an unsettling series of encounters with mental instability in his mother, who had been hospitalized for the first time when he was three. Her struggles with the torments of psychic uncertainty were seriously disruptive events in Ginsberg's otherwise unremarkable boyhood, but Ginsberg felt deep sympathy for his mother's agony and also was touched by her warmth, love, and social conscience. Although not exactly a "red diaper baby," Ginsberg had adopted a radical political conscience early enough to decide to pursue labor law as a college student, and he never wavered from his initial convictions concerning the excesses of capitalism. His passionate call for tolerance and fairness had roots as much in his mother's ideas as in his contacts with the "lamblike youths" who were "slaughtered" by the demon Moloch: his symbol for the greed and materialism of the United States in the 1950's. In conjunction with his displeasure with what he saw as the failure of the government to correct these abuses, he carried an idealized conception of "the lost America of love" based on his readings in nineteenth century American literature, Walt Whitman and Henry David Thoreau in particular, and reinforced by the political and social idealism of contemporaries such as Kerouac, Snyder, and McClure.

Ginsberg brought all these concerns together when he began to compose "Howl." However, while the social and political elements of the poem were immediately apparent, the careful structural arrangements were not. Ginsberg found it necessary to explain his intentions in a series of notes and letters, emphasizing his desire to use Whitman's long line "to *build up* large organic structures" and his realization that he did not have to satisfy anyone's concept of what a poem should be, but could follow his "romantic inspiration" and simply write as he wished, "without fear." Using what he called his "Hebraic-Melvillian bardic breath"—a rhythmic pattern similar to the cadences of the Old Testament as employed by Herman Melville—Ginsberg wrote a three-part prophetic elegy, which he described as a "huge sad comedy of wild phrasing."

"HOWL"

The first part of "Howl" is a long catalog of the activities of the "angelheaded hipsters" who were his contemporaries. Calling the bohemian underground of outcasts, outlaws, rebels, mystics, sexual deviants, junkies, and other misfits "the best minds of my generation"—a judgment that still rankles many social critics—Ginsberg produced image after image of the antics of "remarkable lamblike youths" in pursuit of cosmic enlightenment, "the ancient heavenly connection to the starry dynamo in the machinery of night." Because the larger American society had offered them little support, Ginsberg summarized their efforts by declaring that these people had been "destroyed by madness." The long lines, most beginning with the word "who" (which was used "as a base to keep measure, return to and take off from again"), create a composite portrait that pulses with energy and excitement. Ginsberg is not only lamenting the destruction—or self-destruction—of his friends and acquaintances, but also celebrating their wild flights of imagination, their ecstatic illuminations, and their rapturous adventures. His typical line, or breath unit, communicates the awesome power of the experiences he describes along with their potential for danger. Ginsberg believed that by the end of the first section he had expressed what he believed "true to eternity" and had reconstituted "the data of celestial experience."

Part 2 of the poem "names the monster of mental consciousness that preys" on the people he admires. The fear and tension of the Cold War, stirred by materialistic greed and what Ginsberg later called "lacklove," are symbolized by a demon he calls Moloch, after the Canaanite god that required human sacrifice. With the name Moloch as a kind of "base repetition" and destructive attributes described in a string of lines beginning with "whose," the second part of the poem reaches a kind of crescendo of chaos in which an anarchic vision of frenzy and disruption engulfs the world.

In part 3, "a litany of affirmation," Ginsberg addresses himself to Solomon, a poet he knew from the Psychiatric Institute; he holds up Solomon as a kind of emblem of the victim-heroes he has been describing. The pattern here is based on the statement-counterstatement form of Christopher Smart's *Jubilate Agno* (1939; as *Rejoice in the Lamb*, 1954), and Ginsberg envisioned it as pyramidal, "with a graduated longer response to the fixed base." Affirming his allegiance to Solomon (and everyone like him), Ginsberg begins each breath unit with the phrase "I'm with you in Rockland" followed by "where . . ." and an exposition of strange or unorthodox behavior that has been labeled "madness" but that to the poet is actually a form of creative sanity. The poem concludes with a vision of Ginsberg and Solomon together on a journey to an America that transcends Moloch and madness and offers utopian possibilities of love and "true mental regularity."

During the year that "Howl" was written, Ginsberg wondered whether he might use the same long line in a "short quiet lyrical poem." The result was a poignant tribute to his "old courage teacher," Whitman, which he called "A Supermarket in California," and a meditation on the bounty of nature, "A Strange New Cottage in Berkeley." He continued to work with his long-breath line in larger compositions as well, most notably the poem "America," which has been accurately described by Charles Molesworth as "a gem of polyvocal satire and miscreant complaint." This poem gave Ginsberg the opportunity to exercise his exuberant sense of humor and good-natured view of himself in a mock-ironic address to his country. The claim "It occurs to me that I am America" is meant to be taken as a whimsical wish made in self-deprecating modesty, but Ginsberg's growing popularity through the last decades of the century cast it as prophetic as well.

"KADDISH"

Naomi Ginsberg died in 1956 after several harrowing episodes at home and in mental institutions, and she was not accorded a traditional orthodox funeral because a *minyan* (a complement of ten men to serve as witnesses) could not be found. Ginsberg was troubled by thoughts of his mother's suffering and tormented by uncertainty concerning his own role as sometime caregiver for her. Brooding over his tangled feelings, he spent a night listening to jazz, ingesting marijuana and methamphetamine, and reading passages from an old bar mitzvah book. Then, at dawn, he walked the streets of the lower East Side in Manhattan, where many Jewish immigrant families had settled. A tangle of images and emotions rushed through his mind, organized now by the rhythms of ancient Hebrew prayers and chants. The poem that took shape in his mind was his own version of the Kaddish, the traditional Jewish service for the dead that had been denied to his mother. As it was formed in an initial burst of energy, he saw its goal as a celebration of her memory and a prayer for her soul's serenity, an attempt to confront his own fears about death, and ultimately, an attempt to come to terms with his relationship to his mother.

"Kaddish" begins in an elegiac mood, "Strange now to think of you gone," and proceeds as both an elegy and a kind of dual biography. Details from Ginsberg's childhood begin to take on a sinister aspect when viewed from the perspective of an adult with a tragic sense of existence. The course of his life's journey from early youth and full parental love to the threshold of middle age is paralleled by Naomi's life as it advances from late youth toward a decline into paranoia and madness. Ginsberg recalls his mother "teaching school, laughing with idiots, the backward classes—her Russian speciality," then sees her in agony "one night, sudden attack . . . left retching on the tile floor." The juxtaposition of images ranging over many years reminds him of his own mortality, compelling him to probe his subconscious mind to face some of the fears that he has suppressed about his mother's madness. The first part of the poem concludes as the poet realizes that he will never find any peace until he is able to "cut through—to talk to you—" and finally to write her true history.

The central incident of the second section is a bus trip the twelve-year-old Ginsberg took with his mother to a clinic. The confusion and unpredictability of his mother's behavior forced him to assume an adult's role, for which he was not prepared. For the first time, he realizes that this moment marked the real end of childhood and introduced him to a universe of chaos and absurdity. As the narrative develops, the emergence of a nascent artistic consciousness, poetic perception, and political idealism is presented against a panorama of life in the United States in the late 1930's. Realizing that his growth into the poet who is revealing this psychic history is closely intertwined with his mother's decline, Ginsberg faces his fear that he was drawing his newfound strength from her as she failed. As the section concludes, he squarely confronts his mother's illness, rendering her madness in disjointed scraps of conversation while using blunt physical detail as a means of showing the body's collapse: an effective analogue for her simultaneous mental disorder. There is a daunting authenticity to these details, as Ginsberg speaks with utter candor about the most intimate and unpleasant subjects (a method he also employs in later poems about sexual contacts), confirming his determination to bury nothing in memory.

This frankness fuses Ginsberg's recollections into a mood of great sympathy; he is moved to prayer, asking divine intervention to ease his mother's suffering. Here he introduces the actual Hebrew words of the Kaddish, the formal service that had been denied his mother because of a technicality. The poet's contribution is not only to create an appropriate setting for the ancient ritual but also to offer a testament to his mother's most admirable qualities. As the second section ends, Ginsberg sets the power of poetic language to celebrate beauty against the pain of his mother's last days. Returning to the elegiac mode (after Percy Bysshe Shelley's "Adonais"), Ginsberg has a last vision of his mother days before her final stroke, associated with sunlight and giving her son advice that concludes, "Love,/ your mother," which he acknowledges with his own tribute, "which is Naomi."

The last part of the poem, "Hymmnn," is divided into four sections. The first is a prayer for God's blessing for his mother (and for all people); the second is a recitation of some of the circumstances of her life; the third is a catalog of characteristics that seem surreal and random but coalesce toward the portrait he is producing by composite images; and the last part is "another variation of the litany form," ending the poem in a flow of "pure emotive sound" in which the words "Lord lord lord," as if beseeching, alternate with the words "caw caw caw," as if exclaiming in ecstasy.

By resisting almost all the conventional approaches to the loaded subject of motherhood, Ginsberg has avoided sentimentality and reached a depth of feeling that is overwhelming, even if the reader's experience is nothing like the poet's. The universality of the relationship is established by its particulars, the sublimity of the relationship by the revelation of the poet's enduring love and empathy.

The publication of "Kaddish" ended the initial phase of Ginsberg's writing life. "Howl" is a declaration of poetic intention, while "Kaddish" is a confession of personal necessity. With these two long, powerful works, Ginsberg completed the educational process of his youth and was ready to use his craft as a confident, mature artist. His range in the early 1960's included the hilarious "I Am a Victim of Telephone," which debunked his increasing celebrity, the gleeful jeremiad "Television Was a Baby Crawling Toward That Deathchamber," the generously compassionate "Who Be Kind To," and the effusive lyric "Why Is God Love, Jack?" A tribute to his mentor, "Death News," describes his thoughts on learning of Williams's demise.

"Kral Majales"

In 1965, after he had been invited to Cuba and Czechoslovakia, Ginsberg was expelled from each country for his bold condemnation of each nation's policies. In Prague, he had been selected by students (including young Václav Havel) as Kral Majales (king of May), an ancient European honor that has lasted through centuries of upheaval. In the poem "Kral Majales"—published accompanied by positive and negative silhouettes of the smiling poet, naked except for tennis shoes and sporting three hands bearing finger cymbals, against a phallic symbol—he juxtaposed communist and capitalist societies at their most dreary and destructive to the life-enhancing properties of the symbolic May King: a figure of life, love, art, and enlightenment. The first part of the poem is marked by discouragement, anger, and sorrow mixed with comic resignation to show the dead end reached by governments run by a small clique of rulers. However, the heart of the poem, a list of all the attributes that he brings to the position of Kral Majales, is an exuberant explosion of joy, mirth, and confidence in the rising generation of the mid-1960's. Written before the full weight of the debacle in Vietnam had been felt and before the string of assassinations that rocked the United States took place, Ginsberg reveled in the growth of what he thought was a revolutionary movement toward a utopian society. His chant of praise for the foundations of a counterculture celebrates "the power of sexual youth," productive, fulfilling work ("industry in eloquence"), honest acceptance of the body ("long hair of Adam"), the vitality of art ("old Human poesy"), and the ecumenical spirit of religious pluralism that he incarnates: "I am of Slavic parentage and Buddhist Jew/ who worships the Sacred Heart of Christ the blue body of Krishna the straight back of Ram the beads of Chango." In a demonstration of rhythmic power, the poem builds until it tells of the poet's literal descent to earth from the airplane he took to London after his expulsion. Arriving at "Albion's airfield" with the exultation of creative energy still vibrating through his mind and body, he proudly presents (to the reader or listener) the poem he has just written "on a jet seat in mid Heaven." The immediacy of the ending keeps the occasion fresh in the poet's memory and alive forever in the rhythms and images of his art.

"Witchita Vortex Sutra"

The Prague Spring that was to flourish temporarily in events such as the 1965 May Festival was crushed by Soviet tanks in 1968. By then, the United States had become fully involved in the war in Southeast Asia, and Ginsberg had replaced some of his optimism about change with an anger that recalled the mood of the Moloch section of "Howl." In 1966, he was in Kansas to read poetry, and this trip to the heartland of the United States became the occasion for a poem that is close to an epic of American life as the country was being torn apart. "Witchita Vortex Sutra," one of Ginsberg's longest poems, combines elements of American mythological history, personal psychic exploration, multicultural interaction, and prophetic incantation. The poem is sustained by a twin vision of the United States: the submerged but still vital American spirit that inspired Whitman and the contemporary American realities by which "many another has suffered death and madness/ in the Vortex." A sense of a betrayal informs the narrative, and the poet is involved in a search for the cause and the cure, ultimately (and typically) discovering that only art can rescue the blighted land.

The first part of the poem depicts Kansas as the seat of American innocence, where the spirit of transcendental idealism is still relatively untouched by American actions in Vietnam. Whitman's dream of an open country and worthy citizens seems to remain alive, but events from the outside have begun to reach even this sheltered place. The land of Abraham Lincoln, Vachel Lindsay, William Jennings Bryan, and other American idealists is being ruined by the actions of a rogue "government" out of touch with the spirit of the nation. The poet attempts to understand why this is happening and what consequences it has for him, for any artist. After this entrance into the poem's geopolitical and psychic space, the second part presents, in a collage form akin to Ezra Pound's *Cantos* (1925-1972), figures, numbers, names, and snatches of propaganda about the conflict in Vietnam. Following Pound's proposal that a bad government corrupts a people by its misuse of language, Ginsberg begins an examination of the nature of language itself to try to determine how the lies and deceptions in "black language/ writ by machine" can be overcome by a "lonesome man in Kansas" who is "not afraid" and who can speak "with ecstatic language": that is, the true language of human need, essential human reality. Calling on "all Powers of imagination," Ginsberg acts as an artist in service to moral being, using all the poetic power, or versions of speech, that he has worked to master.

Ginsberg's "ecstatic language" includes, in particular, the lingo of the Far Eastern religions he has learned in his travels. To assist in exorcising the demons of the West, he implores the gods of the East (fitting, since the war is in the East) to merge their forces with those of the new deities of the West, whose incarnation he finds in such American mavericks as the musician Dylan. He summons them as allies against the Puritan death-wish he locates in the fanaticism of unbending, self-righteous zealots such as Kansas's Carrie Nation, whose "angry smashing ax" began "a vortex of hatred" that eventually "defoliated the Mekong Delta." Through the poem, Ginsberg has cast the language artist as the rescuer, the visionary who can restore the heartland to its primal state as a land of promise and justice. In an extraordinary testament to his faith in his craft, Ginsberg declares, "The war is over now"—which, in a poem that examines language in "its deceits, its degeneration" (as Charles Molesworth says), "is especially poignant being only language."

THE FALL OF AMERICA

Other poems, such as "Bayonne Entering NYC," further contributed to the mood of a collection titled *The Fall of America*, but Ginsberg was also turning again toward the personal. In poems such as "Wales Visitation," a nature ode written in the spirit of the English Romantics, and "Bixby Canyon," which is an American West Coast parallel, Ginsberg explores the possibilities of a personal pantheism, attempting to achieve a degree of cosmic transcendence to compensate for the disagreeable situation on earth. His loving remembrance for Beat poet Cassady, "On Neal's Ashes," is another expression of this elegiac inclination, which reaches a culmination in *Mind Breaths*.

MIND BREATHS

"Mind Breaths," the title poem of the collection *Mind Breaths*, is a meditation that gathers the long lines of what Ginsberg has called "a chain of strong-breath'd poems" into a series of modulations on the theme of the poet's breath as an aspect of the wind-spirit of life. As he has often pointed out, Ginsberg believes that one of his most basic principles of organization is his ability to control the rhythms of a long line ("My breath is long"). In "Mind Breaths," he develops the idea that the voice of the poet is a part of the "voice" of the cosmos—a variant on the ancient belief that the gods spoke directly through the poet. Ranging over the entire planet, Ginsberg gradually includes details from many of the world's cultures, uniting nations in motive and design to achieve an encompassing ethos of universality. Beneath the fragmentation and strife of the world's governments, the poet sees "a calm breath, a silent breath, a slow breath," part of the fundamentally human universe that the artist wishes to inhabit.

PLUTONIAN ODE

In the title poem of *Plutonian Ode*, Ginsberg offers another persuasive poetic argument to strengthen the "Mind-guard spirit" against the death wish that leads some to embrace "Radioactive Nemesis." Recalling, once again, "Howl," in which Moloch stands for the death-driven impulses of humankind gone mad with greed, Ginsberg surveys the history of nuclear experimentation. The poem is designed as a guide for "spiritual friends and teachers," and the "mountain of Plutonian" is presented as the dark shadow-image of the life force that has energized the universe since "the beginning." Addressing himself, as well, to the "heavy heavy Element awakened," Ginsberg describes a force of "vaunted Mystery" against which he brings, as always, the "verse prophetic" to "wake space" itself. The poem is written to restore the power of mind (which is founded on spiritual enlightenment) to a civilization addicted to "horrific arm'd, Satanic industries"—an echo of Blake's injunctions at the dawn of an era in which machinery has threatened human well-being.

"Birdbrain"

The tranquility of such reveries in poems such as "Mind Breaths" did not replace Ginsberg's anger at the social system but operated more as a condition of recovery or place of restoration, so that the poet could venture back into the political arena and chant, "Birdbrain is the ultimate product of Capitalism/ Birdbrain chief bureaucrat of Russia." In the poem "Birdbrain," published in *Collected Poems, 1947-1980*, Ginsberg castigates the idiocy of organizations everywhere. His humor balances his anger, but there is an implication that neither humor nor anger will be sufficient against the forces of "Birdbrain [who] is Pope, Premier, President, Commissar, Chairman, Senator!" In spite of his decades of experience as a political activist, Ginsberg never let his discouragement overcome his sense of civic responsibility. The publication of *Collected Poems, 1947-1980* secured Ginsberg's reputation as one of the leading writers of late twentieth century American literature.

White Shroud

The appearance in 1986 of *White Shroud* revived Ginsberg's political orations; in this work, he identifies the demons of contemporary American life as he sees them: "yes I glimpse CIA's spooky dope deal vanity." There is a discernible sense of time's passage in "White Shroud," which is a kind of postscript to "Kaddish." Once again, Ginsberg recollects the pain of his family relationships: His difficulties in dealing with aging, irascible relatives merges with his responsibility to care for those who have loved him, and his feeling for modern America fuse with his memories of the Old Left past of his immigrant family. The poem tells how Ginsberg, in search of an apartment, finds himself in the Bronx neighborhood where his family once lived. There he meets the shade of his mother, still berating him for having abandoned her, but now offering him a home as well. There is a form of comfort for the poet in his dream of returning to an older New York to live with his family, a return to the "lost America," the mythic America that has inspired millions of American dreams.

Cosmopolitan Greetings

Ginsberg in the 1990's expressed his introspective side with lyric sadness in such poems as "Personals Ad" (from *Cosmopolitan Greetings*), in which he communicates his quest for a ". . . companion protector friend/ young lover w/empty compassionate soul" to help him live "in New York alone with the Alone." With the advent of his seventh decade, he might have settled for a kind of comfortable celebrity, offering the substance of his literary and social experiences to students at the Graduate Center of the City University of New York and to countless admirers on reading tours throughout the nation. Instead, he accepted his position as the primary proponent and spokesperson for his fellow artists of the Beat generation, and he continued to write with the invention and vigor that had marked his work from its inception. Acknowledging his perspective as a "poet professor in autumn years" in "Personals Ad," Ginsberg remains highly conscious of ". . . the body/ where I was born" (from "Song," in *Howl, and Other Poems*), but his focus is now on the inescapable consequences of time's passage on that body in poems that register the anxieties of an aging man trying to assess his own role in the cultural and historical patterns of his era.

The exuberance and the antic humor that have always been a feature of Ginsberg's poetry of sexual candor remain, but there is a modulation in tone and mood toward the rueful and contemplative. Similarly, poems presenting strong positions about social and governmental policies often refer to earlier works on related subjects, as if adding links to a chain of historical commentaries. Although few of Ginsberg's poems are as individually distinctive as the "strong-breath'd poems" such as "Howl," "Kaddish," or "Witchita Vortex Sutra," which Ginsberg calls "peaks of inspiration," Ginsberg's utilization of a characteristic powerful rhythmic base figure drives poems such as "Improvisation in Beijing." "On Cremation of Chogyam Trungpa, Vidadhara," "Get It," and "Graphic Winces" offer statements that are reflections of fundamental positions that Ginsberg has been developing throughout his work.

"Improvisation in Beijing," the opening poem, is a poetic credo in the form of an expression of artistic ambition. Using the phrase "I write poetry . . ." to launch each line, Ginsberg juxtaposes ideas, images, data, and assertion in a flux of energetic intent, his life's experiences revealing the desire and urgency of his calling. Ginsberg has gathered his responses to requests for his sources of inspiration: from the explicitly personal "I write poetry to make accurate picture my own mind" to the overtly political ". . . Wild West destroys new grass & erosion creates deserts" to the culturally connected "I write poetry because I listened to black Blues on 1939 radio, Leadbelly and Ma Rainey" to the aesthetically ambitious in the concluding line, "I write poetry because it's the best way to say everything in mind with 6 minutes or a lifetime."

"On Cremation of Chogyam Trungpa, Vidadhara," a tribute to a spiritual guide, reverses the structural thrust of "Improvisation in Beijing" so that the lines beginning "I noticed the . . ." spiral inward toward a composite portrait built by "minute particulars," Ginsberg's term for Williams's injunction "No ideas but in things." Ginsberg concentrates on specifics in tightly wound lines that present observations of an extremely aware, actively thoughtful participant: "I noticed the grass, I noticed the hills, I noticed the highways,/ I noticed the dirt road, I noticed the cars in the parking lot." Eventually, the poet's inclusion of more personal details reveals his deep involvement in the occasion, demonstrating his ability to internalize his guide's teaching. The poem concludes with a summation of the event's impact, a fusion of awe, delight, and wonder joining the mundane with the cosmic. Typically at this time in his life, Ginsberg acts from a classic poetic position, speaking as the recorder who sees, understands, and appreciates the significance of important events and who can find language adequate for their expression.

The collection, like Ginsberg's other major volumes, contains many poems that are not meant to be either especially serious or particularly profound. These works include poems written to a musical notation ("C.I.A. Dope Calypso"), poetic lines cast in speech bubbles in a "Deadline Dragon Comix" strip, three pages of what are called "American Sentences" (which are, in effect, a version of haiku), and a new set of verses to the old political anthem, "The Internationale," in which Ginsberg pays homage to the dreams of a social republic of justice while parodying various manifestations of self-important propagandists and salvationists.

The poems in the volume that show Ginsberg at his most effective, however, occur in two modes. Ever since his tribute to Whitman, "A Supermarket in California," Ginsberg has used the lyric mode as a means of conveying his deeply romantic vision of an idealized existence set in opposition to the social disasters he has resisted. These are poems of appreciation and gratitude, celebrating the things of the world that bring delight. "To Jacob Rabinowitz" is a letter of thanks for a translation of Catullus. "Fun House Antique Store" conveys the poet's astonishment at finding a "country antique store, an/ oldfashioned house" on the road to "see our lawyer in D.C." The lovingly evoked intricate furnishings of the store suggest something human that is absent in "the postmodern Capital." Both of these poems sustain a mood of exultation crucial to a lyric.

The other mode that Ginsberg employs is a familiar one. Even since he described himself as "Rotting Ginsberg" in "Mescaline" (1959), Ginsberg has emphasized physical sensation and the extremes of sensory response as means for understanding artistic consciousness, a mind-body linkage. Some of the most despairing lines Ginsberg has written appear in these poems— understandable considering the poet's ailments, including the first manifestations of liver cancer, which Ginsberg endured for years before his death. Nonetheless, the bright spirit that animates Ginsberg's work throughout is present as a counterthrust.

"In the Benjo," which has been placed at the close of the collection, expresses Ginsberg's appreciation for Snyder's lessons in transcendent wisdom and epitomizes a pattern of affirmation that is present in poems that resist the ravages of physical decline ("Return to Kral Majales"), the loss of friends ("Visiting Father & Friends"), the sorry state of the world ("You Don't Know It"), and the fraudulent nature of so-called leaders ("Elephant in the Meditation Hall"). In these poems, as in many in earlier collections, Ginsberg is conveying the spirit of an artistic age that he helped shape and that his work exemplifies. As Snyder said in tribute, "Allen Ginsberg showed that poetry could speak to our moment, our political concerns, our hopes and fears, and in the grandest style. He broke that open for all of us."

COLLECTED POEMS, 1947-1997

Collected Poems, 1947-1997 is a massive chronological compilation—combining *Collected Poems, 1947-1980*, *White Shroud*, *Cosmopolitan Greetings*, and *Death and Fame*—that gathers virtually every poem Ginsberg ever wrote, from his first published effort, "In Society" (1947), to his last written work, "Things I'll Not Do (Nostalgia)," finished just days before he died. The volume incorporates drawings, photographs, sheet music, calligraphy, notes, acknowledgments, introductions, appendixes, and all the other addenda included in the previous publications that collectively reveal Ginsberg's far-reaching interests and his enormous skill. Ginsberg's entire body of work portrays the poet's growth as a craftsperson, a seeker of truth, a spokesperson for his generation, and ultimately as a human being.

Even in his earliest work, "In Society"—which alludes to his homosexuality and includes epithets that polite society would deem vulgar—Ginsberg demonstrated that no subject was unworthy of consideration, no phrase taboo. Though his topics from the beginning were sometimes controversial, the format of his poems was still restrained and formal because he had not yet rejected his father's traditionalist ways. Such poems as "Two Sonnets" (1948), with their conventional fourteen-line structures and rhyme schemes, would not look out of place in collections of William Shakespeare or Edmund Spenser. Indeed, much of Ginsberg's early work (in the first section, "Empty Mirror: Gates of Wrath, 1947-1952") constitutes rhyming verse as the poet experimented with meter, line length, and language in his fledgling efforts to find a unique voice. Subject matter, too, is fairly traditional: love poems, contemplation of nature, and musings on life, death and religion. With few exceptions, the titles of these poems—"A Very Dove," "Vision 1948," "Refrain," "A Western Ballad," "The Shrouded Stranger," "This Is About Death," "Sunset," "Ode to the Setting Sun"— give little indication of Ginsberg's pixie-like humor or his coming break with literary convention.

Part 2 of the collection ("The Green Automobile, 1953-1954") provides the first inkling that Ginsberg was beginning to discover the appropriate form of expression for ideas too large to be otherwise contained. The long poem "Siesta in Xbalba and Return to the States," an impressionistic work based on Ginsberg's travels in Mexico, sets the stage for the angry, dynamic, no-holds-barred compositions that would follow and characterize the bulk of his poetic career. The main part of Ginsberg's career is collected in eleven sections: "Howl, Before and After: San Francisco Bay Area (1955-1956)," "Reality Sandwiches: Europe! Europe!" (1957-1959)," "Kaddish and Related Poems (1959-1960)," "Planet News: To Europe and Asia (1961-1963)," "King of May: America to Europe (1963-1965)," "The Fall of America (1965-1971)," "Mind Breaths All over the Place (1972-1977)," "Plutonian Ode (1977-1980)," "White Shroud: Poems, 1980-1985," "Cosmopolitan Greetings: Poems, 1986-1992," and "Death and Fame: Poems, 1993-1997."

At the very end of his life, as he lay dying, Ginsberg, like someone reviewing the span of his existence in clarifying flashes, seemed to return full circle to where he had begun. Brief bursts of inspiration, such as "American Sentences," are whimsical, epigram-like in nature. Other final thoughts, including "Sky Words," "Scatological Observations," "My Team Is Red Hot," "Starry Rhymes," "Thirty State Bummers," and "Bop

Sh'bam," are almost childlike ditties in conventional verse forms such as rhyming couplets and quatrains.

Collected Poems, 1947-1997 captures the essence of an artist who, like Whitman before him, exploded the notion of what poetry could or should be. Mostly, though, it lays bare the mind and soul of an individual of consummate craft, a person of fierce intelligence and insatiable curiosity, a human blessed with playful wit, undying optimism, all-encompassing compassion and unstinting generosity for other people.

OTHER MAJOR WORKS

NONFICTION: *Indian Journals*, 1963; *The Yage Letters*, 1963 (with William Burroughs); *Indian Journals, March 1962-May 1963: Notebooks, Diary, Blank Pages, Writings*, 1970; *Allen Verbatim: Lectures on Poetry, Politics, Consciousness*, 1974; *Gay Sunshine Interview*, 1974; *Visions of the Great Rememberer*, 1974; *To Eberhart from Ginsberg*, 1976; *As Ever: The Collected Correspondence of Allen Ginsberg and Neal Cassady*, 1977; *Journals: Early Fifties, Early Sixties*, 1977, 1992; *Composed on the Tongue: Literary Conversations, 1967-1977*, 1980; *Allen Ginsberg Photographs*, 1990; *Snapshot Poetics: A Photographic Memoir of the Beat Era*, 1993; *Journals Mid-Fifties, 1954-1958*, 1995; *Deliberate Prose: Selected Essays, 1952-1995*, 2000; *Family Business: Selected Letters Between a Father and Son*, 2001 (with Louis Ginsberg); *Spontaneous Mind: Selected Interviews, 1958-1996*, 2001; *The Letters of Allen Ginsberg*, 2008 (Bill Morgan, editor); *The Selected Letters of Allen Ginsberg and Gary Snyder*, 2009 (Morgan, editor).

EDITED TEXT: *Poems for the Nation: A Collection of Contemporary Political Poems*, 2000.

MISCELLANEOUS: *Beat Legacy, Connections, Influences: Poems and Letters by Allen Ginsberg*, 1994; *The Book of Matyrdom and Artifice: First Journals and Poems, 1937-1952*, 2006.

BIBLIOGRAPHY

Baker, Deborah. *A Blue Hand: The Tragicomic, Mind-Altering Odyssey of Allen Ginsberg, a Holy Fool, a Lost Muse, a Dharma Bum, and His Prickly Bride in India.* New York: Penguin, 2009. A well-researched study of the life-changing travels in India undertaken by Ginsberg and various companions in search of enlightenment, and the aftereffects of the journeys on the poet's work and attitudes.

Edwards, Susan. *The Wild West Wind: Remembering Allen Ginsberg.* Boulder, Colo.: Baksun Books, 2001. A fond and enlightening reminiscence from an author, teacher, artist, and metaphysician who worked for twenty years alongside Ginsberg at Naropa University.

Felver, Christopher, Lawrence Ferlinghetti, and David Shapiro. *The Late Great Allen Ginsberg: A Photo Biography.* New York: Running Press, 2003. A compendium of images and impressions of the poet from all stages of his life, with contributions from many of those who knew him and worked or performed alongside him, including Philip Glass, Ray Manzarek, Ed Sanders, Norman Mailer, Peter Orlovsky, Gary Snyder, Gregory Corso, William Burroughs, and Lawrence Ferlinghetti.

Ginsberg, Allen. *Howl: Original Draft Facsimile, Transcript, and Variant Versions, Fully Annotated by Author, with Contemporaneous Correspondence, Account of First Public Presentation.* New York: Harper Perennial Modern Classics, 2006. An in-depth examination of Ginsberg's first important work, which resulted in charges of obscenity—eventually dismissed—and which made the poet a household name.

Landas, John. *The Bop Apocalypse.* Champaign: University of Illinois Press, 2001. An illuminating account of the religious aspects and elements of the work of Ginsberg, Jack Kerouac, and William Burroughs. Particularly good on the historical dynamics operating in the writers' lives.

Miles, Barry. *The Beat Hotel: Ginsberg, Burroughs, and Corso in Paris, 1958-1963.* New York: Grove Press, 2000. A narrative chronicle of the Beats in Paris from the "Howl" obscenity trial to the invention of the cut-up technique. Based on firsthand accounts from diaries, letters, and many original interviews.

Morgan, Bill. *I Celebrate Myself: The Somewhat Private Life of Allen Ginsberg.* New York: Viking Press, 2006. Morgan drew on unpublished letters and journals to create an extensive, full-length biography, the first to be published after Ginsberg's death. Morgan veers away from lending his own opinion and chronicles rather than interprets Ginsberg's life; however, he manages to highlight the events that inspired Ginsberg to write his unique brand of poetry.

Podhoretz, Norman. *Ex-Friends: Falling Out with Allen Ginsberg, Lionel and Diana Trilling, Lillian Hellman, Hannah Arendt, and Norman Mailer.* New York: Encounter Books, 2000. Podhoretz, the conservative editor of *Commentary*, presents a different and highly entertaining perspective on the infighting that went on among the New York intellectual community of which Ginsberg was a part during the 1950's and 1960's.

Raskin, Jonah. *American Scream: Allen Ginsberg's "Howl" and the Making of the Beat Generation.* Berkeley: University of California Press, 2006. Describes Ginsberg's composition and presentation of his groundbreaking poem against the twin backdrops of the poet's personal life and the era in which it was created.

Trigillo, Tony. *Allen Ginsberg's Buddhist Poetics.* Carbondale: Southern Illinois University Press, 2007. This scholarly study focuses on the poet's adoption of Buddhism and its effect on Ginsberg's work, in terms of form, content, and spirituality.

Leon Lewis
Updated by Jack Ewing

ANTHONY HECHT

Born: New York, New York; January 16, 1923
Died: Washington, D.C.; October 20, 2004

PRINCIPAL POETRY

A Summoning of Stones, 1954
The Seven Deadly Sins, 1958
Aesopic, 1967
The Hard Hours, 1967
Millions of Strange Shadows, 1977
The Venetian Vespers, 1979
A Love for Four Voices: Homage to Franz Joseph Haydn, 1983
Collected Earlier Poems, 1990
The Transparent Man, 1990
Flight Among the Tombs, 1996
The Darkness and the Light, 2001
Collected Later Poems, 2003

OTHER LITERARY FORMS

Critical pieces by Anthony Hecht (hehkt) have been compiled as *Obbligati: Essays in Criticism* (1986). He has also worked as a translator, publishing a version of Aeschylus's *Seven Against Thebes* (1973; with Helen Bacon) and of Voltaire's *Poem upon the Lisbon Disaster* (1977).

ACHIEVEMENTS

An admirer of John Crowe Ransom, Allen Tate, and George Santayana, Anthony Hecht maintained the wit, precision, and intellectual rigor of the modernist voice for decades following World War II. He avoided a variety of trends in American poetry, including confessional poetry and didactic antiwar poetry, during the 1960's and 1970's. However, his focus on issues surrounding art and human experience and on ethics and questions of human evil throughout history brought Hecht major recognition. In 1968, he won the Pulitzer Prize in poetry for *The Hard Hours*. He received the Russell Loines Award of the American Academy of Arts and Letters in 1968 and was elected to membership of that academy in 1970. He served as chancellor for the Academy of American Poets from 1971 to 1997. In 1983, Hecht was a corecipient of the Bollingen Prize (with John Hollander), and from 1982 to 1984, he was consultant in poetry (poet laureate) to the Library of Congress. He has won a variety of other awards, including the Prix de Rome (1951), the Eugenio Montale Award (1984), the Ruth Lilly Poetry Prize (1988), the Aiken Taylor Award in Modern American Poetry (1989), the Wallace Stevens Award (1997), the Corrington Award for Literary Excellence from Centenary College of Louisiana (1997-1998), the Frost Medal (2000), the Ambassador Book Award (2002), and a Los Angeles Times Book Prize (2003). He was the recipient of Guggenheim Fellowships (1954, 1959), Ford Foundation Fellowships (1960, 1968), a Rockefeller Fellowship (1967), and an Academy of American Poets Fellowship (1969). He has also received honorary doctorates from Bard College, Georgetown University, Towson State University, and the University of Rochester.

BIOGRAPHY

Anthony Evan Hecht was born in New York City on January 16, 1923. He was graduated from Bard College in 1944 and spent the next three years in Europe and Japan as a rifleman in the U.S. Army. He was also briefly in the Counter-Intelligence Corps. With his unit, Hecht discovered the site of mass graves in an annex area of the Buchenwald concentration camp. This shattering experience would shape his worldview and influence the direction of his poetry.

Upon his return from Europe, Hecht took several teaching jobs, moving around from the Middle West to New England and finally back to New York. He spent a year at Kenyon College between 1947 and 1948 and studied with John Crowe Ransom, who was editing *Kenyon Review* and published several poems by the young poet. Hecht embraced Ransom's New Critical perspective and soon afterward continued his tutelage under the Fugitives, working informally with Allen Tate. He went on to take a master's degree from Columbia University in 1950.

His first book, *A Summoning of Stones*, appeared in 1954, the same year as his marriage to his first wife, the mother of their two sons. In 1971, Hecht was married to Helen D'Alessandro, who bore his third son. Over several decades, Hecht taught in a number of colleges and universities, including Kenyon College, the University of Iowa, New York University, Smith College, and Bard College. At the University of Rochester, he was the John H. Dean Professor of Poetry and Rhetoric from 1967 to 1982; during this time, he also spent brief periods as a visiting lecturer at Washington University, Harvard University, and Yale University. In 1982, for two years, Hecht was appointed poetry consultant to the Library of Congress. He went on to join the graduate faculty at Georgetown University. His career also led him to spend some time abroad, as a Fulbright professor in Brazil and a trustee of the American Academy in Rome.

ANALYSIS

Terms such as "baroque," "neoclassical," "meditative," "realistic," "manneristic," "metaphysical," and "pessimistic" as well as "optimistic" have been used to describe Anthony Hecht's poetry. These varying descriptions reflect not so much transitions in the course of his poetry as the depth and complexity of his work. His poems are unpretentiously finely wrought, reflecting his interest in Greek and Roman poetry and seventeenth century poetry in addition to the work of the generation of poets that directly preceded him, including such writers as Ransom, Tate, and W. H. Auden. Hecht has also translated poems by writers including Joseph Brodsky, Charles Baudelaire, Guillaume Apollinaire, Voltaire, and Joachim du Bellay. His view of tradition is not unlike the one expressed in T. S. Eliot's essay "Tradition and the Individual Talent." Hecht is also very much aware of history, from the battles of the ancients to the wars of the twentieth century. Many of his poems are very serious, addressing such themes as death and carnage, while others are light and playful. His treatment of history and attention to the history of poetic convention set his work apart from that of many American poets of the latter part of the twentieth century.

A SUMMONING OF STONES

Selected poems from Hecht's first volume, *A Summoning of Stones*, reappear in his *Collected Earlier Poems*. Among these, "La Condition Botanique," "A Poem for Julia," and "Alceste in the Wilderness" have received considerable critical attention. "La Condition Botanique" treats the relationship between humanity and nature, especially the human attempt to order the natural world. The meditation is highly structured with a rhyme scheme, *abccba*. It moves great distances in time and space, from the Romans to Marie Curie, from Mexico to Brooklyn, from Ezekiel to the Buddha, suggesting the unending quest for order and stasis. Human endeavor is treated with some degree of humor. For example, the opening of "La Condition Botanique" is ironic:

> Romans, rheumatic, gouty, came
> To bathe in Ischian springs where water steamed,
> Puffed and enlarged their bold imperial thoughts, and   which
> Later Madame Curie declared to be so rich
> In radioactive content as she deemed
> Should win them everlasting fame.

Some of the stanza breaks are rhymically counterpointed through the enjambment between the last line of one stanza and the first line of the next. Hecht's amusing catalog, which moves at a quick pace structurally and thematically, echoes the flux of the world.

"Alceste in the Wilderness" takes the main character of the seventeenth century comedy of manners and pursues the disillusionment of the misanthrope of Molière (Jean Baptiste Poquelin) in the heart of Africa, far removed from the pretense of French society. Alceste finds a monkey corpse as "heat gives his thinking cavity no quarter,/ For he is burning with the monkey's fever." His exile in the wild stands in ironic contrast to the affected manners of the world he rejected. This combination is furthered by the poet's adherence to poetic convention, employing an *abbaab* rhyme scheme and iambic meter for images of death and corruption.

"A Poem for Julia" is meditative, opening with a description of a painting of a madonna by Hans Memling, a fifteenth century Flemish painter. The name Julia has resonances in the course of poetry and calls to mind Proteus's beloved in William Shakespeare's *Two Gentlemen of Verona* (pr. c. 1594-1595) and Robert Herrick's poems, including "Upon Julia's Clothes" and "Upon Julia's Voice." After addressing the painting by Memling, the speaker considers the human desire to transcend death. On one level, then, the poem addresses the relationship between art and the world; it also treats the relationship between art and history. For example, "a small, foul-minded clergyman" considered that Michelangelo's *Last Judgment* was "a lewd and most indecent show/ Of nakedness, not for a sacred place."

Although Hecht celebrates artifice, like William Butler Yeats in "Byzantium," "A Poem for Julia" identifies its genesis in nature. Related to the theme of art as opposed to the real and physical is the subject of spirit and the eternal. To close six long stanzas of blank verse, the poet presents the perpetual balance of spirit and nature:

> The heart is ramified with an old force
> (Outlingering the blood, out of the sway
> Of its own fleshy trap) that finds its source
> Deep in the phosphorous waters of the bay,
> Or in the wind, or pointing cedar tree,
> Or its own ramified complexity.

Thus, the heart perceives nature as transcendent, but the persona makes no direct statement. Still, since the poem is for "Julia," the poet suggests that love is central to the painter's vision and the poet's craft. Through the name, the poet gracefully acknowledges the role of convention in art. Through the literary allusions and the description of a painting, "A Poem for Julia" ingeniously deals with art in self-referential metaphors.

THE HARD HOURS

Hecht opens his first book with a philosophical epigraph, quoting George Santayana: "To call the stones themselves to their ideal places, and enchant the very substance and the skeleton of the world." In contrast, he opens his second book, *The Hard Hours*, published thirteen years later, with a dedication to his two sons. Reflecting this difference, many of the poems in the latter book are thematically more personal and structurally less ordered than those in *A Summoning of Stones*. History is also treated with less distance and more emotion. A number of poems in *The Hard Hours* have been the subject of numerous critical discussions.

"Rites and Ceremonies," a ten-page meditation on the Buchenwald concentration camp and religious persecution through the ages, has received, possibly, the most attention of any of Hecht's poems. It illustrates many facets of his sensibility and orientation. The poem is structurally complex and is thematically immersed in human history—a history rife with accounts of cruelty. "Rites and Ceremonies" reveals the poet's personal exploration of major theological considerations. Finally, the poem echoes Eliot in places and thereby pays homage to a great modernist, but this also serves to highlight Hecht's perceptions as opposed to those of Eliot. Whereas Eliot presents the transcendent through images of the world and timelessness through temporal images, Hecht treats the human condition through references to historical events in which humanity is bound by its brutality. Whereas Eliot gives thanks for the divine sacrifice of love, Hecht mourns the sacrifice of human life and makes only ironic reference to the Bible. Hecht's Jewish background contributes to his perspective.

Like Eliot's *Four Quartets* (1943), "Rites and Ceremonies" is in four parts, and each is composed of statements, counterstatements, and variations. The second part is titled "The Fire Sermon," like a section in Eliot's *The Waste Land* (1922). Hecht's poem is also conversational in places and includes quite a few literary references. It differs from Eliot's poetry, however, in that no revelation is at hand, only words and prayers and the poet's acute attention to the problem of evil and the grim history of the Jews in Christian hands.

The persona, who seems very close to the poet, speaks in several tones. The first part, "The Room," opens in praise of God and is psalmlike in rhythm and diction. This prayer refers to a post-Holocaust world that is both the source of the poet's desire to pray to God and the cause of his skepticism. Biblical allusions in "Rites and Ceremonies" ring with irony. The poem begins, "Father, adonoi, author of all things," and alludes to the birth of the Messiah:

> Who was that child of whom they tell
> in lauds and threnes?
> whose holy names all shall pronounce
> Emmanuel,
> which being interpreted means,
> *"Gott mit uns"*?

The allusion is highly ironic as it echoes Matthew 1:23, in which an angel tells Joseph of Isaiah's prophecy and says that a virgin will bear a son to be called Emmanuel (which means "God with us"). The biblical allusion, punctuated by a question mark, is followed by a description of Buchenwald. In an understated tone, Hecht describes the signs of the millions killed and the method of extermination.

"Rites and Ceremonies" thereby opens with a contemplation of a place in twentieth century Germany where suffering was so great that questions are raised concerning the efficacy of language and prayer. Hecht then considers other events in previous centuries that also defy reason. In the second part, "The Fire Sermon," he treats several infamous incidents that took place in medieval Europe and considers the relationship between God and humanity—or perhaps more accurately, he questions the will of God as it is perceived by human beings.

Noting that a shipful of men died on Easter, the speaker asks, "Was it a judgment?" In reference to the death of hundreds of friars during Lent, he says that the Catholic Church decided that this was not a judgment. Finally, the speaker recounts the execution of Jews throughout Europe because two Jews had allegedly confessed, under torture, to poisoning the wells; it was believed that purging the Jews would end the plague. This belief, along with the Crusaders' slaughter of the heathen, was based on the assumption that people can discern God's will and help carry it out. The Church's position is rendered irrational—highly suspect, at best, and at worst self-serving. The tone here is matter-of-fact, and the images are unembellished—the speaker saying, for example, "Even as here in the city of Strasbourg,/ And the Jews assembled upon them [platforms],/ Children and all, and tied together with a rope."

The third part of "Rites and Ceremonies," "The Dream," begins, "The contemplation of horror is not edifying,/ Neither does it strengthen the soul," but continues by describing the death of three medieval saints—Lucy, Cecilia, and Lawrence. The speaker then switches to the public scourging of the Jews during Lent, which was described by the poet Joachim du Bellay. Thus Hecht suggests that the history of brutality is a long one. "Rites and Ceremonies" is a version of the story of human tragedy updated by the grim addition of the Holocaust.

The final section, "Words for the Day of Atonement," confronts the troubling theological issue of the cause of human suffering. The accepted view, that it is a consequence of sin, has been challenged in the previous sections of the poem. The speaker now says, discursively, "Merely to have survived is not an index of excellence,/ Nor given the way things go,/ Even of low cunning." He goes on to ask, "And to what purpose, as the darkness closes about/ And the child screams in the jellied fire,/ Had best be our present concern." This is followed by an allusion to Eliot's "The Hollow Men" through the repetition of a litany: "The soul is thine, and the body is thy creation:/ O have compassion on thy handiwork./ The soul is thine, and the body is thine." Whereas Eliot contrasts the mundane world of humanity to the kingdom of Heaven, Hecht's focus is on the here and now. Even as he makes a reference to the Christian promise of salvation in Matthew 10:30 ("Even the hairs of your head are numbered"), Hecht's imagery remains rooted in human history." "Rites and Ceremonies" closes with a consideration of the Holocaust. The images have a tragic literal significance:

> Neither shall the flame
> Kindle upon them, nor the fire burn
> A hair of them, for they
> Shall be thy care when it shall come to pass,
> And calling on thy name
> In the hot kilns and ovens, they shall turn
> To thee as it is prophesied, and say,
> *"He shall come down like rain upon mown grass."*

The last line, from Psalm 72, is highly ambiguous, since the psalm itself has been interpreted in several ways. In the Anglican tradition, it has been viewed as being messianic; therefore, the ending may be considered optimistic, as it makes a mystical leap to the promise of salvation. However, this is rendered ironic by the graphic imagery of the Holocaust. The psalm, however, is most often interpreted in Jewish tradition as a prayer for a king's moral integrity and his just treatment of his subjects. The simile is taken to suggest, metaphorically, fertility resulting from his gentleness as a ruler. Thus, "Rites and Ceremonies" calls attention not only to the relationship between God and humanity but also to how humanity governs itself. The history of the treatment of the Jews is a grim reminder of a monstrous flaw in the makeup of humanity.

This is also dealt with in "More Light! More Light!"—a poem dedicated to Heinrich Blücher and his wife, Hannah Arendt, author of *Eichmann in Jerusalem: A Report on the Banality of Evil* (1963). In rhymed couplets, "More Light! More Light!" juxtaposes a medieval heretic's death to the murder of a Pole and several Jews by the Nazis. The first stanza includes the heretic's prayer, "I implore my God to witness that I have made no crime." His death, however, is agonizing, because the sack of gunpowder does not ignite: "His legs were blistered sticks on which the black sap/ Bubbled and burst as he howled for the Kindly Light." There is no sign of this light in the poem. The poet continues with an equally graphic description of the murder of a Pole, who was shot and left to bleed to death because he refused to kill two Jews. The absence of God is implied as the narrator says, "No light, no light in the blue Polish eye." Although the heretic may die with more dignity because of his faith, God does not appear to intercede for him or the Pole. Instead of a sign of salvation, "More Light! More Light" ends on a powerful image of death: "Ghosts from the ovens" settle on the dead Pole's eyes "in a black soot." The notion of transcendence is strictly limited to the heretic's vision. If there is any transcendent quality conveyed in the poem, it is evil. The title, quoting what are thought to be Johann Wolfgang von Goethe's final words, imbues the stanzas that follow with irony.

In "It Out-Herods Herod. Pray You, Avoid It," Hecht confronts the meaning of the Holocaust on a personal level; he confesses to his children as they sleep that he could not "have saved them from the gas." His inability to protect them from monstrous evil is contrasted with his children's feeling of security, for they think him omnipotent.

The title resonates on several levels. First, the extermination of children during the Holocaust is compared to Herod's slaughter of the innocents (Matthew 2) or possibly it "out-Herods" the ruler's brutality. The quotation comes from act 3 of *Hamlet, Prince of Denmark* (pr. c. 1600-1601), where Hamlet advises the actors not to overact. The reference suggests that the speaker is reminding himself of his own limitations and his desire to avoid an exaggerated sense of power. In *The Hard Hours*, Hecht considers the meaning of Buchenwald both intellectually and emotionally.

Other poems in this volume that have received considerable critical attention include "A Hill" and "The Dover Bitch: A Criticism of Life." "A Hill" is another poem in which little distance appears to separate the speaker from the poet. It subtly conveys the speaker's loss of innocence as he comes into contact with a world that has a troubling underside. Reminiscent of some of Robert Frost's poetry, "A Hill" is ambiguous. The speaker is in a setting that leads him to envision another setting; this in turn calls to mind a childhood recollection. Hecht suggests that there is a dynamic relationship between the objects of the world and human consciousness, since the speaker's view of a hill is related to a hill that he recalls from childhood. As in Frost's poetry, Hecht's settings reveal something about the speaker's consciousness and also something about the poet's philosophical perspective; both poets portray a post-Edenic world.

"The Dover Bitch," on the other hand, is a light, whimsical poem and represents another dimension of Hecht's craft. It parodies Matthew Arnold's "Dover Beach." Whereas Arnold's speaker makes a series of profound observations on the nature of the world and fate and presents an idealized relationship with his love, Hecht's speaker informally discusses his relationship with the same woman. He claims that she treats him right and he gives her a good time. He concludes,

> and perhaps it's a year
> Before I see her again, but there she is,
> Running to fat, but dependable as they come.
> And sometimes I bring her a bottle of *Nuit d'Amour*.

"Dover Bitch" counters the idealism and philosophical abstraction of "Dover Beach" with realism. By parodying the masterly Victorian poet, who addresses the nature of reality, Hecht indirectly raises the question of the relationship between poetry and reality, including that in his own verse. Finally, Hecht comically yanks Arnold's poem from its Victorian context and into the second half of the twentieth century. Hecht's attention to the history of poetry has several different kinds of manifestations in his own work; it has steeped some of his poems with meaning, and it has been the source of the wit and humor in others.

MILLIONS OF STRANGE SHADOWS

Millions of Strange Shadows was published ten years after *The Hard Hours*. Although some critics consider this to be a transitional work, the poet's meditative stance endures. In addition, his preoccupation with the relationship between art and the world is expressed. "Dichtung und Wahrheit" (poetry and truth, or fiction and reality) wrestles with that very issue. The title is the one Goethe gave to his autobiography. The first part, written mostly in alternating tetrameter and trimeter lines, portrays two renderings of men: first, the famous sculpture of *The Discus Thrower*, and second, a photograph of several soldiers, including Hecht. The poet asks, "How can such fixture speak to us?" Both the sculptor's chisel and the camera "deal in a taxidermy/ Of our arrested flights." Here are philosophical questions going back to Socrates, including the relationship between stasis and motion, its rendering in art, and the ways in which the present is interpreted in art when it has become part of the past.

The second part of "Dichtung und Wahrheit" uses a longer line. It begins by invoking Wolfang Amadeus Mozart, whose music is often considered the measure of order and beauty. Hecht continues to pursue the relationship between the world and art. They are held in a dynamic balance as the speaker says, "We begin with the supreme donnée, the world," and quotes a person in a theatrical presentation who says, "We begin with the supreme donnée, the word." As in the poetry of Auden, the reader is left to question his or her own views, because the poem is intellectually challenging and presents no simple resolution.

"Apprehensions," which deals with Hecht's childhood, is according to several critics one of the best poems in *Millions of Strange Shadows*. It is written in blank verse in a conversational tone. Private and public worlds merge in "Apprehensions." Incidents in the poet's childhood are associated with cataclysmic world events, including the contemporaneous stock market crash and the Holocaust, which followed a decade later. As in many of Hecht's poems, there is an underlying symmetry. While the poem presents the child's and, ultimately, the poet's confrontation with painful reality, including his brother's illness, his father's suicide attempt, his governess's cruelty, and the brutality of the Holocaust, "Apprehensions" also presents the speaker's epiphanic perception of the beauty of the world—although a fallen one.

The strongest image is of the Teutonic governess, who craves lurid details in the popular press. She is "replete with the curious thumb-print of her race,/ That special relish for inflicted pain." "Apprehensions" closes with the speaker's dream of her, years after he knew her, in which their "relationship/ grew into international proportions." He envisions her as the infamous female concentration camp commandant, and he hears her say to him, "I always knew/ That you would come to me, that you'd come home." Although the poem appears to address childhood apprehensions, it reveals the American Jewish poet's empathy with the Jews of Europe, who were governed by rulers who created ghettos and camps that made the lurid stories of the tabloids look like tales for children.

THE VENETIAN VESPERS

Hecht's call for existentially responsible behavior also comes across in "Deodand," in *The Venetian Vespers*, published in 1979. On one level, it is a response to Pierre-Auguste Renoir's painting titled *Parisians Dressed in Algerian Costume*. The theme of the relationship between art and the world resurfaces. Based on the painting, the poet begins by describing a group of women in Paris who don exotic Arabic garments. They seem to be completely unaware of the inauthenticity of their antics. The speaker asks, "What is all this but crude imperial pride,/ Feminized, scented and attenuated,/ The exploitation of the primitive . . . ?" The second part of the poem switches to a description of the torturing of a French Legionnaire during the Algerian struggle for independence from France. The Algerians cut off his hands and feet, dressed him in a woman's wig and skirt, and paraded him through the streets.

The juxtaposition of these two descriptions and the role reversals convey the speaker's existentialism and refusal to embrace a political ideology. Although the young Legionnaire was involved in the French colonization of Algeria, he was a pawn in his own country's policy and in turn became the victim of terrible cruelty. Hecht examines some of the implicit cultural ramifications of the superficially pleasing images in Renoir's painting.

"The Venetian Vespers," a long six-part narrative in blank verse, also reveals the poet's compassion. Critics have compared it to Eliot's "Gerontion" in theme and have compared Hecht's speaker to Eliot's Prufrock. "The Venetian Vespers," a meditation on Venice, presents the psychological landscape of the speaker, a middle-aged American expatriate. He lost his parents long ago and is wifeless and childless. Through image motifs Hecht addresses the pain of aging and loneliness, the emptiness of contemporary life, the longing for transcendent meaning, and the particular history of one man. Humor is another dimension of human experience Hecht treats; the speaker notes that "the ochre pastes and puddings of dogshit/ Keep us earthbound in half a dozen ways,/ Curbing the spirit's tendency to pride."

In other places, however, the language and thought are elevated: "Morning has tooled the bay with bright inlays/ Of writing silver, scattered scintillance." The speaker also describes landscapes from his past, such as his uncle's A&P store in Lawrence, Massachusetts. The reader learns that his parents were Latvian immigrants, and that his father went west and his mother died when he was six.

While "The Venetian Vespers" is a narrative poem, it includes numerous allusions to works by authors such as Thomas Mann, Marcel Proust, and Lord Byron, and references to artists and composers. Introduced by two epigraphs, one from Shakespeare's *Othello, the Moor of Venice* (pr. 1604) and the other from John Ruskin's *The Stones of Venice* (1879), "The Venetian Vespers" is yet another means by which Hecht explores art and its meaning.

Finally, the poem explores the meaning of human behavior. The speaker, a pacifist, served as a medic in the army. He saw the shooting of an acquaintance, which he describes in graphic terms: "Enemy machine-gun fire/ . . . had sheared away/ The top of his cranium like a soft-boiled egg." This soldier had carried with him a book of etiquette instead of sentimental mementos in the field, and the speaker confesses that "he haunts me here, that seeker after law/ In a lawless world." "The Venetian Vespers," therefore, is an extended effort rich in engaging philosophical and psychological perspectives.

THE TRANSPARENT MAN

The Transparent Man, published in 1990, includes several narratives. "See Naples and Die" presents an account of a marriage that dissolves as the couple vacations in Italy. The theme of loss is also pursued in "The Transparent Man," whose speaker is a young woman dying of leukemia. In the style of a dramatic monologue, she addresses a visitor, Mrs. Curtis. Completely aware of her bleak prognosis, she calmly reveals that her father does not visit her because the thought that she will predecease him is too painful. External and internal landscapes overlap in the poem through the poet's skillful presentation of unified imagery. For example, the speaker compares her disease to "a sort of blizzard in the bloodstream,/ A deep, severe, unseasonable winter." In turn, the physical landscape of autumn is compared to the brain. She says that the sycamores and beeches outside her window resemble "magnificent enlargements/ Of the vascular system of the human brain." In the conclusion of the poem, the speaker considers the trees outdoors and what they seem to suggest about the larger scheme of things. Hecht's treatment of nature again calls to mind the poetry of Frost, in which images of nature reflect human experience.

Hecht also presents love as a central force in human experience. In another monologue, "Devotions of a Painter," the speaker claims, "I am enamored of the . . . corrupted treasures of this world," and he concludes, "Against the Gospel let my brush declare:/ 'These are the anaglyphs and gleams of love.'" Sexual love is celebrated in a masquelike poem, "A Love For Four Voices: Homage to Franz Joseph Haydn." Here the two sets of lovers from Shakespeare's *A Midsummer Night's Dream* (pr. c. 1595-1596) are identified with the four instruments in a string quartet, and they engage in a kind of musical dialogue. The epilogue directly relates art and love. Thus, on several levels, Hecht associates these themes.

The poet refers to artistic convention in several humorous poems of this collection, including "Eclogue of the Shepherd and the Townie" and "Humoresque." Thus, *The Transparent Man* reveals both Hecht's consistency and his development over the course of his career. It reveals him as having a remarkable range, from the agonizing contemplation of genocide to the graceful construction of witty parodies. All his work is tempered by both his extensive knowledge of the history of poetry and his intellectual rigor.

THE DARKNESS AND THE LIGHT

Hecht moves into the twenty-first century with *The Darkness and the Light*, further displaying his range of style, emotion, intellectual cachet, and modern-day references. Hecht culls from this range in this collection, in which he seems convinced that the sumptuous beauty he calls forth in a number of poems cannot compensate for the ravages of time. In "Memory," for example, a shaft of light striking some brass andirons in the late afternoon becomes "the dusty gleam of temporary wealth." These forty-four short lyrics are the quintessential "later work" of a poet—alternately fiery and wistful, looking back over past darkness and strife to a promise of light and rest and to a personal pantheon (Baudelaire, Horace, Goethe) represented here in nine translations.

Hecht also creates poems from biblical stories—Lot's wife, Saul and David, the witch of Endor, and Abraham—and he speaks as Bible characters. These are not mere retellings, but ferocious reinterpretations. Haman, villain of the story of Esther, is frighteningly eloquent as a hangman serving the Third Reich. With ease, Hecht makes the reader feel terror, an emotion that few poets know how to convey.

Surprisingly, in a volume given to the acerbic, burning emotions of an aging man, it is notable that the showcase work is a love poem. "Rara Avis in Terris" is a dizzying display of a full range of tones, from adoration to sarcasm, fury to awe. "Hawks are in the ascendant," it opens, and he does mean "some jihad, some rash all-get-out/ Crusade" to which people perhaps are all too well accustomed in the twenty-first century. This gives way to a different scene, brilliantly pointed before rising to its own occasion: "But where are the mild monogamous lovebirds. . . ." Such is Hecht's art that the reader sees them: "Lightly an olive branch they bear,/ Its deathless leafage emblematic of/ A quarter-century of faultless love."

COLLECTED LATER POEMS

Less than a year before Hecht's death, *Collected Later Poems* was published, gathering together his highly acclaimed, final three volumes: *Transparent Man*, *Flight Among the Tombs*, and *The Darkness and the Light*. Hecht's acute sense of classical tragedy infused in the everyday and mundane is evident in the poems of this late-life collection. The sharp, satirical wit that won Hecht the Pulitzer in *The Hard Hours* plays an equally significant role here. However, the scope of tenderness in this book differs from that of earlier volumes. There is a more recognizable compassion to be found in Hecht's *Collected Later Poems* that balances classical tragedy with jest and consecration.

The Transparent Man explores various manifestations of loss, but other prevalent themes include devotion, wonder, and reverence. In "Meditation," a "sacred conversation" takes place between an orchestral performance, the silent statues of martyred saints, and the speaker, who hears a group of indifferent children at play. Hecht remembers how those ". . . torments, deaths, renunciations,/ Made in the name of love . . . served as warrant// For the infliction of new atrocities." Nevertheless, the voices of the children, the "viols and lutes," and the cautionary sculptures surrounding him warrant recognition of something holy and worth attending.

The collection's final book, *The Darkness and the Light*, continues Hecht's exploration of love and loss through translations of Goethe, Horace, and others. The title of the opening poem, "Late Afternoon in Love: The Onslaught of Love" suggests the theme of what is to follow: the blurred line between slaughter and deep affection. Hecht sees "puddled oil" as "a miracle of colors" and a contribution to the "evening's perfection." This may seem a strange perfection, but it poignantly suggests Hecht's "sacred conversation" between the darkness and the light—a concept previously explored in his haunting collection of poems, *Flight Among the Tombs*.

Flight Among the Tombs is not just a book of poems. In this volume, Hecht's gross ironies are married to the sinister woodcuts of Leonard Baskin. Each woodcut depicts Death (a skull-and-bones figure robed in the traditional black habit) in some unexpected profession. In one poem, Death is an Oxford don; in another, he is a Mexican revolutionary. In another, Death is playing "peekaboo" in a nursery, grimly twisting rhymes: "Weep, baby, weep!/ No solaces in sleep./ Nightmare will ruin your repose/ And daylight resurrect your woes."

Though self-deprecating, wry, and at times almost silly, Death is not just the Fool parading his advantage for the reader's bemusement. Death is also a relentless social critic. In "Death the Copperplate Printer," historical, Christian torture devices are referenced ironically as tools of progress. The wheel—Catherine's wheel and the spokelike structure of Andrew's cross— alludes to methods of technological gain as well as the brutality inflicted on those who were often instigators of social progress. "This is no metaphor," Death asserts, evoking the sixteenth century Catholic martyr who was crushed to death, Margaret Clitherow: "A pious woman, even as she prayed/ Was cheated of her breath// I'm always grateful for such human aid."

In the oil of Hecht's wit and cynicism, a spectrum of affections and devotions can be found. It is no wonder that critics such as Harold Bloom have ranked Hecht among the masters: Ransom, Auden, James Merrill, and even Henry James and Marcel Proust.

OTHER MAJOR WORKS

NONFICTION: *Obbligati: Essays in Criticism*, 1986; *The Hidden Law: The Poetry of W. H. Auden*, 1993; *On the Laws of the Poetic Art*, 1995; *Anthony Hecht in Conversation with Philip Hoy*, 1999; *Melodies Unheard: Essays on the Mysteries of Poetry*, 2003.

TRANSLATIONS: *Seven Against Thebes*, 1973 (with Helen Bacon; of Aeschylus); *Poem upon the Lisbon Disaster*, 1977 (of Voltaire).

EDITED TEXTS: *Jiggery Pokery: A Compendium of Double Dactyls*, 1966 (with John Hollander); *The Essential Herbert*, 1987.

BIBLIOGRAPHY

Alvarez, A. "The Darkness and the Light." *The New York Review of Books* 49, no. 8 (May 9, 2002): 10-13. A perceptive and informative discussion of Hecht's poetry and its evolution in terms of Hecht's formative experiences.

Fairchild, B. H. "In Memoriam: Anthony Hecht." *Sewanee Review* 113, no. 3 (Summer, 2005): 463-469. After Hecht's death, the poet Fairchild remembers his friend and expresses admiration for both Hecht the poet and the man.

_____. "Motion and Stasis in the Poetry of Anthony Hecht." *Yale Review* 95, no. 3 (July, 2007): 50. Fairchild analyzes Hecht's poetry, finding it full of energy, motion, and sustained action.

German, Norman. *Anthony Hecht*. New York: Peter Lang, 1989. This book-length study presents a chronological discussion of Hecht's books of poetry, beginning with *A Summoning of Stones* and ending with *The Venetian Vespers*. It also contains some useful biographical information and an index of subjects and poems.

Hammer, Langdon. "Two Formalists." *American Scholar* 74, no. 1 (Winter, 2005): 51-59. Hammer compares and contrasts the poetry of Hecht and Thomas Gunn, who both began publishing at about the same time.

Hecht, Anthony. *Anthony Hecht in Conversation with Philip Hoy*. London: Between the Lines, 1999. Hoy sent Hecht a list of one hundred questions, to which Hecht responded with detailed written replies. Followed by more questions and considerable revision and rewriting prior to the final presentation, Hecht's responses are very revealing and offer a reflective, self-aware portrait of the artist in contemplation of his life and work.

Lea, Sydney, ed. *The Burdens of Formality: Essays on the Poetry of Anthony Hecht*. Athens: University of Georgia Press, 1989. A book-length consideration of Hecht's writing, with essays covering the main themes, subjects, and formal qualities of his poems by placing them in artistic, social, and historical contexts. With an appendix that outlines the basic chronology of Hecht's life and a thorough bibliography.

Lieberman, Laurence. *Unassigned Frequencies: American Poetry in Review, 1964-1977*. Urbana: University of Illinois Press, 1977. This collection includes a short essay on W. S. Merwin and Hecht that was originally published in 1968. The author focuses on Hecht's realism.

Ricks, Christopher B. *True Friendship: Geoffrey Hill, Anthony Hecht, and Robert Lowell Under the Sign of Eliot and Pound*. New Haven, Conn.: Yale University Press, 2010. Contains the Anthony Hecht Lectures in the Humanities at Bard College given by Ricks in 2007. Discusses Hecht and other poets, placing Hecht in context and examining influences.

Kathy Rugoff; Sarah Hilbert
Updated by Steven Brown

HEINRICH HEINE

Born: Düsseldorf, Prussia (now in Germany); December 13, 1797
Died: Paris, France; February 17, 1856
Also known as: Christian Johann Heinrich Heine

<small>PRINCIPAL POETRY</small>
Gedichte, 1822 (*Poems*, 1937)
Tragödien, nebst einem lyrischen Intermezzo, 1823 (*Tragedies, Together with Lyric Intermezzo*, 1905)
Buch der Lieder, 1827 (*Book of Songs*, 1856)
Deutschland: Ein Wintermärchen, 1844 (*Germany: A Winter's Tale*, 1892)
Neue Gedichte, 1844 (8 volumes; *New Poems*, 1858)
Atta Troll, 1847 (English translation, 1876)
Ein Sommernachtstraum, 1847 (*A Midsummer Night's Dream*, 1876)
Romanzero, 1851 (English translation, 1859)
Gedichte, 1851-1857 (4 volumes; *Poems*, 1937)
Letzte Gedichte und Gedanken, 1869 (*Last Poems and Thoughts*, 1937)
Atta Troll, and Other Poems, 1876 (includes *Atta Troll* and *A Midsummer Night's Dream*)
Heinrich Heine: The Poems, 1937
The Complete Poems of Heinrich Heine, 1982

<small>OTHER LITERARY FORMS</small>
Although Heinrich Heine (HI-nuh) is best remembered for his verse, he also made significant contributions to the development of the feuilleton and the political essay in Germany. Experiments with prose accelerated his rise to fame as a writer. Among the most important of his nonfiction works are *Reisebilder* (1826-1831 ; *Pictures of Travel*, 1855), a series of witty essays that are spiced with poetic imagination and penetrating social commentary; *Zur Geschichte der neueren schönen Litteratur in Deutschland* (1833; *Letters Auxiliary to the History of Modern Polite Literature in Germany*, 1836), which was later republished and expanded as *Die romantische Schule* (1836; *The Romantic School*, 1876) and constitutes Heine's personal settlement with German Romanticism; *Französische Zustände* (1833; *French Affairs*, 1889), a collection of sensitive newspaper articles about the contemporary political situation in France; and *Vermischte Schriften* (1854), a group of primarily political essays.

Heine's attempts to create in other genres were unsuccessful. During his student years in Berlin, he began a novel, *Der Rabbi von Bacherach* (1887; *The Rabbi of Bacherach*, 1891), but it remained a fragment. Two dramas, *Almansor* and *William*

Ratliff, published in *Tragedies, Together with Lyric Intermezzo*, failed on the stage, although *William Ratliff* was later employed by Pietro Mascagni as the basis of an opera.

ACHIEVEMENTS

Second only to Johann Wolfgang von Goethe in impact on the history of German lyric poetry in the nineteenth century, Heinrich Heine was unquestionably the most controversial poet of his time. He was a major representative of the post-Romantic literary crisis and became the most renowned love poet in Europe after Petrarch, yet for decades he was more celebrated abroad than in Germany. Anti-Semitism and negative reactions to his biting satire, to his radical inclinations, and to his seemingly unpatriotic love of France combined to prevent any consistent approbation in Heine's homeland. Nevertheless, he became the first Jewish author to break into the mainstream of German literature in modern times.

Heine's poetic reputation is based primarily on *Book of Songs*, which went through twelve editions during his lifetime. The collection achieved immediate popularity with the public and was well received by critics; since 1827, it has been translated into more than fifty languages. Lyrics that became part of the *Book of Songs* were set to music as early as 1822, and within a year after the book appeared, Franz Schubert used six poems from the "Heimkehr" ("Homecoming") section in his famous cycle *Schwanengesang* (1828; "Swan Song"). Robert Schumann's *Dichterliebe* (1840; love poems) features musical settings for sixteen poems from *Tragedies, Together with Lyric Intermezzo*. By 1840, Heine's works had become prime texts for German songs. In all, more than three thousand pieces of music have been written for the creations of Heine's early period.

In 1835, four years after he went into self-imposed exile in France, Heine's works were banned in Germany, along with the writings of the social reform and literary movement Junges Deutschland (Young Germany). The critics rejected him as a bad influence on Germany's youth. His immediate popularity waned as conflicts with government censors increased. In the late nineteenth century, attempts to reclaim his works for German literature touched off riots, yet by then his enchanting lyrics had become so ingrained in German culture that it was impossible to expel them. The measure of Heine's undying significance for German poetry is perhaps the fact that even the Nazis, who formally prohibited his works once again, could not exclude his poems completely from their anthologies of songs.

BIOGRAPHY

Heinrich Heine was born Chaim Harry Heine, the son of a Jewish merchant. He spent his early years working toward goals set for him by his family. His secondary education ended in 1814 when he left the Düsseldorf Lyceum without being graduated. After failing in two apprenticeships in Frankfurt, he was sent to Hamburg to prepare for a

Heinrich Heine
(Library of Congress)

career in commerce under the direction of a wealthy uncle. While there, he fell in love with his cousin Amalie. This unfulfilled relationship was a stimulus for verse that the young poet published in a local periodical. In 1818, his uncle set him up in a retailing enterprise, but within a year Harry Heine and Co. was bankrupt. Acknowledging that his nephew was unsuited for business, Uncle Salomon at last agreed to underwrite his further education.

Between 1819 and 1825, Heine studied in Bonn, Berlin, and Göttingen. His university years were very important for his development as a poet. While in Bonn, he attended lectures given by August Wilhelm von Schlegel, whose interest in his work stimulated Heine's creativity. In the fall of 1820, he moved to Göttingen. Besides law, he studied German history and philology until January, 1821, when he challenged another student to a duel and was expelled from the university. He continued his studies in Berlin and was rapidly accepted into prominent literary circles. Included among the writers with whom he associated were Adelbert von Chamisso, Friedrich Schleiermacher, and Christian Dietrich Grabbe. Rahel von Varnhagen helped in the publication of Heine's first collection of poems in 1822, and he quickly became known as a promising talent.

During a visit to Hamburg in 1823, he met Julius Campe, who afterward published all Heine's works except a few commissioned essays that he wrote in Paris. Literary success persuaded him away from the study of law, but at his uncle's request Heine returned to Göttingen to complete work toward his degree. In the summer of 1825, he passed his examinations, though not with distinction. To facilitate a public career, he was baptized a Protestant, at which time he changed his name to Heinrich.

Travel was a significantly formative experience for Heine. Vacations in Cuxhaven and Norderney provided initial powerful impressions of the sea that informed the two North Sea cycles of the *Book of Songs*. Journeys through the Harz Mountains in 1824, to England in 1827, and to Italy the following year provided material for the *Pictures of Travel* series that elevated him to the literary mainstream of his time. Exposure to foreign points of view also aroused his interest in current political questions and led to a brief involvement as coeditor of Johann Friedrich von Cotta's *Politische Annalen* in Munich in 1827 and 1828.

When continued efforts to obtain permission to practice law in Hamburg failed, Heine moved to Paris in 1831, where he began to write articles for French and German newspapers and journals. Heine loved Paris, and during the next few years friendships with Honoré de Balzac, Victor Hugo, George Sand, Giacomo Meyerbeer, and other writers, artists, and composers contributed to his sense of well-being. When the German Federal Diet banned his writings, making it impossible for him to continue contributing to German periodicals, the French government granted him a modest pension.

The 1840's were a stormy period in Heine's life. In 1841, he married Cresence Eugénie Mirat (whom he called Mathilde), his mistress of seven years. Her lack of education and understanding of his writings placed a strain on their relationship and later contributed to the poet's increasing isolation from his friends. After returning from Hamburg in 1843, Heine met Karl Marx. Their association sharpened Heine's political attitudes and increased his aggressive activism. Salomon Heine's death in 1844 unleashed between the writer and his cousins a struggle for the inheritance. Eventually they reached an accommodation that guaranteed an annuity in exchange for Heine's promise not to criticize family members in his writings.

After a collapse in 1848, Heine spent his remaining years in unceasing pain. An apparent venereal disease attacked his nervous system, leaving him paralyzed. Physical infirmities, however, did not stifle his creative spirit, and from the torment and loneliness of his "mattress grave," he wrote some of the best poetry of his career.

ANALYSIS

Unlike many poets, Heinrich Heine never stated a formal theory of poetry that could serve as a basis for interpreting his works and measuring his creative development. For that reason, confusion and critical controversy have clouded the picture of his oeuvre, resulting in misunderstandings of his literary orientation and intentions. The general concept that he was a poet of experience is, at the very least, an oversimplification. To be sure, immediate personal observations of life were a consistent stimulus for Heine's writing, yet his product is not simply a stylized reproduction of individual encounters with reality. Each poem reveals a reflective processing of unique perceptions of people, milieus, and events that transforms seemingly specific descriptions into generally valid representations of humankind's confrontation with the times. The poet's ability to convey, with penetrating exactitude, feelings, existential problems, and elements of the human condition that correspond to the concerns and apperceptions of a broad readership enabled him to generate lyrics that belong more to the poetry of ideas than to the poetry of experience.

A characteristic of Heine's thought and verse is a purposeful poetic tension between the individual and the world. The dissonance between the artistic sensibility and reality is presented in unified constructs that represent qualities that were missing from the poet's era: unity, form, constancy, and continuity. By emphasizing condition rather than event, Heine was able to offer meaningful illustrations in the juxtaposition of antithetical concepts: sunny milieu and melancholy mood, pain and witticism, affirmation and negation, enchantment of feeling and practical wisdom of experience, enthusiasm and pessimism, love and hate, spirit and reality, tradition and anticipation of the future. The magic and power of his verse arise from his ability to clothe these dynamic conflicts in deceptively simple, compact forms, pure melodic sounds and rhythms, and playfully witty treatments of theme, substance, motif, and detail.

More than anything else, Heine was a poet of mood. His greatest strengths were his sensitivity and his capacity to analyze, create, and manipulate feeling. A colorful interchange of disillusionment, scorn, cynicism, rebellion, blasphemy, playful mockery, longing, and melancholy is the essence of his appeal to the reader's spirit. The goal, however, is not the arousal of emotion but rather the intensification of awareness, achieved by drawing the audience into a desired frame of feeling, then shattering the illusion in a breach of mood that typifies Heine's poetry.

Although he was not a true representative of any single German literary movement, Heine wrote poems that reflect clear relationships to definite intellectual and artistic traditions. Both the German Enlightenment and German Romanticism provided him with important models. In matters of form, attitude, and style, he was a child of the Enlightenment. Especially visible are his epigrammatic technique and the tendency toward didactic exemplification and pointed representation. Gotthold Ephraim Lessing was his favorite among Enlightenment authors. Heine combined the technical aspects of Enlightenment literary approach with a pronounced Romantic subjectivity in the handling of substance, theme, and motif, particularly in the examination of self, pain, experience, and condition. The absolute status of the self is a prominent characteristic of his works. In the emancipation of self, however, he carried the thoughtful exploration of personal individuality a step beyond that of the early Romantics and in so doing separated himself from them. Other Romantic traits in his lyrics include a dreamy fantasy of feeling and a pronounced element of irony. Where Friedrich Schlegel employed irony to transcend the restrictive material world and unite humankind with a spiritual cosmos, Heine used it to expand the self to encompass the cosmos. The feature of Romanticism with which Heine most consciously identified was the inclination of Joseph von Eichendorff and others toward simple musical poems modeled on the German folk song. Heine specifically acknowledged the influence of Wilhelm Müller, whose cultivation of pure sound and clear simplicity most closely approximated his own poetic ideal.

In many respects, the polish of language and form that marked Heine's *Book of Songs* was never surpassed in later collections. At most a strengthening of intonation, an increase in wit, a maturing of the intellect subtly and gradually enhanced his writings with the passing years. Nevertheless, his literary career can be divided into four distinct phases with regard to material focus and poetic concern.

EARLY YEARS

Heine's initial creative period encompassed his university years and reached its peak in the mid-1820's. In *Poems*, the cycle of verse in *Tragedies, Together with Lyric Intermezzo*, and, finally, *Book of Songs*, the young poet opened a world of personal subjectivity at the center of which is a self that undergoes unceasing examination. Consciousness of the self, its suffering and loneliness, is the essence of melodic compositions that include poems of unrequited love, lyrical mood pictures, satires, romances, confessions, and parodies. Lines and stanzas deftly reflect Heine's ability to feel his way into nature, the magic of legend, and the spiritual substance of humankind, while the poetic world remains a fragmentary manifestation of the subjective truthfulness of the moment.

THE SELF AS A MIRROR OF THE TIMES

A major change in orientation coincided with Heine's move to Paris. The political upheaval in France and the death of Goethe signaled the end of an artistic era, and Heine looked forward to the possibility of a different literature that would replace the subjectivity of Romanticism with a new stress on life, time, and reality. He was especially attracted to the Saint-Simonian religion, which inspired within him a hope for a modern doctrine that would offer a new balance between Judeo-Christian ideals and those of classical antiquity. The lyrics in *New Poems*, the major document of this period, reveal a shift in emphasis from the self per se to the self as a mirror of the times. Heine's poetry of the 1830's is shallower than his earlier creations, yet it effectively presents the inner turmoil, confusion, and splintering of the era as Heine experienced it. Accompanying a slightly faded reprise of earlier themes is a new view of the poet as a heathen cosmopolitan who affirms material reality and champions the moment as having eternal value.

Political radicalization

The third stage in Heine's career is best described as a period of political radicalization. It most visibly affected his poetry during the mid-1840's, the time of his friendship with Marx. In the aggressively satirical epics *Atta Troll* and *Germany: A Winter's Tale*, he paired sharp criticism of contemporary conditions with revelations of his love for Germany, specifically attacking his own critics, radical literature, militant nationalism, student organizations, the German hatred of the French , the fragmented condition of the German nation, and almost everything else that was valued by the establishment.

Last of the Romantics

Profound isolation and intense physical pain provided the catalyst for a final poetic reorientation after Heine's physical collapse in 1848. Some of the poems that he wrote in his "mattress grave" are among his greatest masterpieces; they reflect a new religiosity in spiritual penetration of the self. In *Romanzero* and other late poems, the poet becomes a kind of martyr, experiencing the world's illness in his own heart. The act of suffering generates a poetry of bleak glosses of the human condition, heartrending laments, and songs about death unequaled in German literature.

Although Heine styled himself the last of the Romantics, a significant difference in approach to substance distinguishes his early poems from those of the Romantic movement. Where Clemens Maria Brentano and Eichendorff celebrated existence as it opened itself to them, Heine sang of a life that had closed its doors, shutting him out. The dominant themes of his *Book of Songs* are longing and suffering as aspects of the experience of disappointed love. Combining the sentimental pessimism of Lord Byron with the objective portrayal of tangible reality, he succeeded in exploring love's frustrations and pain more effectively, more impressively, and more imaginatively than any of his forerunners and contemporaries had done. In dream images, songs, romances, and sonnets that employ Romantic materials yet remain suspicious of the feelings that they symbolize, the poet transformed the barrier that he felt existed between himself and the world into deceptively simple, profoundly valid treatments of universal problems.

Book of Songs

The poems of *Book of Songs* are extraordinarily flexible, self-contained productions that derive their charm from the combination of supple form and seemingly directly experienced and personally felt content. Colorful sketches of lime trees, an ancient bastion, a city pond, a whistling boy, gardens, people, fields, forests, a mill wheel, and an old tower contribute to a world of great fascination and sensual seduction. The verse is often bittersweet, however, focusing not on the sunny summer landscape but on the sadness of the poet who does not participate in a beauty that mocks him. The forceful presentation of the individual's isolation and conflict with the times represented a fresh direction in poetry that contributed greatly to Heine's early popularity. At the same time, the carefully constructed tension between the poet and his surroundings established a pattern that became characteristic of all his works.

An extremely important feature of these early lyrics is the break in mood that typically occurs at several levels, including tone, setting, and the lyricist's subjective interpretation of his situation. The tone frequently shifts from emotional to conversational, from delicate to blunt, while the settings of the imagination are shattered by the banal reality of modern society. As the poet analyzes his position vis-à-vis his milieu, his positive feeling is broken by frustration and defeat, his hope collapses beneath the awareness of his delusion, and his attraction to his beloved is marred by her unthinking cruelty. There is never any resolution of these conflicts, and the poem itself provides the only mediation between the writer and a hostile world.

Among the most exquisite compositions in *Book of Songs* are the rustically simple lyric paintings from "Die Harzreise" ("The Journey to the Harz") and the rhythmically powerful, almost mystical studies from the two cycles of "Die Nordsee" ("The North Sea"). Filled with the fairy-tale atmosphere of the Rhine and the Harz Mountains, "The Journey to the Harz" poems exemplify Heine's ability to capture the compelling musicality and inner tone of the folk song and to combine these elements with an overwhelming power of feeling in the formation of an intense poetry of mood. In "The North Sea," he cultivated a new kind of language, anticipating twentieth century verse in free rhythms that sounded the depths of elemental human experience. Constant motion, changing patterns of light , play of wind, and movement of ships and fish combine as parts of a unified basic form. Heine pinpointed the individuality of the ocean in a given moment, reproducing atmosphere with precision and intensifying impact through mythological or human ornamentation. The rolling flow of impression is a consistent product of Heine's poetic art in its finest form.

NEW POEMS

Two years after moving to Paris, Heine published *Letters Auxiliary to the History of Modern Polite Literature in Germany*, his most significant theoretical treatise on literature and a work that marked his formal break with Romanticism. The major poetic document of this transition to a more realistic brand of expression is *New Poems*, a less integrated collection than *Book of Songs*, containing both echoes of early themes and the first fruits of his increased political commitment of the 1840's. *New Poems* attests strongly a shift in approach and creative concern from poetry as an absolute to the demand for contemporary relevance.

The first cycle of *New Poems*, "Neuer Frühling" ("New Spring"), returns to the motifs that dominate the "Lyric Intermezzo" and "Homecoming" segments of *Book of Songs* yet presents them with greater polish and distance. New variations portray love as a distraction, a nuisance that causes emotional turmoil in the inherent knowledge of its transitoriness. The tone and direction of the entire volume are established in the prologue to "New Spring," in which the poet contrasts his own subjection to the hindering influence of love with the strivings of others in "the great struggle of the times."

Among the other sections of the book, "Verschiedene" ("Variae"), with its short cycles of rather acidic poems about the girls of Paris, its legendary ballad "Der Tannhäuser" ("Tannhäuser"), and its "Schöpfungslieder" ("Songs of Creation"), is the least coherent, most disturbing group of poems that Heine ever wrote. Campe, his publisher, decried the lyricist's creation of what he called "whore and chamber-pot stories" and was extremely reluctant to publish them. Nothing that Heine wrote, however, is without artistic value, and there are nuggets of brilliance even here. Despite its artificiality and seeming inconsistency with Heine's true poetic nature, "Tannhäuser," for example, must be regarded as one of his greatest masterpieces. The deeply psychological rejuvenation of the old folk epic, which served as the stimulus for Richard Wagner's opera, reflects the poet's all-encompassing and penetrating knowledge of the human heart.

"Zeitgedichte" ("Poems of the Times"), the concluding cycle in *New Poems*, sets the pattern for Heine's harsh political satire of the 1840's. Some of the lyrics were written expressly for Karl Marx's newspaper *Vorwärts*. Most of them are informed by homesickness, longing, and the bitter disappointment that Heine felt as the expected dawn of spiritual freedom in Germany failed to materialize in the evolution of a more cosmopolitan relationship with the rest of Europe. Powerful poems directed against cultural, social, and political dilettantes anticipate the incisively masterful tones of his most successful epics of the period, *Atta Troll* and *Germany: A Winter's Tale*; irreverent assaults on cherished institutions, superficial political activism, and his own critics accent his peculiar love-hate relationship with his homeland.

ROMANZERO

Regarded by many critics as Heine's finest collection of poems, *Romanzero* presents his final attempts to come to grips with his own mortality. Rich in their sophistication, more coherent in tone than the lyrics of *New Poems* or even the *Book of Songs*, the romances, laments, and melodies of *Romanzero* reveal the wit, irony, and epigrammatic style for which Heine is famous in the service of a new, peculiarly transparent penetration of the self. Dominant in the poems is the theme of death, which confronts the individual in many forms. A new religiosity is present in the acknowledgment of a personal God with whom the poet quarrels about a divine justice that is out of phase with humankind's needs. Individual creations pass through the spectrum of human and religious history and into the future in the expectation of a new social order. Bitter pessimism unmasks the dreams of life, pointing to the defeat of that which is noble and beautiful and the triumph of the worse human being over the better as the derisive law of the world. Voicing the mourning and bitter resistance of the tormented soul, Heine transforms personal confrontation with suffering and death into a timeless statement of universal experience.

Romanzero is divided into three main parts, each of which projects a substantial array of feeling: seriousness, despair, goodness, compassion, a longing for faith, bitterness, and mature composure. The first section, "Historien" ("Stories"), is composed of discursive, sometimes rambling narrative ballads and romances dealing with the tragedies of kings, heroes, and poets. Some of them process through a temporal distance such typical Heine themes as the yearning for love, clothing them in historical trappings. Others, such as the cruel poem "Vitzliputzli" that ends the cycle, are profound discourses on humans' inhumanity toward their own kind. The poems of "Lamentationen" ("Lamentations"), the second major section, are directly confessional in form: deeply moving cries of anguish, sublime expressions of horror, statements of longing for home. The "Lazarus" poems that conclude this portion of *Romanzero* are especially vivid documents of the poet's individual suffering in a world where God seems to be indifferent. In "Hebräische Melodien" ("Hebrew Melodies"), the last segment of the collection, Heine presented the essence of his reidentification with Judaism. Three long poems explore the broad dimensions of Jewish culture, history, and tradition, ending with an almost sinister medieval disputation between Christian and Jew that evolves into a tragicomic anticlerical satire. Thumbing his nose at irrational action, intolerance, and superstition, the poet offers a dying plea for humanism.

No other volume presents Heine so thoroughly in all his heights and depths, perfection and error, wit and seriousness. Captivating for the directness of despairing and contrite confession, repelling for its boastful, sometimes vicious cynicism, *Romanzero*, as perhaps no other work in the history of German lyric poetry, reveals the hubris of the problematic individual and penetrates the facade of the bright fool's drama that is life.

OTHER MAJOR WORKS

LONG FICTION: *Der Rabbi von Bacherach*, 1887 (*The Rabbi of Bacherach*, 1891).

SHORT FICTION: *Aus den Memoiren des Herrn von Schnabelewopsky*, 1910 (*The Memoirs of Herr von Schnabelewopski*, 1876).

PLAYS: *Almansor*, pb. 1821 (English translation, 1905); *Der Doktor Faust*, pb. 1851 (libretto; *Doktor Faust*, 1952).

NONFICTION: *Briefe aus Berlin*, 1822; *Reisebilder*, 1826-1831 (4 volumes; *Pictures of Travel*, 1855); *Die Bäder von Lucca*, 1829 (*The Baths of Lucca*, 1855); *Französische Zustände*, 1833 (*French Affairs*, 1889); *Zur Geschichte der neueren schönen Literatur in Deutschland*, 1833 (*Letters Auxiliary to the History of Modern Polite Literature in Germany*, 1836); *Der Salon*, 1834-1840 (4 volumes; *The Salon*, 1893); *Zur Geschichte der Religion und Philosophie in Deutschland*, 1835 (*On the History of Religion and Philosophy in Germany*, 1876); *Die romantische Schule*, 1836 (expansion of *Zur Geschichte der Religion und Philosophie in Deutschland*; *The Romantic School*, 1876); *Über die französische Bühne*, 1837 (*Concerning the French Stage*, 1891-1905); *Shakespeares Mädchen und Frauen*, 1838 (*Shakespeare's Maidens and Ladies*, 1891);

Ludwig Börne: Eine Denkschrift von H. Heine, 1840 (*Ludwig Börne: Recollections of a Revolutionist*, 1881); *Les Dieux en exil*, 1853 (*Gods in Exile*, 1962); *Lutetia: Berichte über Politik, Kunst, und Volksleben*, 1854 (*Lutetia: Reports on Politics, Art, and Popular Life*, 1891-1905); *Vermischte Schriften*, 1854 (3 volumes); *De l'Allemagne*, 1855 (2 volumes).

MISCELLANEOUS: *The Works of Heinrich Heine*, 1891-1905 (12 volumes).

BIBLIOGRAPHY

Cook, Roger F., ed. *A Companion to the Works of Heinrich Heine*. Rochester, N.Y.: Camden House, 2002. A collection of essays that examine Heine's work; topics include the eroticism, Jewish culture, mythology, and modernity in his poems.

Heady, Katy. *Literature and Censorship in Restoration Germany: Repression and Rhetoric*. Rochester, N.Y.: Camden House, 2009. This work on the censorship of literature that occurred in Restoration Germany examines how the intellectual and political climate affected Heine.

Hermand, Jost, and Robert C. Holub, eds. *Heinrich Heine's Contested Identities: Politics, Religion, and Nationalism in Nineteenth-Century Germany*. New York: Peter Lang, 1999. A collection of essays concerning Heine's identity, which was formed and reformed, revised and modified, in relationship to the politics, religion, and nationalism of his era. The essays offer an understanding of Heine's predicaments and choices as well as the parameters placed on him by the exigencies of the time.

Justis, Diana Lynn. *The Feminine in Heine's Life and Oeuvre: Self and Other*. New York: Peter Lang, 1997. Heine's literary representations of women and interactions with women vividly demonstrate his position as a marginal German-Jewish writer of the nineteenth century. Heine, like many Jews of that era, internalized the European cultural stereotype of the Jew as "woman," that is, as essentially inferior and marginal.

Pawel, Ernst. *The Poet Dying: Heinrich Heine's Last Years in Paris*. New York: Farrar, Straus and Giroux, 1995. In this biography of Heine, Pawel portrays a poet at the height of his creativity in the last eight years of his life, when he was confined to his bed with a mysterious ailment.

Phelan, Anthony. *Reading Heinrich Heine*. New York: Cambridge University Press, 2007. Examines Heine's poetry from the earliest to his last, and argues that Heine is a major contributor to the articulation of modernity.

Lowell A. Bangerter

DAVID IGNATOW

Born: Brooklyn, New York; February 7, 1914
Died: East Hampton, New York; November 17, 1997

PRINCIPAL POETRY

Poems, 1948
The Gentle Weight Lifter, 1955
Say Pardon, 1961
Figures of the Human, 1964
Earth Hard: Selected Poems, 1968
Rescue the Dead, 1968
Poems, 1934-1969, 1970
Facing the Tree, 1975
Selected Poems, 1975 (Robert Bly, editor)
Tread the Dark: New Poems, 1978
Sunlight: A Sequence for My Daughter, 1979
Whisper to the Earth, 1981
Leaving the Door Open, 1984
New and Collected Poems, 1970-1985, 1986
Shadowing the Ground, 1991
Against the Evidence: Selected Poems, 1934-1994, 1993
I Have a Name, 1996
At My Ease: Uncollected Poems of the Fifties and Sixties, 1998
Living Is What I Wanted: Last Poems, 1999

OTHER LITERARY FORMS

David Ignatow (ihg-NAH-toh) published several volumes of prose, including *The Notebooks of David Ignatow* (1973); *Open Between Us* (1980), a collection of lectures, interviews, essays, and reviews; and *The One in the Many: A Poet's Memoirs* (1988). In addition, Ignatow published a substantial number of short stories in various small magazines in the 1940's and 1950's. Many of these are collected in *The End Game, and Other Stories* (1996). His letters, a treasure trove of personal, aesthetic, and philosophical insight, are collected in *Talking Together: Letters of David Ignatow, 1946-1990* (1992).

ACHIEVEMENTS

Because of his deliberate eschewal of traditional poetic techniques, including rhyme and meter, and his firm insistence on the "plain style" in contradiction to prevailing modes of the day, David Ignatow endured a long period of public and academic neglect, not unlike that endured by his idol and warm supporter, William Carlos Williams. Also like Williams, he was an early victim of T. S. Eliot's extraordinary success, which has tended to cast much modern American poetry in a convoluted Donne-shadowed mold, despite Eliot's own sympathetic openness to free verse.

Ignatow's first two collections, *Poems* and *The Gentle Weight Lifter*, were decidedly the work of a poet at odds with the dominant mandarin sensibility of the period. The first collection occasioned an enthusiastic review by Williams in *The New York Times* (November 21, 1948), a review that led to a friendship between the two men. Although conversational in style, the poems' simplicity of diction and syntax, their almost clumsy rejection of conventional lyricism, and their steadfast metaphoric sparseness placed them outside the mainstream of contemporary aesthetics, causing more than one critic to label their author a "naif" or "primitive." Randall Jarrell's more accurate review of *The Gentle Weight Lifter* in the *Yale Review* (Autumn, 1955) characterized Ignatow's poetry as "humane, unaffected, and unexciting," noting that he lacked Williams's "heights and depths."

From the beginning, Ignatow proclaimed himself "a man with a small song," identifying most strongly with Walt Whitman and Williams in terms of wanting to articulate the travails and tragedies of the ordinary citizen in his own language. A strong chord of social and political protest inevitably accompanied such a program, and not a little of Ignatow's value resided in his willingness to confront the inequities he saw all around him.

However, it must have become increasingly evident to Ignatow that very few of the poems in his first two books were clear successes, for all their integrity of purpose and manner, and that something more was needed if he hoped to achieve the same sort of understated suggestiveness that Ernest Hemingway, an admired fellow writer, had achieved in his best short stories. He had to find a method that could weld Hemingway's lean but loaded sentences to the plain style learned from Williams and the kind of parabolic structures encountered in the Bible (an important source); that is, he needed to use narrative as metaphor but he needed to free it from the innate limitations of a prose mode by more direct confrontations with unconscious forces. Allegory was an obvious answer, as in Stephen Crane's neglected verse, but the specific modernist approach was found in the nightmare revelations of the Surrealists, which seemed to complement perfectly readings in Charles Baudelaire and Arthur Rimbaud.

Consequently, beginning with *Say Pardon*, Ignatow's deceptively modest story-poems started to illuminate deeper, darker undercurrents, started to probe Freudian streams with relentless innocence. In "The Dream," a stranger approaches "to fall down at your feet/ and pound his head upon the sidewalk" until "your life takes on his desperation," even after waking. Like Baudelaire, Ignatow remained a poet of urban landscapes, committed to a moral exploration of humanity's most ambitious and ambiguous invention, yet he never lost his spiritual roots in a Jewish past in his search for godhead and ideal certitudes. In the book's title poem, for example, he advises, "Say pardon/ and follow your own will," but two poems later, "The Complex" addresses the dilemma of a father whose "madness is to own himself/ for what he gives is taken," while another poem, "And I Said," envisions "God" behind "my enemy."

The tension energizing his strongest poems, an ethical and psychological matrix of contending defiance and guilt, often entails a transformation of public material into family dramas, spotlighting an ambivalent father figure, a wronged wife, a victimized son. A prolific writer intent on processing every vagrant bit of daily experience, however trivial, Ignatow published more poems than he should have, far too frequently lapsing into sententious whimsy or belaboring the obvious. This contributed, no doubt, to his dismissal by many academics. It was not until the 1970's and the publication of *Poems, 1934-1969* and *Selected Poems* that the true extent of his contribution to American literature was appreciated, climaxing in the award of the prestigious Bollingen Prize in 1977 and reconfirming the truism that risk taking and pratfalls are ever the hallmarks of the serious artist.

Fellow poets were more ready to concede and celebrate the sly art beneath Ignatow's rough surfaces—at least poets who shared his concern for establishing an alternative aesthetic closer to the Whitman-Williams line of descent, ranging from Charles Reznikoff to the Deep Image school of Robert Bly, James Wright, and Diane Wakoski. They helped bring Ignatow's verses to the forefront of contemporary American poetry—Bly in particular, through his choices for the *Selected Poems*.

In later years, belying his age, Ignatow continued to evolve, another sign of genuine talent, and relaxed enough, at last, to appreciate poetic stances at the opposite end of the scale, including a growing comprehension of Eliot's technical radicalism and intelligence. If *Tread the Dark* exhibited symptoms of possible fatigue, compulsive reiteration of death threats and near self-parodies, these were since denied in the moving *Sunlight: A Sequence for My Daughter* and *Whisper to the Earth*, in which the concluding "With Horace" epitomizes Ignatow's determination to dig for rocks, to strike off "his fire upon stone."

Ignatow received the National Institute of Arts and Letters Award (1964), two Guggenheim Fellowships (1965 and 1973), the Shelley Memorial Award (1966), and the Bollingen Prize (1977). In 1992, Ignatow received the Frost Medal along with American poet Adrienne Rich.

B IOGRAPHY

Born February 7, 1914, in Brooklyn, New York, the son of Russian immigrant parents, Max and Yetta (Reinbach) Ignatow, David Ignatow had the misfortune to graduate from New Utrecht High School in 1932: "I stepped out of high school into the worst economic, social, and political disaster of our times, the Great Depression." He did enroll at Brooklyn College but lasted only half a semester, subsequently schooling himself in literary matters by reading Ernest Hemingway, Walt Whitman, Friedrich Nietzsche, Arthur Schopenhauer, Søren Kierkegaard, the Russian novelists, the French poets of the previous century, and the Bible. He worked in his father's commercial pamphlet bindery, running a machine or delivering the finished pamphlets by hand-truck, and wrote stories and poems in his spare hours. Oppressed by the tedious labor, and by an ambivalent, often heated relationship with a hard-driving father, Ignatow envisioned literature as an escape. With his mother's aid, he managed to secure an appointment as a reporter for the WPA (Works Project Administration) Newspaper Project. The year before, his short story "I Can't Stop It" had appeared in *The New Talent* magazine, earning a place on Edward J. O'Brien's Honor List in his *The Best American Short Stories* annual in 1933.

Ignatow was finally able to leave the family business and home in 1935, when he found a cheap apartment in Manhattan's East Village, where he became a part of the literary scene and met artist Rose Graubart, whom he married two years later. Their son, David, was born in 1937. Financial difficulties plagued the young couple, and from 1939 to 1948, Ignatow was forced to work at a series of low-paying jobs, as night clerk at the sanitation department, as a health department clerk, as an apprentice handyman in the lathe workshop at the Kearny Shipyards in New Jersey, and, for five years, as night admitting clerk at Beth Israel Hospital in New York. It was during his last year at Beth Israel that his first collection, *Poems*, appeared and garnered an enthusiastic review from William Carlos Williams. Williams, in fact, emerged as a friend, as did Charles Reznikoff, and these two poets probably exerted the most enduring influence on Ignatow's career.

The year 1955 proved to be crucial in Ignatow's life. *The Gentle Weight Lifter* was published; he was asked to edit the Whitman Centennial issue of the *Beloit Poetry Journal*; and his son began to exhibit the signs of mental illness that would eventually result in his being institutionalized. A daughter, Yaedi, was born the next year, and Ignatow became closely associated with *Chelsea* magazine. In 1961, his third volume of poetry, *Say Pardon*, was published by Wesleyan University Press—destined to remain his publisher for almost two decades—but money was still a pressing problem, and Ignatow worked as a paper salesperson in the years between 1962 and 1964, also serving as an auto messenger for Western Union on the weekends. During the same interval, he spent a year as poetry editor of *The Nation* and gave a poetry workshop at the New School for Social Research.

The publication of *Figures of the Human* helped to earn him an award from the National Institute of Arts and Letters in 1964, his first significant token of recognition. This was followed by a Guggenheim Fellowship a year later. In 1966, he also won the Shelley Memorial Award and was a visiting lecturer at the University of Kentucky. Other academic posts came his way: at the University of Kansas in 1966 and at Vassar College from 1967 to 1969. He then accepted positions as poet in residence at York College

(CUNY) and as adjunct professor at Columbia University. Editorial assignments included extended stints with *Beloit Poetry Journal* and *Chelsea*, and in 1972, he was among the first associate editors connected with the founding of *American Poetry Review*, a connection that was dissolved near the decade's end when he and a group of fellow editors resigned in protest over what they perceived as implicit unfairness in the magazine's attitude toward women and minority groups.

In 1973, Ignatow was granted a second Guggenheim Fellowship, but the award that had the most to do with bringing his name before a broader audience was the Bollingen Prize of 1977. The publication of *The Notebooks of David Ignatow*—selections from his journals that the poet hoped, in vain, would result in a wider readership for his poetry— had made clear the terrible cost of being a writer, particularly an antiestablishment writer, in the United States. It also demonstrated with high principle, brutal candor, and almost claustrophobic narcissism the ultimate advantages and limitations of constantly translating self into truth. Ignatow's career achieved ironic completeness with his election to the presidency of the Poetry Society of America in 1980. He died on November 17, 1997.

ANALYSIS

In his poetry written in the 1930's and 1940's, later gathered in the first section of *Poems, 1934-1969*, David Ignatow projected an abiding concern for both the well-made poem, however occasionally denuded of conventional lyric devices, and a reformer's vision of realistic life—in the city, in the streets, in the homes of the poor and outcast, who are romantically linked with the artist's difficult lot. The subjects were traditional—marriage, murder, sex, love's complexities, adolescence, the death of Franklin D. Roosevelt—but their treatment exhibited a diverting ability to make sudden leaps from the banal to the profound, always in language direct enough to disarm. "Autumn Leaves," for example, moves skillfully from an ordinary image of the leaves as Depression victims to a vivid figure of God sprawling beneath a tree, gaunt in giving, "like a shriveled nut where plumpness/ and the fruit have fed the worm." This kind of dramatic shift epitomizes Ignatow's focus on social injustice and his often bitter struggle with a religious heritage and the questionable place of deity in a scheme of things so geared to grind down human hopes.

Surprisingly, many of the early poems betray a professional smoothness and a reliance on metaphor and balanced lines that one might not expect from a disciple of Williams; there is scant sense in these poems of a language straining for experimental intensities. "The Murderer," an undeniable failure, marked by simplistic psychology but true to its author's identification with the underclass, can only express love for "those who cart me off to jail" in easy prose: "I love them too/ for the grief and anger/ I have given." More relevant, the murderer had killed with a knife, that most intimate of weapons, which reappears again and again in the Ignatow canon, a reflection of the menace and death lurking behind every scene of ordinary existence, as well as symbolic reminder of murderous impulses and contrary fears of castration by the father and his capitalistic society.

POEMS

In *Poems*, which is a bundle of furies, Ignatow's rage against America's hunger for money, "our masterpiece" (according to a poem of that title), rarely escapes self-imposed boundaries. Occasionally, as in "At the Zoo," a quiet pathos gives modest dimensions their proper subject: an elephant trapped and separated from his real self, like the poet of course, in "stingy space and concrete setting." Repeatedly, however, as in "Come!" and "The Poet Is a Hospital Clerk," Ignatow underestimates his audience, wherein lies the innate danger of such songs, and settles for either blatant self-abasement—"I have said it before, I am no good"—or political invective: "Come, let us blow up the whole business;/ the city is insane." At his best, he can produce "Europe and America," merging anger against world ills with ambivalence toward his father, the knife resurfacing in a climax of fused violences:

> My father comes of a small hell
> where bread and man have been kneaded
>   and baked together.
> You have heard the scream as the knife fell;
> while I have slept
> as guns pounded offshore.

THE GENTLE WEIGHT LIFTER

Working with a larger canvas and a surer touch, *The Gentle Weight Lifter* evinces a growing dependence on narrative means and on verbal portraits and mirrors of the people who define Ignatow's imagination. The collection is not unlike Edgar Lee Masters's urbanized *Spoon River Anthology* (1915), although it is brightened by exotic historic additions and splashes of darker Kafkaesque tones. In its quest for parallel lives and allegorical configurations, the collection ranges back in time to ancient Greece, to Oedipus at Colonnus in "Lives II"—tellingly centered on the father, not Antigone, his head in her lap as "he thought surely some cover/ could be found for him"—to Nicias in "The Men Sang," a parable about the poet's generic function, and to the Old Testament in "The Pardon of Cain," which captures Cain in the "joy" of having freed himself from death's insidious allure.

Though not yet prevalent, surrealistic perspectives, when they do appear, tend to be founded on absurd juxtapositions of mythic and modernist elements, as in "News Report," where "a thing" arises from a sewer to run amok among urban females—primeval sexuality rampant in a city field. Each victim describes her special view, "one giving the shaggy fur, the next the shank bone/ of a beast." In the end, the creature is an obvious refugee from Greek mythology, "the red teeth marks sunk into the thigh/ and the smell of a goat clinging tenaciously." Throughout the book, there is a stubborn quest for philosophic truths at variance with contemporary culture, and the governing voice, confounding Ignatow's own aesthetic, often resounds with a pedant's dense lexicon, as in "The Painter," a sensitive inquiry into a particular artist's world, which has a fourth stanza beginning: "These are not dreams, and the brush stroke is the agent./ At the hour of appropriate exhaustion, leaving the field/ of canvas, she ravens on the transient bread and cheese."

This is far from streamlined narrative terseness, far from the language of the person in the street, and it points up *The Gentle Weight Lifter*'s uneasy transitional quality, despite several remarkable poems, and its abrupt swings between simple allegorical spareness and thicker meditative measures.

SAY PARDON

In *Say Pardon*, much of the uncertainty has disappeared, carrying Ignatow's main voice and means closer to the spare slyness that distinguishes his final style. In *Babel to Byzantium* (1968), James Dickey salutes the collection's "strange, myth-dreaming vision of city life" and isolates, with acute accuracy, its basic modus operandi as "an inspired and brilliantly successful metaphysical reportage." Since it announces a greater willingness to accept a surrealistic path to unconscious resources, without jettisoning conversational immediacy and treasured social and moral concerns, one of the key poems is "How Come?" A naked, unpretentious self funnels the experience into Everyman's tale: "I'm in New York covered by a layer of soap foam." The conceit, whimsy in service of darker designs, is logically developed, radio newscasts informing him of the foam's spread to San Francisco, Canada, and the Mexican border, climaxing with "God help the many/ who will die of soap foam." Light fantasy has suggested the paradox of drowning in cleanliness, next to American godliness, the pollution of scientific and commercial advances against nature.

The relaxed speech is matter-of-fact, contrasting scaffolding for a surreal flight, not quite as jagged as it will later become in Ignatow's continued effort to simulate urban realities, and the situation adeptly yokes "what-if" fantasy to persistent reformist despair. More touching, though no less characteristic, are two poems about the author's institutionalized son, "In Limbo" and "Sunday at the State Hospital," the former a brief statement of grief, insisting that "there is no wisdom/ without a child in the house," and the latter recounting a visit in which the son cannot eat the sandwich his father has brought him:

> My past is sitting in front of me
> filled with itself
> and trying with almost no success
> to bring the present to its mouth.

A poem called simply "Guilt" lays bare the emotional core of these and other family verses: "Guilt is my one attachment to reality."

Jewish guilt, the anxiety bred of childhood training in a context that conditions love to obedience, outsider status, and unresolved Oedipus complexes, must forever seek release not only in the past, but in a specific religious ethos as well. Thus, the last section of *Say Pardon* is a procession of spiritual selves that assumes a living godhead, who proffers salvation (from guilt, rage, hatred) through the act of loving fatherhood, the "Lord" claiming "you will win your life/ out of my hands/ by taking up your child." These lines are from "I Felt," second in the series of twelve poems, after "The Mountain Is Stripped," in which the poet had conceded, "I have been made frail with righteousness:/ with two voices. I am but one person." Because of its inveterate opposition to his rational espousal of liberal dogma and experimental openness, this conservative streak in Ignatow's consciousness, which helps to fuel his moral indignation, generates the lion's share of the tension in some of his strongest poetry. It also explains how such a cosmopolitan individual could, as revealed in *The Notebooks of David Ignatow*, react with abhorrence to homosexuality, viewing it as a degeneration into self-love.

"And I Stand," third in the series, ostensibly a declaration, has the impact of a prayer in its speaker's avowal not to kill his enemy, standing and gazing, instead, past "my enemy at Him." Noah, Samson, and Job, three personifications of a volatile man-god fulcrum, are considered for antithetical urges, their stories rephrased, until the final poem, "The Rightful One," confronts a divine visitation, a New Testament Christ to replace the Old Testament's paternal fierceness, full of forgiveness, "his hair long, face exhausted, eyes sad," with pardon again based on selfless parenthood: "Bless your son . . ./ . . . And the Rightful One/ was gone and left a power to feel free." Redemption is not the reader's, however, ideal or otherwise, since boredom is the normal response when any dramatic conflict flattens out into a species of George Santayana's "animal faith," intimating that belief, in this case, is either forced or without sufficient doubt.

FIGURES OF THE HUMAN

Figures of the Human is free of such overt metaphysical gestures toward mental entropy, and more potent as a result. Its first section concentrates on those human figures whose crimes and tragedies populate the daily tabloids; it is tuned to the violence, urban and sudden, that Ignatow deems typical of modern life. A victim, for example, of a random, fatal assault in his own home is elegized in "And That Night." The poem's attitude is one of primitive awe: "You bring up a family in three small rooms,/ this crazy man comes along/ to finish it off." Note how the language refuses mandarin remoteness, and savors instead the vernacular tongue of victim and reporter. Another victim, a nine-year-old girl raped and thrown off a tenement roof, is the voice in "Play Again," which enables Ignatow to grant her (at the brink of poor taste) a sacrificial mission:

> The living
> share me among them. They taste
> me on the ground, they taste me
> in the air descending.

Salvation comes, saving the poem, with a beautiful death plea, as the child and author ask readers to play again "and love me/ until I really die, when you are old/ on a flight of stairs." A poem called "Two Voices," echoing Alfred, Lord Tennyson, underscores the almost schizophrenic division in self of which the poet is always aware; the retreat into "Baudelaire, Whitman, Eliot" versus the need for active involvement in a present tense is translated into a suicidal leap into a winter lake, which is daring, if deadly, because it challenges "the weather," nature itself.

The rest of *Figures of the Human*, three further sections, varies its approach with frequent recourse to personal days and ways—"My mind is green with anxiety/ about money"—and surreal fantasies, one of which, the brief "Earth Hard," has a delicious Blakean air:

> Earth hard to my heels
> bear me up like a child
> standing on its mother's belly
> I am a surprised guest to the air.

Childhood is an issue in the title poem also, questing after "the childhood spirit" of a maddened beloved for the impulse that impels art as well: "Then are we loved, hand drawing swiftly/ figures of the human struggling awake." This is mission and theme combined, dream explicating experience, and a reply to the savage urge that brings back the "knife" in other poems.

RESCUE THE DEAD

Whatever else it accomplishes, *Figures of the Human* demonstrates the firm command Ignatow had obtained over his unique aesthetic, culminating, four years later, in *Rescue the Dead*, his finest, most consistently effective volume of verse, which is, at times, his most autobiographical. As the title avers, the major goal of the book is to revive the past, the personal dead and strangers and the dead in spirit. A handful of its poems have already been recognized for the virtuoso performances they are, among them "The Boss" and "The Bagel," first and last in the initial section, which is introduced by a "Prologue" that offers up parents "who had small/ comfort from one another." The larger arrangement of the section, which evolves from a bitter portrait of a sinning father into the playful absurdity of a man turning into a rolling bagel, has the additional weight of a small sequence about the father: five poems, beginning with the "Prologue" and concluding with his "Epitaph," which prays: "Forgive me, father,/ as I have forgiven you/ my sins."

The Freudian chain has thus been broken, at least for the moment, at least within the limits of the poem, and "Nourish the Crops," the next poem, can proceed to the other father, God, realizing self as the "product of you to whom all life/ is equal." The proposition here is the same frightening one, minus deity, facing Albert Camus and Jean-Paul Sartre in the 1950's, modern man's existential dilemma vis-à-vis an indifferent cosmos. In spite of conflicting religious restraints, for Ignatow, the pivotal answer must be imagination, ceaseless reworkings of the Romantic heritage he had forsworn, and an alter ego in pursuit of a bagel, sounding like Williams and Wright, tumbling head over heels, "one complete somersault/ after another like a bagel/ and strangely happy with myself." In the title poem, the climb to redemption is pitted against paradox—"Not to love is to live"—and has the poet conceding his incapacity to choose love over life and asking that you "who are free/ rescue the dead." A powerful poem at the end of the second section, "The Room," reconfirms the crucial role of imagination in the battle against loneliness, emotional and physical, again seeking, with fluid lyricism, escape from loss of self and others—his bed constructed from "the fallen hairs/ of my love, naked, her head dry"—through a magical transformation, the persona flying around his dark room like a bat or angel.

The fourth section of *Rescue the Dead* is the weakest by far, its lapses made glaring by the general excellence of section three, which focuses on rituals of survival in breathless contrast to the violence of the real world (inner and outer), circling from the murder of innocence in England to a derelict, who returns, like "a grey-haired foetus," to his mother while asleep, and two ignored children in the "East Bronx," sharpening their "knives against the curb." The failure of the section stems from a stubborn determination to fashion vehicles of protest, blunt weapons to combat what is perceived as massive public wrongs, such as the Vietnam War and the Medgar Evers incident, and even contains a poem about "Christ" and dares add the coda of "In My Childhood," a facile memory of a yellow canary and a boy with an air gun. Returning to more complex private visions to tap a wellspring, the fifth section recoups some of the lost poetic energy, humming appreciations, never without saving shadows, of a put-upon wife, a foraging bum, an old love, and so on. It peaks with "Omen," a sentimental grab for love from sylvan nature that beats false, but provides a smooth thematic entry to the sixth and final section of eleven poems about poetry, three of which are dedicated to admired fellow craftspeople, Denise Levertov, Marianne Moore, and Williams.

Like Stanley Kunitz, whom he closely resembles in his search for paternal, mystical salvation amid alien corn, Ignatow summons up Dante for validation in "Anew," commencing, "Dante forgot to say,/ Thank you, Lord, for sending me/ to hell." The apex of the sequence is "Walk There," an allegorical walk in a dark wood, full of fear, before a heaven is glimpsed: "Ahead, is that too the sky/ or a clearing?/ Walk there." The desire is credible and is honestly earned by prior struggles with private and public demons, but the poetry that inevitably concludes an Ignatow collection, mirroring Dante's *Paradiso*, never equals in intensity and metaphoric convolutions the engrossing journey through infernal regions that got him there.

In the year before his death, Ignatow looked back over this amazingly prolific period and decided that many poems not collected in his several volumes of those decades were worthy enough to be given a new life. Thus, in *At My Ease: Uncollected Poems of the Fifties and Sixties*, Ignatow gathered a rich second harvest.

FACING THE TREE

Facing the Tree is more of a mixed bag than its predecessors, sure of its technique and confident in voice, and including a growing fondness for prose poems, that most dangerous invitation to self-indulgence. The voice of "Reading the Headlines" mates, typically, personal and social anguish: "I have a burial ground in me where I place the bodies/ without fuss or emotion." Whimsy alternates with stark tragedy as the naïve but shrewd narrator reacts to an evil world by laboring to extract some psychological and spiritual truths from its surface madness, filtered, always, through the mesh of a receptive self. The poems that work efficiently, such as "Letter to a Friend," "My Own Line," "The Refuse Man," "Autumn," "In Season," and several untitled prose poems, are those that remember to keep near the taut edge of the parabolic methodology that Ignatow has perfected, avoiding the glibness and rhetorical excess that ruin so many others in the book, notably where they are attached to political frames, such as "My President Weeps" and "Now Celebrate Life and Death."

TREAD THE DARK

Tread the Dark is similarly confident in style and speech, but its obsession with death and the absence of adequate counter-moods numb the reader to its occasional brilliance and successes, such as "The Abandoned Animal," "Death of a Lawn Mower," "The Dead Sea," "The Forest Warden," "An Account in the Present Tense . . . ," "Midnight," and two untitled pieces, numbered 46 and 80. All the poems are numbered, stressing their author's conception of them as a series structured on the leitmotif of death. In treading the dark, fighting off oblivion with imagination, the poet too often treads familiar waters, flounders into pretentiousness and embarrassing archness, appropriately reaching a nadir in "Epilogue," a short coda that has the persona, aware of being watched by trees ("tall gods") in his study, bow over his typewriter and start "the ceremony/ of a prayer." A year later, the publication of the highly charged *Sunlight* sequence demonstrated that the decline signaled by *Tread the Dark* was temporary.

WHISPER TO THE EARTH

Although not equal to Ignatow's strongest volumes, *Whisper to the Earth* is ripe with readiness, open to new modes, and at peace with the softer hues of twilight and autumn and the death they prefigure. Divided into five sections, the collection's first group of poems, with a single exception, approach nature directly, forsaking urbanscapes in favor of garden meditations on apples and trees and stones, a strategy for resolving death fears, so that entering the grave will "be like entering my own house." In a poem for his daughter, "For Yaedi," Ignatow claims that when he dies he wants it said, "that I wasted/ hours in feeling absolutely useless/ and enjoyed it, sensing my life/ more strongly than when I worked at it." Elegies fittingly dominate the next two sections, but the ones for his father and mother—"Kaddish," "The Bread Itself," "A Requiem," and "1905"—can be counted among the most evocative poems he has ever written, regardless of their mellow reordering of the past to concentrate on his parents' genuine gifts to him. The father is forgiven by way of a comprehension of his own harsh youth in Russia, and the mother is celebrated as the "bread" that sustained him. Tension here is less important than the positive electricity of love heightening the language out of itself and its narrative solidity.

The fourth section, "Four Conversations," is the weakest series in the book, a sequence of dialogues that seems to lead toward Wallace Stevens, but its experimental boldness reflects credit on Ignatow's resolve not to surrender to old age's penchant for self-parody and safe repetitions. In the final section, the prose poem holds sway, at its tightest in "I Love to Fly," which uses a dream to good effect. The climax is in "With Horace," an identification with the Roman poet that accepts the Sabine Farm wisdom of his retreat from the city to use the experience of his late years as a new tool for penetrating nature's rock hardness.

LATER POEMS

Death is once again center stage in *Shadowing the Ground*, which can be read either as a book-length poem or an ordered sequence of (untitled) poems built around a unifying theme. These sixty-five terse pieces, most only ten lines or fewer, reexamine past deaths of wife and parents and meditate on the poet's death to come. Ignatow's lonely, sagacious voice seems highly restrained, emotion checked by a lifetime of brooding wisdom. *I Have a Name* is a late return to a more characteristic manner, showing the aged poet still exercising a full range of powers. Finally, and posthumously, Ignatow left readers with *Living Is What I Wanted*. Written in the year preceding his death, these poems close a brilliant career in which a poet's courage to acknowledge and grapple with death through all life's turnings has taken him to the inevitable shore. As ever, Ignatow's writings hover between a stoic, intellectual detachment and an honest display of deep emotion.

OTHER MAJOR WORKS

SHORT FICTION: *The End Game, and Other Stories*, 1996.

NONFICTION: *The Notebooks of David Ignatow*, 1973; *Open Between Us*, 1980; *The One in the Many: A Poet's Memoirs*, 1988; *Talking Together: Letters of David Ignatow, 1946 to 1990*, 1992.

EDITED TEXT: *The Wild Card: Selected Poems, Early and Late*, 1998 (by Karl Shapiro; with Stanley Kunitz).

BIBLIOGRAPHY

Ignatow, David. "An Interview with David Ignatow." Interview by Leif Sjöberg. *Contemporary Literature* 28 (Summer, 1987): 143-162. Ignatow explains the influence of Walt Whitman and William Carlos Williams on his poetry. Whitman, he says, wrote about everyday life, and Williams wrote in everyday speech. These two influences were Ignatow's salvation in the 1930's and through the 1950's, when the fashion in poetry was lofty abstraction.

_____. "It's Like Having Something in the Bank: An Interview with David Ignatow." Interview by Lynn Emanuel and Anthony Petrosky. *American Poetry* 3 (Winter, 1986): 64-85. Offers valuable insight into Ignatow's poetic philosophy. Ordinary life is his subject, and he tries to show it in a new way. Essential to understanding Ignatow.

_____. *The Notebooks of David Ignatow*. Chicago: Swallow Press, 1973. Ignatow allows the reader into his creative process by means of these journals. He offers biographical details as well as insight into his philosophy of writing poetry.

_____. *The One in the Many: A Poet's Memoirs*. Middletown, Conn.: Wesleyan University Press, 1988. Ignatow presents his essays on poetry written over a period of four decades. In them, he reveals that he was obsessed with a single artistic quest: to uncover the human dimension beneath the technical structure of poetic theory.

Mazzaro, Jerome. *Postmodern American Poetry*. Urbana: University of Illinois Press, 1980. Mazzaro outlines Ignatow's work, as well as that of six other modern American poets. He includes biographical references and an index. A good, quick overview useful to any student.

Ray, David. "The Survivor's Art: The Notebook of David Ignatow." *Kansas Quarterly* 24/25 (1992/1993): 219-233. A detailed analysis of the demons that tormented Ignatow and fed his art. Ray's retrospective look at this volume is a springboard to a fine discussion of Ignatow's themes and of the creative process.

Terris, Virginia R., ed. *Meaningful Differences: The Poetry and Prose of David Ignatow*. Tuscaloosa: University of Alabama Press, 1994. Though Terris is clearly an Ignatow partisan, she has gathered more than forty critical voices in a balanced, wide-ranging survey of critical opinion on Ignatow's work.

Wakoski, Diane, Linda M. Wagner, and Milton Hindus. "David Ignatow: Three Appreciations." *American Poetry* 3 (Winter, 1986): 35-51. Wakoski praises Ignatow's use of simple American language, as opposed to a more stylized British idiom. Wagner points out that Ignatow achieves the rhythms of spoken speech through idiomatic phrasing rather than colloquial word choice. Hindus explains the reason that Ignatow and his literary predecessors, William Carlos Williams and Walt Whitman, have been so rarely anthologized.

Edward Butscher
Updated by Philip K. Jason

STANLEY KUNITZ

Born: Worcester, Massachusetts; July 29, 1905
Died: New York, New York; May 14, 2006

PRINCIPAL POETRY

Intellectual Things, 1930
Passport to the War: A Selection of Poems, 1944
Selected Poems, 1928-1958, 1958
The Testing-Tree, 1971
The Coat Without a Seam: Sixty Poems, 1930-1972, 1974
The Terrible Threshold: Selected Poems, 1940-1970, 1974
The Lincoln Relics, 1978
The Poems of Stanley Kunitz, 1928-1978, 1979
The Wellfleet Whale and Companion Poems, 1983
Passing Through: The Later Poems, New and Selected, 1995
The Collected Poems, 2000

OTHER LITERARY FORMS

Stanley Kunitz (KYEWN-ihts) published numerous essays, interviews, and reviews on poetry and art. These are collected in *A Kind of Order, a Kind of Folly: Essays and Conversations* (1975) and in *Next-to-Last Things: New Poems and Essays* (1985). In addition, he made extensive translations of modern Russian poetry, most notably in *Poems of Akhmatova* (1973, with Max Hayward) and *Story Under Full Sail* by Andrei Voznesensky (1974), and he edited and cotranslated Ivan Drach's *Orchard Lamps* (1978) from the Ukrainian.

ACHIEVEMENTS

In more than seven decades of writing poetry, Stanley Kunitz produced a corpus of work that is notable for its cohesiveness, its courageous explorations of the modern psyche, and its ever-broadening sympathies that adumbrate (with some fierce reservations and caveats) the unity of human experience. In language that always sustains a high degree of passionate dignity, never falling prey to the hortatory or didactic, Kunitz boldly knocked again and again on the doors of his obsessions with family, love, memory, and identity to demand that they surrender their secret meanings.

From the start of his career, Kunitz paid consummate attention to matters of form, as bespeaking, to use his borrowed phrase, "a conservation of energy." Indeed, on numerous occasions, Kunitz spoke of form as a constant in art, as opposed to techniques and materials, which vary according to time and cultural necessity. Nevertheless, Kunitz's later poems surprised his readers with their fresh embodiments: journal poems, prose poems, and free verse. At the same time, the poems retain the characteristically impassioned, sometimes bardic voice of the earlier work, a voice that constitutes an unbroken thread running through all his poetry.

In many ways, Kunitz's work declares allegiance to the "flinty, maverick side" of American literature, the side inhabited by Henry David Thoreau and Walt Whitman, and holds to humanistic values, independent judgment, self-discipline, and a distrust of power in all its modern manifestations, particularly in the hands of the state. At the same time, the poems bear witness to the individual's spiritual yearnings in an age of decreasing sanctity at all levels. Although not explicitly a religious poet ("I'm an American freethinker, a damn stubborn one . . ."), Kunitz wrote poems that, nevertheless, remind readers of the tragic consequences that befall humans at the loss of that dimension. His achievement was "to roam the wreckage" of his own humanity in a way that was both highly personal and representative and to ennoble that pursuit with the transformative powers of his art.

Kunitz was honored with the Lloyd McKim Garrison Medal for poetry (1926), a Levinson Prize from *Poetry* magazine (1956), the Pulitzer Prize in poetry (1959), the Lenore Marshall Poetry Prize (1980), the Bollingen Prize for Poetry (1987), the National Book Award in Poetry (1995), and the Shelley Memorial Award (1995) and the Frost Medal (1998), both from the Poetry Society of America. He became a member of the American Academy of Arts and Letters in 1963. He served as chancellor for the Academy of American Poets from 1970 to 1996 and as consultant in poetry to the Library of Congress from 1974 to 1976 and poet laureate consultant in poetry from 2000 to 2001. In 1996, President Bill Clinton presented Kunitz with a National Medal of Arts. In 2002, Kunitz was awarded the Massachusetts Book Medal for lifetime achievement. He received a Guggenheim Fellowship in 1945, an Academy Award in Literature from the National Institute of Arts and Letters in 1959, and the Academy of American Poets Fellowship in 1968 as well as a grant from the Ford Foundation.

BIOGRAPHY

The son of immigrants, Stanley Jasspon Kunitz was born July 29, 1905, in Worcester, Massachusetts. Kunitz's father, Solomon, descended from Russian Sephardic Jews, committed suicide shortly before Stanley was born—an event that was to haunt the poet and that stands behind some of his most important and best-known poems. His mother, Yetta Helen, of Lithuanian descent, opened a dry-goods store to support herself, her son, and two older daughters and to repay accumulated debts. Reared principally by his sisters and a succession of nurses, Kunitz grew up with his father's book collection, into which, as he put it, he would "passionately burrow." Though his mother shortly remarried, his stepfather, of whom he was fond, died before Kunitz reached his teens.

Educated in Worcester public schools, Kunitz edited the high school magazine, played tennis, and graduated valedictorian of his class. Kunitz won a scholarship to Harvard, where he majored in English and began to write poetry, subsequently winning the Lloyd McKim Garrison Medal for poetry in 1926. He graduated summa cum laude in the same year, and he took his M.A. degree from Harvard the following year. He worked briefly as a Sunday feature writer for the Worcester *Telegram*, where he had worked summers during college. He also completed a novel, which he later "heroically destroyed."

In 1927, Kunitz joined the H. W. Wilson Company as an editor. With Wilson's encouragement, he became editor of the *Wilson Bulletin*, a library publication (known now as the *Wilson Library Bulletin*). While at Wilson, he edited a series of reference books, including *Authors Today and Yesterday: A Companion Volume to "Living Authors"* (1933; with Howard Haycraft and Wilbur C. Hadden), *British Authors of the Nineteenth Century* (1936; with Haycraft), *American Authors, 1600-1900: A Biographical Dictionary of American Literature* (1938; with Haycraft), and *Twentieth Century Authors: A Biographical Dictionary of Modern Literature* (1942; with Haycraft).

In 1930, Kunitz married Helen Pearse (they were divorced in 1937) and published his first collection of poems, *Intellectual Things*. The book was enthusiastically received by reviewers. Writing in *Saturday Review of Literature*, William Rose Benét observed, "Mr. Kunitz has gained the front rank of contemporary verse in a single stride." In 1939, Kunitz married a former actress, Eleanor Evans (from whom he was divorced in 1958), a union that produced his only child, Gretchen.

Kunitz's tenure with the H. W. Wilson Company was interrupted by World War II, during which he served as a noncommissioned officer in charge of information and education in the Air Transport Command. His second collection, *Passport to the War*, appeared in 1944. A reviewer of that volume for *The New York Times Book Review* noted, "Kunitz has now (it seems) every instrument necessary to the poetic analysis of modern experience." After receiving a Guggenheim Fellowship in 1945, Kunitz began a second career as an itinerant teacher, first at Bennington College, at the behest of his friend, the poet Theodore Roethke, then at a succession of colleges and universities, including the State University of New York at Potsdam, the New School for Social Research, Queens College, Brandeis University, the University of Washington, Yale University, Princeton University, and Rutgers University's Camden Campus.

In 1958, Kunitz married the artist Elise Asher and published *Selected Poems, 1928-1958*, which was awarded the Pulitzer Prize in poetry in 1959. During the 1960's, though based in New York City and Provincetown, Massachusetts, Kunitz was a Danforth Visiting Lecturer at colleges and universities throughout the United States. He also lectured in the Soviet Union, Poland, Senegal, and Ghana. He translated poems by Russian poet Andrei Voznesensky, which were published in *Antiworlds and the Fifth Ace* (1967). He continued to edit for the Wilson Company (with Vineta Colby, *European Authors: 1000-1900: A Biographical Dictionary of European Literature*, 1967).

In 1968, along with artist Robert Motherwell and novelist Norman Mailer, he helped found the Fine Arts Work Center in Provincetown, a resident community of young artists and writers, and in 1969, he assumed the general editorship of the Yale Series of Younger Poets.

The Testing-Tree, a volume of poems and translations, appeared in 1971, prompting Robert Lowell to assert in *The New York Times Book Review*, "once again, Kunitz tops the crowd, the old iron brought to the white heat of simplicity." In 1974, Kunitz was appointed consultant in poetry to the Library of Congress. In addition to *The Testing-Tree* and the collected volume *The Poems of Stanley Kunitz, 1928-1978*, a book of essays and conversations titled *A Kind of Order, a Kind of Folly*, as well as three volumes of translations, appeared during the 1970's.

Kunitz published a thematic volume of old and new poems, *The Wellfleet Whale and Companion Poems*, in a limited edition in 1983, with the new poems later incorporated in *Next-to-Last Things*, published in 1985. In recognition of his lifetime achievement, Kunitz was chosen as the first New York State poet, for the term 1987-1989.

Kunitz's next volume of poems, *Passing Through*, received the National Book Award in Poetry in 1995. In 1998, he received the Frost Medal from the Poetry Society of America. From 2000 to 2001, Kunitz served a second term as poet laureate consultant in poetry to the Library of Congress. Kunitz died in 2006, at the age of one hundred.

ANALYSIS

Stanley Kunitz constantly sought to achieve higher and higher ground, both in his thoughtful aesthetic and in his themes. Kunitz's first poems were composed after the initial wave of modernism, led, in poetry, by T. S. Eliot and Ezra Pound, had crested. They resemble, to some extent, the earlier, tightly organized, ironic poems of Eliot, though the influence of the seventeenth century Metaphysical poets, particularly George Herbert (again an indirect influence of Eliot, who was largely responsible for the resurgence of interest in the Metaphysicals), is probably more preponderant. Moreover, by the 1920's, the work of Sigmund Freud had successfully invaded American arts and provided the introspective poet with a powerful tool for the analysis of self and culture.

INTELLECTUAL THINGS

The poems of *Intellectual Things* sketch many of the themes that would later be subject to elaboration and enrichment: the figure of the regenerative wound that is both the fresh scar of loss and the font of the power to transform experience into art; humans' willful capriciousness (the "blood's unreason") and the inevitable cargo of guilt; and the search for the father, which is ultimately the search for identity, authority, and tradition. These topics pervade Kunitz's later poems as crucially as they pervaded his early verse.

Eloquent and formally rigorous, the poems in this first collection show a poet already mature in his medium, writing of his "daily self that bled" to "Earth's absolute arithmetic/ of being." Characterized by paradox and a wish for transcendence (though that wish is frequently denied or diverted to another object), the early poems often poise on niceties of intellection—though they are also fully felt—and suggest transport by language rather than the transcendence to which they aspire. From the first, Kunitz's poems have typically employed the language and images of paradox. In "Change," the opening poem to his first collection, humankind is "neither here nor there/ Because the mind moves everywhere;/ And he [sic] is neither now nor then/ Because tomorrow comes again/ Foreshadowed. . . ." In more characteristically personal poems, such as "Postscript," the poet observes, in what will develop into one of his ongoing themes, the self's phoenixlike destruction and subsequent regeneration: "I lost by winning, and I shall not win/ Again, except by loss." The losses Kunitz traces in *Intellectual Things* are those of past life (or of a past one that was denied), symbolized by the loss of his father, and the loss of love. In "For the Word Is Flesh," the poet admonishes his dead father: "O ruined father dead, long sweetly rotten/ Under the dial, the time-dissolving urn,/ Beware a second perishing. . . ." The second death is the doleful fate of being erased from the memories of the living. In a memorable passage that presages a later, more famous poem ("Father and Son"), Kunitz writes, "Let sons learn from their lipless fathers how/ Man enters Hell without a golden bough"—that is to say, uninstructed.

Some of the finest effects attained in *Intellectual Things* can be attributed to a high degree of control over phrasing, combined with the use of rhyme as a tool of force reminiscent of Alexander Pope, as in "Lovers Relentlessly": "Lovers relentlessly contend to be/ Superior in their identity.// The compass of the ego is designed/ To circumscribe intact a lesser mind. . . ." Kunitz uses rhyme also as a vehicle of wit, as in the shorter, three-beat lines of "Benediction": "God banish from your house/ The fly, the roach/ the mouse// That riots in the walls/ Until the plaster falls. . . ."

PASSPORT TO THE WAR

Passport to the War retains much of the density and bardic resonance of *Intellectual Things*, but the range of subject matter is broader: The self must now take its transformations into account against the background of recent history, for which regeneration is entirely problematic: "One generation past, two days by plane away,/ My house is dispossessed, my friends dispersed,/ My teeth and pride knocked in, my people game/ For the hunters of manskins in the warrens of Europe." To the question "How shall we uncreate that lawless energy?" the poet can only defer to the determinisms of time: "I think of Pavlov and his dogs/ And the motto carved on the broad lintel of his brain:/ "Sequence, consequence, and again consequence." If the shadow of history casts the representative self in a darker hue, the poet, like Matthew Arnold before him, clings to what is most central to the life of the individual: "Lie down with me, dear girl, before/ My butcher-boys begin to rave./ 'No hope for persons any more,'/ They cry, 'on either side of the grave.'/ Tell them I say the heart forgives/ The World." The strange weapons of intimacy and charity would seem ill-suited as protection in a brutal world, but the sacramental element, the desire to raise the supposed commonplace, remains one of the bolts of a civilization unravaged by history. If history is the inevitable backdrop of our mortality, so do a representative mortal's most private strivings and sufferings themselves constitute a part of its fabric: "What the deep heart means,/ Its message of the big, round, childish hand,/ Its wonder, its simple lonely cry,/ The bloodied envelope addressed to you,/ Is history, that wide and mortal pang."

The visionary "Father and Son," perhaps Kunitz's best-known poem, establishes, in surrealistic images full of longing and regret, the poet's existential fate in the context of history. "Whirling between two wars," he follows "with skimming feet,/ The secret master of my blood . . . whose indomitable love/ Kept me in chains." Addressing his father "At the water's edge, where the smothering ferns lifted/ Their arms. . . ." The poet asks for his father's instruction: "For I would be a child to those who mourn/ And brother to the foundlings of the field . . ./ O teach me how to work and keep me kind." Yet the summons brings only a shocking specter of discontinuity: "Among the turtles and the lilies he turned to me/ The white ignorant hollow of his face." One senses that what the poet asks is already, in some way, self-provided, though minus the love so deeply rooted in biology that it has the status of a cultural given. As war and upheaval expose these roots, one senses the poet's implication that, in a metaphorical sense, all are orphans.

"Open the Gates," another well-known visionary lyric, delivered in a grave voice that eerily suggests posthumous utterance, finds the poet "Within the city of the burning cloud," standing "at the monumental door/ Carved with the curious legend of my youth." Striking the door with "the great bone of my death," the poet stands "on the terrible threshold," where he sees "the end and the beginning in each other's arms." The seamless and incestuous image suggests the allegorical figures of Sin and Death in John Milton's *Paradise Lost* (1667, 1674), and the allusion holds to the extent that both figures are determinants of human fate. At the same time, the emphasis is less on moral conditioning than on the endlessly reforming fate of the human, as felt from the inside, in contrast with the wholeness of a life, glimpsed, so to speak, from a vantage somehow apart from it. Our lives, as William Shakespeare said, are "rounded with a sleep," and it is a matter of indifference whether one attempts an artificial distinction between the two sleeps, except that one's only knowledge takes place as human and forever from the vantage of one looking outward (even when looking inward). As for the question of inside versus outside, no other consciousness has yet much to contribute to the subject.

SELECTED POEMS, 1928-1958

In 1958, after another long hiatus, Kunitz published his *Selected Poems, 1928-1958*, more than a third of which are new poems. The new poems take up the modern subject of otherness, as in "The Science of the Night," in which the speaker contemplates his sleeping beloved: "Down the imploring roads I cannot take/ Into the arms of ghosts I never knew." Even if he could track her to her birth, he admits, "You would escape me." He concludes, "As through a glass that magnifies my loss/ I see the lines of your spectrum shifting red,/ The universe expanding, thinning out,/ Our worlds flying, oh flying, fast apart." Always a time-bewitched poet, Kunitz brings to this and other new poems in the volume an added sense of urgency, for they are imbued with a love and desire that is unintentionally but nevertheless increasingly rearranged by the shifting weight of years.

THE TESTING-TREE

With amiable, if slow, regularity, Kunitz's fourth volume, *The Testing-Tree*, marks a departure from the rhetorical shimmer and elevated diction displayed in the previous collections. Written in a less knotty, more transparent syntax and style, the poems confront the upheavals of the 1960's, the guilt of failed marriage and inadequate parenthood, the ravages of time past ("the deep litter of the years"), and the inexplicable urge to carry on in the face of public and private failures: "In a murderous time/ the heart breaks and breaks/ and lives by breaking." The consolations of this volume, though sparse, strike the reader as all the more authentic for their scrupulous lack of facade, which, however, in no way implies a lessening of charity on the part of the poet.

One of the most notable poems in *The Testing-Tree* is "King of the River," a poem of the skewed hopes and unclear motives that disfigure and sometimes break a life but that are finally overtaken, with individual life itself transcended and transfigured by the relentless biological urge to perpetuate the species. The poem, whose central symbol is the chinook salmon swimming upstream to spawn, seeks to rebut the materialist's claim that "there is no life, only living things." By addressing the fish throughout as "you," the poet clearly implicates the reader in an allegory of life: "If the water were clear enough,/ if the water were still,/ but the water is not clear . . . If the knowledge were given you,/ but it is not given,/ for the membrane is clouded/ with self-deceptions." The psychological phrase helps swing the pointed finger around to the reader. "If the power were granted you/ to break out of your cells,/ but the imagination fails . . . If the heart were pure enough, but it is not pure . . . " continues the litany of denial that underpins the allegory. The salmon ("Finned Ego") thrashes to a place of which it has no knowledge, for "the doors of the senses close/ on the child within." The blind, headlong rush to "the orgiastic pool" brings about dreadful change ("A dry fire eats you./ Fat drips from your bones") into something "beyond the merely human," where, despite the "fire on your tongue," promising that "The only music is time/ the only dance is love,/ you would admit/ that nothing compels you/ any more . . . but nostalgia and desire,/ the two-way ladder/ between heaven and hell." At the "brute absolute hour" when the salmon spawns only to die, when "The great clock of your life/ is slowing down,/ and the small clocks run wild," he ("you") stares into the face of his "creature self" and finds "he is not broken but endures," but at a price: He is "forever inheriting his salt kingdom,/ from which he is banished/ forever." The "forever" that rounds the conclusion, like a little sleep, suggests that the victory of life's mission to perpetuate itself is ironically accomplished at the loss of the human's vaunted objectivity and understanding.

In "Robin Redbreast," Kunitz reveals a similar, but distinct, necessity. In "the room where I lived/ with an empty page" (a room identified in "River Road" from the same volume as one the poet inhabited after his second divorce), the poet hears the squawking of blue jays tormenting a robin, "the dingiest bird/ you ever saw." Going out to pick up the bird "after they knocked him down," in order to "toss him back into his element," he notices the bullet hole that "had tunneled out his wits." The hole, cut so clean it becomes a window, reveals "the cold flash of the blue/ unappeasable sky." The sky's indifference to the poet's sympathy for the bird ("Poor thing! Poor foolish life!") or to his own condition (he lives "in a house marked 'For Sale'") provides the chilling backdrop for a revelation of the necessity for human charity toward all living things. The poem knowingly alludes to a passage in "Father and Son": "For I would be . . . brother to the foundlings of the field/ And friend of innocence and all bright eyes." As with that earlier poem, "Robin Redbreast" finds no consolation in received wisdom, either from a father's love or the heavens. What charity there is exists (as do humans) in what scientists dryly refer to as "terminal structure."

Memory is more directly the subject of "The Magic Curtain," a cultural tour of the United States during the 1920's. A paean to his nurse, Frieda, the poem affectionately recounts his happy childhood adventures with this blue-eyed, Bavarian maid, while his mother, "her mind already on her shop," unrolled "gingham by the yard,/ stitching dresses for the Boston trade." Frieda, identified as his "first love," in secret complicity with the knowing child, bestows "the kinds of kisses mother would not dream" and serves as his guide to the melodramatic, romantic world of the motion pictures where, during reels of *The Perils of Pauline* (1914), Keystone Kops, and Charlie Chaplin, "School faded out at every morning reel." The films also offer a hint of the glamorous world beyond for Frieda, who takes her cue in a cinematic cliché and runs off "with somebody's husband, daddy to a brood." Although the poet's mother never forgives her this abandonment, the older poet, returning to her in the sanctuary of memory, eagerly does, for each has in a different way unknowingly conspired in fulfilling the dreams of the other.

The uneasy subject and situation of parents (and parent figures) weighs heavily, if somewhat obliquely, in the poems of *The Testing-Tree*. In fact, the volume opens with "Journal for My Daughter," a poem in which the poet, in nine free-verse sections, confronts his own hesitations and guilt in the upbringing of his only child. He imagines himself through her eyes as beckoning "down corridors,/ secret, elusive, saturnine." Now that, he hopes, the smoke of these misgivings has cleared, he declares, "I propose/ that we gather our affections." Looking back over his role in her life, he recounts his absence ("his name was absence") but claims, "I think I'd rather sleep forever/ than wake up cold/ in a country without women." He recounts, too, drunken nights of bonhomie with his friend, the poet Theodore Roethke, "slapping each other on the back,/ sweaty with genius," while she "crawled under the sofa." While he confesses that he is now "haggard with his thousand years," he declares his solidarity with her 1960's protests: "His heart is at home/ in your own generation," and to prove it, he equates her misspelled slogan *"Don't tred on me"* with the *"Noli me tangere!"* he used "to cry in Latin once." Though it seems implausible that one would cry out in Latin anyplace outside the Vatican or a course in Tudor poets, the point is well made. Recalling "the summer I went away," he carries her outside "in a blitz of fireflies" to observe her first eclipse. To this image he adds Samuel Taylor Coleridge's carrying his crying son outside and catching the reflection of stars in each of his suspended tears. The heavens and the natural world are captured, comfortably diminished, and naturalized as a way of sanctioning human folly and love. The reverse of this coin is that it is an illusion, a pint-sized reflection of a placid cosmos that will momentarily evaporate.

The book's title poem, composed in four sections of unrhymed tercets, concerns a ritualistic childhood game of stone-throwing ("for keeps") at a specific oak tree able to confer magic gifts: one hit for love, two for poetry, three for eternal life. In the summers of his youth, searching for "perfect stones," he is master "over that stretch of road . . . the world's fastest human." Leaving the road that begins at school at one end and that at the other tries "to loop me home," he enters a field "riddled with rabbit-life/ where the bees sank sugar-wells/ in the trunks of the maples." There, in the shadow of the "inexhaustible oak,/ tyrant and target," he calls to his father, *"wherever you are/ I have only three throws/ bless my good right arm."* In the final section, he recalls a recurring dream of his mother "wearing an owl's face/ and making barking noises." As "her minatory finger points," he steps through a cardboard door and wonders if he should be blamed for the dirt sifting into a well where a gentle-eyed "albino walrus huffs." Suddenly the scene shifts, and the highway up which a Model A chugs becomes the road "where tanks maneuver,/ revolving their turrets." He concludes, "It is necessary to go/ through dark and deeper dark/ and not to turn." With the clear implication that the poet is mindful of his approaching mortal hour, with or without his father's blessing, he cries, "Where is my testing-tree?/ Give me back my stones!"

The Testing-Tree differs from the first three volumes in being composed of nearly a quarter translations, all from postrevolutionary Russian poetry. It was during the 1960's that Kunitz met and befriended two of the Soviet Union's best-known poets, Yevgeny Yevtushenko and Andrei Voznesensky, and, in collaboration with Max Hayward, translated a selection of poems by a third, Anna Akhmatova. Clearly, the poems enabled Kunitz, with the aid of this fortuitous ventriloquism, to take aim at the brutality and inhumanity of the modern political bureaucracy, whether Soviet or American. In Yevtushenko's "Hand-Rolled Cigarettes," for example, the common man's practice of rolling cigarettes in papers torn from *Pravda* and *Izvestia*, the two chief organs of state propaganda, gives rise to a dandy send-up of the bureaucrat's contempt for the common man: "Returning late, the tired fisherman/ enjoys his ladled kvass's tang,/ and sifts tobacco at his ease/ onto some bureaucrat's harangue."

THE POEMS OF STANLEY KUNITZ, 1928-1978

The Poems of Stanley Kunitz, 1928-1978, like *Selected Poems, 1928-1958*, contains a section of new poems, titled "The Layers." Here, the poet returns to the garden of his obsessions—father, family, time, the wounds of guilt, and memory—in poems of reconciliation and commemoration. In the opening poem, "The Knot," the poet imagines that the knot "scored in the lintel of my door" keeps "bleeding through/ into the world we share." Like a repressed thought, the knot wants more than anything to grow out again, to become a limb: "I hear it come/ with a rush of resin/ out of the trauma/ of its lopping-off." Characteristically, the poet associates the wound with a door, a threshold. It is as though something in nature has had to be tamed to effect the domestic tranquillity so delicately limned here, but its desire to return to its true nature is such that it "racks itself with shoots/ that crackle overhead." Identifying a part of his own nature with that of the knot, the poet completes the metaphor: "I shake my wings/ and fly into its boughs."

Kunitz returns to the theme of the lost father in "What of the Night?" and "Quinnapoxet." In the former, the poet wakes in the middle of the night "like a country doctor," having imagined, "with racing heart," the doorbell ringing. It is a messenger (Death) whose "gentle, insistent ring" finds the poet "not ready yet" and realizing "nobody stands on the stoop." Suddenly the poem switches focus from the grown son to the father: "When the messenger comes again/ I shall pretend/ in a childish voice/ my father is not home." His father has, in actuality, never been home, but in a deeper, metaphorical sense, he has never left home. In this light, just as the grown man must receive the messenger at the end of his life, so the son must protect the father in memory from the "second death," the oblivion of forgetting. The poet's task of remembering is obligatory, as his question earlier in the poem recognizes: "How could I afford/ to disobey that call?" "Quinnapoxet" takes place on a mysterious fishing trip where, on a dusty road similar to the one described in "Father and Son," the poet describes a hallucinatory vision of his mother and father "commingling with the dust/ they raised." His mother admonishes him for not writing, and the poet's response is simple: "I had nothing to say to her." Yet for his father who walks behind, "his face averted . . . deep in his other life," the poet, too awestruck to attempt speech, touches his forehead with his thumb, "in deaf-mute country/ the sign for father."

One of the most original of the new poems in this volume is "A Blessing of Women," a prose poem inspired by an exhibit of early American women painters and artisans mounted by the Whitney Museum. In the form of a litany, the poem briefly describes, in dignified understatement, the works and lives of five of the representative women: an embroiderer, a quilter, and three painters, "a rainbow-cloud of witnesses in a rising hub-bub." He blesses them and greets them "as they pass from their long obscurity, through the gate that separates us from our history."

"Our history" is again the subject of "The Lincoln Relics," a meditation on Lincoln's passage from the "rawboned, warty" mortal "into his legend and his fame." Written not long after the Watergate trauma during Kunitz's tenure at the Library of Congress, the poem alludes to that episode by invoking the ancient struggle between idealism and ma-terialism, no less fierce in Lincoln's day than in ours: "I saw the piranhas darting/ be-tween the roseveined columns,/ avid to strip the flesh/ from the Republic's bones." The source of Lincoln's, the sacrificial redeemer's, strength is identified as his "secret wound"—that is to say, "trusting the better angels of our nature." It is this trust, evoked by the humble but talismanic relics—a pocketknife, a handkerchief, a button—found on his person after the assassination, that makes "a noble, dissolving music/ out of homely fife and drum."

The title poem of the new section, "The Layers," looks forward to the possibilities of new art. The poet has "walked through many lives" and from the present vantage sees "milestones dwindling/ toward the horizon/ and the slow fires trailing/ from the aban-doned camp-sites." To the question, "How shall the heart be reconciled/ to its feast of losses?" the answer comes "In my darkest night" from a "nimbus-cloud voice" that thunders, "Live in the layers,/ not on the litter." Though the poet admits, "I lack the art/ to decipher it," he concludes, "I am not done with my changes."

NEXT-TO-LAST THINGS

Kunitz's *Next-to-Last Things* makes at least three important additions to his poetic canon. A dream poem, "The Abduction," begins with the image of the beloved stum-bling out of a wood, her blouse torn, her skirt bloodstained; she addresses the poet with the mysterious question, "Do you believe?" Through the years, he says, "from bits/ from broken clues/ we pieced enough together/ to make the story real." Led into the presence of "a royal stag,/ flaming in his chestnut coat," she was "borne/ aloft in triumph through the green,/ stretched on his rack of budding horn." In the next verse paragraph, the poet discloses that the episode was "a long time ago,/ almost another age" and muses on his sleeping wife (recalling, with the same image, the theme of otherness in "The Sci-ence of the Night"): "You lie in elegant repose,/ a hint of transport hovering on your lips." His attention shifts "to the harsh green flares," to which she is indifferent, that "swivel through the room/ controlled by unseen hands." The night world outside is "childhood country,/ bleached faces peering in/ with coals for eyes." His meditation leads him to realize that "the shapes of things/ are shifting in the wind," and concludes, "What do we know/ beyond the rapture and the dread?" echoing William Butler Yeats's famous question, "How can we know the dancer from the dance?" As a poem of trans-formation, "The Abduction" does not lend itself easily to interpretation—partly by design—for, at a very basic level, the preternatural images of transformation are rooted in undisclosed biographical events. As a poet of knowledge, however, Kunitz is poignant in his recognition that when people sleep, when they are most themselves, they are also most withdrawn and indifferent to their surroundings, even, or especially, from those they love. Yet by acknowledging, even honoring, the terms of this indifference, one most surely understands the unselfish nature of love.

"Days of Foreboding" begins with the announcement, "Great events are about to happen." The poet has seen migratory birds "in unprecedented numbers" picking the coastal margin clean. Turning to himself, he observes, "My bones are a family in their tent/ huddled over a small fire/ waiting for the uncertain signal/ to resume the long march." He too is migratory, warmed by the small fire of his heart. Presumably, the "uncertain signal" is in some way keyed to the signal by which the migratory birds decide to move on—that is, it is keyed to nature. Moreover, while the signal is uncertain in terms of time and origin, it is nevertheless inevitable. The ultimate phrase, "the long march," sings with historical resonance and the promise of an irreversible transformation at the end. In this poem and in others, Kunitz accepts the awful fact of mortality, not by making an abstraction of it but by naturalizing both it and the patch of history that is the bolt of time and circumstance given for its completion. Avoiding the need for consolation, it is a brave and existential view.

Certainly the centerpiece of *Next-to-Last Things* is the five-part meditative elegy, "The Wellfleet Whale," composed, like "The Testing-Tree," in tercets. Kunitz has noted that much of contemporary meditative poetry suffers from "the poverty of what it is meditating on," but this poem, occasioned by the beaching of a finback whale near the poet's home on Cape Cod, is rich in its suggestion that life's secret origins can be, if not revealed, then somehow embodied by the evocativeness of language, which is itself, as the poet notes elsewhere, "anciently deep in mysteries." The poem begins by ascribing to the whale, both Leviathan and deliverer of Jonah, Christ's precursor, the gift of language: "You have your language too,/ an eerie medley of clicks/ and hoots and trills. . . ." That language, to which humans are denied access (just as historical man, exiled from Eden, can no longer hear the music of the spheres), becomes only "sounds that all melt/ . . . with endless variations,/ as if to compensate/ for the vast loneliness of the sea." In the second section of the poem, the whale's arrival in the harbor is greeted with cheers "at the sign of your greatness." Unlike man, the whale in its element seems "like something poured,/ not driven," his presence asking "not sympathy, or love,/ or understanding,/ but awe and wonder," responses appropriate to deity. Yet by dawn, the whale is stranded on the rocks, and the curious gather in: "school-girls in yellow halters/ and a housewife bedecked/ with curlers, and whole families in beach/ buggies. . . ." As the great body is slowly crushed by its own weight, the Curator of Mammals arrives to draw the requisite vial of blood, someone carves his initials on the blistered flanks, and seagulls peck at the skin. The poet asks, "What drew us, like a magnet, to your dying?" and answers, "You made a bond between us." This unlikely company, "boozing in the bonfire night," stands watch during the night as the whale enters its final agony and swings its head around to open "a blood-shot, glistening eye/ in which we swam with terror and recognition." The terror is that of witnessing "an exiled god" and the recognition that the creature, bringing with it "the myth/ of another country, dimly remembered" is "like us,/ disgraced and mortal," like all beings, and "delivered to the mercy of time." Despite the desecrations visited upon the creature, it remains an emissary from that other "country," the country of myth and inspired origin that stands at the beginning of human memory—and thus of identity—and so supervenes upon the noble disenchantment of the poem.

PASSING THROUGH

Passing Through, published when Kunitz was ninety years old, is a slim volume that adds nine new poems to the body of Kunitz's work. Some of the poems in this collection are drawn from *The Testing-Tree, Next-to-Last Things*, and "The Layers." The title of the collection comes from a poem, "Passing Through," that Kunitz wrote on his seventy-ninth birthday and published in *Next-to-Last Things*. In this poem, he looks back on his childhood and amplifies his quest for identity. Saying that his family never observed anniversaries, he matter-of-factly states, "my birthday went up in smoke/ in a fire at City Hall that gutted/ the Department of Vital Statistics." He goes on to say that only because a census report noted that "a five-year-old White Male/ [was] sharing my mother's address/ at the Green Street tenement in Worchester" did he have any identity at all. However, he concludes that "Maybe I enjoy not-being as much/ as being who I am," and continues whimsically, saying that—at seventy-nine, mind you—"I'm passing through a phase."

Similar in its quest for identity is "The Sea, That Has No Ending," which begins with the questions "Who are we? Why are we here,/ huddled on this desolate shore,/ so curiously chopped and joined?" The eternal sea, the forever sea, the sea that has always been and will always be, "The sea that has no ending,/ is lapping at our feet." Kunitz recounts, "How we long for the cleansing waters/ to rise and cover us forever!" Here he juxtaposes immortality and mortality, human time and eternity, reiterating forcefully his persistent concerns with time and space.

In his selection of poems for this volume, the author included a range of works that detail ancient and modern events, broadly global and intensely personal occurrences, and events both real and mythical. On one hand, he celebrates the flight of Apollo 11 (the first to transport humans to the Moon); on the other, he tells of the struggles of Roman gladiators.

"Around Pastor Bonhoeffer," his homage to Dietrich Bonhoeffer, who stood four-square against Adolf Hitler and his reign of terror in Nazi Germany, is stylistically among his most successful poems. Short, clipped lines capture the tension of the situation:

Kyrie eleison: Night
like no other night, plotted
and palmed,
omega of terror,
packed like a bullet
in the triggered chamber.

THE COLLECTED POEMS

Coincident with his being appointed the poet laureate of the United States in 2000, when he was ninety-five years old, *The Collected Poems* is the first collection of Kunitz's poems since the publication in 1979 of *The Poems of Stanley Kunitz, 1928-1978* by W. W. Norton. This volume, drawing on all the earlier volumes, provides readers with the full range of Kunitz's remarkably varied work. Reading through the entire volume, which is arranged chronologically, one becomes fully aware of the themes that most affected the poet and his work: innocence and love, including the loss of each; parental relationships, particularly the father-son relationship of which he was deprived by his father's suicide shortly before his birth; a tragic element connected with personal disappointments; and an overwhelming optimism, articulated well in "The Long Boat," where Kunitz writes, "He loved the earth so much/ he wanted to stay forever." Kunitz was always aware of the tenuous relationship of time in human terms to eternity, which is a global concept. The poet urged young writers always to be explorers. In his ninth decade of life, Kunitz continued to be an explorer, seeking out new experiences and writing about them in new and uniquely wonderful ways.

The tension that is everywhere apparent between noble disenchantment and hard-won acceptance demonstrates the ruling dialectic in Kunitz's poems. At the very least, it reveals the long trail of a poetic career (poetic careers have been built on much less); at its most resplendent, this dialectic embodies, through its variously charted interests, experiences, and investigations, a reason for the mind's commitment to the things of this world. Standing simultaneously in their singular and typical natures, they suggest the duality that is both a curse and triumph and lead to an appreciation and understanding, as individuals rebound endlessly between the two, of the transformations that must be endured to ensure survival.

OTHER MAJOR WORKS

NONFICTION: *A Kind of Order, a Kind of Folly: Essays and Conversations*, 1975; *Interviews and Encounters with Stanley Kunitz*, 1993 (Stanley Moss, editor).

TRANSLATIONS: *Antiworlds and the Fifth Ace*, 1967 (with others; of Andrei Voznesensky's poetry); *Stolen Apples*, 1971 (with others; of Yevgeny Yevtushenko's poetry); *Poems of Akhmatova*, 1973 (with Max Hayward; of Anna Akhmatova); *Story Under Full Sail*, 1974 (of Voznesensky's poetry); *Orchard Lamps*, 1978 (of Ivan Drach's poetry).

EDITED TEXTS: *Living Authors: A Book of Biographies*, 1931; *Authors Today and Yesterday: A Companion Volume to "Living Authors,"* 1933 (with Howard Haycraft and Wilbur C. Hadden); *The Junior Book of Authors*, 1934, 2d edition 1951 (with Haycraft); *British Authors of the Nineteenth Century*, 1936 (with Haycraft); *American Authors, 1600-1900: A Biographical Dictionary of American Literature*, 1938 (with Haycraft); *Twentieth Century Authors: A Biographical Dictionary of Modern Literature*, 1942, 7th edition 1973 (with Haycraft); *British Authors Before 1800: A Biographical Dictionary*, 1952 (with Haycraft); *Twentieth Century Authors: A Biographical Dictionary of Modern Literature, First Supplement*, 1955, 7th edition 1990 (with Vineta Colby); *European Authors, 1000-1900: A Biographical Dictionary of European Literature*, 1967 (with Colby); *Contemporary Poetry in America*, 1973; *The Essential Blake*, 1987; *The Wild Card: Selected Poems, Early and Late*, 1998 (by Karl Shapiro; with David Ignatow); *The Wild Braid: A Poet Reflects on a Century in the Garden*, 2005 (with Genine Lentine).

MISCELLANEOUS: *Next-to-Last Things: New Poems and Essays*, 1985.

BIBLIOGRAPHY

Barber, David. "A Visionary Poet at Ninety." *The Atlantic Monthly* 277, no. 6 (June, 1996): 113-120. This article includes a biographical survey and a brief review of some of the poet's earlier works before turning to a heartfelt appreciation of *Passing Through*. Barber names Kunitz a "visionary" and sees his poetry as "transfiguring."

Campbell, Robert. "God, Man, and Whale: Stanley Kunitz's *Collected Poems* Show His Work Is All of a Piece." Review of *The Collected Poems*. *The New York Times Book Review*, October 1, 2000, p. 6. This review of Kunitz's poems, collected and published in his ninety-fifth year, offers comments about the broad spectrum of this poet's writing over seven decades. One of the most insightful brief overviews of Kunitz in print.

Henault, Marie. *Stanley Kunitz*. Boston: Twayne, 1980. A good introduction to Kunitz for the beginning reader. Presents biographical detail and criticism of his poetry, discussing his themes, form, and techniques, and the "interior logics" of his poems. A sympathetic study lamenting the fact that Kunitz has not received the wide critical recognition he deserves.

Kunitz, Stanley. "An Interview with Stanley Kunitz." Interview by Peter Stitt. *Gettysburg Review* 5, no. 2 (Spring, 1992): 193-209. Offers a transcript of a 1990 interview and features a new poem, "The Chariot," with commentary by Kunitz.

_____. "Translating Anna Akhmatova: A Conversation with Stanley Kunitz." Interview by Daniel Weissbort. In *Translating Poetry: The Double Labyrinth*, edited by Weissbort. Iowa City: University of Iowa Press, 1989. An explanation of the history of the translation project, with a discussion of the methods employed by Kunitz and Max Hayward.

Lowell, Robert. "On Stanley Kunitz's 'Father and Son.'" In *The Contemporary Poet as Artist and Critic*, edited by Anthony Ostroff. Boston: Little, Brown, 1964. Analyzes "Father and Son" and takes issue with a number of images in this poem, such as an orange being "nailed." Despite his unfavorable response, Lowell acknowledges that Kunitz has "never published an unfinished and unfelt poem."

Orr, Gregory. *Stanley Kunitz: An Introduction to the Poetry*. New York: Columbia University Press, 1985. A full-length criticism of Kunitz, noting that love and art are the two ways in which this poet seeks his identity. Discusses the key image, which Orr maintains is the single most important element in Kunitz's work. The chapter on *The Testing-Tree* is particularly recommended.

Plummer, William. "New Beginnings: At Ninety-five, Fledgling Poet Laureat Stanley Kunitz Finds Fresh Wood." *People Weekly* 54 (October 30, 2000): 159-160. Written for a popular audience, this overview of Kunitz's life and work emphasizes that the poet has continued to grow. An excellent, humane assessment of a life of creative endeavor.

Vinson, James, ed. *Contemporary Poets*. 3d ed. New York: Macmillan, 1980. The entry on Kunitz, by Michael True, examines his poetry as it retraces the "myth of the lost father." Cites his devotion to craft and the high standards he strove to maintain throughout his work. Notes Kunitz's earlier works as being more intellectual and his later ones as being more oriented toward feelings.

Weisberg, Robert. "Stanley Kunitz: The Stubborn Middle Way." *Modern Poetry Studies* 6 (Spring, 1975): 49-57. In this sympathetic article, Weisberg laments that Kunitz's "impressive" canon has aroused little critical interest. In discussing *Selected Poems, 1928-1958*, however, he criticizes Kunitz for being a "reincarnation of John Donne" but praises "The Words of the Preacher" for the energy that his other metaphysical lyrics lack. Includes an analysis of *The Testing-Tree*.

David Rigsbee
Updated by R. Baird Shuman

DENISE LEVERTOV

Born: Ilford, Essex, England; October 24, 1923
Died: Seattle, Washington; December 20, 1997

PRINCIPAL POETRY

The Double Image, 1946
Here and Now, 1957
Five Poems, 1958
Overland to the Islands, 1958
With Eyes at the Back of Our Heads, 1959
The Jacob's Ladder, 1961
City Psalm, 1964
O Taste and See: New Poems, 1964
Psalm Concerning the Castle, 1966
The Sorrow Dance, 1966
A Marigold from North Vietnam, 1968
Three Poems, 1968
A Tree Telling of Orpheus, 1968
The Cold Spring, and Other Poems, 1969
Embroideries, 1969
Summer Poems, 1969, 1970
A New Year's Garland for My Students: MIT, 1969-1970, 1970
Relearning the Alphabet, 1970
To Stay Alive, 1971
Footprints, 1972
The Freeing of the Dust, 1975
Chekhov on the West Heath, 1977
Modulations for Solo Voice, 1977
Life in the Forest, 1978
Collected Earlier Poems, 1940-1960, 1979
Pig Dreams: Scenes from the Life of Sylvia, 1981
Wanderer's Daysong, 1981
Candles in Babylon, 1982
Poems, 1960-1967, 1983
The Menaced World, 1984
Oblique Prayers: New Poems with Fourteen Translations from Jean Joubert, 1984
Selected Poems, 1986
Breathing the Water, 1987

Poems, 1968-1972, 1987
A Door in the Hive, 1989
Evening Train, 1993
Sands of the Well, 1996
The Stream and the Sapphire: Selected Poems on Religious Themes, 1997
The Great Unknowing: Last Poems, 1999
Making Peace, 2006 (Peggy Rosenthal, editor)

OTHER LITERARY FORMS

The Poet in the World (1973) gathers prose articles, reviews, criticism, statements to the press, and tributes to fellow poets by Denise Levertov (LEHV-ur-tawf). *Light Up the Cave* (1981), her second volume of prose pieces, includes three short stories, articles on the nature of poetry and politics, speeches and political commentary, and memoirs and notes on other writers—Hilda Morley, Michele Murray, Bert Meyers, Rainer Maria Rilke, and Anton Chekhov. Of particular interest are the pages on dream, memory, and poetry and the details of her arrest and imprisonment experience as a war protester.

Levertov also wrote a novella, *In the Night: A Story* (1968), and the libretto for an oratorio, *El Salvador: Requiem and Invocation* (pr. 1983). With Kenneth Rexroth and William Carlos Williams, she edited *Penguin Modern Poets Nine* (1967). She produced translations of other poets' works, including *In Praise of Krishna: Songs from the Bengali* (1967, with Edward C. Dimock, Jr.), *Selected Poems,* by Eugene Guillevic (1969), and *Black Iris,* by Jean Joubert (1988). Her final prose work, *Tesserae* (1995), consists of autobiographical fragments that composed a "mosaic" of the poet's life.

ACHIEVEMENTS

Denise Levertov's first book of poems, *The Double Image,* was published in England in 1946. It brought her to the attention of British and American critics and poets such as Kenneth Rexroth and Robert Creeley. Eleven years later, her first American book was published, followed by many volumes of poems and several translations of other poets' work. She taught at many institutions, including Vassar College; Drew University; City College of New York; University of California, Berkeley; Massachusetts Institute of Technology; Brandeis University; Tufts University; and Stanford University. As the poetry editor of *The Nation* in the 1960's, she influenced the critical reception of new poets. She was elected to the American Academy of Arts and Letters. Her many awards include the Bess Hokin Prize from *Poetry* magazine in 1960, a Guggenheim Foundation Fellowship in 1962, a National Institute of Arts and Letters Award in 1965, the Lenore Marshall Poetry Prize in 1976 for *The Freeing of the Dust,* both the Elmer Holmes Bobst Award and the Shelley Memorial Award in 1983, the Frost Medal in 1990, the Lannan Literary Award for Poetry in 1993, an Academy of American Poets Fellowship in 1995, and a Washington State Book Award in 1996.

BIOGRAPHY

Born near London, England, in 1923, Denise Levertov was reared in a multicultural environment: Welsh and Russian, Jewish and Christian. On her mother's side, her lineage was Welsh. Beatrice Spooner-Jones, her mother, was a daughter of a physician and great-granddaughter of a tailor, teacher, and preacher, Angell Jones, made famous by Daniel Owen, "the Welsh Dickens," in the novel *Hunangofiant Rhys Lewis* (1885). Beatrice Spooner-Jones had a beautiful singing voice and a stock of stories to tell of Welsh life. She loved to travel, and in Constantinople, where she was a teacher in a Scottish mission, she met a young Russian Jew, Paul Peter Levertoff, who had converted to Christianity. They were married in London, where he was ordained to the Anglican priesthood. His great passion in life was reconciliation between Christians and Jews. A daughter, Olga, was born to the couple, and seven years later, a second daughter, Denise.

In some ways, Denise felt like an only child. She never attended a public or private school; her mother, her only teacher, read many classic works of fiction to her. She visited museums and libraries in London and studied ballet for many years; for a time, she considered a career in dance. When World War II came, she entered nurse's training and worked in a number of London public hospitals caring for children, the aged, and the poor. She had been writing poems since childhood and published her first volume of poems in England shortly after the war.

Levertov met and married an American writer, Mitchell Goodman, who was studying abroad. They lived in Europe until 1948, returning to Europe from New York for a period in 1950-1951. Her son Nikolai was born in 1949. In 1956, she became an American citizen. For the next thirty years, she published more than a dozen volumes of poetry with the same publisher, New Directions. During the Vietnam era, she wrote and spoke passionately against the war; in 1972, with Muriel Rukeyser and Jane Hart, she traveled to Hanoi. In the years of nuclear bomb testing in the air, she participated in the movement toward a test-ban treaty and the elimination of nuclear weapons. Later, she vigorously supported protests against American involvement in civil wars in El Salvador, Honduras, and Nicaragua. She lived in Mexico for a number of years: Indeed, her mother grew to love Mexico and remained with a family in Oaxaca for twenty years before her death in 1977. After spending much of the last decade of her life in the Pacific Northwest, Levertov died in Seattle, Washington, on December 20, 1997.

ANALYSIS

Denise Levertov published about six hundred poems. Despite this large number of works, her poems revolve around a few preoccupations and questions that continuously engaged her attention: the meaning of life, the issues of justice that have arisen in the twentieth century, and more personal concerns that have to do with friendships, family relationships, and immediate thoughts and feelings. Since the lyric poem captures a moment of intense feeling and thought (it is the most compressed form of literature), chronological analysis of Levertov's work gives access to a record of the poet's unfolding life. Levertov seems to have been uniquely placed in her family and time to inherit two great streams of lyric power—the Welsh gift of song and speech and the profound religious thought of her priest father's Jewish-Christian search for truth.

With such a combination of parental influences, the themes that prevail in Levertov's poetry—the nature and form of poetry, and the moral obligations of the poet to society—are hardly surprising. She once said that the Hasidic or mystical beliefs in her father's Jewish heritage gave her an ease and familiarity with spiritual mysteries. For the purpose of analysis, one can study these three areas of her concern—poetry, morality, and mystery—but in her poems they often appear not separately but together, coloring the mosaic of her words. She combines the skills of a craftsperson and those of an artist, the vision of moral integrity and spiritual insight.

EARLY INFLUENCES

A young poet must establish her voice and style. Levertov learned from modernist poets such as Charles Olson and William Carlos Williams, who used concrete, everyday words and familiar settings and events to convey profound truths. She drew also from Welsh hymn-singing lines. Lines and line breaks are essential to the sound quality of her poetry. Some of her inspiration comes from dreams, images, and dream sounds. Naturally, the technical apparatus of poetry-making absorbs her interest as a poet and teacher of poetry writing: How should journals be used? How should a poet revise drafts? How does one evaluate poetry and distinguish what is good from what is bad? Who are the great poets of the twentieth century?

As to the second preoccupation in Levertov's poetry, the integrity of moral vision, the twentieth century has provided abundant evidence of the human capacity for sin as well as visionary leadership in the fight against evil. The age-old oppression of Jews by Christians flared into monstrous proportions as millions of innocent women, children, and men were gassed in death camps in Europe. The shock of this discovery in 1945 as World War II came to a close must have been intense for the young poet-nurse whose father was both Jew and Christian. In later decades, she felt an imperative to protest the horror and injustice of war. The effort to end the Vietnam War brought women together before the women's movement had gathered full force. The sight of children mutilated and burned by napalm aroused the conscience of many "unpolitical" people. Levertov's actions and her words expressed the outrage of many citizens. She explored the relevance of poetry to politics and questioned the moral responsibility of the poet in a time of peril. What use should be made of the gift of speech?

Early in her career, Levertov expressed her vision of unity in the physical and spiritual worlds. "Taste and See," the title poem of her seventh volume, has a biblical sound. Insisting that one cannot know a divinity apart from what is given to the senses, she probes the meaning of physical experience—a life affirmation—and considers its relationship to religious values. Decades before the general public awakened to the need to respect the physical world, Levertov spoke of the mystery in the objects people taste, touch, and see: the Moon, food, a glass of water. She found both happiness and wisdom in the realization of mystery. Increasingly, in her later poetry, the value of mystical and religious experience became her theme.

RELIGIOUS SIGNIFICANCE

Levertov links the imagination with truth in poetry; thus, the poem has a religious significance. As "religion" literally means "binding anew," she finds connections to be the essence or truth of imagination. In the poem "A Straw Swan Under the Christmas Tree," she writes, "All trivial parts of/ world-about-us speak in their forms/ of themselves and their counterparts! . . . one speech conjuring the other." The human emotion of sympathy depends on understanding the connections in animate and also inanimate life. "May the taste of salt/ recall to us the great depths about us," she writes in "The Depths." The principle of interrelated form applies even in the extreme case of Nazi leader Karl Adolf Eichmann. In "During the Eichmann Trial," she says that if one looks accurately into another face, or into a mirror, one sees "the other," even Eichmann. This oneness is a mystery, and something Eichmann did not know: "We are members/ one of another."

One should not conclude, however, that the truth of imagination Levertov seeks is an intellectual truth. Unlike the poet Dante, who moves from love and care in the physical world to a spiritual and intellectual understanding of love, Levertov remains firmly based in the physical realm, however far along the mystical path she may travel. Perhaps in the modern age the presence of evil within and without is so strong that the poet dares not abandon her mooring in the physical "real" world that needs so much assistance. Humanity is "a criminal kind, the planet's nightmare" (as she quotes Robinson Jeffers in the poem "Kith and Kin"). The truth she continually explores remains the connection in the patterns of human and natural life. Courage is a necessity, and models of courage may be found in her lean, economical poetic voice.

DICTION AND IMAGERY

A "speaking-voice" quality in Levertov's poems results from the open form of uneven line lengths. In keeping with the tone of a human voice in natural and varied cadences, her diction neither startles nor challenges the reader with rare and exotic words in the manner of Marianne Moore or Edith Sitwell. She "tunes up" or increases the vibrancy of her poems by making them "tight," with no excess words or phrases. She often omits subjects and verbs, punctuating a fragment as though it were a sentence, and alternates or intersperses fragments with complete sentences. Another skill is accuracy in word choice, using the best word to evoke the scene, the object, the person, or the feeling she is describing. She can change the feeling of a line by inserting words from another collocation—sets of words often found together. For example, in a late poem, "Those Who Want Out," from *A Door in the Hive*, she describes people who are designing permanent colonies in space—their optimism, their love of speed and machines that are "outside of nature." Then a closing line judges them with icy and stern tone in six one-syllable words with biblical power: "They do not love the earth." This use of sparse, plain Anglo-Saxon English for a "stopper" of great power is found frequently in William Shakespeare.

Along with devices of diction, poetic speech uses images to convey truth. Levertov's images are most frequently from the natural world—plants, animals, and landscapes—and of everyday household objects. "In the Unknown" takes the reader to the poet's home: "As if the white page/ were a clean tablecloth,/ as if the vacuumed floor were a primed canvas." In "To the Muse," she describes the body as the house one lives in and the place to find one's inner poetry. There are many rooms in this house, and when the Muse seems to have departed, she is hiding, like a lost gold ring. One has forgotten to make a place for her, and to bring her back, one needs to attend to the house, find some flowers to decorate it, and be alert to the Muse with all one's senses. Images of caves, mirrors, water, cloud, shadow, and moon fill her poems to make her feelings and ideas accessible to the common reader.

ROLES OF THE POET

In harmony with her use of diction and form, Levertov expressed a modest view of the poet: a person who can articulate feeling through the medium of language. She refused the exalted aura of a supersensitive person whose feelings are beyond the reach of ordinary human beings. Glorification by "temperament" was never attractive to her and was as suspect as misplaced romantic adulation—not a twentieth century ideal. It was the process of writing, not the result, that fascinated her. She saw poems as structures of meaning and sound that convey feelings accurately. The poet must revise and polish until the poem is complete. Technical skill with diction, form, rhythm, syntax, and sound—above all, sound—raises a poem from mediocrity to perfection. As a teacher, she had much experience to share. From her essays and articles on the subject of poetry one can gain information about many technical aspects of her craft. Her poems are more readily understood when one is familiar with these principles.

VERSIFICATION

Like many young poets, Levertov experimented in her early writings with various rhyme schemes, tones, and forms. A 1946 poem, "Folding a Shirt," uses Dante's interlacing terza rima rhyme pattern for six stanzas: *aba bcb cdc ded efe fgf*. "Midnight Quatrains" rhymes the second and fourth end words of each stanza. There are dramatic poems in dialogue form and ballads. Typically, however, Levertov's poems have no end rhyme or regular meter. (The lack of regular rhyme and stressed beats in most modern poetry has been attributed to the chaos and irregularity in the twentieth century— poetry reflects life.) Her rhythm is subtle, moving with the line break. Uneven lines are the rule, not the exception. The placement of words and indentations create rhythmic ebb and flow, abrupt interruptions, slow pauses, and dramatic suspense. The eye follows a varied typography that signals rhythm with blank space and black ink, like a design for reading aloud. The "melos" or song quality of such an open form comes from the rightness of the line length—the line's appropriate length in the poem's internal system of meanings.

As well as obtaining rhythm by a masterful use of line breaks, Levertov excels in the construction of sentences within the poem. Often a poem is built like an argument: a proposition followed by a rebuttal, in the way of a sonnet. The poem's syntax often matches the idea of the poem. In "The Prayer," the poet is praying to Apollo at Delphi for the flame of her poetry to be maintained. As if the poem were the flame, it keeps going until the poet breaks the sentence when she begins to wonder whether the god is mocking her. The sentence ends at the same time that her belief in the god falters. The second sentence, a reprise, says that the flame is flickering, and perhaps it is some other god at work. In a very sensual poem, "Eros at Temple Stream," she pictures lovers bathing near a river, soaping each other with long, slippery strokes—their hands as flames. The poem's syntax—one long sentence with no punctuation at its close—mirrors the meaning.

NARRATIVE AND DRAMATIC POEMS

In Levertov's narrative and dramatic poems, she set the stage quickly. A mini-play, "Scenario," opens bluntly: "The theater of war. Offstage/ a cast of thousands weeping." A poem about animal life at the dump begins, "At the dump bullfrogs/ converse as usual." Often these poems begin with brief noun phrases, as in "A Hunger": "Black beans, white sunlight." Levertov's impulse for story and drama resulted in a number of long poem sequences and poetic plays. "Staying Alive," with its prologue and four parts with entr'actes, vividly recalls events and feelings at the height of the Vietnam War protests and the People's Park struggle in Berkeley, California, in 1969. In 1983, an oratorio, *El Salvador: Requiem and Invocation*, was performed at Harvard University; the text by Levertov was set to music by the composer W. Newell Hendricks. Using the structures of the Johann Sebastian Bach passions and George Frideric Handel and Franz Josef Haydn oratorios, Levertov wrote voices for a narrator, Archbishop Oscar Romero, a questioner, nuns, and a chorus. She studied the speeches of the murdered archbishop and quoted his words as well as passages from Mayan prayers. The work was given to help fund-raising efforts of relief organizations active in Central America.

POLITICAL POEMS

That the poet should be also a political person came as an early and natural revelation to Levertov. Her first published poem, "Listening to Distant Guns" (1940), tells of hearing "a low pulsation in the East" that "betrays no whisper of the battle scream." She actually heard the guns of World War II from the south coast of England, to where she, along with many young people, had been evacuated from the city of London. She herself was safe, but the war was very near. She describes the dismal feelings of the English people in "Christmas 1944," when no celebration could hide the blackout curtains on the windows, the knowledge of "fear knocking on the door" of so many Europeans. She gives a welcome: "Come in, then poverty, and come in, death:/ This year too many lie cold, or die in cold." During her impressionable teens and early twenties, she was surrounded with war. Although two decades would pass before her active involvement in the American antiwar movement, she had already expressed her grief at the mass destruction war brings.

In "On the Edge of Darkness: What Is Political Poetry?" (originally a lecture delivered at Boston University in 1975), Levertov defends the idea that a lyric poem can be simultaneously intimate, passionate, and political. Indeed, there is a long history of poets speaking out their political ideas—generally, though not always, in defense of liberty and peace. Contemporary "political" poets usually participate actively in the struggles of which they write. Specific issues give rise to topical poetry on race, class, environment, and gender problems. These poems, like the songs associated with the struggles, change the feelings of the listeners and readers; they alter the awareness of a community. The standards of aesthetic value apply to this poetry as to all other; it should arouse the whole being of the listener: mind, senses, and spirit.

ANTIWAR POETRY

By 1966, Levertov was writing poems about the war in Vietnam. The most influential and famous of these is probably "Life at War." Speaking for her contemporaries, she tells of war's pervasive influence in her century—"We have breathed the grits of it in, all our lives"—and then begins a long lament over the damage war has done to people's imaginations. The modern imagination, she argues, is "filmed over with the gray filth of it," because humankind (and here she lists wonderful and praiseworthy achievements and powers of human beings) "whose language imagines *mercy* and *lovingkindness*," can schedule the burning of children's bodies. "Burned human flesh/ is smelling in Vietnam as I write." As a former nurse, Levertov can bring her sensual awareness into her passionate denunciation of modern war. The poem closes with a statement that humankind needs the "deep intelligence" that living at peace can give. The violence to human imagination from war comes from its insult to intelligence.

Other antiwar poems were composed in the form of dialogues such as questions and answers about Vietnamese people or a narrator questioning a bomber pilot. Levertov's poems also protest the false language of war communiqués. She pays tribute to the young men and women antiwar activists—those who die, those who live, those who go to jail. One poem honors her friend and fellow poet Muriel Rukeyser, who went to Vietnam with her in 1972. Both women had sons who were teenagers at the time and faced the possibility of being drafted into the military.

MARRIAGE AND FAMILY LIFE

Family life, and in particular marriage, inspired many of Levertov's most memorable poems. In keeping with her insistence on the beauty of sensual experience, she celebrated the joy of marriage. The short poem "Bedtime" puts the contentment of fulfilled love in natural terms: "We are a meadow where the bees hum,/ mind and body are almost one." "Hymn to Eros" praises the "drowsy god" who quietly circles in "a snowfall hush." Two beautiful poems to her son, Nikolai, are spaced years apart—one before his birth, "Who He Was," and one, "The Son," as he becomes a man. The first tells of his conception, gestation, and birth, and the second of skills he has gained.

The death of love and the contemporary difficulties in male-female relationships also provide subjects for notable poems. The much-quoted "About Marriage" begins with a cry for freedom, "Don't lock me in wedlock, I want/ marriage, an/ encounter," and concludes, "I would be/ met/ and meet you/ so,/ in a green/ airy space, not/ locked in." As the women's movement and the antiwar movement seemed to merge, the desire for peace and independence became the message of many women writers and poets. "The Ache of Marriage" compares marriage to Jonah's life in the belly of a whale; the poet and her spouse are looking for joy, "some joy/ not to be known outside it." Marriage is not discarded as an ideal, but its confinement brings problems to women who feel an urge to work in a wider field. In "Hypocrite Women," Levertov tells women that they should not be ashamed of their "unwomanly" traits but should admit boldly the truth of their lives.

The nature of another woman-to-woman relationship is explored in the "Olga" poems. Levertov's sister, older by seven years, was estranged from her family for many years. Her death brought a recollection and definition of the two lives that were linked in dream and memory but separated by behavior, circumstances, and distance. The gaze of her sister's eyes haunts the poet: "eyes with some vision/ of festive goodness in back of their hard, or veiled, or shining,/ unknowable gaze." Poems to her mother and father join poems to other poets as Levertov continually seeks and writes about the connections in her life. Rilke, Rukeyser, Boris Pasternak, Robert Duncan, and Pablo Neruda are some of the poets she addressed in poems.

TRAVEL AND DREAMSCAPES

Reflecting the world consciousness typical of Americans in the second half of the twentieth century, Levertov traveled widely. Many of her poems describe the people and places she visited in Europe, Mexico, the United States, and Asia. Distant places remain alive in memory with sensual evocations—dreamscapes. The perfume of linden trees in blossom in an ancient European town is recalled in "The Past." Feelings of comfortable married happiness mingle with the beauty of the setting. The poem "In Tonga" describes the life of sacred bats hanging in their caves, squeaking in night flight. The poet muses about them, "If they could think/ it would not be of us." "Poem from Manhattan" builds a prayer and invocation to New York City through its power, energy, and hope—"city, act of joy"—to its desolation—"city, gesture of greed." Moral and spiritual awareness accompanies the poet's sensory connections to the world.

MYSTICISM

The mystical and religious tones of Levertov's poetry can be traced from their beginnings to their full flowering in the poems of the 1980's collected in two volumes, *Breathing the Water* and *A Door in the Hive*. The daughter of a clergyman who was steeped in mystical Jewish Hasidism, Levertov showed her familiarity with religious texts in early poems. "Notes of a Scale" gives four moments of wonder; its reference note directs the reader to Martin Buber's *Tales of the Hasidim: The Early Masters* (1975). The poem "Sparks" includes passages from the Old Testament book of Ecclesiastes. In this work, Levertov moves easily from the ancient Hebrew text to the circumstances of a modern life. Not only Jewish mysticism but also Christian tradition inspired her poetry. Later poems take as their themes the annunciation to Mary, Jesus' parable of the mustard seed, and the path of Calvary.

Levertov's religious poetry is deeply imbued as well with thoughts on the lives and works of religious saints and writers. Saint Thomas Didymus, Julian of Norwich, William Blake, William Everson, and W. H. Auden are evoked in various poems. One should remember, also, that she translated religious poetry of the Bengali Vaishnava faith. Collaborating with the scholar Edward C. Dimock, Jr., she published this fascinating poetry under the title *In Praise of Krishna: Songs from the Bengali*. The warm emotional and erotic content of these poems has a kinship to Levertov's sensual approach to religious mysticism.

DREAM-BASED POEMS

Access to religious symbols often comes in dreams. The immensely influential biblical accounts of dream visions (those of Ezekiel, Daniel, and John of Patmos, among others) echo in texts from every century. Many of these dream visions were part of Levertov's own home educational fare. She wrote of two childhood dreams. One consisted of a violent transformation from a rustic scene of happiness to a scene of burning and devastation. The other recurring dream was of a large country house made of a warm pink stone; its name was Mazinger Hall. These two dreams, like the later ones she used in poems, carry emotional content of joy and sorrow, gain and loss, security and terror. Gradually, her dream material was transformed into poems that evoke similar feelings in her readers.

In Levertov's early dream-based poems, the process of transferring a dream to a poem involved describing the dream content. The poet explained that later, after analytical work on her dreams, she abandoned that objectivity and gave her images stronger and clearer emotional force to present the dream content more directly to the reader. A third stage in this process came with the realization that the dream needs a literary form that cannot be imposed but must be listened for. Several times she found that a dream worked only as a prose tale. The stories "Say the Word" and "A Dream" began as poems that she transformed to a rhythmic prose. The experience of using dream material for a work of art teaches the poet that the poem must be not only visually clear but also morally or emotionally significant for the reader. An expression that is too private does not make an effective poem.

Another kind of dream poem may result from an auditory message received in a dream state, or as a combined visual and auditory dream. Levertov experienced each type and made poems of them. In "The Flight," she retells a vision of the poet and mystic William Blake, who spoke the words, "The will is given us that we may know the delights of surrender." She waited several years before composing a poem about that experience, to avoid a too-literal transcription. Again, an auditory message was received in a dream about Pasternak. The visual scene disappeared from memory, but the words remained. In both instances, as Levertov explains, the quality of the resulting poem came from the poet's willingness to recognize and absorb a hidden quality that lay beyond the superficial appearances. Some dream images may indicate the questions or problems present at that moment in the poet's life. In that case, the truth of the life and the truth of the dream provide an interplay that makes a powerful poem.

HONEY OF THE HUMAN

The religious message that hums (a favorite Levertov verb) throughout her poetry is the oneness of all life: all human beings, animals, trees, and the great elements of earth, air, fire, and water. The vision of air and water blended comes in poems about bees, honey, and ocean currents that hold "my seafern arms." The cleansing properties of honey in the hive, she writes in "Second Didactic Poem," neutralize even the poison of disease organisms. That hive with its transforming power may be the same as human activity—"honey of the human." Transformation may also move in the opposite direction, from a joyful morning self-confidence to a rapid pace that diminishes the person ("Remembering"). These apparent divisions between good and evil in a person's emotional life can be harmonized from a point of view that is wide enough to encompass the other side, or opposite, in what is experienced.

Certain lines of Levertov's poetry shine as lighthouse beacons across the restless waters of human experience: for example, "We are one of another" ("A Vision"), the lovely love song "We are a meadow where the bees hum" ("Bedtime"), and "To speak of sorrow/ works upon it" ("To Speak"). Why do these lines hum in the mind years after they are first encountered? In them one finds three qualities that characterize Levertov's poetic work: music, morality, and mysticism. Her best poems are true lyrics—songs, in their flowing rhythms and enchanting sound patterns of vowel and consonant combinations. Moreover, she teaches the lessons modern Americans need to hear, about respect for natural life and for unprotected, helpless human beings, especially children and the elderly. Then there is the wonder she shares in the magic of common things—the "gleam of water in the bedside glass" ("Midnight Gladness") and the moonlight crossing her room ("The Well"). Levertov said, "There is no magic, only facts"; her magic is found in accurate and loving observation of everyday shapes, colors, and sounds.

LEGACY

Beyond her mastery of the poem's form and even beyond the thought content, Levertov's poetry nevertheless can be appreciated for the qualities of the poet herself. During the 1960's, before the women's movement had strengthened the fragile position of women poets, when a cult of death followed the suicides of Anne Sexton and Sylvia Plath, Levertov lamented their loss, not only because they were fine poets but also because their deaths would confirm a popular conception of the poet as abnormally sensitive, often on the edge of madness. For her, alcoholism and nervous breakdowns were not signs of poetic talent. Creativity, she wrote, belongs to responsible, mature adults who take citizenship seriously. In the late 1960's and 1970's, she put this antiromantic view to the service of the peace and women's rights movements—marching, protesting, speaking against social injustices. She called attention to the political poets imprisoned in many countries. In the 1980's, she produced poetry of great beauty on the human and material sources of her spiritual inspiration.

Indeed, one of her last volumes of poetry, *Sands of the Well*, showed the beginning of a pronounced shift from her poems of social engagement to a more all-encompassing focus on a spirituality that transcended simple Christianity. Her lasting legacy was to show that a poet in the United States can support herself economically. Generously and with humor, she shared with students the fruits of her years of practicing her craft. In all these ways, she modeled a high standard for both poetry and the poet.

OTHER MAJOR WORKS

LONG FICTION: *In the Night: A Story*, 1968.

PLAY: *El Salvador: Requiem and Invocation*, pr. 1983 (libretto; music by W. Newell Hendricks).

NONFICTION: *The Poet in the World*, 1973; *Light Up the Cave*, 1981; *New and Selected Essays*, 1992; *Tesserae*, 1995; *The Letters of Robert Duncan and Denise Levertov*, 2004 (Robert J. Bertholf and Albert Gelpi, editors).

TRANSLATIONS: *In Praise of Krishna: Songs from the Bengali*, 1967 (with Edward C. Dimock, Jr.); *Selected Poems*, 1969 (of Eugene Guillevic); *Black Iris*, 1988 (of Jean Joubert).

EDITED TEXTS: *Penguin Modern Poets Nine*, 1967 (with Kenneth Rexroth and William Carlos Williams); *The Collected Poems of Beatrice Hawley*, 1989.

BIBLIOGRAPHY

Felstiner, John. "Poetry and Political Experience: Denise Levertov." In *Coming to Light: American Women Poets in the Twentieth Century*, edited by Diane Wood Middlebrook and Marilyn Yalom. Ann Arbor: University of Michigan Press, 1985. Shows that Levertov awakens human sensitivity—male and female—by insisting on the sacramental quality of all physical presence. In poetry, she finds hope while facing the horrors of war in Central America, in Vietnam, and in American cities. Felstiner's words on the oratorio *El Salvador: Requiem and Invocation* are particularly worthwhile.

Gelpi, Albert, and Robert J. Bertholf, eds. *Robert Duncan and Denise Levertov: The Poetry of Politics, the Politics of Poetry*. Stanford, Calif.: Stanford University Press, 2006. This collection of essays discusses the friendship between Duncan and Levertov that was broken up during the Vietnam War by their differing viewpoints of the role of the poet in politics.

Lacey, Paul A. "Denise Levertov: A Poetry of Exploration." In *American Women Poets*, edited by Harold Bloom. New York: Chelsea House, 1986. Considers the influence of Hasidism in Levertov's poetry: She treats the miraculous in a matter-of-fact tone. Her weakness in the early poetry, Lacey says, stemmed from an inability to deal seriously with evil in the world. Later, however, she grew into the political consequences of what it means to be, as she says, "members one of another."

Levertov, Denise. Interviews. *Conversations with Denise Levertov*. Edited by Jewel Spears Brooker. Jackson: University Press of Mississippi, 1998. Collects interviews with Levertov conducted by various interviewers from 1963 to 1995. The most common themes addressed are faith, politics, feminism, and poetry.

Marten, Harry. *Understanding Denise Levertov*. Columbia: South Carolina University Press, 1988. One of the most important studies of Levertov in book form, Marten's analysis covers four decades of poetry. Individual chapters give an overview, a history of the earliest poetry, an analysis of the volumes that established her reputation, a consideration of her public voice, and a discussion of spiritual dimension in her later development. The annotated bibliography of critical articles is particularly helpful.

Rodgers, Audrey T. *Denise Levertov: The Poetry of Engagement*. Rutherford, N.J.: Fairleigh Dickinson University Press, 1993. Examines Levertov's political commitment to antiwar themes in particular, placing poems on this topic in relation to

Levertov's earlier work and her life. The author had access to Levertov herself and to previously unpublished letters in the preparation of this study.

Wagner-Martin, Linda. *Denise Levertov*. New York: Twayne, 1967. Although written when Levertov was in mid-career, this biography, survey of poems, and bibliography provide an excellent introduction to the poet's life and work. Seven chapters discuss Levertov's family and education in England, her poetic themes and forms, and influences from modernist poets. Includes a chronology and notes.

Doris Earnshaw
Updated by Leslie Ellen Jones

PHILIP LEVINE

Born: Detroit, Michigan; January 10, 1928

OTHER LITERARY FORMS

Philip Levine (luh-VEEN) has published a collection of interviews, *Don't Ask* (1981), in the University of Michigan's Poets on Poetry series. A series of autobiographical essays make up *The Bread of Time* (1994). Levine selected and translated *Tarumba: The Selected Poems of Jaime Sabines*, with Ernesto Trejo (1979) and *Off the Map: Selected Poems of Gloria Fuertes*, with Ada Long (1984).

ACHIEVEMENTS

Philip Levine has received a number of poetry awards, most significantly the Pulitzer Prize for *The Simple Truth* in 1995. Other awards include Frank O'Hara Prizes (1973, 1974), an Academy Award in Literature from the American Academy of Arts and Letters (1973), the Harriet Monroe Memorial Prize (1976), the Lenore Marshall Poetry Prize (1977) for *The Names of the Lost*, the Levinson Prize from *Poetry* magazine (1979), the National Book Critics Circle Award (1979) for *Ashes* and *Seven Years from Somewhere*, and the National Book Award in Poetry (1980) for *Ashes*. *What Work Is* earned the poet the National Book Award, a Los Angeles Times Book Prize, and a Silver Medal from the Commonwealth Club of California. He also was awarded the Ruth Lilly Poetry Prize (1987), the Northern California Book Award in poetry (1988), a second Silver Medal from the Commonwealth Club of California for *The Mercy*, and a Fred Cody Award for lifetime achievement in 2004. He received two Guggenheim Fellowships (1974, 1981).

BIOGRAPHY

Philip Levine was born in Detroit of Russian-Jewish immigrant parents; his experiences of the Depression and World War II in that city play a central role in his poetry. In an interview, Levine said that he spent most of his childhood fighting against people who attacked him because he was Jewish. His father died when he was young (apparently in 1933, according to the poem titled "1933"), and both his parents often appear in his many poems that explore the past. According to Levine, the workers he knew as a child and as a young man had a great effect on him; various immigrant anarchists have affected his politics. After his 1954 marriage to Frances Artley, they had three sons: Mark, John, and Theodore.

Because Levine often writes from personal experience, it is possible to draw a picture of him and his relationships from his poems. He has written many poems about his grandparents, parents, brother, sister, wife, and each of his three sons. Not all the "facts" in his work, however, may necessarily be true. The poems do reveal much about the writer, but the poet's tendency to fictionalize must be kept in mind.

After holding a number of jobs, including working in a foundry, Levine attended Wayne State University, where he studied under John Berryman, receiving a B.A. degree in 1950 and an M.A. in 1955. He refused to serve in the Korean War, and although this was clearly a political protest on his part, he was declared 4-F for psychological reasons. He earned a master of fine arts in creative writing from the University of Iowa in 1957 and won a fellowship to attend Stanford University. He taught at California State University, Fresno, from 1958 to 1992. He has also taught at Tufts University, the University of Cincinnati, the National University of Australia (Canberra), Vassar College, Columbia University, New York University, and Brown University. He has given readings of his poetry throughout the United States and often reveals a comic side of his

Philip Levine

character that is not always obvious in his poetry. Levine was actively opposed to the Vietnam War, and his first trip to live in Spain in the late 1960's was, in part, to escape from the United States. In Spain, the Levines lived near the Catalan city of Barcelona, the stronghold of the anarchists during the Spanish Civil War; Levine has said that Barcelona reminds him of the Detroit of his childhood. He has had an interest in the Spanish Civil War (1936-1939) for many years. Levine sympathizes with the losing Republicans but identifies with the anarchists rather than the communists or Socialists; he made Spain and that war the subject of some of his most memorable poems. Levine served as chair of the Literature Panel of the National Endowment for the Arts (1984-1985) and as a chancellor of the Academy of American Poets (2000-2006). He became a member of the American Academy of Arts and Letters in 1997.

ANALYSIS

Philip Levine's most important achievements in the early part of his career are the collections *Not This Pig* and *They Feed They Lion*. In the best poems of these two books, Levine reflects the influence of the Surrealist and political poets of Spain and South America and takes on the subject of the city with a remarkable vitality. Along with

James Wright, Allen Ginsberg, Denise Levertov, and Robert Bly, Levine has managed to incorporate politics into his poetry, going far beyond the immediate protest reaction to the Vietnam War. He writes about the working poor without condescension and with an empathy that puts him clearly in the tradition of Walt Whitman and William Carlos Williams; these poems are often about survivors, people who have suffered in their lives but refuse to quit.

When Levine issued a new version of his first book *On the Edge*, he added to the title the words "and over," declaring the direction of his dark and fierce poetry. His poems examine a world of evil, loneliness, and loss, where a poem titled "Hymn to God in My Sickness" can only be a cry of unbelief. Paradoxically, there is a strong faith in human nature running throughout Levine's work. His is a poetry of community that at times holds out some distant but powerful dream of a better society. Often he dramatizes the lives of the anarchists of the Spanish Civil War and celebrates their nobility and courage. His work expresses admiration for those who suffer but who do not give in and for those who fight against prejudice and pain. Many of his poems employ a second-person voice; although these people often have specific addressees, Levine introduces them to the reader as a brother or sister in order to say "Your life is mine."

Levine is one of the most overtly urban poets in the United States. His hometown of Detroit—its factories and foundries, its dead-end jobs, its dirt and smoke, its dying lives—plays a central part in his imagination. It is the city he escaped from—or tried to—to Fresno, California, a place often depicted by him as lonely and sad, a silent place where "each has his life/ private and sealed." Then there is the third city, Barcelona, Spain, where Levine often seems most at home, where he feels a greater sense of community and history, even though he carries what he sees as the political burden of America with him.

ON THE EDGE

The second poem in Levine's first book, *On the Edge*, "Night Thoughts over a Sick Child," sets off a central image and theme of his work, presenting the speaker helpless before the boy's suffering, with no faith in the efficacy of prayer. He finds the situation intolerable and refuses to justify it in any way:

> If it were mine by one word
> I would not save any man,
> myself or the universe
> at such cost: reality.

There is nothing for him to do but to face "the frail dignity/ of surrender." The mixture of suffering and helplessness, anger and sadness, points toward many of Levine's later poems.

In this early volume, Levine is writing rather formal poetry, metrical or syllabic, with rhymes or off-rhymes. In poems about World War II and the Algerian War, he shows his concern for the public causes of suffering. In "Gangrene," he draws an ugly picture of torture, "the circus of excrement," and ends with a self-righteous address to the reader as being secretively thrilled by these descriptions of torture even though he fakes boredom. In later volumes, Levine achieves a more satisfactory tone of identification with suffering of this kind.

Probably the best poem in *On the Edge* is "For Fran," a picture of the poet's wife as gardener, an image that appears also in later poems. She is seen preparing the flower beds for winter, and she becomes—for the poet—the person who bears the promise of the future: "Out of whatever we have been/ We will make something for the dark." These final lines can be taken as a kind of motto for Levine's later poetry: his attempt to make something in the face of the dominant darkness.

Not This Pig

Levine's second volume, *Not This Pig*, is the key work in his development as a poet. There are some poems that are like the tightly ordered style of *On the Edge*, but a number of them indicate a new direction—more open, riskier, and more original. The fact that he is moving away from syllabics and rhyme—as did most poets of his generation in the 1960's—is not the main source of this originality; rather, a more daring language is in evidence, opening his work to a wider and deeper range.

"The Midget," which draws on his experiences in Spain, is a fine example of this new range. In a café where the anarchists planned the burning of the bishop of Zaragoza, the speaker sits on a December day—off-season, no tourists—amid the factory workers and other laborers. A midget in the bar begins to sing of how he came from southern Spain "to this terrible/ Barcelona" and tells them all that he is "big in the heart, and big down/ here, big where it really counts." The midget confronts the speaker with talk of his sexual prowess and insists that he "feel this and you'll believe." The speaker tries to turn away from him, buy him off with a drink, but the midget insists, tugging at him and grabbing his hand. The midget ends up sitting in his lap, singing of "Americas/ of those who never left." The others in the bar turn away in disgust, and then the drunken speaker begins to sing to the midget. In the final section, the poem goes beyond anecdote, stepping off into an eerie, mysterious world where the midget and the speaker merge in their opposition. They are both singers, old world and new, both strangers and outcasts. They come together in the brotherhood of those who are different and find the pain of being human.

The title of this volume comes from a brilliant tour de force, "Animals Are Passing from Our Lives," a poem told from the point of view of a pig. At first the pig seems complacent, going off to market "suffering children, suffering flies,/ suffering the consumers." He has no intention, however, of giving in, playing the human fool as the boy who drives him along believes he will. He will not "turn like a beast/ cleverly to hook his teeth/ with my teeth. No. Not this pig." This can be taken as a kind of slogan for the entire book, Levine's "Don't tread on me." In a somewhat similar vein is the poem "Baby Villon," about a 116-pound fighter who was robbed in Bangkok because he was white, in London because he was black; he does not give in—not this pig—he fights back. Different as they are, the poet and Villon become one: "My imaginary brother, my cousin,/ Myself made otherwise by all his pain."

Levine identifies with these tough losers, even though he admits that their pains are greater than his and that their toughness surpasses his. His attitude toward suffering is evident in his often-anthologized poem "To a Child Trapped in a Barbershop." In mock seriousness, he tells the six-year-old that his case is hopeless and advises the child not to drink the Lucky Tiger because "that makes it a crime/ against property and the state." "We've all been here before," he informs the boy; we have all suffered the fears of the barbershop and the sharp instruments, but "we stopped crying." The boy should do the same and welcome the world of experience, its difficulties, fears, and pains.

THEY FEED THEY LION

In his next full-length volume, *They Feed They Lion*, and in the chapbooks *Red Dust* and *Pili's Wall*, Levine pushes further the discoveries that were made in poems such as "The Midget." As he said in his statement in *Contemporary Poets of the English Language*, he was influenced by the Surrealistic Spanish and South American poets Miguel Hernández, Rafael Alberti, Pablo Neruda, and César Vallejo. These poets not only showed the way to a greater freedom of language but also were political poets affected deeply by the Spanish Civil War. Possibly, though, the greatest reason for the renewed vigor of Levine's work is the discovery of his hometown of Detroit as a subject for his poetry. This city is at the heart of *They Feed They Lion*, and it provides the starting point for some of the finest of Levine's poems.

In "Coming Home," Levine returns to the city in 1968 and finds Detroit an affront to nature, a riot-torn city with "the eyes boarded up." The auto factories' dirt and smoke dominate the hellish landscape: "We burn this city every day." In "The Angels of Detroit" sequence, however, the poet repeatedly expresses his sympathy for the workers, people such as Bernard:

> His brothers are factories and
> bowling teams, his mother is the
> power to blight, his father
> moves in all men like a threat,
> a closing of hands, an unkept
> promise to return.

Out of such beaten lives comes Levine's most remarkable poem, the title poem, "They Feed They Lion." As that title illustrates, the poem breaks away from conventional language and syntax. It is a chant celebrating the workers who come "out of burlap sacks, out of bearing butter . . . out of creosote, gasoline, drive shafts, wooden dollies." "They lion grow," the refrain proclaims, "From 'Bow Down' come 'Rise Up.'" It is a cry of and for the workers and praise of their resiliency and courage.

Levine draws on his Spanish experience to praise the sausage and the culture it comes from in the poem "Salami." The poet draws a picture of a Spanish man rebuilding an old church all by himself, caring for his retarded child, and praying each night with "the overwhelming incense/ of salami." Then the poem returns to the speaker—so different from the old man—waking from a nightmare, full of guilt, fear, and chaos. He discovers his son sleeping peacefully, feeling that each breath of the boy carries a prayer for him, "the true and earthly prayer/ of salami." The salami gathers the figures of the poem into a community and draws from Levine an expression of reverence. It is an "earthly prayer," a praise of life in all its harshness and the beauty that, at times, comes from it.

After Levine establishes his distinctive voice, he continues with a series of five volumes to mine the ore he had discovered in *They Feed They Lion*. None of these later volumes has quite the excitement and explosiveness of the earlier ones, yet all of them contain excellent poems. During this period, Levine often moves back and forth between personal and political poems, although sometimes the personal and political merge.

Despite the difficulties of his life, despite encounters with prejudice and brutality, he often looks back with pleasure to the child who thought he could be happy. Now he knows that the earth will "let the same children die day/ after day." There is nothing one can do except "howl your name into the wind/ and it will blow it into dust." Everything is ashes, and the best wish a man can make is to become "a fine flake of dust that moves/ at evening like smoke at great height/ above the earth and sees it all."

In the meantime, the poet seems to say, one can travel, looking for landscapes of greater beauty and intensity than the cities of the United States. In the poem "Seven Years from Somewhere," Levine speaks of an experience, apparently in Morocco, where he was lost and a group of laughing Berber shepherds came to help him, even though they did not share a common language. One of the shepherds took his hand in an effort to communicate with him. After traveling on to "Fez, Meknes, Tetuan, Ceuta, Spain, Paris, here," he awakens to a world where no one takes his hand, and he remembers the shepherd's gesture:

> as one holds a blue egg
> found in tall grasses
> and smile and say something
> that means nothing, that
> means you are, you
> are, and you are home.

Human touch represents the hope that resides at the heart of many of Levine's best poems, and these poems show the way toward his directly political poetry. The poet Bly in "Leaping Up into Political Poetry," the introduction to *Forty Poems Touching on Recent American History* (1970), argues that one has to be an inward poet to write about outward events successfully, that "the writing of political poetry is like the writing of personal poetry, a sudden drive by the poet inward." Levine fits this notion of political poetry better than almost any other modern American poet, often exploring his own life while at the same time exploring the lives of the Spanish anarchists of the Civil War. He admits that someone else "who has suffered/ and died for his sister the earth" might have more to say than he, yet he feels the necessity to speak for those who have no other spokesperson.

In "For the Fallen," Levine visits the graves in Barcelona of the leading anarchists who were executed during the war. After describing the sight of the graves amid the noise of the city, he remembers himself as a schoolboy in Detroit going on with his own life at the same time that the heroes were killed. The boy and the workers who are trudging home from their dreary jobs know, in some mysterious way, that there was an important relationship between the men in Barcelona and them. After all these years the feeling the poet has for these men can "shiver these two stiff/ and darkening hands."

SWEET WILL AND A WALK WITH TOM JEFFERSON

In *Sweet Will* and *A Walk with Tom Jefferson*, Levine began a subtle but important shift in his poetry. Overall, the tough bitterness appears less often; a quieter, more meditative element begins to dominate the feeling of these longer poems. Reviewers have been equally divided in regretting this change or praising it. The poems often still have a strong narrative quality as Levine draws on events of his past or creates other speakers to reflect on their pasts. The harsh world of Detroit's neighborhoods and factories has become even more central to his work, but the poems sometimes end on surprisingly quiet notes. This is still, however, the work of Levine; the horizons of hope remain darkened by storm clouds.

Levine sometimes gives the speaking roles in his poems to others who tell their stories. The speaker in "Voyages" (from *Sweet Will*) has spent his early life working on ships on the Great Lakes, but one day, he impulsively jumps ship and makes his way to another life. He settles for a middle-class existence and in the final lines insists—too strenuously—that he does not miss what he left behind:

> Not once has the ocean wind changed
> and brought the taste of salt
> over the coastal hills and through
> the orchards to my back yard, Not once
> have I wakened cold and scared
> out of a dreamless sleep
> into the dreamless life and cried
> and cried for what I left behind.

The speaker in "Buying and Selling" (from *A Walk with Tom Jefferson*) spends his life traveling the country buying and selling automotive parts, but once, at the age of twenty, he "wept in the Dexter-/ Davison branch of the public library/ over the death of Keats in the Colvin/ biography." The successful buying day ends on a note of sadness, a sadness for his lost youth, like "the sadness of children/ themselves, who having been abandoned believe/ their parents will return before dark."

When Levine is the speaker, a sad note of acceptance becomes the dominant tone. In the ironically titled "I Sing the Body Electric" (from *A Walk with Tom Jefferson*), Levine pictures himself crossing the continent to bring audiences poems about the wars of which they never heard. In "Picture Postcards from the Other World" (from *A Walk with Tom Jefferson*), however, he imagines a reader, like himself: a middle-aged man or woman who "having lost whatever faiths he held goes on/ with only the faith that even more/ will be lost." He hopes to bring such a reader his gift of language, even if it comes down to saying "nothing and saying it perfectly."

In the 1980's, Levine's meditative narratives became lengthier, and in the title poem of *A Walk with Tom Jefferson*, he moved on to his largest canvas. Tom Jefferson is an elderly black Detroit factory worker, but his famous namesake drifts like a ghost at the heart of this ambitious poem. The narrator walks with Tom through his bombed-out landscape of Detroit's inner city, blocks left to rot after the riot of 1967. When Tom was only a child, his family came from Alabama to work in the automobile industry for five dollars a day, but Tom still recalls the world of his childhood.

The narrator muses on the lives destroyed by this industrial system that could not match their "ordinary serviceable dreams" and views the landmarks of the city with hatred—the Renaissance Center that "Ford built/ to look down on our degradation" and the auto plant "where he broke first our backs/ and then the rest." Tom Jefferson, however, still plants his yearly vegetable garden: a habit brought from Alabama. The garden flourishes amid the wreckage of the ghetto. Tom is a believer, and his refrain of "That's Biblical" helps him interpret the sufferings of his life. The American Dream of the other Jefferson, the poem suggests, ended in the ugliness of cities like Detroit, but this Jefferson continues to survive and believe.

What Work Is

Levine's collections of the 1990's demonstrate his continued poetic vitality and increasing depth of vision. Both *What Work Is* and *The Simple Truth* were winners of major literary awards, bringing Levine a level of recognition long deserved.

What Work Is takes a great leap in energy and affects most of his volumes of the 1990's. This brilliant collection solidifies and extends Levine's lifelong concern with the exploited cogs in the industrial machine—the blue-collar workers. Nowhere is Levine's voice more assured, more capable of telling particularity, more sympathetically engaged than in these works. In poems such as "Coming Close," Levine's own subtle mastery of craft embraces and exemplifies the work ethic he applauds. The four-beat lines and roughly patterned consonance let the reader feel the machinery and its interaction with the worker—its penetration. The book's masterpiece, found in the center of the collection, is the long poem "Burned." In this extended story and exfoliating image of the disasters of life in a factory town, Levine gives the reader, once and for all, the dark side of the American Dream.

THE SIMPLE TRUTH AND THE MERCY

In both *The Simple Truth* and *The Mercy*, Levine allows memory to replay events that go back decades. Always a poet whose work snuggles up near sentimentality, he manages even in these late, somewhat nostalgic poems to avoid crossing the line, to keep the language of emotion in check while letting the emotion itself rise out of the material. Levine's memories of his mother and the questions that remain about the father he never knew feed some of his finest work; the title poem of *The Mercy* considers the meaning of his mother's voyage on the ship that brought her to the United States and is one of his best poems in the volume. The anger of his youth now somewhat subdued and at the same time complicated by even greater depths of thought and feeling, Levine in his seventies has clearly achieved a major and permanent place in the literature of his era.

BREATH

Breath contains thirty free-verse poems with references to breath or wind; Levine constantly reminds the reader that without breath, there is death, but with breath, there is life. The symbolism of the title is apparent on reviewing the Old Testament use of the word "ruach," which can mean "wind," "breath," "spirit," or "mind." The son of Russian-Jewish immigrant parents and the author of "Old Testament" (from *The Simple Truth*), Levine would be familiar with the word "ruach" and its meaning. Levine breathes life back into the deceased by speaking their names and remembering their lives. He states in "My Father in the Wind" that the wind or one's breath ". . . can carry all the voices of the living/ and the dead. . . ." This poem is about his grandfather, who hung himself and continued ". . . swinging/ in no wind . . ." until Levine's father found him and cut him down. In "Invention of the Fado," Levine notes, ". . . again the dead have found/ a way into the hearts we swore were stone." He uses plain language, yet many lines are lyrical.

Levine expresses sentimentality, especially in his references to the deceased who remain important to him, whether they are unknown to others or famous people. Lesser-known deceased include his grandfather ("My Father in the Wind") and a visiting relative ("On a Photo of Simon Karaday"). Other characters are famous, including the writer F. Scott Fitzgerald in "The Two," Dinah Washington and the bebop pianist Bud Powell in "52nd Street," the poet John Keats in "Keats in California," musician Charlie

Parker in "The Genius," and the musicians Clifford Brown, Max Roach, Miles Davis, and Lester Young in "Naming."

Like breath and life, music pervades the poems in *Breath*. Despite the somber references to death, the reader realizes that Levine finds solace in memories and song. Even the epigraph to *Breath* (from the beginning lines of "Call It Music," the last poem in the collection) contains hints of hope, of music, and of life itself: "Some days I catch a rhythm, almost a song/ in my own breath."

Levine blends into his poems some historical events; "Dust" recalls the dust storms of the Great Depression. In "Naming," he describes his brother's return from World War II in the summer of 1945; the two brothers become united by things they cannot share. These two poems are the longest in *Breath*; "Naming" has twenty-five parts, each with fifteen lines and an octet and a septet, and "Dust" has five sections. In this collection, Levine also gives status to such everyday events as the end of a workday in "When the Shift Was Over" and to a meal at a café in "Breakfasts with Joachim." His geographical settings include the Amsterdam Railway Station in "Dutch Treat," the river near Detroit that he compares in "Naming" to the River Styx in Greek mythology, and the Ontario residence of his great-uncle in "A View of Home."

OTHER MAJOR WORKS

NONFICTION: *Don't Ask*, 1981; *The Bread of Time*, 1994; *So Ask: Essays, Conversations, and Interviews*, 2002; *A History of My Befuddlement*, 2010.

TRANSLATIONS: *Tarumba: The Selected Poems of Jaime Sabines*, 1979 (with Ernesto Trejo); *Off the Map: Selected Poems of Gloria Fuertes*, 1984 (with Ada Long).

EDITED TEXTS: *Character and Crisis: A Contemporary Reader*, 1966 (with Henri Coulette); *The Essential Keats*, 1987.

BIBLIOGRAPHY

Brouwer, Joel. "The Stubbornness of Things." Review of *The Mercy*. *Progressive* 68, no. 8 (August, 1999): 44. This observant and respectful review singles out key passages from representative poems to illustrate Levine's fascination with the past and his "obsessive desire to get it right."

Buckley, Christopher, ed. *On the Poetry of Philip Levine: Stranger to Nothing*. Ann Arbor: University of Michigan Press, 1991. This first comprehensive look at the poet's career offers both important reviews chronologically arranged and a series of essays that focus on different aspects of Levine's work.

Jackson, Richard. "The Long Embrace, Philip Levine's Longer Poems." *Kenyon Review* 11 (Fall, 1989): 160-169. A detailed analysis of three long poems of Levine: "Letters for the Dead" (from *1933*), "A Poem with No Ending" (from *Sweet Will*), and "A Walk with Tom Jefferson," the title poem of the 1988 volume. He singles out the most recent poem as the most successful in sustaining intensity throughout a long poem.

Knight, Jeff Parker. Review of *The Simple Truth*. *Prairie Schooner* 71, no. 2 (Summer, 1997): 179-182. Knight claims that Levine measures the tension between truth and reality in *The Simple Truth* and in his other poems. Attending also to matters of craft, Knight praises "the perspective gained from an attentive lifetime."

Levine, Philip. "A Conversation with Philip Levine." Interview by Davidson College students. *TriQuarterly* 95 (Winter, 1995/1996): 67-82. In a conversation with Davidson College students, Levine comments on his style, the biographical sources for his subjects, and the situation of contemporary American poetry. The interview is a very rich ramble.

_____. "A Conversation with Philip Levine." Interview by Alan Fox. In *Rattle Conversations: Interviews with Contemporary American Poets*, edited by Fox. Los Angeles: Red Hen Press, 2008. Levine discusses what he wrote and why he had to write it.

Mariani, Paul. "Keeping the Covenant." Review of *A Walk with Tom Jefferson*. *Kenyon Review* 11 (Fall, 1989): 170-171. This laudatory review compares Levine to Walt Whitman and William Carlos Williams. Mariani concludes that Levine's poetry has kept its covenant with the dispossessed.

Stein, Kevin. "Why 'Nothing Is Past': Philip Levine's Conversation with History." In *Private Poets, Worldly Acts: Public and Private History in Contemporary American Poetry*. Athens: Ohio University Press, 1996. Stein explores the way in which the past impinges on the present in Levine's work. Levine carries on a dialogue with the past to reach "an understanding of the self that transcends the self."

Tillinghast, Richard. "Poems That Get Their Hands Dirty." *The New York Times Book Review*, December 18, 1991, p. 7. Compares Levine's *What Work Is* to Turner Cassity's *Between the Chains* (1991) and Adrienne Rich's *An Atlas of the Difficult World: Poems, 1988-1991* (1991).

Vendler, Helen. "All Too Real." *The New York Review of Books* 28 (December 17, 1981): 32-36. An all-out attack on Levine's poetry, an exception to the usual praise heaped on it. Vendler criticizes the metrics, the anecdotal subjects, and what she calls the sentimentality of the poetry. She notes that Levine's notion of the real is too limited.

Michael Paul Novak; Philip K. Jason
Updated by Anita Price Davis

OSIP MANDELSTAM

Born: Warsaw, Poland, Russian Empire (now in Poland); January 15, 1891
Died: Vtoraya Rechka, near Vladivostok, Soviet Union (now in Russia); probably
December 27, 1938

PRINCIPAL POETRY
Kamen, 1913 (enlarged 1916, 1923; *Stone*, 1981)
Tristia, 1922 (English translation, 1973)
Stikhotvoreniya, 1928 (*Poems*, 1973)
Complete Poetry of Osip Emilievich Mandelstam, 1973
Voronezhskiye tetradi, 1980
The Voronezh Notebooks: Poems, 1935-1937, 1996

OTHER LITERARY FORMS

Osip Mandelstam (muhn-dyihl-SHTAHM) was writing essays on Russian and European literature as early as 1913. Many of the theoretical essays were collected, some in considerably revised or censored form, in *O poezii* (1928; *About Poetry*, 1977). These, as well as his otherwise uncollected essays and reviews, are available in their original and most complete versions in *Sobranie sochinenii* (1955, 1964-1971, 1981; *Collected Works*, 1967-1969). Mandelstam's prose was not republished in the Soviet Union, with the exception of his single most important essay, "Razgovor o Dante" ("Conversation About Dante"), written in 1933 but not published until 1967, when an edition of twenty-five thousand copies sold out immediately and was not reprinted. Mandelstam's prose has been seen both as a key to deciphering his poetry and as a complex body of nonpoetic discourse of great independent value. All his prose has been translated into English.

ACHIEVEMENTS

Osip Mandelstam's poetry won immediate praise from fellow members of Russian literary circles, and he now holds an indisputable position as one of Russia's greatest poets. Like many of his contemporaries, however, Mandelstam experienced anything but a "successful" literary career. His work appeared often in pre-Revolutionary journals, but Mandelstam was not among the writers whom the Bolsheviks promoted after 1917. By 1923, the official ostracism of independent poets such as Mandelstam was apparent, though many continued writing and publishing whenever possible. Mandelstam did not write poetry between 1925 and 1930, turning instead to prose forms that were as inventive and as idiosyncratic as his verse. Attempts to discredit him intensified after 1928. He was arrested twice in the 1930's and is believed to have died while in transit to a Siberian labor camp.

Even during the "thaw" under Premier Nikita Khrushchev, Mandelstam's works were kept out of print, and it was not until 1973 that his "rehabilitation" was made credible by the publication of his poetry in the prestigious *Biblioteka poeta* (poet's library) series. That slim volume was reissued. During the Soviet era in Russia, scholarly writing about Mandelstam, although limited, appeared; his name was mentioned in many but by no means all studies of literature. Official publications, such as textbooks or encyclopedias, relegated him to minor status and often commented disparagingly on his "isolation" from his age. The deep respect commanded by his poetry in the Soviet Union was nevertheless measured by the evolution of scholarly interest in his work.

Mandelstam's reputation outside Russia was initially slow in developing because of the extreme difficulty in obtaining reliable texts of his works and because of the scarcity of information about the poet. As texts and translations became available, Mandelstam's reputation grew steadily. The single most important factor in making his work known in the West was the publication of two volumes of memoirs by his wife, Nadezhda Mandelstam. *Vospominania* (1970; *Hope Against Hope: A Memoir*, 1970) and *Vtoraya kniga* (1972; *Hope Abandoned*, 1974), issued in Russian by émigré publishers and translated into many Western languages, are the prime source of information concerning Mandelstam's life. Works of art in their own right, they also provide invaluable insights into his poetry.

BIOGRAPHY

Osip Emilievich Mandelstam was born in Warsaw, Poland, on January 15, 1891. His family moved almost immediately to St. Petersburg, where Mandelstam later received his education at the Tenischev School (as did Vladimir Nabokov only a few years later). Mandelstam's mother was a pianist; his father worked in a leather-tanning factory. Little is known about Mandelstam's childhood or young adulthood; he recorded cultural rather than personal impressions in his autobiographical sketch, *Shum vremeni* (1925; *The Noise of Time*, 1965).

Mandelstam took several trips abroad, including one to Heidelberg, where he studied Old French and the philosophy of Immanuel Kant at the University of Heidelberg from 1909 to 1910. He returned to St. Petersburg University's faculty of history and philology but seems never to have passed his examinations. Mandelstam had a highly intuitive approach to learning that foreshadowed the associative leaps that make his poetry so difficult to read. His schoolmate Viktor Zhirmunsky, later a prominent Formalist critic, said of Mandelstam that he had only to touch and smell the cover of a book to know its contents with a startling degree of accuracy.

Mandelstam had been writing in earnest at least as early as 1908, and he began publishing poems and essays in St. Petersburg on his return from Heidelberg. By 1913, his literary stance was defined by his alliance with the Acmeists, a group dedicated to replacing the murky longing of Russian Symbolism with a classical sense of clarity and with a dedication to the things of this world rather than to the concepts they might symbolize. Among the acquaintances made in the Acmeist Guild of Poets, Mandelstam formed a lifelong friendship with the poet Anna Akhmatova.

The ideological positions taken by poets were soon overwhelmed by the political upheavals of the decade. Mandelstam did not serve in World War I. He greeted the Revolution with an enthusiasm typical of most intellectuals; he grew increasingly disappointed as the nature of Bolshevik power became apparent. Mandelstam worked in several cultural departments of the young Soviet government, moving between Moscow and St. Petersburg (renamed Leningrad) in connection with these and other jobs. In May, 1919, he met and later married Nadezhda Yakovlevna Khazina. The civil war parted the Mandelstams at times, but they were virtually inseparable until Mandelstam's second arrest in 1938. Nadezhda Mandelstam became far more than her husband's companion and source of strength. She recorded his poems after he had composed them mentally; she memorized the poems when it became clear that written texts were in jeopardy; and she ensured her husband's poetic legacy many years after his death with her two volumes of memoirs and her lifelong campaign to have his poems published.

An early indication of Mandelstam's difficulties came in 1925, when the journal *Rossiya* rejected *The Noise of Time*. Living in or near Leningrad after 1925, Mandelstam busied himself with popular journalistic articles, children's literature, translations, and, by the end of the decade, hack editorial work. Although he published volumes of poetry, prose, and literary criticism in 1928, an attempt to entrap him in a plagiarism scandal the same year demonstrated the general precariousness of his status under the new regime. Nikolai Bukharin, who saved Mandelstam more than once, arranged a trip to Armenia and Georgia that proved crucial in ending his five years of poetic silence. Mandelstam wrote a purgative account of the plagiarism trial, *Chetvertaia proza* (1966; *Fourth Prose*, 1970), as well as poetry and prose inspired by the Armenian land and people.

After the journey, Mandelstam and his wife lived in near poverty in Moscow. Though he gave several readings, Mandelstam saw his prose work *Puteshestviye v Armeniyu* (1933; *Journey to Armenia*, 1973) denounced soon after its publication in the periodical *Zvezda*. On May 13, 1934, Mandelstam was arrested, ostensibly for a poem about Stalin's cruelty; the act of reciting such a poem even to a few friends was characteristic of his defiance of the authorities and of the Soviet literary establishment, which he openly despised. Bukharin again intervened, and the terms of exile were softened considerably. First sent to Cherdyn, the Mandelstams were allowed to select Voronezh, a southern provincial city, as the place where they would spend the next three years.

Mandelstam attempted suicide in Cherdyn and suffered intense periods of anxiety whenever Nadezhda Mandelstam was away, even briefly. He could find little work in Voronezh. Despite periods of near insanity, Mandelstam wrote (and actively sought to publish) three notebooks of poems in Voronezh. In May, 1937, the couple returned to

Moscow, where Mandelstam suffered at least one heart attack. Heart ailments had plagued him for years, and throughout his poetry, shortness of breath was always to be a metaphor for the difficulty of writing.

In the fall of 1937, a final respite from the hardships of Moscow was arranged. In the sanatorium in Samatikha, Mandelstam was again arrested in the early morning of May 2, 1938. In August, he was sentenced to five years' hard labor for counterrevolutionary activities. In September, he was sent to a transit camp near Vladivostock, from which he wrote to his wife for the last time. The actual circumstances of Mandelstam's death will probably never be known. The conditions of the camp almost certainly drove him, and not a few others, to the point of insanity. In 1940, his brother Aleksandr received an official statement that Mandelstam had died December 27, 1938, of heart failure.

Nadezhda Mandelstam lived another forty-two years, sustained by her friendship with Anna Akhmatova and by her commitment to preserving her husband's poems for a generation that could read them. As Mandelstam's works began appearing in print, Nadezhda Mandelstam published her two invaluable volumes of memoirs, *Hope Against Hope* and *Hope Abandoned*. On December 31, 1980, she achieved her great wish, an achievement rare enough for Russians of her generation: She died in her own bed.

ANALYSIS

In Osip Mandelstam's first published essay, "O sobesednike" (1913; "On the Addressee"), he describes the ideal reader as one who opens a bottle found among sand dunes and reads a message mysteriously addressed to the reader. Mandelstam's poetry, like the message in the bottle, has had to wait to find its reader; it also demands that a reader be aggressive and resourceful. His poems are intensely dependent on one another and are frequently comprehensible only in terms of ciphered citations from the works of other poets. The reader who wishes to go beyond some critics' belief that Mandelstam's lexicon is arbitrary or irrational must read each poem in the context of the entire oeuvre and with an eye to subtexts from Russian and European literature.

ACMEISM

Mandelstam's attempt to incorporate the poetry of the past into his works suited both the spirit and stated tenets of Acmeism, a movement he later defined as a "homesickness for world culture." Mandelstam always saw the Acmeist poets as the preservers of an increasingly endangered literary memory. "True" poetry could arise only from a celebration of its dependence on the old. Poetry plows up the fields of time, he wrote; his own poems bring forth rich layers of subsoil by their poetics of quotation. Apparently opaque lyric situations, when deciphered, yield transparent levels of meaning. Mandelstam especially loved the myths of Greece and Rome, though his quotations are most often from nineteenth and twentieth century Russian poets.

Using another metaphor, perhaps the most typical metaphor for the Acmeists, Mandelstam wrote in the early 1920's that Russian poetry has no Acropolis. "Our culture has been lost until now and cannot find its walls." Russia's words would build its cultural edifices, he predicted, and it is in the use of the word that one must seek the distinctive feature of Mandelstam's poetry.

"HAPPILY NEIGHING, THE HERDS GRAZE"

An example of Mandelstam's use of quotations will indicate how far interpretation of his poetry must stray from the apparent lyric situation. Referring to Mandelstam's first collection of poems, *Stone*, Kiril Taranovsky has noted that a line in the poem "S veselym rzhaniem pasutsia tabuny" ("Happily Neighing, the Herds Graze") quotes Alexander Pushkin's famous statement, "My sadness is luminous." Mandelstam's line is "In old age my sadness is luminous." Nineteen years later, Mandelstam wrote, in a poem memorializing Andrei Bely, "My sadness is lush." The epithet here comes from the *Slovo o polku Igoreve* (c. 1187; *The Tale of the Armament of Igor*, 1915), but the syntax still recalls Pushkin. Interpreting the stylized line "My sadness is lush" thus requires knowing Pushkin and *The Tale of the Armament of Igor*, to say nothing of Mandelstam's first quotation of Pushkin in "Happily Neighing, the Herds Graze" or the often ornate works of Andrei Bely.

In "Happily Neighing, the Herds Graze," Pushkin's presence is also felt in the poem's seasonal setting, his beloved autumn. The month mentioned, August, suggests Augustus Caesar, and the ancient Roman context is as significant as the Pushkinian overtones. The poem thus has more to do with the ages of human culture than with grazing herds; the poem contrasts the "classical spring" of Pushkin's golden age of Russian literature with the decline of Rome. The dominant color in the poem is gold, specifically the dry gold of harvest. Russia in 1915 resembled Rome during its decline, as the Romanov dynasty faced its end, so that three historical periods come to bear on an interpretation of this apparently pastoral poem. The rise and decline of civilizations do not upset this poet, for whom the cyclical nature of the seasons suggests that historical change is itself cyclical. As Mandelstam wrote in 1918, "Everything has been before, everything will repeat anew. What is sweet to us is the moment of recognition." To achieve such moments, the reader must allow Mandelstam's metaphors to acquire meaning in more than one context. The contexts will border on one another in surprising ways, but it is his peculiar gift to his readers that when they read his poems, they see past poets and past ages of man from new vantage points.

STONE

Mandelstam's first volume of poetry, *Stone*, was published in 1913, with successive enlargements in 1916 and 1923. *Stone* contains short lyrics, many of only three or four quatrains. The title evokes the volume's dominant architectural motifs. Aside from the well-known triptych of cathedral poems in *Stone*, there are also poems of intimate interiors, designs in household utensils, and seashells. The patterns of crafted objects or complex facades allow Mandelstam to write in *Stone* about the structures of language, about how poems may best be written. At times, his metapoetic statements emerge completely undisguised. A landscape is described by the technical language of poetics in "Est' ivolgi v lesakh" ("There Are Orioles in the Woods"), in which the birds' singing is measured by the length of vowel sounds, their lines ringing forth in tonic rhythms. The day "yawns like a caesura."

Mandelstam pursues the probable relationship between the oriole and the poet in "Ia ne slyxal rasskazov Ossiana" ("I Have Not Heard the Tales of Ossian"). Here, a raven echoing a harp replaces the oriole; the poem's persona intones, "And again the bard will compose another's song/ And, as his own, he will pronounce it." Mandelstam contrasts his own heritage with that of another land, as distinct as the singing of birds and men. Despite the differences between the battles of Russian soldiers and the feigned tales of Ossian, the poet's entire received heritage is "blessed," "the erring dreams of other singers" ("other" connotes "foreign" as well as "not oneself" in Russian). It is in making the dreams his own that the poet finds victory.

In "Est' tselomudrennye chary" ("There Are Chaste Charms"), Mandelstam concludes with an equally victorious quatrain. The poem has evoked household gods in terms derived from classical Rome and from eighteenth century poetry. After three quatrains of listening to ancient gods and their lyres, the poet declares that the gods "are your equals." With a careful hand, he adds, "one may rearrange them."

Among the poems that both assert and demonstrate Mandelstam's strength as an independent poet is "Notre Dame," the shortest and most clearly Acmeist of his three 1912 cathedral poems. The Acmeists consistently praised the Gothic optimism of medieval architecture and art, and they shared that period's devotion to art as high craft. In "Notre Dame," Mandelstam praises the church's "massive walls," its "elemental labyrinth." The cathedral becomes both that which the poet studies and that from which he is inspired to create something of his own. The outstretched body of Adam furnishes a metaphor for the opening description of the cathedral's vaulted ceiling. Adam's name, and his having been "joyful and first," had once provided an alternative name for Acmeism, Adamism, which never took hold. The name "Adam," nevertheless, invokes in "Notre Dame" the poetic principles of the movement, its clarity, its balance, its sense of the poem as something visibly constructed. "Notre Dame" is as close to a programmatic statement in verse as Mandelstam ever came; the poem does what a Gothic cathedral should do, "revealing its secret plan from the outside."

TRISTIA

Mandelstam's second volume, *Tristia*, appeared in 1922. Compared to the architectural poems of *Stone*, many drawing on the Roman tradition in classical culture, *Tristia* depends more on the myths of ancient Greece. It evokes the landscape of the Mediterranean or Crimean seas to frame tender, interiorized poems. The title is the same as that of a work by Ovid, written during his exile, and the connotations of *tristia*, both emotional and literary, resonate throughout the volume, though the title was not initially of Mandelstam's choosing. The title poem, "Tristia," addresses the difficulties of separation, the science of which the speaker says he has studied to the point of knowing it well. There are several kinds of separation involved, from women seeing men off to battle in stanza 1 to men and women facing their particular deaths in stanza 4. The poet feels the difficulty of moving from one kind of separation to another in stanza 3, where he complains, "How poor is the language of joy." Ovid's exile has been a continuous event since he wrote his *Tristia* (after 8 C.E.). There is joy in recognizing the repetition of historical and personal events; Mandelstam here performs his usual chronological sleight of hand in juxtaposing several ages in history, rising toward divinations of the future in the final stanza.

The moment of recognition or remembrance is sought after in vain in "Ia slovo pozabyl, chto ia khotel skazat'" ("I Have Forgotten the Word I Wanted to Say"). Like its companion poem "Kogda Psikheia-zhizn' spuskaetsia k teniam" ("When Psyche-Life Descends to the Shades"), the poem evokes the failure to remember poetic words as a descent into Hades. The close correspondence between these two psyche poems is characteristic of Mandelstam: The presentation of variants demonstrates his belief that the drafts of a poem are never lost. These poems also demonstrate the general Acmeist principle that there is no final or closed version of any work of literature.

PSYCHE POEMS

In the psyche poems, mythological figures are mentioned, such as Persephone or Antigone for their descent into the Underworld or for their devotion to the funeral ritual, respectively. The river mentioned in both poems is not Lethe, the river of forgetfulness, but Styx, the boundary of Hades. Forgetfulness plagues both poems, however; "I Have Forgotten the Word I Wanted to Say," a formula repeated in one poem, equates the fear of death's oblivion with the loss of poetry. The images of the dry riverbed, of birds that cannot be heard, of a blind swallow with clipped wings—all suggest an artist's sterility. It is the dead who revive an ability to remember (hence their avoidance of the river Lethe), to recognize meanings as significant as those of the divining women at the end of "Tristia." With the slowness so crucial to the entire volume, something develops in "I Have Forgotten the Word I Wanted to Say." In "When Psyche-Life Descends to the Shades," the soul is slow to hand over her payment for crossing the river. The "unincarnated thought" returns to the Underworld, but the black ice of its remembered sound burns on the poet's lips. For Mandelstam, lips (like breathing), suggest the act of composing poetry, so that these twin poems conclude with a kind of optimism, however fearful.

Several poems in *Tristia* treat the social causes of Mandelstam's fear of poetic failure, among them two of his most famous: "Sumerki svobody" ("The Twilight of Freedom") and "V Peterburge my soidomsia snova" ("In Petersburg We Shall Meet Again"). Both poems respond to the Revolution of 1917 ambiguously if not pessimistically. The sun both rises and sets in "The Twilight of Freedom," where the "twilight" of the title could mean "sunset" as well as "dawn." "In Petersburg We Shall Meet Again" also chooses an ambiguous source of light; the sun is buried and the "night sun" illuminates the final stanza.

Images from the psyche poems reappear with more pronounced political overtones. In "The Twilight of Freedom," there are immobilized swallows, bound into "fighting legions." The people appear as both powerful and restrained, expressing perfectly Mandelstam's perception of the Revolution as potentially empowering but finally overpowering. In "In Petersburg We Shall Meet Again," the "blessed, meaningless word" that the poet feared forgetting in the Psyche poems seems miraculously renewed. The poem displays terrifying sights and sounds, from ominous patrols to whizzing sirens, yet the speaker clings to his "word" as if oblivious of everything else. The poem closes with a crowd leaving a theater, where the end of the performance suggests the end of an entire culture. Yet, as in the exhortation to be brave in "The Twilight of Freedom," the poetic voice affirms its power to live beyond the threats of "Lethe's cold" or the "Soviet night." What endures in *Tristia*, though with difficulty, is what seemed immutable in *Stone*: faith in the word as the center of Russian culture.

POEMS

In 1928, Mandelstam published a volume of poems comprising revised versions of *Stone* and *Tristia*, as well as some twenty new poems. Several had appeared in the second edition of *Tristia*. These poems are even less optimistic than the ambiguous poems of *Tristia*; they are permeated by a fear of disorder that so threatened Mandelstam's voice that he ceased writing poems altogether from 1925 to 1930. The city arches its back threateningly in "In Petersburg We Shall Meet Again"; the back is broken in "Vek" ("The Age"). The age is dying in "Net, nikogda nichei ia ne byl sovremennik" ("No, I Was Never Anyone's Contemporary"), a poem whose first line discloses as well as any of his works Mandelstam's alienated state of mind. The source of light in these poems is not the sun, not even the occluded or nighttime sun, but stars that look down menacingly from the evening firmament. The air is steamy, foamy, dark, and watery, as impossible to breathe as the sky is to behold. Not being able to breathe, like not being able to speak, conveys Mandelstam's extraordinary difficulty in writing during this period.

"SLATE ODE" AND "THE HORSESHOE FINDER"

Two of Mandelstam's most startling and most difficult poems date from the early 1920's: "Nashedshii podkovu" ("The Horseshoe Finder") and "Grifel' naia oda" ("Slate

Ode"). The poems test and affirm poetry's ability to endure despite the shifting values of the age. "The Horseshoe Finder" binds together long, irregular verse lines without rhyme (a new form for Mandelstam) by repeating and interweaving clusters of consonants. Rejecting the slow realizations of *Tristia*, the poem moves quickly from one metaphorical cluster to another. Finding the horseshoe, also a talismanic emblem for poetry in "Slate Ode," is like finding the bottled message in Mandelstam's essay "On the Addressee." The past can still be transmitted in "The Horseshoe Finder": "Human lips . . . preserve the form of the last spoken word," but these lips "have nothing more to say."

"LENINGRAD"

Mandelstam resumed writing poetry in 1930, and, had the official literary establishment not been forcing him out of print, there could easily have emerged a third volume of verse from the poems written in Moscow and Voronezh. A clear task unites many of these poems, a task of self-definition. The fate of the poet has become a metaphor for the fate of the culture, so that intensely personal poems avoid all solipsism. The triangular relationship "world-self-text" emerges as a conflict to be resolved anew in each poem. Mandelstam returned to Leningrad, "familiar to the point of tears." In his poem "Leningrad," Mandelstam proclaims against all odds, echoing the famous Pushkin line, that he does not want to die. Death moves inevitably through the poem, though, as his address book leads only to "dead voices"; the poet lives on back stairs, awaiting guests who rattle a ball and chain.

Mandelstam was arrested for the often-quoted epigram about Stalin; describing "cockroach whiskers" and "fat fingers, like worms," the poem was perhaps his angriest of the period. The secret police could have arrested Mandelstam, however, for any number of works from the early 1930's. Hatred of the "songs" with which the Soviets had supplied the new age, disgust at the ethos of the Socialist Utopia, and fear that Russia's genuine cultural heritage would perish are frequent themes. Mandelstam wanted no part of the changes around him; he names himself as the "unrecognized brother, an outcast in the family of man" in a poem dedicated to Anna Akhmatova, his dear friend and fellow poet who also suffered ostracism.

In the South and in Moscow, Mandelstam was befriended by several biologists. They inspired him to read Jean-Baptiste Lamarck, Charles Darwin, and other authors who in turn provided Mandelstam with a new metaphor for expressing his dislike of the age's paeans to "progress." In "Lamarck," Mandelstam chooses to occupy the lowest step on the evolutionary ladder rather than join in the false advances urged by the government. These steps bring humankind down in the evolutionary chain, observes the poet, toward species that cannot hear, speak, or breathe—toward those that do not produce poetry. The age, in copious images of the silence of deafness, has grown dumb; self-definition nears self-denigration as the surrounding cultural edifices crumble and threaten to bring the new Soviet literature down with them.

Destruction, pain, death, terror—these are the themes that dominate the post-1930 poems to a degree that would separate them from the poems written before 1925 even if there were no other distinctions. As Mandelstam wrote poems inspired by the chaos around him, so also the poems formally demonstrated the pervasiveness of chaos. Disintegration became both subject matter and structuring principle: The late poems demonstrate an openness, fragmentation, and avoidance of conventional poetic diction, meter, and rhyme that would have been inconceivable in the beautifully formed poems of *Stone* or *Tristia*. The early predilection for exact rhyme is reshaped by an admixture of near rhymes of all sorts. The poems grow rich in internal paronomasia, where interweavings of sounds create controlling structures in lines that seem otherwise arbitrarily ordered. The rhythms grow freer during the 1930's as well. Mandelstam had used free verse in the 1920's, as in "The Horseshoe Finder," and returned to it for longer, more complex works such as "Polnoch' v Moskve" ("Midnight in Moscow"). Conventionally metered poems include aberrant lines of fewer or more metrical feet or with entirely different schemes; conversely, the free verse of "Midnight in Moscow" permits interpolated lines of perfect or near-perfect meter.

The spontaneity that the late poems explore represents the final version of Mandelstam's longstanding commitment to the openness of the poetic text. Including fragments of conversation and unconventional constructions in these poems, Mandelstam was converting the destructive chaos around him to his own ends. Hence the fluidity of "cross-references" in his poetry, particularly in the late verse, where there are not only "twin" or "triplet" poems, as Nadezhda Mandelstam called them, but also entire cycles of variants, among them the poems on the death of Bely in 1934. Moving beyond the concrete referentiality of the early poems, the late Mandelstam dramatizes rather than describes the act of self-definition. The communicative act between poet and reader overrides the encoding act between poet and world, as the reader is drawn deeply into the process of decoding the poet's relationships with his world and his poems.

Mandelstam's confidence that a reader would someday seek to understand even his most labyrinthine poems shines through unexpectedly during the late period. There are love poems to his wife and others—among the most remarkable is "Masteritsa vinovatykh vzorov" ("Mistress of Guilty Glances")—as well as poems wherein renunciation yields extraordinary strength. Mandelstam's enduring gift, long after he had himself fallen victim to the society at odds with him, was to find strength in the deepest threats to his identity. Hence, the halfhearted desire to write an ode to Stalin, which might save his wife after his own death, gave rise instead to a host of deeply honest poems that were as hopeful as they were embattled. Though the simple longings of the late poems may be futile, the act of recording his desires into completely threatened poems represents Mandelstam's typical achievement in the late works.

OTHER MAJOR WORKS

SHORT FICTION: *Yegipetskaya marka*, 1928 (*The Egyptian Stamp*, 1965).

NONFICTION: *O prirode slova*, 1922 (*About the Nature of the Word*, 1977); *Feodosiya*, 1925 (autobiography; *Theodosia*, 1965); *Shum vremeni*, 1925 (autobiography; *The Noise of Time*, 1965); *O poezii*, 1928 (*About Poetry*, 1977); *Puteshestviye v Armeniyu*, 1933 (travel sketch; *Journey to Armenia*, 1973); *Chetvertaia proza*, 1966 (wr. 1930 or 1931; *Fourth Prose*, 1970); *Razgovor o Dante*, 1967 (*Conversation About Dante*, 1965); *Selected Essays*, 1977; *Slovo i kul'tura: Stat'i*, 1987.

CHILDREN'S LITERATURE: *Dva tramvaya*, 1925; *Primus*, 1925; *Kukhnya*, 1926; *Shary*, 1926.

MISCELLANEOUS: *Sobranie sochinenii*, 1955, 1964-1971, 1981 (*Collected Works*, 1967-1969); *The Complete Critical Prose and Letters*, 1979.

BIBLIOGRAPHY

Baines, Jennifer. *Mandelstam: The Later Poetry*. New York: Cambridge University Press, 1976. Scholarly treatment of Mandelstam's poems written in Moscow and Voronezh in the 1930's. The study of these poems has been somewhat neglected because of their enigmatic nature.

Brown, Clarence. *Mandelstam*. New York: Cambridge University Press, 1973. The best authority on Mandelstam in the English-speaking world presents his seminal work, covering all aspects of Mandelstam's life and work. Brown's analyses of Mandelstam's poems are particularly valuable.

Broyde, Steven. *Osip Mandelstam and His Age: A Commentary on the Themes of War and Revolution in the Poetry, 1913-1923*. Cambridge, Mass.: Harvard University Press, 1975. A detailed analysis of Mandelstam's poems inspired by, and centered on, war and revolution. There are many citations of poems, in Russian and in English.

Cavanagh, Clare. *Osip Mandelstam and the Modernist Creation of Tradition*. Princeton, N.J.: Princeton University Press, 1995. Places Mandelstam within the modernist tradition of T. S. Eliot and Ezra Pound of reflecting a "world culture" divorced from strict national or ethnic identity.

Glazov-Corrigan, Elena. *Mandel'shtam's Poetics: A Challenge to Postmodernism*. Toronto, Ont.: University of Toronto Press, 2000. Analyses Mandelstam's thoughts on poetry and art in the context of the major postmodern literary debates and traces their development throughout his writings. Describes Mandelstam's intellectual world and its effect on his evolution as a thinker, specifically, on differences in his attitude toward language.

Mandelstam, Nadezhda. *Hope Against Hope: A Memoir*. New York: Atheneum, 1970. The first volume of memoirs written by Mandelstam's wife, dealing with biographical details but also with the genesis of many of Mandelstam's poetms.

_____. *Hope Abandoned*. New York: Atheneum, 1974. The second volume of the memoirs.

Pollack, Nancy. *Mandelstam the Reader*. Baltimore: The Johns Hopkins University Press, 1995. A study of Mandelstam's late verse and prose. The two genres receive approximately equal treatment, but the analyses of poems tend to be deeper.

Prsybylski, Ryszard. *An Essay on the Poetry of Osip Mandelstam: God's Grateful Guest*. Translated by Madeline G. Levine. Ann Arbor, Mich.: Ardis, 1987. A noted Polish scholar treats Mandelstam's attraction to, and reflection of, Greek and Roman classicism, the musical quality of his poetry, his affinity to architecture and archaeology, and other features of the poetry. The author places Mandelstam in the framework of world literature.

Zeeman, Peter. *The Later Poetry of Osip Mandelstam: Text and Context*. Amsterdam: Rodopi, 1988. Detailed interpretations and analyses of Mandelstam's poems written in the 1930's. Zeeman uses primarily contextualization and historical reconstruction in his discussion of the poems, some of which are among the most difficult of all Mandelstam's poems.

Stephanie Sandler

HOWARD NEMEROV

Born: New York, New York; March 1, 1920
Died: University City, Missouri; July 5, 1991

OTHER LITERARY FORMS

Though known primarily for his poetry, Howard Nemerov (NEHM-eh-rawf) wrote novels—*The Melodramatists* (1949), *Federigo: Or, The Power of Love* (1954), and *The Homecoming Game* (1957)—and short stories, collected in *A Commodity of Dreams, and Other Stories* (1959) and *Stories, Fables, and Other Diversions* (1971). Two verse dramas, *Endor* and *Cain*, are included with his collection *The Next Room of the Dream*. His criticism and reflections on the making of poetry are to be found in various volumes: *Poetry and Fiction: Essays* (1963), *Reflexions on Poetry and Poetics* (1972), *Figures of Thought: Speculations on the Meaning of Poetry, and Other Essays* (1978), *New and Selected Essays* (1985), and *The Oak in the Acorn: On "Remembrance of Things Past" and on Teaching Proust, Who Will Never Learn* (1987). *Journal of the Fictive Life* (1965) is a series of candid autobiographical meditations.

ACHIEVEMENTS

As a poet, novelist, critic, and teacher, Howard Nemerov was a man of letters in the eighteenth century tradition. He was identified with no particular school of poetry. Scholar Peter Meinke says that Nemerov's work explores the dilemma of "the existential, science-oriented (or science-displaced) liberal mind of the twentieth century." Almost every available award came to Nemerov; his honors included the Bowdoin

Prize from Harvard University (1940), a *Kenyon Review* Fellowship in Fiction (1955), a National Institute of Arts and Letters Award (1961), a Guggenheim Fellowship (1968-1969), the Theodore Roethke Memorial Poetry Prize (1968) for *The Blue Swallows*, an Academy of American Poets Fellowship (1970), the Levinson Prize from *Poetry* magazine (1975), the Pulitzer Prize and National Book Award (both 1978), the Bollingen Prize from Yale University (1981), the Aiken Taylor Award in Modern American Poetry (1987), and the presidential National Medal of Art (1987). He served as a consultant in poetry to the Library of Congress from 1963 to 1964 and again as poet laureate consultant in poetry from 1988 to 1990. The National Institute of Arts and Letters (1960-1991), the American Academy of Arts and Sciences, and Alpha of Massachusetts all claimed him as a member. He served as chancellor for the Academy of American Poets from 1976 to 1991.

Nemerov was the poet of the modern person. His deep division of temperament and his interest in science illustrated the fragmentation and scientific bent of the twentieth century. His sense of the tragic nature of the human condition and his spiritual questing with no subsequent answers reflected the twentieth century search for meaning. Although his poetry has a decidedly religious quality, Nemerov appeared to resolve his spiritual questions by honoring life's mystery rather than by adopting specific beliefs.

BIOGRAPHY

Howard Stanley Nemerov was born in New York City on March 1, 1920, to David and Gertrude (Russek) Nemerov. His wealthy parents were also cultivated and saw to it that their son was well educated. They sent him first to the exclusive private Fieldston Preparatory School, where he distinguished himself as both scholar and athlete. Nemerov then entered Harvard University, where he began to write poetry, essays, and fiction. In his junior year, he won the Bowdoin Prize for an essay on Thomas Mann. Nemerov graduated in 1937 and immediately entered the Royal Air Force Coast Command as an aviator, based in England. Subsequently, he joined the Eighth United States Army Air Force, which was based in Lincolnshire. On January 26, 1944, Nemerov was married to Margaret (Peggy) Russell (a union that produced three sons, David, Alexander, and Jeremy Seth). In 1945, when he was discharged as a first lieutenant from the Air Force, the Nemerovs moved to New York City to settle into civilian life.

During this time, Nemerov chose, against his father's wishes, to become a poet. This was a hard decision, for tradition decreed that, as the only son, he should carry on the family business. As a "Jewish Puritan of the middle class," Nemerov felt the separation from custom. In his *Journal of the Fictive Life* (1965), he credits his emphasis on work to a "guilty acknowledgment that I became a writer very much against the will of my father."

Because poetry customarily brings more pleasure than money, Nemerov left New York after a year to join the faculty at Hamilton College in Clinton, New York. In 1948, he became a member of the English department of Bennington College and taught there until, in 1966, he went to Brandeis University in Massachusetts. During his stay at Brandeis, Nemerov also held interim teaching appointments. He left Brandeis in 1969 to become the Hurst Professor of Literature at Washington University in St. Louis. He became Washington University's Edward Mallinckrodt Distinguished University Professor of English in 1976. He completed a writer-in-residency at the University of Missouri at Kansas City in April, 1991, shortly before his death from cancer in July.

ANALYSIS

Howard Nemerov's poetry revolves about the theme of the absurd place of humankind within the large drama of time. It also illustrates his divided temperament, about which he wrote in *Journal of the Fictive Life*, "I must attempt to bring together the opposed elements of my character represented by poetry and fiction." These conflicts—the romantic-realist, the skeptic-believer, the scientist-poet—reflect the fragmentation and angst of modern existence. He did not employ scientific terms in a sentimental manner in his poetry but included nebulae, particles, and light-years as true poetic subjects, not simply metaphors for human concerns. Nemerov was a Renaissance man in his breadth and an eighteenth century man of letters in his satire, wit, and respect for form. His spiritual questions and his refusal of any orthodoxy, whether religious or artistic, made him a twentieth century existentialist.

Like any great figure, however, Nemerov defied categorization. He lived his life in and for literature in an age that values, as he wrote in his *Journal of the Fictive Life*, "patient, minute analysis"; he gave himself to "the wholeness of things," "the great primary human drama" in a time when some consider that loving the human story is "unsophisticated, parochial, maybe even sinful."

Many writers reach a plateau; Nemerov kept growing. In his evolution, he became less bitter and more loving. As he became more complex, his language grew simpler, elegantly expressing his subtle mind and his ultimate sadness at the tragic position of humanity in the universe. Nemerov's divided nature shows in his poetry's empiricism and acceptance of objective reality and his subjective, poetic self that searched, perhaps futilely, for a definite Word of God.

THE IMAGE AND THE LAW AND GUIDE TO THE RUINS

Nemerov's first three poetry collections, *The Image and the Law*, *Guide to the Ruins*, and *The Salt Garden*, demonstrate his growth from a somewhat derivative writer to a mature poet with a distinctive voice. *The Image and the Law* is based on his dual vision, what he called "poetry of the eye" (the image) and "poetry of the mind" (the law). He tries to illustrate the "everpresent dispute between the two ways of looking at the world." *The Image and the Law*, as a first book, was competent, but was criticized for lack of unity and for being derivative. Critics found too many echoes of T. S. Eliot, W. H. Auden, William Butler Yeats, and Wallace Stevens—admittedly Nemerov's models.

Nemerov's second book, *Guide to the Ruins*, drew the same complaint, as did *The Salt Garden*. The latter collection, however, was recognized as exhibiting the beginning of his "most characteristic voice, a quiet intelligent voice brooding lyrically on the strange beauty and tragic loneliness of life," as Peter Meinke has described it.

In *The Image and the Law* and *Guide to the Ruins*, not only is Nemerov practicing what he has learned from Yeats, Eliot, and others, but he also starts to purge himself of war-won realizations. Although *The Image and the Law* deals mainly with the city, war, and death, it also contains religious imagery and wit. His poems wail, like an Old Testament lament—"I have become a gate/ To the ruined city, dry" ("Lot's Wife"). The poems in *The Image and the Law* exhibit ironic detachment as well as seriousness, for to Nemerov "the serious and the funny are one." The dualism in the poems is suggested in the title.

Guide to the Ruins has a broader scope than his first collection and reveals artistic growth. The "ruins" are those created in World War II, although the war is not actually over. Again, there is duality in the poems; the poet feels trapped between art-faith and science-reality, but sides with neither wholeheartedly. His tension between the two produces a Dostoevskian religious agony that visits Christianity, but consistently returns to Judaism. Several poems in *Guide to the Ruins* unite war and religion into a pessimism that will become more evident in later works. Paradoxically, and typical of his dualistic vision, he celebrates life not only in spite of war but also because of it.

THE SALT GARDEN

The Salt Garden, while still exhibiting some derivation, exhibits not only the poet's own voice but also a "center," that center being Nemerov's interest in nature. True to his double vision, he contrasts "brutal" nature with "decent" humankind. The link between the two is found in liquids such as ocean and blood, which combine into humankind's "salt dream," the call of the subconscious toward wildness. The poems in *The Salt Garden* range from a decent, rational man's reflection on his garden to the nightmarish, Freudian dream "The Scales of the Eyes." A brilliant combination of the "civilized" and the "wild" is found in "I Only Am Escaped Alone to Tell Thee." By degrees, this poem shows the submerged anguish of a prosperous nineteenth century woman. The whalebone stays of her corset are a central image, leading to other images of sea, mirrors, and light, until "the black flukes of agony/ Beat at the air till the light blows out." *The Salt Garden* treats not only humanity, "brutal" nature, and the link between the two, but also death as a part of "time's ruining stream." Water, sea, and blood are beyond moral categories; they are the substance of life. In this respect, according to Julia Bartholomay in *The Shield of Perseus: The Vision and Imagination of Howard Nemerov* (1972), Nemerov's perspective is biblical. Water is creative and purifying; it "sanctifies that which it permeates and recreates, for all objects are but fleeting forms on the changing surface of eternity."

MIRRORS AND WINDOWS

Nemerov's interest in nature, which is first evident in *The Salt Garden*, continues in *The Next Room of the Dream*, *Mirrors and Windows*, and *The Blue Swallows*. Nature, in these poems, has objective reality; it is never merely a projection of human concerns. Like Robert Frost, Nemerov not only describes nature as something "other" than himself but also brings philosophical issues into his nature poems. In *Mirrors and Windows*, Nemerov indicates that poetry helps make life bearable by stopping it in a frame (poem). It sheds no light on the meaning of life or death; it only reveals life's beauty or terror.

THE NEXT ROOM OF THE DREAM

The Next Room of the Dream, a collection of poems and two verse plays, illustrates Nemerov's decision to stay close to what he calls in *Journal of the Fictive Life* the "great primary human drama." His plays *Cain* and *Endor*, based on biblical themes, illustrate his humanitarianism as well as his quest for ultimate truth. This quest is ironically expressed in "Santa Claus," which begins, "Somewhere on his travels the strange Child/ Picked up with this overstuffed confidence man," and ends, "At Easter, he's anonymous again,/ Just one of the crowd lunching on Calvary."

Nemerov's plays, however, provide no spiritual resolution to humankind's questions. Stanley Knock in *The Christian Century* comments, "Nemerov succeeds only in revealing the devastating emptiness of contemporary beliefs." The poem "Nothing Will Yield" sums up Nemerov's perception of human helplessness in the face of reality; even art is no solution, although poets will continue to speak "holy language" in the face of despair. In *The Next Room of the Dream*, the poems become simpler, with more precise natural descriptions and more obvious compassion for humankind.

Nemerov's dark vision mellows in his later work. In two later collections of poetry, *Gnomes and Occasions* and *Sentences*, the emphasis is spiritual, the tone elegiac. In *The Western Approaches*, the topics range from speculation about fate ("The Western Approaches") to the sterility of space travel ("The Backward Look").

THE BLUE SWALLOWS

The Blue Swallows, published twenty years after his first collection, indicates further growth in Nemerov's technique and development of his philosophy of "minimal affirmation." In this book, Nemerov's paradoxical view of humanity as both helpless and indomitable is expressed in images of gulls and swallows that circle around this world, only to find it illusory and strange. His duality is expressed in symbols of physics and theology, again underlining the division between science-reality and art-faith. According to his philosophy of minimal affirmation, human beings may be crushed, but they rise "again and again," as in the end of "Beyond the Pleasure Principle." The final emphasis of the poem is simultaneously on the absurdity of life and death and the inexplicable resilience of humankind. "Beyond the Pleasure Principle" expresses the central theme of *The Blue Swallows*, a theme that was to remain constant in Nemerov's works until his later years.

"RUNES"

Critics have commented profusely on Nemerov's witty pessimism and urbane helplessness. Though Bartholomay acknowledges Nemerov's dualistic nature, she finds other meanings in his poems besides wit and hopelessness. She sees Nemerov as a witty sophisticate who responds to life bitterly, yet she also points out his capacity to be "philosophical, subjective, lyrical, or even mystical."

To support this contention she calls attention to "Runes," considered by many to be Nemerov's finest poem. Mutability is the theme of "Runes," but with a recognition of the mystery of life. The poem expresses pessimism but avoids nihilism, attacking the emptiness of modern life while affirming "the stillness in moving things." "Runes" is religious in that it is concerned with the mystery of creation and finds resolution in total submission to life's riddle.

The major artistic triumph of "Runes" is the integration of external and internal through which its paradox is resolved. This unity is achieved through the brilliant treatment of three reflexive images: two objective images—water and seed—and a subjective image—thought itself. "Runes" is perhaps the most complete expression of Nemerov's philosophy of minimal affirmation. In it Nemerov returns to the mystery of creation, in which he finds the beginnings of art. Imagination is reality's agent, revealing "the divine shadow of nature's signature on all things."

GNOMES AND OCCASIONS

Gnomes and Occasions consists of epigrams, riddles, meditations, and reflections, all poems that stress origins and ends. They have the epigrammatic style of wisdom literature—pithy, sage, and provocative. The language is rife with references to the Bible, priests, grace, and God, as well as nature. There are also the characteristic wit, irony, and doubt, as expressed in "Creation Myth on a Moebius Band":

> This world's just mad enough to have been made
> By the Being his beings into Being prayed.

Nemerov's interest in nature is also apparent in this book, in poems such as "Late Butterflies" and "The Rent in the Screen," a lyric dedicated to science writer Loren Eiseley. Nemerov's sharp observations of nature are here transformed into melancholy, sometimes irony. "The Rent in the Screen" ends by commenting on the lives of moths and men, "How brief a dream." Compassion for the fate of butterflies in winter ends with the dry "We take our pity/ Back in the house,/ The warm indoors."

THE COLLECTED POEMS OF HOWARD NEMEROV

The publication of *The Collected Poems of Howard Nemerov* in 1977 led to a critical revaluation of Nemerov's work. This collection (which includes all his poetry written through 1977) exhibits "a gradual intensifying of a unified perspective," according to critic Phoebe Pettingell. The effect of *The Collected Poems of Howard Nemerov* is to delineate the depth and breadth of Nemerov's insights. Throughout the volume certain questions recur—questions having to do with the nature of reality and the role of poetry in revealing the world's appearances and sometimes, perhaps, what lies beyond appearances.

SENTENCES

Despite the increasingly religious quality of his language, Nemerov, as usual, does not make specific religious statements. It is poetry, if anything, that comes closest to being an intercessor between God and humanity, and this link is the theme of *Sentences.* Here Nemerov applies his belief that "in the highest range the theory of poetry would be the theory of the Incarnation, which seeks to explain how the Word became Flesh." In a letter to Robert D. Harvey, he wrote,

> Poetry is a kind of spiritual exercise, a (generally doomed but stoical) attempt to pray one's humanity back into the universe; and conversely an attempt to read, to derive anew, one's humanity from nature . . . In the darkness of this search, patience and good humour are useful qualities. Also: the serious and the funny are one. The purpose of poetry is to persuade, fool or compel God into speaking.

Indeed, the main theme of *Sentences* is the coherence art gives to life's randomness. In accordance with his theory of connecting through the power of art, the book is divided into sections titled "Beneath," "Above," and "Beyond"; these sections correspond to sex and power (beneath), metaphysics and poetry (above), and human destiny (beyond). The first section is ironic, the middle is speculative, and the last is moving. Critics generally disliked the first part of *Sentences*, but applauded the other two sections.

INSIDE THE ONION AND WAR STORIES

After *Sentences*, Nemerov published another stunning poetry collection, *Inside the Onion*. The title wryly implies his subjective-objective, romantic-realist nature. In this book, Nemerov blends the homely and the humorous into poems that avoid the dramatic and highlight the commonplace, making it arresting.

War Stories contains forty-six poems grouped into three parts: "The War in the Streets," "The War in the Air," and "The War in the Heavens." This volume is Nemerov at his metaphysical best, grounding his spiritual musings in everyday experience. His interest in science and modern events is linked to literature—for example, the advent of

Halley's Comet is hailed in the language of the speech in the Anglo-Saxon epic *Beowulf* (c. 1000) that compares humankind's life to a swallow's brief flight through a mead hall. These poems range from an elegy for a student to explorations of subtle psychological insights to profound spiritual observations: "Though God be dead, he lived so far away/ His sourceless light continues to fall on us" ("The Celestial Emperor").

OTHER MAJOR WORKS

LONG FICTION: *The Melodramatists*, 1949; *Federigo: Or, The Power of Love*, 1954; *The Homecoming Game*, 1957.

SHORT FICTION: *A Commodity of Dreams, and Other Stories*, 1959; *Stories, Fables, and Other Diversions*, 1971.

PLAY: *Endor: Drama in One Act*, pb. 1961 (verse play).

NONFICTION: *Poetry and Fiction: Essays*, 1963; *Journal of the Fictive Life*, 1965; *Reflexions on Poetry and Poetics*, 1972; *Figures of Thought: Speculations on the Meaning of Poetry, and Other Essays*, 1978; *New and Selected Essays*, 1985; *The Oak in the Acorn: On "Remembrance of Things Past" and on Teaching Proust, Who Will Never Learn*, 1987.

EDITED TEXT: *Poets on Poetry*, 1965.

MISCELLANEOUS: *A Howard Nemerov Reader*, 1991.

BIBLIOGRAPHY

Bartholomay, Julia A. *The Shield of Perseus: The Vision and Imagination of Howard Nemerov*. Gainesville: University Press of Florida, 1972. Discusses Nemerov's poetic techniques and recurrent themes. Provides detailed information about the poet drawn from his letters and conversations. An excellent source.

Burris, Sidney. "A Sort of Memoir, a Sort of Review." *Southern Review* 28 (Winter, 1992): 184-201. Burris presents a memoir of Nemerov as well as critiques of *A Howard Nemerov Reader* and *Trying Conclusions*.

Kinzie, Mary. "The Signature of Things: On Howard Nemerov." In *The Cure of Poetry in an Age of Prose: Moral Essays on the Poet's Calling*. Chicago: University of Chicago Press, 1993. Examines the body of Nemerov's work.

Knock, Stanley F., Jr. "Renewal of Illusion." *Christian Century*, January 16, 1962, 85-86. In this review of Nemerov's verse drama *Endor*, Knock shows how Nemerov transports an Old Testament story into the context of existentialism and the Cold War. Rather than "see ourselves as others see us," as poet Robert Burns advised, Nemerov finds hope not in the stripping of illusion, but in its renewal.

Labrie, Ross. *Howard Nemerov*. Boston: Twayne, 1980. A standard biography in Twayne's United States Authors series. Includes an index and a bibliography.

Meinke, Peter. *Howard Nemerov*. Minneapolis: University of Minnesota Press, 1968. One of the most comprehensive books on Nemerov insofar as general knowledge is concerned. It covers not only biographical data but also the effect some life incidents had on his work. Includes brief comments on Nemerov's major works, tracing Nemerov's rise to literary prominence.

Nemerov, Alexander. "Modeling My Father." *American Scholar* 62 (Autumn, 1993). A notable biographical piece.

Potts, Donna L. *Howard Nemerov and Objective Idealism: The Influence of Owen Barfield.* Columbia: University of Missouri Press, 1994. Potts contends that Nemerov was profoundly influenced by the objective idealism of British philosopher Barfield. Includes excerpts from the thirty years of correspondence between the two and selections of Nemerov's poetry.

Vaughan, David K. *Words to Measure a War: Nine American Poets of World War II.* Jefferson, N.C.: McFarland, 2009. Vaughan provides an examination of war poets, contrasting those who became famous before and during World War II, with those who became known as poets after the war, such as Nemerov.

Mary Hanford Bruce

GEORGE OPPEN

Born: New Rochelle, New York; April 24, 1908
Died: Sunnyvale, California; July 7, 1984

OTHER LITERARY FORMS

In addition to his poetry, George Oppen (AHP-uhn) published several reviews and essays. Of these, two are central to an understanding of his work: "The Mind's Own Place," published in *Kulchur*, in 1963, and "A Letter," published in *Agenda*, in 1973. Oppen's many published interviews and his extensive correspondence with both American and British writers provide an in-depth look into Oppen's poetics and his sense of poetry's place in the contemporary world; *The Selected Letters of George Oppen* was published in 1990.

ACHIEVEMENTS

In a long and distinguished career, George Oppen never wavered from that which Ezra Pound in 1934 noted of his work: its commitment to sustained seriousness, craftsmanship, and individual sensibility. Out of this commitment, Oppen created one of the most moving and complex bodies of poetry of the twentieth century.

Oppen was one of the original Objectivist poets; his work can be associated with that of William Carlos Williams, Pound, and the Imagists. However, more than any other poet associated with that group, he was to develop a radical poetics of contingency, a poetics as wary of formalist assumptions about art as it is about naïve realism in poetry. His unique combining of imagery and rhetoric, the breadth of his subject matter, and its nearly populist strain have made his work extremely important to younger poets.

With the receipt of the Pulitzer Prize in poetry in 1969 and an award for his distinguished contribution to poetry from the National Endowment for the Arts and with increasing critical attention (much of it contained in _George Oppen: Man and Poet_, published in 1981), Oppen's place in twentieth century poetry is beginning to be recognized as one of major significance.

George Oppen was born on April 24, 1908, in New Rochelle, New York, into a moderately wealthy Jewish family. His father, George August Oppenheimer, was a diamond merchant. Oppen's mother committed suicide when he was four years old. His father remarried in 1917 and the next year moved his family to San Francisco, a city which has been both an inspiration and a resource for much of Oppen's poetry. In 1926, at Oregon State University, Corvallis, he met Mary Colby. They were married in 1927, the same year that the family shortened its name to Oppen. Of their relationship, Mary wrote that it was not simply love but the discovery that "we were in search of an aesthetic within which to live." For both, it meant distancing themselves from their pasts and striking out into new territory, both geographical and psychic. This departure was not so much a break with the past as a desire to obtain distance from and insight into it, for in this, as in all their subsequent travels, the Oppens sought to live close to, and understand, ordinary working people.

Together, the Oppens hitchhiked to New York City, completing the last leg of the journey on a barge through the Erie Canal. In New York, they met Louis Zukofsky and Charles Reznikoff, whose friendship and influence were to shape Oppen's poetry significantly over the years. These poets, with the encouragement of Williams and Pound, formed themselves into the Objectivists, one of the most significant groupings in the field of twentieth century poetry, and began publishing one another's work.

In 1930, the Oppens traveled to France and Italy, meeting Pound and Constantin Brancusi; returning to the United States, the couple became involved in labor organizing and other left-wing political movements, an involvement which for Oppen ultimately led to a twenty-five-year hiatus from writing poetry. In 1940, they had a daughter, and two years later, Oppen was fighting in Europe with the Allied forces.

After the war and living in California, the Oppens were investigated by the Federal Bureau of Investigation for their old left-wing politics. This situation led the Oppens to flee to Mexico during the McCarthy period, where Oppen began to write poetry again. This work, collected in _The Materials_, and touching on the themes of Oppen's past, his travels, and his sense of contemporary urban life, brought Oppen immediate recognition as a unique and powerful voice in contemporary poetry.

In 1960, the Oppens returned to the United States, living alternately in New York, San Francisco (where they eventually settled), and Maine, places which play a prominent role in Oppen's poetry. Oppen died in Sunnyvale, California, southeast of San Francisco, in 1984.

ANALYSIS

In one of George Oppen's poems, the poet is being driven around an island off the coast of Maine by a poor fisherman and his wife. The landscape, the lobster pots and fishing gear, the harbor, and the post office are noted, and the poet is, unaccountably, moved by a nearly metaphysical sense of passage. The experience is at once intimate and remote, and the poet is moved to exclaim to himself: "Difficult to know what one means/ —to be serious and to know what one means—." Such lines could be emblems for Oppen's entire career, for, of contemporary poets, none has more searchingly investigated through poetry the attempt to mean, to examine how language is used, and so to account for the very vocabulary of modernity.

For Oppen, inquiry is synonymous with expression. In a world of mass communication and of a debased language riddled with preconceptions about the nature of reality, the poet, according to Oppen, must begin in a completely new way; he must begin, as he says in one poem, "impoverished of tone of pose that common/ wealth of parlance." In Oppen, this is not so much a search for a language of innocence or novelty as it is a resolve against making use of certain historical or elegiac associations in language, a desire on the part of the poet not to be bewitched (as the philosopher Ludwig Wittgenstein warned) by conventional ways of speaking and of making poetry.

Oppen's entire body of work can be seen as a modern test of the poet's capacity to articulate. The terms of his poetry are the common meanings of words as they attempt to render the brute givens of the world of appearance. For this reason, Oppen has called his work "realist"; it is realist in the sense that it is "concerned with a fact (the world) which it did not create." In a way, the subject of all Oppen's poetry is the nature of this encounter, whether with the world or with others. The task for the poet is neither to beautify sentimentally nor to categorize such encounters but to render their living quality, to make the poet's relatedness to the facts into something felt. As Oppen acknowledges in one of his poems, "Perhaps one is himself/ Beyond the heart, the center of the thing/ and cannot praise it/ As he would want to."

DISCRETE SERIES

In all Oppen's work, there is an attempt to render the visual datum accurately and precisely; this is in keeping with the Imagist and Objectivist techniques at the root of Oppen's poetics. The aim of the technique, however, is more philosophical than literary; it is to establish the material otherness of the visual event. In the poems, objects and landscapes obtrude and reveal their existence as though seen for the first time. *Discrete Series*, Oppen's first book, is nearly procedural in its epistemological insistence on what is seen. The short lyrics which compose its contents are less like poems than they are the recording of eye movements across surfaces juxtaposed with snatches of statement and remembered lines from older poetry and fiction. The white space of the page surrounding these elements becomes a field of hesitations, advances, and reconsiderations, and the burden of meaning in the poem resides in the reader's recomposition of the fragmented elements. It is as though a crystal or prism had been interposed between poet and subject.

By the time Oppen had resumed writing poetry in the late 1950's, he had greatly modified his reliance on visual sense as a source of knowledge. One of the chief distinctions of his poetry remains its persuasive powers of registration, as in a poem written in the 1960's where "the north/ Looks out from its rock/ bulging into the fields," or from a poem of the 1970's where the sun moves "beyond the blunt/ towns of the coast . . . fishermen's/ tumbled tumbling headlands the needle silver/ water. . . ." Such imagery evokes the solidity and palpability of the world, and, at the same time, suggests its ungainliness and its obdurate self-referential quality which contrasts sharply with the usual visual clichés.

This sense of the visual, however, is for Oppen only one element in a dialectical occasion in which poetic truth resides neither in the object nor in the poet but in the interaction between the two. If, as Oppen would insist, the poet's ultimate aim is truth, then what is seen has the possibility of being a kind of measure: Seeing precedes its verbalization and therefore offers an opportunity for an open response to the world. This opportunity is hedged about with all one's conditioned reflexes, the material which the poet must work through to arrive at a sense of the real. It is through this struggle that Oppen's poetics, though they are concerned with ambiguity and paradox, strive for a clarity that is both immediate and complex. Oppen has described this as an attempt to write poetry which "cannot not be understood."

THE MATERIALS

This process can be seen at work in *The Materials*, the first of Oppen's major collections to be written and published after his twenty-year hiatus from the world of poetry. The book's underlying theme, carried through its forty poems, is clearly signaled in its epigraph from the philosopher Jacques Maritain, "We awake in the same moment to ourselves and to things." Oppen's "subjects" are these awakenings, which are capable of transcending the usual notions of self and society. In one of the book's major poems, "The Return," amid "the dim sound of the living," the impingement of the natural world becomes a moment in which "We cannot reconcile ourselves./ No one is reconciled, tho we spring/ From the ground together—." Nor is this estrangement eased by a sense of history or community; these are fictions in their way, and to look closely at them is to feel "The sense of that passage, is desertion, betrayal, that we are not innocent of loneliness." The poem ends with an image of the poet's old neighborhood "razed, whole blocks of a city gone," in which "the very ceremony of innocence" has been drowned.

In Oppen, such loss of innocence is not to be mourned; rather, it is the very beginning of a purer association between individuals and between the individual and the world, based on a language shorn of old, inauthentic mythologies. "Leviathan," the last poem in *The Materials*, insists that "Truth also is the pursuit of it," that "We must talk now. Fear/ is fear. But we abandon one another."

THIS IN WHICH

Oppen's next book, *This in Which*, is an exploration of the nature of such "talk." Here the poet's search is for a "substantial language of clarity, and of respect," based on a willingness to look fully, without illusion, at the human condition. It is "possible to use words," the poet says, "provided one treat them as enemies./ Not enemies—Ghosts which have run mad." Comparing modern consciousness to that of the primitive Mayans and their mythic view of life, "the poor savages of ghost and glitter," Oppen reminds the reader that it is necessary to examine squarely the "terror/ the unsightly/ silting sand of events." The critic Hugh Kenner, in discussing Oppen's method of stripping language of its historical associations, suggests that an apt motto for his work (and for that of the other Objectivist poets) might be "No myths." "Art," Oppen warns, "also is not good for us/ unless . . . it may rescue us/ as only the true/ might rescue us."

OF BEING NUMEROUS

These themes, the need for a demythologizing poetics and a language adequate to render the fullness of reality, are brought to culmination in *Of Being Numerous*, the book-length poem that many critics consider to be Oppen's masterpiece. *Of Being Numerous* is concerned with the deepest notions of community and the basis on which community might be established: what is meant by humanity, ethics, and love. The poem is, in a sense, an interrogation of these terms, an attempt to discover whether they can truthfully be retained in the light of what humanity has become. For Oppen, the word "community" represents, in the present, an expression of the individual's psychic needs, of the effect of anxiety on contemporary life. Hence, in Oppen's view, the very notion of community is, at best, flawed and irrational. Humanity, the poem tells us, is "bewildered/ by the shipwreck/ of the singular"; thus, "we have chosen the meaning/ of being numerous." Given this situation, there is now only "a ferocious mumbling in public/ of rootless speech." Against this mumbling, Oppen seeks to set the truth-value of poetic speech. The poem attempts, not to lull one into another false sense of community, but to clear the air of bankrupt sentimentality about community and to genuinely reestablish it on a recognition of one another's essential aloneness. This is to discover, the poem continues, "Not truth, but each other." The poem's last word, "curious," overshadows the argument of the poem, for it is Oppen's intention to lead the reader to this understanding, not by rational means, but by the dynamics of aesthetic response. In such a response is to be found "our jubilation/ exalted and as old as that truthfulness/ which illumines speech."

SEASCAPE AND PRIMITIVE

Oppen's last works, beginning with *Seascape* and continuing through his final collection, *Primitive*, involve a radical departure from the poetry that had come before. In the earlier poems, especially in *Of Being Numerous*, Oppen created a restrained but rhetorically powerful amalgam of statement and imagery, a poetry which, like a Socratic dialogue, aimed at undermining conventional thought and attitude. In the later poems, the chaos and flux of life and the ever-partial mythologizing that language enacts are embodied in a troubled and moving voice that seems to embrace deeply the contingency and indeterminacy of life.

In these poems, syntax, punctuation, and rhythm are wrenched into a compelling new tone; words and phrases are enjambed and repeated, then modified into a poetic architecture which in its cadence expresses a new urgency, as in this excerpt from *Seascape*:

> Pride in the sandspit wind this ether this other
>   this element all
> It is I or I believe
> We are the beaks of the ragged birds
> Tune of the ragged birds' beaks.

Such poetry seems at once immensely sophisticated and primordial; it is sophisticated inasmuch as behind its strange and powerful technique lies the history of the use and misuse of language. At the same time, it strikes the reader as a kind of first poetry, fashioned out of an unconditioned and open sense of life.

Such poems range across all the characteristic themes of poetry, love, death, politics, and being; yet the ambiguity of their claims, rather than diminishing them, adds a new, previously unheard richness to the verse. This richness is in the service not only of the present but also of history.

As Oppen notes in *Primitive*, harking back to the very beginning of his career and his insistence on the visual, "the tongues of appearance/ speak in the unchosen journey . . . the words out of that whirlwind his." In Oppen, this "unchosen journey" has been transformed into a powerful poetry of both collective and individual pain and loss, into a desire to make "a music more powerful," a music meant to redeem humanity "till other voices wake us or we drown."

OTHER MAJOR WORKS

NONFICTION: "The Mind's Own Place," 1963; "A Letter," 1973; *The Selected Letters of George Oppen*, 1990; *George Oppen: Selected Prose, Daybooks, and Papers*, 2008 (Stephen Cope, editor).

BIBLIOGRAPHY

Barzilai, Lyn Graham. *George Oppen: A Critical Study.* Jefferson, N.C.: McFarland, 2006. This study of Oppen looks at his literary style and contains chapters examining *The Materials* and *Primitive.*

Freeman, John, ed. *Not Comforts, but Vision: Essays on the Poetry of George Oppen.* Budleigh Salterton, Devon, England: Interim Press, 1985. This volume, intended to introduce Oppen to British readers, contains contributions by poets and critics. The essays survey Oppen's work rather than analyze the poems.

Hatlen, Burton, ed. *George Oppen, Man and Poet.* Orono: National Poetry Foundation, University of Maine, 1981. This homage dedicated to Oppen and his wife is an anthology of twenty-eight articles and two separate bibliographies, all but six published for the first time. The essays are well organized, and good bibliographies appear in notes. Two essays give political and philosophical contexts to the poetry. Contains an index and two personal memoirs by Mary Oppen.

Ironwood 5 (1975). This special issue devoted to Oppen contains, among other things, an "Introductory Note on Poetry" by Charles Tomlinson; seven poems by the poet; an interview, photographs, and memoirs by Charles Reznikoff and Mary Oppen; and a critical essay by Rachel Blau DuPlessis. Includes a bibliography.

Ironwood 13 (Fall, 1985). This second special issue on the poet contains a number of excellent essays, memoirs, and appreciations. This volume contains more critical work than the first volume, and a different selection of critics, poets, and scholars is presented.

Nicholls, Peter. *George Oppen and the Fate of Modernism.* New York: Oxford University Press, 2007. Drawing on the Oppen archive, Nicholls investigates the sources of the innovative poetics of Oppen, who tried to avoid what he regarded as the mistakes of the modernists.

Paideuma 10 (Spring, 1981). This journal, normally dedicated to Ezra Pound studies, is a memorial to Oppen. It contains a collection of more than thirty appreciations, poems, explications, biographical sketches, and memorials, and it begins with Pound's preface to Oppen's *Discrete Series.* This, like the 1975 *Ironwood* special issue, is really a commemorative collection of material on the poet's life and work.

Shoemaker, Steve, ed. *Thinking Poetics: Essays on George Oppen.* Tuscaloosa: University of Alabama Press, 2009. A collection of essays examining various aspects of Oppen's poetry, including his worldview.

Weinfield, Henry. *The Music of Thought in the Poetry of George Oppen and William Bronk.* Iowa City: University of Iowa Press, 2009. Oppen and William Bronk were very different in their background and orientation, but still formed a close friendship. Weinfield examines their correspondence and their poetry to find they were both extraordinary thinkers who shared a pursuit of questions of meaning and value.

Michael Heller

JOEL OPPENHEIMER

Born: Yonkers, New York; February 18, 1930
Died: Henniker, New Hampshire; October 11, 1988

OTHER LITERARY FORMS

In addition to writing book reviews and critiques, introductions, and jacket blurbs, Joel Oppenheimer (AHP-puhn-hi-muhr) worked on the primary level as a printer and typographer. He was also a regular columnist for *The Village Voice* from 1969 to 1984.

Oppenheimer wrote several plays that have been performed off-off-Broadway: *The Great American Desert* (pr. 1961), *Miss Right* (pr. 1962), and *Like a Hill* (pr. 1963). Oppenheimer's collection of short stories, *Pan's Eyes*, was published in 1974. Through the aficionado's eyes, he has viewed popular American culture in *The Wrong Season* (1973) and *Marilyn Lives!* (1981). *The Wrong Season* re-creates the year 1972 from the point of view of a disappointed New York Mets baseball fan. With interviews, photographs, personal narrative, and poems, *Marilyn Lives!* looks at the life of Marilyn Monroe.

ACHIEVEMENTS

For the first fifteen years of his writing career, Joel Oppenheimer worked, in the tradition of William Carlos Williams or Wallace Stevens, outside the university to support himself and his writing, mostly as a production manager for printing firms. Beginning in 1969, he became an active presence at various universities, teaching and giving poetry readings. His work was recognized by his appointments as director of the St. Mark's Poetry Project and the New York City Teachers and Writers Collaborative, as well as by such awards as the Creative Artists Public Service Fellowship (1971) and the National

Endowment for the Humanities (1980). In addition, he held poet-in-residence positions at the City College of New York and at New England College and visiting professorships at St. Andrews Presbyterian College in North Carolina and the Black Mountain II College at the State University of New York at Buffalo. In his own words, his achievement was that he "made poems and children much of his adult life, and also a living."

BIOGRAPHY

Joel Lester Oppenheimer was born in Yonkers, New York, a son of a leather goods retailer; he was the youngest of three boys. He went to Cornell University (1947-1948), wanting to become an architect, but, compromising with his mother, he enrolled in civil engineering. He left Cornell for the University of Chicago, where he stayed only briefly.

For the next three years (1950-1953), Oppenheimer attended Black Mountain College, enrolled as a painter/writer. Here he met and was influenced by such men as Robert Creeley, Charles Olson, Robert Duncan, and Jonathan Williams. Remembering his grandfather, who had founded a printing union, Oppenheimer tried to start his own press. He shortly abandoned it, however, after completing only one or two jobs.

Leaving Black Mountain, Oppenheimer worked in various print shops for the next fifteen years, mostly as a production person, mediating between advertisers' demands and the printer's experience. He worked first in Washington, D.C. (living in Olson's apartment), and later in Rochester, New Hampshire; Provincetown, Massachusetts; and New York City.

For two years beginning in 1966, Oppenheimer directed the Poetry Project at St. Mark's in the Bowery, followed by one year directing the New York City Teachers and Writers Collaborative. In 1969, he began writing for *The Village Voice*, and after teaching part-time at the City College of the City University of New York, in 1970, he was offered a part-time but untenured position as poet-in-residence. On leave from City College, he taught, again as poet-in-residence, at New England College in New Hampshire. He also taught poetry workshops and seminars at the State University of New York at Buffalo's "Black Mountain II Summer Arts Program." In 1982, Oppenheimer became associate professor of communications and poet-in-residence at New England College. He died in New Hampshire in 1988.

ANALYSIS

This "sports-loving Jewish intellectual/ writer" ("Dear Miss Monroe"), who "still grew up a jew in/ yonkers new york" admits at one moment that "finally i am through with it, with/ the american dream, a dream that ran through/ all my ancestors who fought here for you/ america" ("17-18 April, 1961"). Don't believe him. Joel Oppenheimer's own language and ideas give him away. His book *On Occasion* includes "Life," the poem, and "Life," a subsection of the collection. Two major sections are titled "Liberty" and "The Pursuit of Happiness."

Not only does the triumvirate of American independence reign throughout his work, but the language of his poetry also shows that he has not abandoned America. Instead of the Christmas jingle "not a creature was stirring, not even a mouse," he writes, "inside the/ window/ not even a/ football game not even/ a haiku disturbing/ us" ("Found Art"). He defines "contra naturam" as "the pot which boils while/ watched" ("The Zoom Lens"). Beginning "The Riddle," he asks, "what/ s gray and comes in quarts"; answering, "is an elephant or my brain." His biblical allusions take the form of "it/ is very hot/ my sweat runneth over, even if/ my belly be not sheaved/ wheat" ("The Bye-Bye Happiness Swing"). He reaffirms or readjusts the platitudes "love *is* a/ many-splendored thing" ("Untitled") and "it's the world we live in/ we can't eat our cake or have it/ either"("Four Photographs by Richard Kirstel"); and he haunts one with an echo of the now classic radio line, "who knows what shadows lurk in the hearts of old girl friends" ("Come On Baby"). As he exclaims in "Poem Written in the Light of Certain Events April 14th, 1967," "finally, i am here, goddamnit!/ i am american, goddamnit!"

POLITICAL POEMS

Only an American would take and insist on such liberties with language. Oppenheimer insists not only that one can take liberties with language, but also that it is language that gives us our liberty and freedom. He vehemently defends that right, to "defend that truth/ that is our inheritance" ("Poem in Defense of Children"). The fight is against those that would take it away—"the first amendment was here/ before mendel rivers or lbj" ("A Dab of Cornpone")—as well as against those who would equally damage individual freedom by manipulation and lies. Echoing Williams's complaint against T. S. Eliot, he rejects language that is not part of and does not express one's own experience: "there is the problem of words, how/ to sound like language, and/ one/ s self" ("The Great American Novel").

Oppenheimer's American heritage runs from Thomas Jefferson through Davy Crockett and Andrew Jackson—"andy/ show them all. once/ a free man ruled the free" ("The 150th Anniversary of the Battle of New Orleans"). His other ancestors include such persons (and literary banners) as Walt Whitman (I sing of myself), William Carlos Williams ("no ideas but in things"), Ezra Pound ("make it new"), and Olson ("form is but an extension of content"). His immediate kin he addresses in "The Excuse":

> dear god, dear olson, dear
> creeley, dear ginsberg, my
> teachers and makers, bring
> me again to light, keep
> me from lies. . . .

These influences are political and literary. Many of Oppenheimer's poems are politically directed, created in the protesting air of the late 1950's and 1960's. Oppenheimer, however, does not separate politics from life, from art, art from politics or life—"after all man is a/ political animal" ("The Innocent Breasts"). All directly affect how one lives, and how one says one wants to live—"we have forgotten/ we once carried a flag into battle that/ read don't/ tread on me" ("17-18 April, 1961").

Life, however, in these United States as he states in "17-18 April, 1961" has somehow found it

> . . . better to lie and hope not
> to get caught, than to behave honorably.
> well, this has been true of the world
> all along, but it was not supposed
> to be true of you, america

Oppenheimer finds that America has ignored the simple tenets of life, liberty, and the pursuit of happiness. Instead of honor and justice, his poem "Keeping It" expresses how one lives by fear and deception:

> the world we live in
> is not what we sing,
> and we are afraid we will
> fall prey to that we
> are most afraid of, the
> truth.

In the world that Oppenheimer perceives, truths about how humans are created are no longer self evident: "we are all incapable/ it seems of living in that/ environment we were created/ for . . ." ("A Prayer"). In "Sirventes on a Sad Occasion" (1967), an old woman loses control of her bowels walking up the stairs to her apartment. She tries to hide the accident, feeling inadequate and inhuman for it. Oppenheimer can only ask, sadly, "this is a/ natural act, why will you/ fear me for it. . . ." Without these truths the world is unnatural, alien, often hostile.

Against such threats, one must preserve one's liberty. "The Surgeon in Spite of Himself" endures his fear because "master of my fate and captain/ of my soul, i know that i will." Liberty, built into the Declaration of Independence, is a fundamental need; Oppenheimer declares, in "A Treatise": "all that matters is/ the built-in mechanism/ of self-preservation."

Oppenheimer's poetry is filled with slogans: "to live my own life" and "to thine own self be true." These might be taken as mere egotistical or selfish desires. Oppenheimer might respond, "So what?" Liberty is necessary to make and define one's self; he insists on a voice, the personal voice and poetic voice being one and the same. Oppenheimer's ideal is the self-made man—Crockett, Jackson, Jefferson, his grandfather who began his own printing union—all men of action who looked to themselves and into themselves for freedoms: "freedoms you might only/ have, anyhow, if you look deep inside/ yourself where all freedom is to be/ found . . ." ("17-18 April, 1961").

Oppenheimer's poems, as one title specifically indicates, provide "Some Suggested Guidelines" as to how one can live freely in this world; and they encourage individual action. His advice starts, of course, with himself. "Notes Toward Lessons to Be Learned at Thirty" advises taking care of his body; it provides advice on coffee, cigarettes, fresh fruit, and "the loveliest ass in the world." "Sirventes Against Waiting" underscores three lessons: "you do what you can . . . what you have to . . . [and] what you want to." Oppenheimer's faith in America, then, comes down to a faith in the self. His declaration of independence is "the simple/ declaration of the/ faith a man must have,/ in his own balls, in/ his own heart" ("Keeping It").

LOVE POEMS

Not all of Oppenheimer's poems are political. Many are love poems—love that varies and that takes as many forms as do the women he invokes—Artemis, Persephone, Diana, Medusa, and Marilyn Monroe. *The Woman Poems* presents his fourfold synthesis of woman—Good Mother, Death Mother, Ecstasy or Dancing Mother, and Stone or Tooth Mother—all embodied in the mythical figure of Mother Goddess. As a true democrat, he loves and lusts after them all, equally. His poems, in addition, are filled with tenderness, affection, and hope—for friends, children, and parents. There is fighting and plain sex; there are elegies, celebrations of births and weddings, and blues. A poem in *New Spaces* celebrates a marriage (and in the process touches on the relationship between art and life); noting that people ask for poems as "blessing on their union," he adds, "the wonder is/ we keep writing/ they keep getting married."

Oppenheimer's definition of happiness invokes the old-time notion of a little peace and quiet—"this much/ will a little quiet do,/ and peace, in our times" ("Modern Times")—and a little honesty and decency. Happiness is having one's own space, "asking for/ space to build our own perimeters/ in defense of such" ("Poem for Soho"). Happiness for Oppenheimer is not so much being happy as pursuing happiness. Happiness is the labors of Hercules, not their completion; or, more apt, the labors of love. It is the act of happiness, not the state, which seems more real. The last poem of *On Occasion* is "The Act":

> as i do
> it is as it is
> does as it does
> as i am it is
> is as is is as
> i do as i do
> as it does as it
> does as it is
> as is is

Containing all active, simple verbs, "The Act" defines, blends with, but does not constrict, personal pronouns and direct objects. The act defines itself and oneself. "The Act" summarizes Oppenheimer's self and his world in language, idea, and act.

OTHER MAJOR WORKS

SHORT FICTION: *Pan's Eyes*, 1974.

PLAYS: *The Great American Desert*, pr. 1961; *Miss Right*, pr. 1962; *Like a Hill*, pr. 1963.

NONFICTION: *The Wrong Season*, 1973; *Marilyn Lives!*, 1981; *Drawing from Life*, 1997.

BIBLIOGRAPHY

Bertholf, Robert J. *Remembering Joel Oppenheimer*. Jersey City, N.J.: Talisman House, 2006. In this work, Bertholf, the editor of *The Collected Later Poems of Joel Oppenheimer*, recalls his relationship with the poet.

Gilmore, Lyman. *Don't Touch the Poet: The Life and Times of Joel Oppenheimer*. Jersey City, N.J.: Talisman House, 1998. Gilmore has done an admirable job of balancing views about Oppenheimer and goes beyond facade to show a man obsessed with magic, routine, and lists. Gilmore provides a very human view of the Black Mountain and Greenwich Village poetry world of the 1950's and 1960's.

Landrey, David W. "Simply Survival: David Budbill and Joel Oppenheimer." *Credences*, n.s. 1 (Fall/Winter, 1981/1982): 150-157. This article explores the two poets' shared quest for life, knowledge, and understanding, their different approaches to their work, and their shared need for a changed sense of self through poetry. Particularly significant is the discussion of Oppenheimer working from the inside out. Several themes are pointed out and short examples given.

Oppenheimer, Joel. "Interview with Joel Oppenheimer." Interview by Christopher Beach. *Sagetrieb* 7 (Fall, 1978): 89-130. An informative interview conducted ten years before the poet's death. Contains Oppenheimer's comments on his contemporaries and poetry in general, interspersed with personal detail. This lengthy document gives an excellent portrait of the poet. His personality surfaces as he reflects on topics and figures in American poetry.

_____. "Joel Oppenheimer Talks About His Poetry." Interview by William Sylvester. *Credences*, n.s. 3 (Fall, 1985): 69-76. This transcription of several conversations with Oppenheimer lets the poet speak for himself about his craft, his career, and his early influences from theater and film. It gives one a strong sense of who Oppenheimer was and what informed his thinking.

_____. *Poetry, the Ecology of the Soul: Talks and Selected Poems*. Edited by David Landrey and Dennis Maloney. Buffalo, N.Y.: White Plains Press, 1983. This excellent collection is preceded by an introductory appreciation by David Landrèy. The volume contains a number of poems, three informative talks, and a bibliography of Oppenheimer's work. The lectures on the Black Mountain poets and on *The Woman Poems* are of particular importance because of what they reveal about the poet's craft.

Thibodaux, David. *Joel Oppenheimer: An Introduction.* Columbia, S.C.: Camden House, 1986. This study provides an overview of Oppenheimer's work and examines closely his literary themes, including the significance of images, motifs, and symbols. Approximately half the book is devoted to poetry. The remainder discusses fiction, drama, and nonfiction prose. An excellent bibliography cites several useful journal articles on specific poems, interviews, and reviews.

Steven P. Schultz

DAN PAGIS

Born: Radautsi, Romania; October 16, 1930
Died: Jerusalem, Israel; July 29, 1986

OTHER LITERARY FORMS

Although Dan Pagis (pah-GEE) is internationally known as a poet, he has written a children's book in Hebrew, *ha-Beitzah she-hithapsah* (1973; the egg that tried to disguise itself). As a professor of medieval Hebrew literature at Hebrew University, he has published important studies on the aesthetics of medieval poetry, including expositions of Moses Ibn Ezra, Judah ha-Levi, Ibn Gabirol, and the other great poets of the eleventh and twelfth centuries who celebrated the colors and images of worldly existence in elegant, formal verse. Pagis's own poems, more understated and conversational than the medieval texts he studied, have been translated into Afrikaans, Czech, Danish, Dutch, Estonian, French, Hungarian, Italian, Japanese, Polish, Portuguese, Romanian, Serbo-Croatian, Swedish, Vietnamese, and Yiddish.

ACHIEVEMENTS

The first generation of Israeli poets often used a collective identity to write poetry of largely ideological content. However, the reaction to previous ideological values that arose in the late 1950's and the 1960's has been described by Hebrew critic Shimon Sandbank as "the withdrawal from certainty." Poets Yehuda Amichai and Natan Zach were at the forefront of this avant-garde movement, a "new wave" that included Dan Pagis, Tuvia Ruebner, Dahlia Ravikovitch, and David Rokeah. These poets of the 1950's turned away from the socially minded national poets, believing in the poet as an individual and using understatement, irony, prosaic diction, and free verse to express their own views.

Most of all, the revolution in Hebrew verse that Pagis, Amichai, and Zach brought about was the perfection of a colloquial norm for Hebrew poetry. Pagis and Amichai especially made efforts to incorporate elements of classical Hebrew into the colloquial diction, with Pagis often calling on a specific biblical or rabbinical text. His poems have appeared in major American magazines, including *The New Yorker* and *Tikkun*.

BIOGRAPHY

Dan Pagis was born in Radautsi, Romania, and was brought up in Bukovina, speaking German in a Jewish home in what was once an eastern province of the Austro-Hungarian Empire. He spent three years in Nazi concentration camps, from which he escaped in 1944. After he arrived in Palestine in 1946, Pagis began to publish poetry in his newly acquired Hebrew within only three or four years, and he became a schoolteacher on a kibbutz.

He settled in Jerusalem in 1956, where he earned his Ph.D. from Hebrew University and became a professor of medieval Hebrew literature. Pagis also taught at the Jewish Theological Seminary in New York, Harvard University, and the University of California, at both San Diego and Berkeley. During his life, he was the foremost living authority on the poetics of Hebrew literature of the High Middle Ages and the Renaissance. He was married and had two children. Pagis died of cancer in Jerusalem in 1986.

ANALYSIS

Reflecting the geographic and linguistic displacements of his life, displacement is a governing concept in Dan Pagis's poetry, in the sense that to "displace" is to remove or put out of its proper place. Although there is a great deal of horror in his poetry, the historical record of that horror is so enormous that Pagis uses displacement to give it expression without the shrillness of hysteria or the bathos of melodrama. Instead, he cultivates a variety of distanced, ventriloquist voices that become authentic surrogates for his own voice. Pagis survived one of the darkest events in human history and managed to set distance from it through the medium of his art. Pagis is a playful poet as well, sometimes using humor and whimsy to transform the displacement of his life from a passively suffered fate into an imaginative reconstruction of reality.

POEMS BY DAN PAGIS

In *Poems by Dan Pagis*, it is apparent why many discussions of Pagis's poems tend to pigeonhole him as a "poet of the Holocaust." The first poem is titled "The Last Ones," and the first-person speaker in the poem speaks for all the Jews left after the Holocaust. Ironically, he states that "For years I have appeared only here and there/ at the edges of this jungle." Nevertheless, he is certain that "at this moment/ someone is tracking me. . . . Very close. Here." The poem ends with the line "There is no time to explain," indicating a collective consciousness that is still running in fear for its life.

A section of the book called "Testimony" contains six Holocaust poems, among them "Europe, Late," the brilliant "Written in Pencil in the Sealed Railway-Car," and the chilling "Draft of a Reparations Agreement." In "Europe, Late," the speaker betrays his innocence by asking what year it is, and the answer is "Thirty-nine and a half, still awfully early." He introduces the reader to the life of the party, dancing the tango and kissing the hand of an elegant woman, reassuring her "that everything will be all right." However, the voice stops midsentence at the end of the poem, "No it could never happen here,/ don't worry so—you'll see—it could."

Often Holocaust themes are placed in an archetypal perspective, as in the widely known poem "Written in Pencil in the Sealed Railway-Car." The speaker is "eve" traveling with her son "abel," and she means to leave a message for her other son. "If you see my other son/ cain son of man/ tell him i"; here the poem ends abruptly, leaving the reader to meditate on the nature of evil.

In "Draft of a Reparations Agreement," the speaker is again a collective voice, the voice of the perpetrators of the Holocaust. The agreement promises that "Everything will be returned to its place,/ paragraph after paragraph," echoing the bureaucratic language in which the whole Nazi endeavor was carried out. In a kind of mordant displacement the draft writer promises "The scream back into the throat./ The gold teeth back to the gums." Also,

> . . . you will be covered with skin and sinews and you
>   will live,
> look, you will have your lives back,
>
> .   .   .   .
> Here you are. Nothing is too late.

The exquisite irony exposes the absurdity of reparations as well as the lunacy of the speaker.

POINTS OF DEPARTURE

In *Points of Departure*, Pagis's voice runs the gamut from horrifying to deceptively whimsical. In "End of the Questionnaire," he creates a questionnaire to be filled out posthumously, with questions including "number of galaxy and star,/ number of grave." "You have the right to appeal," the questionnaire informs the deceased. It ends with the command, "In the blank space below, state/ how long you have been awake and why you are surprised." Ironically, this poem provokes the reader to meditate on the great finality of death.

"The Beginning" is a poem about "the end of creation." Pagis envisions the end as "A time of war," when "distant fleets of steel are waiting." The shadow of the Holocaust hovers over all, as "High above the smoke and the odor of fat and skins hovers/ a yellow magnetic stain." The poet seems to be saying that the Holocaust is the beginning of the end, when "at the zero-hour/ the Great Bear, blazing, strides forth/ in heat."

In a charming cycle in which five poems are grouped under the heading "Bestiary," each poem is rich with humor and whimsy. In the first, "The Elephant," Pagis writes of the pachyderm who ties on sixteen "marvelously accurate wristwatches" and "glides forth smoothly/ out of his elephant fate." Armchairs also become animals in this bestiary: "The slowest animals/ are the soft large-eared leather armchairs" that "multiply/ in the shade of potted philodendrons." Balloons also are animate, as they "fondle one another" and cluster at the ceiling, humbly accepting their limit. However, what is playful suddenly becomes ominous, as

> The soul suddenly leaks out
> in a terrified whistle
> or explodes
> with a single pop.

The darkest poem in this group is the one titled "The Biped." Pagis points out that though he is related to other predatory animals, "he alone/ cooks animals, peppers them,/ he alone is clothed with animals," and he alone "protests/ against what is decreed." What the poet finds strangest is that he "rides of his own free will/ on a motorcycle." "The Biped" becomes an existential comedy through this odd mixture of traits Pagis chooses to juxtapose, including the last three lines of the poem, which state "He has four limbs,/ two ears,/ a hundred hearts."

"Brain"

The highly intellectual poetry of Pagis treats each subject in a style which seems most appropriate. In "Brain" (from *Points of Departure*), he uses several different styles to illustrate the tortured life of this brain in exile, or, what the reader might imagine, Pagis himself. Typical of his later poetry, "Brain" is concerned with the ambivalence of the poet's experience of the world and employs images from the laboratory, popular culture, the Hebrew Bible, and medicine. The poem begins with a reference to religious life, although the "dark night of the soul" here becomes ironically "the dark night of the skull," during which "Brain" discovers "he" is born. In part 2, in a biblical reference, "Brain hovers upon the face of the deep," yet he is not a deity when his eyes develop, he discovers the world complete.

Brain first suspects that he is the whole universe, as an infant is aware only of itself, but then suspects he embodies millions of other brains, all "splitting off from him, betraying him from within." In a sudden shift of tone in part 4, Pagis gives us an image of Brain, looking exactly as one would picture him: "grayish-white convolutions,/ a bit oily, sliding back and forth." Brain sets out to explore the world and makes a friend, with whom he communicates over radio sets in the attic. He questions the friend to find out if they are alike, and when they become intimate Brain asks, "Tell me, do you know how to forget?"

When his life is half over, Brain finds his "bush of veins" enveloping him, snaring him, and in a fit of existential despair, he wonders why he ever spoke, to whom he spoke, and if there is anyone to listen to him. Part 9 is an encyclopedic entry describing the brain, and Brain is embarrassed by so much praise; he commands "Let there be darkness!" and closes the encyclopedia. Brain metamorphoses throughout the poem and starts to think about outer space.

Toward the end of this remarkable poem, Brain is receiving signals from light years away and makes contact with another world, which may be a heart. The discovery is cloaked in the language of science fiction; Brain is both a microcosm and a macrocosm, and he is astounded to find that

> There is a hidden circle somewhere
> whose center is everywhere
> and whose circumference is nowhere;
> . . . so near
> that he will never
> be able
> to see it.

With his new knowledge, his old sarcasm and jokes desert him, along with his fear. Finally, he achieves what he desires; "he no longer has to remember."

"INSTRUCTIONS FOR CROSSING THE BORDER"

The second line of "Instructions for Crossing the Border," "You are not allowed to remember," is typical of the preoccupation with memory that haunts this poet. The advice is positive, almost upbeat: "you are a man, you sit in the train./ Sit comfortably./ You've got a decent coat now." This is sinister advice, considering that the last line is a direct contradiction of the second: "Go. You are not allowed to forget." The voice is that of an official speaking, addressing "Imaginary man." It is a dehumanized voice, one that cannot recognize the man to whom it is speaking; the addressee is only present in the speaker's imagination. Although it is an early poem, using the stripped and spare vocabulary of his early work, "Instructions for Crossing the Border" forecasts the later "Brain" in its preoccupation with obliterating memory.

"HARVESTS"

"Harvests" starts with a deceptively benign image, that of "The prudent field-mouse" who "hoards and hoards for the time of battle and siege." Other benign images follow until an ironic twist in the sixth line, "the fire revels in the wheat," hints at what is ahead. What waits, of course, is the hawk, against whom the mouse's prudence and marvelously tunneled home is no protection at all. To darken the image further, the hawk is both "sharp-eyed" and "punctual," implying that the time of the mouse's demise is determined and no matter how canny he is, the hawk will appear at the appointed time. "Harvests" is a small parable in which Pagis, typically, uses animals to make a statement about the human condition, similar to his whimsical poem "Experiment of the Maze."

OTHER MAJOR WORKS

NONFICTION: *The Poetry of David Vogel*, 1966, fourth edition, 1975; *The Poetry of Levi Ibn Altabban of Saragossa*, 1968; *Secular Poetry and Poetic Theory: Moses Ibn Ezra and His Contemporaries*, 1970; *Hindush u-mascoret be-shirat-ha-hol ha-'Ivrit, Sefarad ve-Italyah*, 1976.

CHILDREN'S LITERATURE: *ha-Beitzah she-hithapsah*, 1973.

BIBLIOGRAPHY

Alter, Robert. "Dan Pagis and the Poetry of Displacement." *Judaism* 45, no. 80 (Fall, 1996). This article places the poet among his peers, primarily Yehuda Amichai and Natan Zach, illuminating Pagis's similarities and differences.

_____. Introduction to *The Selected Poetry of Dan Pagis*. Translated by Stephen Mitchell. Berkeley: University of California Press, 1996. Alter examines the life of Pagis and offers some literary criticism in this introduction to a translation of selected works. Originally published as *Variable Directions* in 1989.

Burnshaw, Stanley, T. Carmi, and Ezra Spicehandler, eds. *The Modern Hebrew Poem Itself.* New York: Holt, Rinehart and Winston, 1989. This book offers a stunning explication of Pagis's poem "The Log Book" and an afterword covering Hebrew poetry from 1965 to 1988. Provides a detailed discussion of the literary world Pagis inhabited and places him securely in the poetic movement of his generation. Each poem is presented in the original Hebrew, in phonetic transcription, and in English translation.

Keller, Tsipi, ed. *Poets on the Edge: An Anthology of Contemporary Hebrew Poetry.* Introduction by Aminadav Dykman. Albany: State University of New York Press, 2010. Contains a selection of poems by Pagis as well as a brief biography. The introduction discusses Pagis and Hebrew poetry in general, placing him among his fellows.

Omer-Sherman, Ranen. "In Place of the Absent God: The Reader in Dan Pagis's 'Written in Pencil in a Sealed Railway Car.'" *Cross Currents* 54, no. 2 (Summer, 2004): 51-61. Discusses teaching Pagis's well-known poem to students and their reactions and understandings. He also briefly outlines Pagis's life and provides analysis of the poem itself.

Sheila Golburgh Johnson

CHARLES REZNIKOFF

Born: Brooklyn, New York; August 31, 1894
Died: New York, New York; January 22, 1976

OTHER LITERARY FORMS

In addition to poetry, Charles Reznikoff (REHZ-nih-kahf) wrote fiction and verse drama and was active as a translator, historian, and editor. His novels include *By the Waters of Manhattan* (1930), a title Reznikoff also used for a later collection of his poetry, and *The Manner "Music"* (1977). The novels, as well as his historical work such as *Early History of a Sewing Machine Operator* (1936), are, like his poetry, sharply observed but detached, nearly autobiographical accounts and impressions of family and working life. Although thematically much of his fiction may be compared with the "proletarian" literature of the 1930's, its spareness and restraint give it a highly individual stamp. Reznikoff also wrote a historical novel, *The Lionhearted* (1944), which portrays the fate of English Jewry during the reign of Richard the Lionhearted.

Reznikoff's verse plays, such as *Uriel Accosta: A Play and a Fourth Group of Verse* (1921) and *"Chatterton," "The Black Death," and "Meriwether Lewis": Three Plays* (1922), extend his interest in the individual in history along dramatic lines. The plays make use of choruslike recitations both to convey offstage occurrence and to develop character much in the manner of the classical theater.

Reznikoff was the editor of the collected papers of Louis Marshall and a translator of two volumes of Yiddish stories and history. Much of his work in law was in writing and editing for the legal encyclopedia *Corpus Juris*. His few prose comments on the art of writing poetry are contained in a slim volume of prose titled *First, There Is the Need* (1977).

ACHIEVEMENTS

A rubric for Charles Reznikoff's career might well read: early, nearly precocious development; late recognition. Reznikoff, without ever seeking to be unique, was one of the twentieth century's most original writers, virtually with the publication of his first work. His abandonment, as early as 1918, of the verse conventions of late nineteenth century poetry and his utilization of proselike rhythms anticipate a kind of American plainsong that is to be found in the work of the most diverse poets writing today. Reznikoff, in reinventing the image as an element of realist rather than symbolic notation, also made a significant contribution to the notion of imagery as the cornerstone of the modern poem.

His highly unconventional and imaginative use of historical materials sets him off from the vogues of confessional and psychological poetry, but only in his later years did literary critics begin to appreciate the unprecedented and original manner in which Reznikoff brought history, both contemporary and biblical, alive. In 1971, he was the recipient of the Morton Dauwen Zabel Award for Poetry from the National Institute of Arts and Letters.

BIOGRAPHY

Born in a Jewish ghetto in Brooklyn and ultimately to live most of his life in New York City, Charles Reznikoff drew, for all his writing, on the very circumstances and surroundings of his life. Like his near-contemporary, William Carlos Williams, the "local" was to be the source of all that was universal in his work. Reznikoff sought out his poems not only in the lives of those around him, in the newly immigrant populations seething in the New York streets, but also in the European and biblical histories and even the customs that these immigrant groups had brought with them to the New World.

Graduating from a high school in Brooklyn, Reznikoff spent a year at the new School of Journalism of the University of Missouri but returned to New York to enter the New York University Law School, a decisive move for both his livelihood and his poetry. The influence of his legal training and his work in law were to affect his notions of poetry profoundly; his love of "the daylight meaning of words," as he put it in one of his autobiographical poems, stemmed from this education, and it was this sense of language that, from the beginning, Reznikoff developed into one of the most unusual and moving bodies of contemporary poetry. Reznikoff actually practiced law only briefly; he worked a number of years for *Corpus Juris*, the legal encyclopedia, however, and maintained his interest in the law throughout his entire career.

Except for short sojourns elsewhere, Reznikoff lived and worked in New York City. One three-year period, however, was spent in Hollywood working for a film producer; this visit was the source of some of Reznikoff's wittiest verse and furnished the background for his novel *The Manner "Music."* On his return to New York from Hollywood, Reznikoff took up freelance writing, editing, and translating.

Reznikoff was one of the city's great walkers; late in his life, he would still stroll for miles on foot through the city's parks and streets. In this regard, he was close to the boulevardiers and *flâneurs* of nineteenth century Paris so aptly described by Walter Benjamin. Like them, he was attracted to the anonymity of the solitary walker, to the possibility of a simultaneous distance and engagement. Out of such walks, Reznikoff fashioned an extraordinary body of poetry, one which only now after his death is receiving adequate critical attention. From younger poets and from those poets around him, George Oppen, Louis Zukofsky, and William Carlos Williams, attention had been there from the beginning. Reznikoff had early discovered something new and of major importance in the writing of poetry and stayed with it, despite neglect, throughout his long and fruitful life.

ANALYSIS

Of all the poets loosely gathered under the Objectivist label coined by Zukofsky for Harriet Monroe's *Poetry* magazine in 1931, none seems to have been quite as "objective" as Charles Reznikoff. In him, legal training and the moral imperative of the Jew as a historical witness combine with the Objectivist and Imagist principles, which guided such writers as Williams and Zukofsky, to produce a body of poetry distinguished by its clarity, judgment, and tact. This notion of witness or bystander, of someone who is at the scene of events but not of the events themselves, is implicit in all of Reznikoff's work. Such titles as *By the Waters of Manhattan: Selected Verse*, *Testimony*, *Separate Ways*, *Going To and Fro and Walking Up and Down*, and *By the Well of Living and Seeing* are indicative of a poetic stance that was to be, as Reznikoff once put it, "content at the periphery of such wonder." This wonder was to embrace both the urban experience, in particular its relation to the life of newly immigrant Jews, but also to range across such topics as early Jewish history, legal proceedings in nineteenth and twentieth century America, and the Holocaust.

THE URBAN ENVIRONMENT

Reznikoff's stance is not so much concerned with a conventional sense of poetic distance or with irony per se as with precision of realization. The modern city, the source of much of Reznikoff's most memorable work, is for him a place one continually passes through, a locus of large anonymous forces encountered tangentially yet which overshadow and overwhelm the experience of the city inhabitant. The truths of the city are multiple, highly individualized, and—in Reznikoff—caught not as part of some grand design but as minor resistance to its forces. Victories and defeats occur not in the towers and offices of government but in street corner and kitchen tableaux in which individual fate is registered. Thus, in his work, the urban environment and the lives caught up in the vast workings of the city and of history tend to remain resolutely what they are, to resist being read analogically or symbolically. The poems hover on the edge of factual materiality with few gestures toward the literary; yet their construction has a cleanliness and freshness found in few other contemporaries. One goes to Reznikoff's work not only for its poetic beauty and its surety of language but also for its historical testimony.

IMAGISM VS. IMAGE

Reznikoff began to publish his work in 1918, when the traditionalist devices of fixed meter and rhyme were already under attack from the modernism of Ezra Pound and T. S. Eliot. However, Reznikoff was not to traffic in the obviously unconventional or extreme writing of the early twentieth century avant-grade. Even the Imagist movement, which certainly influenced Reznikoff and to which he pays homage, was refined and transmuted by him into something that would not be particularly recognizable to the founders of the movement. The "image" of the Imagists was something decidedly literary, something used for its allusive or symbolic effect, whereas in Reznikoff it becomes a construction, made out of observation and precise detail, concerned primarily to render a datum.

This "nonliterary" use of the image characterizes all of Reznikoff's work. His poems strike the reader almost as a kind of low-key reportage, making use of proselike speech rhythms and barely discernible shifts in discourse from statement to simile or metaphor, as in this early example: "Suddenly we noticed we were in darkness/ So we went into the house and lit the lamp/ And sat around, dark spaces about a sun." This shorn-down language inhabits a number of linguistic realms at once; the datum and its meaning for the poet are so inextricably linked that the usual suspension of belief or accounting for poetic license no longer applies. The poetry has about it a "documentary" effect, one that is both tactful and powerful by virtue of its being stripped, it would seem, of any attempt by the poet to persuade.

Reznikoff's poetry can be likened to the photograph, something profoundly and intimately linked to the visible world, and yet, by virtue of the camera angle or constraint of the frame, necessarily and profoundly something selected. Like photographs, in which what is beyond the frame may be hinted at by that which is included, Reznikoff's poems, while framing actual particularities and occasions, resonate with a life of associations far beyond the frame of the image which the language constructs. This image, less metaphoric than informative, becomes a possibility for emotional response but not an occasion for dictating it. If through Reznikoff one sees or knows a certain life intimately, a history, custom or usage, it is because in his work the lyricist and the chronicler are joined with minimal rhetorical flourish.

RECITATIVE

This poetic technique, which Reznikoff called "recitative," stresses the evidential or communicative aspect of language over the figurative; it unites all of Reznikoff's work, from the early *Rhythms* published in 1918 up to and through the late volumes *Testimony* and *Holocaust*. This minimal use of poetic devices such as rhyme, metaphor, or exaggerated imagery results in a restrained tone that balances irony, sarcasm, and humor with emotional distance. It is particularly apt for the short two- or three-line poem (one of Reznikoff's trademarks) that combines a wise knowingness and bleak hilarity, as in: "Permit me to warn you/ against this automobile rushing to embrace you/ with outstretched fender." It also attains a meditative strength, as in: "Among the heaps of brick and plaster lies/ a girder, still itself among the rubbish." Here, the double reading of "still itself" transforms the poem from mere description to enigmatic philosophy.

Such surety of technique makes Reznikoff's poems radiate with both completeness of finish and mystery, as though their author, while knowing much, says little. Indeed, they sustain an aphoristic or epigrammatic tone, even in poems of great length and over a wide variety of subject matter.

In Reznikoff, this reticence has little to do with modesty. Rather, understatement becomes a device for achieving accurate registration, for giving subjects their due in the reader's mind by not imposing attitudes or judgments on experience. It is, in its way, a form of humility, a desire, as Reznikoff noted, that "we, whose lives are only a few words" meet in the thing seen not in the personality of the viewer.

SOLITUDE OF THE MORAL WITNESS

At the very center of Reznikoff's writing, concomitant with the objectivity of his technique, is the aloneness of the moral witness, of a deep and abiding solitude that moved C. P. Snow, in commenting on Reznikoff's work, to regard him as a lonely writer. In Reznikoff, this isolation is less a product of experience than of fundamental choice. As he says of his life in the poem "Autobiography: New York": "I am alone— and glad to be alone . . . I like the sound of the street—but I, apart and alone,/ beside an open window/ and behind a closed door." This desire for isolation, for witnessing as from a distance, can be traced back to the traditions embedded in Jewish religious and philosophical works which influenced him. In the Kabbalistic tradition that informs Reznikoff's work, language, as Gershom Scholem notes, "reflects the fundamental spiritual nature of the world." The Kabbalists, Scholem points out, "revel in objective description." This sacred attitude toward language is manifest in Reznikoff. As he says in one of his poems, "I have learned the Hebrew blessing before eating bread./ Is there no blessing before reading Hebrew?"

Coupled with this respect for language is the influence of Reznikoff's early legal training on his poetic style. As he relates of his law school days: "I found it delightful . . ./ to use words for their daylight meaning/ and not as prisms/ playing with the rainbows of connotation." Like Williams, Reznikoff seems to have thoroughly refused the artifice of high style in favor of the "daylight meaning" of words, to produce a style which is at once humane and communicative.

As Reznikoff's few prose comments on his poetry make clear, craft and technique stem for him from communicative and ethical concerns as opposed to literary ones, and it is this urge to communicate which is his primary motive. One finds in his work that nearly lost sense of the poet as teller of tales as tribal historian. The poet, according to Reznikoff (perhaps in particular the Jewish poet of the People of the Book) stands always with history at his back. For such a poet, the work is not one of self-expression but of a desire to be an agency for those voices lost or denied in time, for individuals caught up in historical forces beyond their control.

JEWS IN BABYLONIA

This urge to reclaim in Reznikoff has deeper implications, however, as demonstrated in one of Reznikoff's longer historical poems, *Jews in Babylonia*, where a collagist technique initially yokes natural phenomena—the passing of seasons, growth of plants, and the behavior of animals—with simple actions of the biblical tradesmen: "Plane the wood into boards; chisel the stone." The rhythms here are stately and the imagery peaceful. As the poem continues, however, the harmony begins to come apart. Now there is "A beast with its load/ and a bit in its mouth" and "the horn gores/ the hoof kicks/ the teeth bite." The shift in tone becomes even more "unnatural": "The bread has become moldy/ and the dates blown down by the wind . . . the dead woman has forgotten her comb." The lines become a litany of ruin and decay which has both historical and metaphysical implications: "But where are the dead of the Flood . . . the dead of Nebuchadnezzar?" until finally the images express a kind of visionary chaos where "the hyena will turn into a bat/ and a bat will turn into a thorn," where what is seen is "the blood of his wounds/ and the tears of her eyes" and "the Angel of Death in time of war/ does not distinguish/ between the righteous and the wicked."

The effect of this technique is to create something that seems at once cinematic and apocalyptic, forcefully in keeping with the historical situation itself while at the same time suggesting both foreboding and prophecy. In this regard, Reznikoff's work is no simple addition or nostalgic reminder of the past but, like the songs and poems of the biblical prophets, a potential guide to personal and social action. As he says of his grandfather's lost poetry in "By the Well of Living and Seeing": "All the verse he wrote was lost—except for what/ still speaks through me/ as mine."

TESTIMONY AND HOLOCAUST

It is in Reznikoff's most difficult and controversial works, *Testimony* and *Holocaust*, that his sense of historical urgency and the need to testify culminate. In these works, Reznikoff may be said to have created a new poetic form (or as some critics have claimed, absence of form) which is meant to do justice to the full weight of humankind's inhumanity to humans. In these two works, legal records—American courtroom proceedings in *Testimony* and the Nuremberg war crimes trials and the accounts of victims and witnesses in the case of *Holocaust*—are unsparingly worked into verse form, shorn of poetic devices. The author's hand appears solely in the austere editing and lineation of the historical record. Here, the "poetic" by its very absence in the poetry seems to be both witness and prosecutor, a reminder to the reader not only of the events that have occurred but also the life, grace, and possibility denied by the events. The works curiously penetrate the reader's consciousness since, by leaving all the individual interpretation, they undermine, in their account of devastating cruelty and horror, the reader's conventional notions of civilization and culture.

Such penetration, accomplished in such a "hands off" manner, has the further effect of evoking and calling to account the reader's humanity. It is this effect that gives Reznikoff's "objectivity" such moral power. This wedding of artistic means and the procedures of the law courts gives Reznikoff's work a unique contemporaneity, one that honors and respects the individual while in no way striving for egocentric novelty. This is a *communitas* at its most moving and profound. It can be said of Reznikoff that he is one of the few contemporary poets to have transformed literary artistry into a major historical vision.

OTHER MAJOR WORKS

LONG FICTION: *By the Waters of Manhattan*, 1930; *The Lionhearted*, 1944; *The Manner "Music,"* 1977.

PLAYS: *Uriel Accosta: A Play and a Fourth Group of Verse*, 1921; *"Chatterton," "The Black Death," and "Meriwether Lewis": Three Plays*, 1922; *"Coral" and "Captive Israel": Two Plays*, 1923.

NONFICTION: *Early History of a Sewing Machine Operator*, 1936; *First, There Is the Need*, 1977; *Selected Letters of Charles Reznikoff, 1917-1976*, 1997.

TRANSLATIONS: *Stories and Fantasies from the Jewish Past*, 1951 (of Emil Cohn); *Three Years in America, 1859-1862*, 1956 (of Israel Joseph Benjamin).

EDITED TEXT: *Louis Marshall, Champion of Liberty: Selected Papers and Addresses*, 1957 (2 volumes).

BIBLIOGRAPHY

Fredman, Stephen. *A Menorah for Athena: Charles Reznikoff and the Jewish Dilemmas of Objectivist Poetry*. Chicago: University of Chicago Press, 2001. An analysis of the poetry of Reznikoff and objectivity in literature. Includes bibliographical references and index.

Gefin, Laszlo K. *Ideogram: History of a Poetic Method*. Austin: University of Texas Press, 1982. Gefin cites Reznikoff as one of the poets who use the synthetical or ideogrammatic method in their poetry. He sees this composition as an "aesthetic form extending from a postlogical and even posthumanist consciousness." In the chapter titled "Sincerity and Objectification," Gefin remarks on the influence of Chinese poetry on Reznikoff and, at the same time, calls him the "Giacometti of poetry," because he pares down his words to bare essentials.

Heller, Michael. "Reznikoff's Modernity." *American Book Review* 2 (July/August, 1980): 3. Reviews a number of Reznikoff's works in the light of modernism. States that this poet stands out in the continuity of his work rather than the more usual modernist discontinuity. Admires Reznikoff's restraint and his ability to allow readers to come to their own conclusions.

Hindus, Milton. *Charles Reznikoff: Man and Poet.* Orono, Maine: National Poetry Foundation, 1984. A full-length study, initially conceived to correct the relative obscurity and neglect of Reznikoff. Half the volume is devoted to the author's personal accounts of Reznikoff's life; the latter half is a compilation of important critical essays on his poetry. Includes a section on his prose and concludes with a useful and thorough annotated bibliography of his works.

Omer-Sherman, Ranen. "Revisiting Charles Reznikoff's Urban Poetics of Diaspora and Contingency." In *Radical Poetics and Secular Jewish Culture*, edited by Stephen Paul Miller and Daniel Morris. Tuscaloosa: University of Alabama Press, 2010. An examination of the urban Jewish culture in Reznikoff's poetry.

Reznikoff, Charles. *Family Chronicle.* New York: Markus Wiener, 1988. A fascinating background account of the Reznikoff family, from their origins in Russia to their immigration to the United States and establishment in New York. Contains three accounts of family members, including "Needle Trade," an autobiographical piece by Reznikoff, and much useful information that illuminates the themes in his poetry.

_____. *Selected Letters of Charles Reznikoff, 1917-1976.* Edited by Milton Hindus. Santa Rosa, Calif.: Black Sparrow Press, 1997. A collection of letters that reveal some of the poet, but much more of the man. Includes an essay by Hindus on Reznikoff's life and work.

Vescia, Monique Claire. *Depression Glass: Documentary Photography and the Medium of the Camera-Eye in Charles Reznikoff, George Oppen, and William Carlos Williams.* New York: Routledge, 2006. Examines photographic and linguistic images in three works—Reznikoff's *Testimony*, Oppen's *Discrete Series* (1934), and Williams's *Collected Poems, 1921-1931* (1934)—as well as camera work by Walker Evans, Lewis Hines, and Alfred Stieglitz to find what is shared between documentary photography and modern poetry.

Michael Heller

ADRIENNE RICH

Born: Baltimore, Maryland; May 16, 1929

OTHER LITERARY FORMS

Adrienne Rich is known primarily for her poetry, but she has produced essays on writing and politics as well: *Of Woman Born: Motherhood as Experience and Institution* (1976) is an analysis of the changing meanings of childbirth and motherhood in Anglo-American culture, in which Rich draws on personal experience as well as sources in mythology, sociology, economics, the history of medicine, and literature to develop her analysis. *On Lies, Secrets, and Silence: Selected Prose, 1966-1978* (1979) is a collection of essays on women writers (including Anne Bradstreet, Anne Sexton, Charlotte Brontë, and Emily Dickinson) and feminism. *Blood, Bread, and Poetry: Selected*

Prose, 1979-1985 (1986) followed with further essays on women writers and feminist criticism. *What Is Found There: Notebooks on Poetry and Politics* (1993) delivers just what the title promises. For several years Rich also coedited, with Michelle Cliff, the lesbian feminist journal *Sinister Wisdom*.

ACHIEVEMENTS

Adrienne Rich's work has been at the vanguard of the women's movement in the United States. Her poems and essays explore her own experience and seek to develop a "common language" for women to communicate their values and perceptions. She has received numerous awards, including two Guggenheim Fellowships, the National Institute of Arts and Letters Award for Poetry (1960), the Shelley Memorial Award of the Poetry Society of America (1971), and the National Book Award (1974) for *Diving into the Wreck*. Other recognitions include the Ruth Lilly Poetry Prize (1986), the Northern California Book Award in poetry (1989), the Bill Whitehead Award (1990), Lambda Literary Awards (1991, 1995, 2001), the Lenore Marshall Poetry Prize (1992), the Academy of American Poets Fellowship (1992), the *Los Angeles Times* Book Prize (1992), the Frost Medal (1992), a MacArthur Fellowship, the Poets' Prize (1993), the Fred Cody Award for lifetime achievement (1994), the Wallace Stevens Award (1996), the Lifetime Achievement Award from the Lannan Foundation (1999), the Bollingen Prize (2003), and the Medal for Distinguished Contribution to American Letters from the National Book Foundation (2006). In 2004, *The School Among the Ruins* earned Rich the National Book Critics Circle Award, the Gold Medal from the Commonwealth Club of California, and the Poetry Center Book Award. She served as chancellor for the Academy of American Poets from 1999 to 2001.

BIOGRAPHY

Adrienne Cecile Rich was born in 1929, into a white, middle-class southern family. Her Jewish father, Arnold Rice Rich, taught medicine at The Johns Hopkins University. Her southern Protestant mother, Helen Jones Rich, was trained as a composer and concert pianist but gave up her career to devote herself to her husband and two daughters. She carried out their early education at home, until the girls began to attend school in fourth grade. Her father encouraged his daughter to read and to write poetry. In his library, she found the work of such writers as Matthew Arnold, William Blake, Thomas Carlyle, John Keats, Dante Gabriel Rossetti, and Alfred, Lord Tennyson. Rich graduated from Radcliffe College in 1951, the year her first volume of poetry was published. She traveled in Europe and England on a Guggenheim Fellowship in 1952-1953.

Rich married Alfred H. Conrad in 1953 and in the next few years gave birth to three sons, David (1955), Paul (1957), and Jacob (1959). She lived with her family in Cambridge, Massachusetts, from 1953 to 1966, but spent 1961-1962 in the Netherlands on

Adrienne Rich
(Library of Congress)

another Guggenheim Fellowship. In 1964, Rich began her involvement in the New Left, initiating a period of personal and political growth and crisis. In 1966, the family moved to New York, where Conrad taught at City College of New York. Rich also began to teach at City College, where she worked for the first time with disadvantaged students. In 1970, Rich ended her marriage, and later the same year, Conrad ended his life. Rich continued teaching at City College and then Rutgers University until 1979, when she moved to western Massachusetts. Poems of these years explore her lesbian relationships.

Rich eventually moved to northern California to continue her active career as poet, essayist, and sought-after speaker. Rich spent time in the 1980's and early 1990's at numerous California colleges and universities, acting as visiting professor and lecturer. Her stops included Scripps College, San Jose State University, and Stanford University. In 1992, she accepted the National Director of the National Writer's Voice Project. In the 1990's, she joined several advisory boards, including the Boston Woman's Fund, National Writers Union, Sisterhood in Support of Sisters in South Africa, and New Jewish Agenda.

ANALYSIS

Adrienne Rich's successive volumes of poetry chronicle a contemporary female artist's odyssey. Her earliest work is a notable contribution to modern poetry. Her later work has broken new ground as she redefines and reimagines women's lives to create a female myth of self-discovery. In her life and work, she has been struggling to break out of patriarchal social and literary conventions, to redefine herself and to create new traditions. W. H. Auden praised her first volume for its stylistic control, its skillful use of traditional themes such as isolation, and its assimilation of influences such as the work of Robert Frost and William Butler Yeats. He wrote: "The poems . . . in this book are neatly and modestly dressed, speak quietly but do not mumble, respect their elders but are not cowed by them, and do not tell fibs."

Since then, however, Rich has been reshaping poetic conventions to develop her own themes and to create her own voice, often a radical (and sometimes a jarring) one. Reviewer Helen Vendler termed *Diving into the Wreck* "dispatches from the battlefield." Central concerns of Rich's poetry include the uses of history and language, the relationship of the individual to society, and the individual's quest for identity and meaning. The home is often a site for the working out of these themes.

A CHANGE OF WORLD

Auden chose Rich's first volume of poetry, *A Change of World*, for the Yale Younger Poets Award. Despite the title, the poems have to do with resisting change. Rich's early training at her father's hands reinforced her allegiance to a literary tradition of meticulous craft, of "beauty" and "perfection." Accordingly, these poems are objective, carefully crafted, and rhymed, with echoes of W. H. Auden, T. S. Eliot, and Robert Frost. A recurring image is that of the home as a refuge that is threatened by social instability ("The Uncle Speaks in the Drawing Room") or natural forces ("Storm Warnings"). The women in these poems remain at home, occupied with women's tasks such as embroidering ("Aunt Jennifer's Tigers"), weaving ("Mathilde in Normandy"), and caring for their families ("Eastport to Block Island"). A central theme of these poems is the use of art as a technique for ordering experience ("Aunt Jennifer's Tigers" and "At a Bach Concert"). "At a Bach Concert" is written in a musically complex form, a variant of the intricate terza rima stanza used by Dante. Rich's poem weaves together many strands of poetic technique (assonance, consonance, internal rhyme, off-rhyme, alliteration) and rhetorical devices (oxymoron and parallelism) into a rich textural harmony to develop the theme that formal structure is the poet's gift of love: "Form is the ultimate gift that love can offer—/ The vital union of necessity/ With all that we desire, all that we suffer."

THE DIAMOND CUTTERS

The theme of artistic control and craft is repeated in Rich's second book, *The Diamond Cutters*. Written when Rich was traveling in Europe as the recipient of a

Guggenheim Traveling Fellowship, this volume is a tourist's poetic diary. Landscape and scenery are prominent. The book blends two moods, nostalgia for a more beautiful past and ironic disillusionment with a present that falls short of perfection (as in "The Ideal Landscape," "Lucifer in the Train," or "The Strayed Village." In a profound way, all the characters in this book are exiles, aliens, uneasy in the places they inhabit. The heroines of poems such as "Autumn Equinox," "The Prospect," and "The Perennial Answer" are dissatisfied with their lives but unable to change. They hold on to history and to the social structures it has produced, refusing to question present conditions. Suppressed anger and unacknowledged tensions lie just beneath the surface of all the poems; the book's tone is passive, flat. Eight years passed before Rich's next book appeared. Its stylistic and thematic changes reflect changes in her outlook.

SNAPSHOTS OF A DAUGHTER-IN-LAW

In her next two books, *Snapshots of a Daughter-in-Law* and *Necessities of Life*, Rich begins to move from conventional poetic forms, to develop her own style, and to deal more directly with personal experience. Her attitudes toward literary tradition, history, and the home have changed markedly. She questions traditional attitudes toward home and family. As she found the patriarchal definitions of human relationships inadequate, her work became more personal and more urgent.

Snapshots of a Daughter-in-Law is written in a looser form than Rich's previous work. Language is simpler, texture less dense. The title poem is a series of vignettes of women's experiences. It fairly bristles with quotations drawn from Rich's wide-ranging reading. According to the poem, male authorities have always defined women in myths and literature. Thus, women lacked a literature of their own in which to define themselves. Rich wrote that she composed the poem "in fragments during children's naps, brief hours in a library, or at 3 A.M. after rising with a wakeful child." Because of these interruptions, she wrote the poem over a two-year period. In this poem, she wrote, "for the first time, directly about experiencing myself as a woman" rather than striving to be "universal." As the title indicates, these are static, fixed vignettes: The women are trapped, denied scope for action and choice.

Another poem in this volume, "The Roofwalker," speaks again of entrapment. The poem's speaker is a builder or architect who is no longer satisfied with the enclosure he has built. The role of the artist is here redefined. Whereas "At a Bach Concert" celebrated the need for objectivity, distance, and form, the speaker of "The Roofwalker" feels constrained by forms: "Was it worth while to lay—/ with infinite exertion—/ a roof I can't live under?" The poet begins to wonder whether her tools—rhyme, alliteration, meter, poetic conventions—are stifling her imagination.

The well-planned house that Rich rejects in "The Roofwalker" is the house of formalist poetry as well. She finds the measured stanzas, rhymed couplets, and blank verse rhythms of her earlier books too rigid for her present purposes. Writing a poem no longer means finding a form for a preconceived idea. Instead, each experience informs its own expression; the poem is not product, but process. The poet, like "The Roof-walker," must break out of the stultifying traditional structure. Like most of her contemporaries, she has come to write in freer forms. Yet Rich never abandons rational structure or rootedness in social context as do some experimental writers.

NECESSITIES OF LIFE

Rich's next book, *Necessities of Life*, continues her movement toward a freer poetic line and toward subjectivity. Where she formerly spoke of history in terms of objects and products of tradition, she now identifies with historical persons (Antinous, Emily Dickinson, and others). A struggle between death and life, between winter and spring, is in process. Indoor-outdoor imagery carries the weight of these tensions. Poems of death and disappearance take place indoors; the expansive, life-enhancing experiences occur outdoors.

These poems are a retreat from the angry stance of "Snapshots of a Daughter-in-Law" and the daring escape of "The Roofwalker." In *Necessities of Life*, Rich feels oppressed by the human world, so she turns to nature for sustenance. *Necessities of Life* establishes a deep relationship with the world of nature; it is one of the "bare essentials" that preserve the heroine in her difficulties. Through a bond with the vegetable and animal world, the world of warmth and light, the book is able to bring life to bear against death and darkness. Nature's cyclical pattern provides clues for survival. Plants move from winter's icy grip into spring's renewal by learning to exist on little. To achieve similar rebirth, humans must consciously will change and force themselves into action. This is the pattern of death and rebirth that structures the book.

LEAFLETS

Rich's first four books are built on linear oppositions. Balanced groups of stanzas articulate dichotomies between art and emotion, control and chaos, passivity and action, indoors and outdoors. Often characters must choose between alternatives. Tension between polarities becomes a controlling force, focusing the poems' energies. In her next books of poetry, Rich would modify the dualistic structure of the earlier books. At the end of *Leaflets*, she introduces the *ghazal*, a series of two-line units that conflate many ideas. These poems are collagelike, offering multiple perspectives.

Prompted by her increasing social concern and the leftist political critique evolving in the middle and later 1960's, Rich turned from personal malaise to political struggle, from private meditation to public discourse. Her jarring tone reflects her anger and impatience with language. Rhythms are broken, speech is fragmented. The poems suggest hurried diary entries. Images of violence, guerrilla warfare, and global human suffering suggest an embattled society. Yet anger is close kin to hope: It asserts the wish to effect change. Therefore, alongside the destruction, symbols of fertility and rebirth appear.

Rich writes of an old tradition dying and a new one struggling to be born. Fear of change dominated her earlier books, but the "will to change" is paramount here. The poems of this period describe Rich's heroines casting off traditional roles and preparing for journeys. The titles of the next three books represent steps in this process. *Leaflets* is a manifesto for public involvement, *The Will to Change* is the determination to move forward, and *Diving into the Wreck*, the first title to contain a verb, is the act itself.

The evolution of *Leaflets* epitomizes Rich's movement from the personal to the political. The first poem, "Orion," is written in regular six-line stanzas and built on a typical pattern of balanced contrast. Indoors and outdoors, feminine and masculine, stagnation and adventure are the poles. The poem is a monologue in which the speaker blames herself for her failures as a woman. In contrast, the last poem in the book, "Ghazals," is a series of unrhymed couplets arranged in a seemingly random conflation of ideas and images. "Ghazals" is a multivoiced political critique of contemporary America. The heroes and heroines of the book are revolutionaries, protesters, and challengers of an old order: Frantz Fanon, Walt Whitman, Galileo, LeRoi Jones (Amiri Baraka), Eldridge Cleaver, and Dian Fossey. Turning her back on a political tradition that she now equates with death and destruction, Rich is saddened and estranged. However, she not only wants to last until the new tradition begins but also will attempt to create that new tradition. To do so, she must substitute new ideas and modes of expression for the old, wishing "to choose words that even you/ would have to be changed by" ("Implosions"). Because the values and attitudes she wants to modify are so deeply entrenched in people's most fundamental assumptions, language itself must be reshaped to provide a vocabulary equal to her task of reconstruction. Consequently, language becomes a crucial issue.

Rich believes that "only where there is language is there world" ("The Demon Lover"). She fears, however, that the English language is "spoiled." If the poet is using the "oppressor's language," how may her words avoid contamination?

THE WILL TO CHANGE

Rich's powerful meditation on language and power "The Burning of Paper Instead of Children" (in *The Will to Change*) draws on her classroom experience with disadvantaged students. Unlike the poet, whose privileged childhood opened the possibilities of language to her, the children of the ghetto find the worlds of literacy and power closed to them. Rich quotes a student whose grammatical awkwardness lends his description of poverty a pointed eloquence: "a child steal because he did not have money to buy it: to hear a mother say she do not have money to buy food for her children . . . it will make tears in your eyes." Because she mistrusts rhetoric, the poet closes her meditation with a prose passage of bald statement.

I am in danger. You are in danger. The burning of a book arouses no sensation in me. I know it hurts to burn. There are flames of napalm in Catonsville, Maryland. I know it hurts to burn.

The typewriter is overheated, my mouth is burning, I cannot touch you and this is the oppressor's language.

Her simple syntax affirms her identification with the disadvantaged student, the oppressed. In her refusal to use complex diction or traditional metrics she argues by implication for a rhetoric of honesty and simplicity.

DIVING INTO THE WRECK

Rich's poetry revises the heroic myth to reflect women's experiences. *Diving into the Wreck* presents questing female heroes for the first time in her work. On their quests, they reconnect with lost parts of themselves, discover their own power, and build commonality with other women. Women's lives are the central focus as Rich's project becomes that of giving voice to women's experience, developing a "common language" that will bring the "dark country" of women's lives into the common light of day. Yet Rich also claims another task for women: They must struggle to redeem an endangered society. She argues that patriarchy's exaggerated aggressiveness, competition, and repression of feeling have led Western civilization to the brink of extinction. The task of reconstruction must be taken up by women. Working for change, the women in this book seek to turn civilization from its destructive paths by persuasion, creation of new myths, or redirection of anger.

To understand and overcome patriarchy's suicidal impulses, Rich attempts to open a dialogue. Almost all the poems in *Diving into the Wreck* are cast as dialogue. Conversation is the book's central metaphor for poetry. The book begins with "Trying to Talk with a Man," a poem that deals with the dangers of an accelerating arms race but also has a deeper subject: the creation of a dialogue between men and women. Considering gender a political issue, Rich calls on men to join her in rethinking gender questions.

The book, however, comes to question the possibility of real communication. "Translations" examines the gulf between the languages spoken by women and men. In "Meditations for a Savage Child," the concluding poem, scientists cannot teach the child to speak.

POEMS: SELECTED AND NEW, 1950-1974

Poems: Selected and New, 1950-1974 includes early unpublished poems and several new ones. In the final poem of this book, "From an Old House in America," Rich uses the home image as a starting point for a reconsideration of American history from a woman's point of view. She reimagines the lives of women, from immigrants to pioneers to the new generation of feminist activists. All are journeying. Simple and direct in language, written in stanzas of open couplets, the poem is a stream-of-consciousness meditation that builds in force as it imagines the unwritten history of North American women and reaches a profound celebration of sisterhood.

Thus, by the end of the book, the woman at home is transformed from the cautious door-closer of "Storm Warnings" (*A Change of World*) into the active participant in history and the questing adventurer eager to define herself by exploration and new experience.

THE DREAM OF A COMMON LANGUAGE

Transformation is the cornerstone of *The Dream of a Common Language* and *A Wild Patience Has Taken Me This Far*. The poet wishes to effect fundamental changes in social arrangements, in concepts of selfhood, in governmental politics, in the meanings of sexuality, and in language. To that end, transformation supplants her earlier idea of revolution.

The title *The Dream of a Common Language* suggests vision, community, and above all a language in which visions and shared experience may be conceived and expressed. Dream is the voice of the nocturnal, unconscious self breaking into daytime existence. The terrain Rich explores here is the unknown country of the self, discovered in dream, myth, vision, and ritual. Like dreams, the poems telescope time and space to make new connections among past, present, and future, between home and world. "Common" signifies that which is communal, habitual, shared, widely used, and ordinary. Rich sets great value on the common, choosing it over the extraordinary.

In *The Dream of a Common Language*, the poet affirms that poetry stems from "the drive/ to connect. The dream of a common language." The book's central section, "Twenty-One Love Poems," orchestrates the controlling themes of women's love, power, language, world. Images of light and dark, dream and reality, speech and silence, home and wanderer structure the sequence. There are in fact twenty-two poems, for Rich has included an unnumbered "Floating Poem." Drawing from the sonnet tradition, Rich breaks formal conventions by varying the poems' lengths and departing from strict rhyme and meter. The sequence records a particular lesbian relationship, its joyous beginnings, the difficulties encountered, and the termination of the relationship. The poems ask questions about the meanings of self, language, and love between women, and about the possibilities of sustaining love in a hostile world. Rich insists on grounding her explorations in the quotidian as well as the oneiric world. To be "at home" in the world requires coming to terms with the ugliness and brutality of the city, the pain and wounds, as well as the beauty of love and poetry. Deliberately, Rich situates the first sonnet of her sequence "in this city," with its "rainsoaked garbage."

Because she wishes to escape false romanticism, Rich seeks to connect the poems firmly to the world of daily life, to avoid sentimentality, and to speak honestly of her feelings. Because she wishes to transform the self-effacing behavior that has typically characterized women in love, she stresses self-awareness and deliberate choice. Caves and circles—images of roundness, completeness, and wholeness—are dominant. Like the homes of Rich's earlier work, they are enclosures; however, the meaning of encirclement has been transformed, for in her new vision, the poet no longer escapes from the world in her narrow room but reaches out to include the world, to bring it within her protected circle.

Poem 21, the final poem of the sequence, is a complex network of dreamlike associations, of ritual and archetypal memory. In the sonnet, Rich moves from dark into light, from the prehistoric into the present, from inanimate nature ("the color of stone") into purposeful consciousness ("more than stone"). She becomes by choice "a figure in the light." The clarity of intelligence—"a cleft of light"—shapes her purpose. In drawing the circle, she deliberately chooses her place.

Particularly in the last three poems of the book, there is a sacramental quality, as Rich affirms her fusion with a world of women working together throughout time. Weaving, cooking, and caring for children, they are crafting beautiful and utilitarian objects such as ceramic vessels, quilts, and clothing. Through these tasks, they create mementos of their lives and carry out the work of making a world.

"Transcendental Etude" is a long meditative poem of great richness and power. It traces the course of birth, death, and rebirth through a creativity that heals splits in the natural world and within the self. The poem begins in the pastoral imagery of an August evening and ranges over the realms of nature and of human life. Rich's vision here transforms the poet's craft. As a poet, she need not be, as she had once feared, an egocentric artist seeking undying fame at the expense of those she loves. Instead, through participation in the life of the physical universe, she articulates the patterns of her own being, of life itself. Thus, Rich's new metaphor of the poet is at once the most daring and the most simple: The poet is a common woman.

Achieving a selfhood that encompasses both creative work and human relationships, egotism and altruism, Rich and her women heal their psychic split in the symbolic return to home, to the full self represented by the circle. The voyage into history, the unconsciousness, the mind is completed in the return.

EXPLORING WOMEN'S SHARED PASTS

The next group of books—*A Wild Patience Has Taken Me This Far*, *Sources*, *The Fact of a Doorframe*, *Your Native Land, Your Life*, and *Time's Power*—continue to develop the themes broached in *The Dream of a Common Language*: exploration of women's shared past, the struggle to be "at home" in a strife-torn world, the vision of transforming the self and the world. Here again the imagery is that of simple, ordinary objects important to women's lives: books, kettles, and beets. Yet these books speak in a more muted voice, the voice of resolution, acceptance, accomplishment, with less anger.

A Wild Patience Has Taken Me This Far is to a large extent a dialogue with nineteenth century women writers and thinkers: the Brontës, Susan B. Anthony, Elizabeth Barrett Browning. "Culture and Anarchy" takes its title from Matthew Arnold's essay on nineteenth century culture. Arnold longed for a literate, elite, verbal culture; Rich, on the other hand, celebrates a world of women's work, both verbal and nonverbal. Here, growing and cooking vegetables, responding to nature's seasonal rhythms, the simple tasks of women's lives, form a valuable cultural matrix out of which arise the heroic actions of individual women.

Rich's poem is a quilting together of the words of historical women (derived from the diaries and letters of Emily Dickinson, Susan B. Anthony, Elizabeth Barrett Browning, and Jane Addams) and meditation on her own life and work. The women's voices here replace the quotations of male words in "Snapshots of a Daughter-in-Law." Again, Rich telescopes time, bringing the earlier women into the circle of her life, joining them in their acts and visions.

In *Sources*, Rich returns to her past and engages in a dialogue with her dead father and husband. She is trying to come to terms with her own life and to put the lives of the others into perspective. *Your Native Land, Your Life* and *Time's Power* continue to develop the persona of the poet as representative woman facing the issues of her country and time. Language and poetry and their relation to history remain foci of concern: in "North American Time" she writes

> Poetry never stood a chance
> of standing outside history.
>
> . . . .
>
> We move   but our words stand
> become responsible
> for more than we intended

In the ruefully ironic "Blue Rock" she writes

> Once when I wrote poems they did not change
> left overnight on the page
>
> . . . .
>
> But now I know what happens while I sleep
> and when I wake the poem has changed:
> the facts have dilated it, or cancelled it.

Time's Power is a book of dialogue, with the poet's mother, her lover, and a cast of historical figures. "Letters in the Family" is a series of imagined letters written by fictionalized historical persons, such as a friend of the Hungarian partisan Chana Senesh or a South African mother writing to her child. The book ends with "Turning," a poem of quest for knowledge. It articulates a question the poet-speaker asks as she tries to understand her ongoing quest: "So why am I out here, trying/ to read your name in the illegible air?"

MIDNIGHT SALVAGE

Rich subtly moves toward a quieter wisdom in *Midnight Salvage*, passing the torch and trying to impart to future readers and writers what she has learned and how she learned it. In doing so, she reminisces of her girlhood and her past selves' varied goals and causes, perhaps best captured in the title poem, an ambitious, eight-section piece that sorts through her history. Her experience with aging and illness brings forth the subject matter of physical torture. "Shattered Head" ranges from one body's devastation ("a life hauls itself uphill") to the betrayal of the many, and by the end of the poem, to the victims of torture or warfare ("who did this to us?"). Her work continues to be combative, yet in this volume, it is in a quiet, more indirect way.

FOX

Fox continues to meld Rich's art with conviction, her familiar attentions to social injustice and intense personal introspection still present. She praises, commemorates, and questions friends and public figures, while also probing what political action means. Her usual strident tone makes a small retreat here, however, and her voice is less edgy, a little more malleable, than in previous collections. As she declares in "Regardless," a poem about loving a man, "we'd love/ regardless of manifestoes I wrote or signed." Yet familiar themes are present, whether she is writing about war in the long, provocative poem "Veterans Day," female identity in the searing title poem, or the violence witnessed by a woman in "Second Sight," and Rich continues to give voice to the most fundamental of feelings.

POETIC EVOLUTION

Rich's successive volumes of poetry reveal her development as poet and as woman. As she breaks out from restrictive traditions, her voice is achieving power and authenticity. From a poet of isolation and withdrawal, of constraint and despair, she has become a seer of wide-ranging communal sympathy and great imaginative possibility. She is redefining in her life and poetry the meanings of language, poetry, love, power, and home. In her earlier life and work, she accepted patriarchal definitions. Consequently, she felt trapped in personal and poetic conventions: a marriage that curbed her creativity, an aesthetic that split form and feeling, a language that ignored her experience, a position of powerlessness.

At first, she spoke in a derivative voice, the language of the "universal." Reluctant to speak as a woman, she echoed the tone of her male poetic ancestors. Because she hesitated to voice her own experience, her early poems are highly polished but avoid emotional depth. She grew to mistrust a language that seemed alien. The fragmented, provisional, stark poems of *Leaflets*, *The Will to Change*, and *Diving into the Wreck* record her groping toward a new language in which to voice her deepest concerns. In subsequent books, she wrote in a freer form, viewing poems as "speaking to their moment."

This stance is particularly noticeable in such works of the 1990's as *An Atlas of the Difficult World*, with its powerhouse title poem, *Dark Fields of the Republic*, and *Midnight Salvage*. These volumes, produced almost on schedule every three or four years, also suggest less urgency and a more relaxed authority as a voice at once personal and representative. In *Fox*, there seems to be a gradual falling off of intensity, a quieter wisdom, as Rich moves into her seventies.

Through the major phases of her career, the transformations of Rich's home imagery parallel her growth of poetic force and political awareness. In early poems, the home was entrapping, because patriarchal voices defined women's roles. As Rich's women became more self-defining, the old relationships were abandoned or modified to fit the real needs of the persons involved. Achieving selfhood, Rich's female heroes came to seize control of their homes, their lives. Through metaphorical journeys exploring the world, women's history, and their own psychic heights and depths, they struggle for knowledge and self-mastery. Healing their tormenting self-division, they grow more "at home" in the world. They recognize and cherish their links to a women's tradition of great power and beauty and to the natural world. In this process, the idea of home has acquired new significance: from frail shelter or painful trap it has grown to a gateway, the starting point for journeys of self-exploration, and the magic circle to which women return so that they may participate in the work of "making and remaking" the world.

OTHER MAJOR WORKS

NONFICTION: *Of Woman Born: Motherhood as Experience and Institution*, 1976; *On Lies, Secrets, and Silence: Selected Prose, 1966-1978*, 1979; *Blood, Bread, and Poetry: Selected Prose, 1979-1985*, 1986; *What Is Found There: Notebooks on Poetry and Politics*, 1993, 2003; *Arts of the Possible: Essays and Conversations*, 2001; *Poetry and Commitment: An Essay*, 2007; *A Human Eye: Essays on Art in Society, 1997-2008*, 2009.

EDITED TEXTS: *The Best American Poetry, 1996*, 1996; *Selected Poems / Muriel Rukeyser*, 2004.

MISCELLANEOUS: *Adrienne Rich's Poetry and Prose: Poems, Prose, Reviews, and Criticism*, 1993 (Barbara Chartesworth Gelpi and Albert Gelpi, editors).

BIBLIOGRAPHY

Cooper, Jane Roberta, ed. *Reading Adrienne Rich: Review and Re-visions, 1951-1981.* Ann Arbor: University of Michigan Press, 1984. A useful collection of reviews and critical studies of Rich's poetry and prose. It includes Auden's foreword to *A Change of World* and other significant essays. The aim is for breadth and balance.

Dickie, Margaret. *Stein, Bishop, and Rich: Lyrics of Love, War, and Place.* Chapel Hill: University of North Carolina Press, 1997. Examination of the poets Rich, Gertrude Stein, and Elizabeth Bishop. Three of the book's nine chapters are devoted to Rich. Bibliography, index.

Estrin, Barbara L. *The American Love Lyric After Auschwitz and Hiroshima.* New York: Palgrave, 2001. Estrin finds a connection between the language of the love lyric and hate speech. Using the specific examples of Rich, Wallace Stevens, and Robert Lowell, she expresses a revisionist critique of twentieth American poetry, supporting the theory that the love lyric is political.

Gelpi, Barbara Charlesworth, and Albert Gelpi, eds. *Adrienne Rich's Poetry and Prose.* New York: W. W. Norton, 1993. This volume in the Norton Critical Edition series presents a significant sampling of Rich's work, biographical materials, and a carefully representative selection of essays (sometimes excerpted) and reviews. It provides a chronology and a list of selected criticism for further study.

Keyes, Claire. *The Aesthetics of Power: The Poetry of Adrienne Rich.* Athens: University of Georgia Press, 1986. Keyes discusses Rich as a feminist poet. Introduction provides a biographical and historical overview. Each of the ten chapters discusses one of Rich's books, from *A Change of World* through *A Wild Patience Has Taken Me This Far.*

Langdell, Cheryl Colby. *Adrienne Rich: The Moment of Change.* Westport, Conn.: Praeger, 2004. This biography of Rich traces her several transformations through analyses of her poems.

Ratcliffe, Krista. *Anglo-American Feminist Challenges to the Rhetorical Traditions: Virginia Woolf, Mary Daly, Adrienne Rich.* Carbondale: Southern Illinois University Press, 1996. A feminist perspective on the rhetoric and literary devices of writers-critics Rich, Virginia Woolf, and Mary Daly. Bibliography, index.

Templeton, Alice. *The Dream and the Dialogue: Adrienne Rich's Feminist Poetics.* Knoxville: University of Tennessee Press, 1994. Templeton finds each of Rich's volumes both responsive to and party to the dominant critical issues at the time of publication. Templeton's exploration of Rich's "feminist poetics" posits feminism as a way of reading literature, so that reading in itself becomes a political act.

Waddell, William S., ed. *"Catch If You Can Your Country's Moment": Recovery and Regeneration in the Poetry of Adrienne Rich.* Newcastle, England: Cambridge Scholars, 2007. A collection of eight essays on Rich's poetry that focuses on the themes of recovery and regeneration. Looks at her development from a poet dealing with feminist personal topics to one dealing with public, political issues.

Yorke, Liz. *Adrienne Rich: Passion, Politics, and the Body.* Newbury Park, Calif.: Sage, 1998. This accessible introduction to Rich's work reviews the process and development of her ideas, tracing her place in the major debates within second-wave feminism. Yorke assesses Rich's contribution to feminism and outlines her ideas on motherhood, heterosexuality, lesbian identity, Jewish identity, and issues of racial and sexual otherness.

Karen F. Stein; Philip K. Jason
Updated by Sarah Hilbert

ISAAC ROSENBERG

Born: Bristol, England; November 25, 1890
Died: Near Arras, France; April 1, 1918

OTHER LITERARY FORMS

Isaac Rosenberg's *Moses* combines poetry with verse drama. Rosenberg's prose, letters, and drawings can be found in two collections of his works, one edited by Gordon Bottomley and Denys Harding and published in 1937 and the other edited by Ian Parsons and published in 1979.

ACHIEVEMENTS

Isaac Rosenberg was one of a group of young poets, including Rupert Brooke, Edward Thomas, and Wilfred Owen, whose lives were tragically cut short by World War I. Rosenberg's early poems were slight; it is as a war poet that his reputation was established, largely through the efforts of his mentor, Gordon Bottomley. What makes him unusual among British poets in general and war poets in particular is his Jewish perspective. That aspect coupled with his working-class background sets his poetry apart from the Georgian tones of Thomas or Brooke, or the upper-class tones of Siegfried Sassoon or Robert Graves.

BIOGRAPHY

Isaac Rosenberg was the son of Barnett Rosenberg and Hacha Davidov. His father was a Lithuanian Jew whose impoverished family had emigrated from Russia to Bristol, England, shortly before Rosenberg's birth. Soon after, they moved to the East End of London, which was then the center of the Jewish immigrant community, a community that existed as a tightly knit group until the 1960's and from which emerged such Jewish writers as the dramatists Bernard Kops and Arnold Wesker.

His father opened his own butcher shop; when that failed, he became an itinerant peddler. The family lived in constant poverty, but it was cohesive, and Isaac Rosenberg grew up in a religious atmosphere. After an elementary school education, Rosenberg showed some artistic promise, and in 1907, he began attending evening classes at

Birkbeck College, an affiliated college of the University of London, set up especially to help poor students. In 1908, he won the Mason Prize for his nude studies as well as several other awards. To earn a living, he became apprenticed to an engraver.

A few people noticed Rosenberg's talent and sponsored him at the Slade, London's most prestigious art school, which he entered in 1911. There he was influenced by such British artists as the Pre-Raphaelites, particularly Dante Gabriel Rossetti, and also by William Blake and the modernist Roger Fry. While continuing to study at the Slade, he struck out as an artist, setting up a studio in 1912 in Hampstead Road. He had also been writing poetry and sent some of it to Laurence Binyon, an established Georgian poet who worked at the British Museum, and some to the *English Review*. He received encouragement from both the poet and the journal, and he decided to publish these poems at his own expense in a twenty-four-page pamphlet.

The next year, he met Edward Marsh, editor of *Georgian Poetry* and an influential literary figure in London. Marsh purchased some of his paintings and encouraged him to go on writing, introducing him to other poets such as the modernists T. E. Hulme and Ezra Pound. Rosenberg was still undecided as to whether he was better as a painter or as a poet.

At this point, Rosenberg's health deteriorated, and he sailed to South Africa to stay with one of his sisters. He remained there during 1914, returning to England in March, 1915. Marsh bought three more of his paintings, and Rosenberg published another volume of verse, again at his own expense. However, with the war on, the literary and artistic scene in London had broken up, and there were no immediate prospects or contacts for him. In the light of this, he decided, reluctantly, to enlist, though feeling no particular patriotism.

He was not in good health, rather underweight and undersized. Nevertheless, he was accepted by the army, joining the "Bantams" of the 12th Suffolk Regiment, later transferring to the King's Own Royal Lancasters. After initial training, he was dispatched to the Somme battle area of northern France in June, 1916. During this time, he wrote a play, *Moses*, and then several other dramatic pieces based loosely on Jewish mythology.

He continued to write poetry, now influenced by his experience of war. By 1916, there were few illusions left about the nature of modern warfare. Rosenberg was able to embrace what he saw and sought some positive response to it. Apart from ten days of leave in September, 1917, and a few short spells in the hospital, he served continuously on or just behind the front lines until his death. He was killed shortly before the end of the war while riding dispatches at night. His body was never recovered. His war poems were first collected and published in 1922 by Gordon Bottomley.

ANALYSIS

Such is the lateness in poetic development in Isaac Rosenberg's short life that the majority of his output could be termed "early." His earliest dated poem is from 1905, but the so-called trench poems, on which his reputation solely depends, did not begin until 1916, when he enlisted and was posted to France. Thus the earlier poems span eleven years, with the best gathered into the 1912 and 1915 collections. The total number of poems gathered by his editors, including all the unpublished ones, is 154, of which only 10 percent represent the war poems.

Even though he did have friendships with several Imagist poets—Imagism being the first flowering of modern poetry—his early poetry, unlike his painting, seems typically Georgian. This movement, spanning the first fifteen years of the twentieth century, is best typified as Romantic in a suburban, restrained way, with the emphasis on nature as recreation and pretty images, being nostalgic in tone and with harmonious versification. Some critics have seen the influence of the Pre-Raphaelite painter-poet Dante Gabriel Rossetti, though the most obvious echoing is that of John Keats, another London city poet, whose poetry is full of woods, light, and shade and heightened sensory perceptions, with nature as an escape for the trapped urban spirit.

"Night and Day"

The long opening poem of the 1912 collection is titled "Night and Day" and apostrophizes the stars as he walks out of the city into the woods. The poet feels himself "set aside," seeking symbolic meaning in nature. Keats's "Sleep and Poetry" forms an obvious comparison. Echoes also sound of E. M. Forster's character Leonard Bast in his novel *Howards End* (1910). Other poems in the volume talk of "Desire" with an interesting religious reference; others show sympathy for the common people, a sympathy Rosenberg was to demonstrate later in his war poems.

Youth

Youth, the 1915 volume, shows in some of its lyrics somewhat more focus and control, but the emotions stay at a very generalized level. "God Made Blind" is more like a poem by Thomas Hardy, England's most senior poet at the time. "The Dead Heroes" shows an entirely conventional view of patriotism at this stage.

"On Receiving News of the War"

The uncollected "On Receiving News of the War," written from Cape Town, South Africa, shows a much less conventional and more genuine response. He writes, "God's blood is shed/ He mourns from His lone place/ His children dead." There is no heroism here, only divine pity. In 1915, he sent some of these poems to Lascelles Abercrombie, one of the most popular of the Georgians, whom Rosenberg considered "our best living poet." Abercrombie found the poems to possess a "vivid and original impulse," though he noted that Rosenberg had not yet found his true voice.

MOSES

Rosenberg was also attracted to dramatic verse. In 1916, he had published _Moses_, which consisted of a small number of poems added to a fragment of what was presumably intended to be a larger dramatic work on the Israelite leader Moses. He took considerable license with the biblical story, placing Moses at the moment he was still a prince of Egypt, but just beginning to find his identity as a Hebrew. The speech rhythms and dramatic ideas show much more poetic talent than anything done before, but there is still too much verbiage to be truly dramatic.

Some of the other poems in the volume are much bolder in their conceptual range than anything before. "God" makes a defiant Promethean statement. "Chagrin" uses the image of Absalom hanging by his hair, linking this to Christ hanging on the cross, quite a new sort of poem. "Marching" is the first soldier poem, with taut strong rhythms. The language is much richer and more imagistic. In the volume as a whole, there is for the first time some awareness of modernism, as there had been for some time in his painting.

THE LILITH THEME

While enlisted, Rosenberg also experimented with another Jewish myth, that of Lilith, mixing it strangely with unicorn myths and even a "Rape of the Sabine Women" theme. In his unpublished papers, there were a number of versions of this, titled variously "The Unicorn" or "The Amulet." As he works through various drafts, the blank verse becomes more dramatic, but his own imagination is revealed as mythic rather than dramatic, and there is no overall conceptual grasp of dramatic ideas or structure. Most of the verse consists of soliloquies or long monologues. Yet when it is considered that most of it was done under the most appalling physical conditions, it shows considerable commitment on the poet's part.

TRENCH POEMS

Once under the pressure of fighting in France, Rosenberg's poetic talents crystallized quickly. Flowery sentiments and unfocused images, typical also of Keats's early style, were, as with Keats himself, left behind, and a genuine unsentimental human sympathy was revealed. "The Dying Soldier" sets the tone: it is lyrical, almost balladic, but it focuses on the pathos of the actual death, not the stark horrors of the overall scene. "In War" shows a great advance in poetic technique: The controlled stanza form displays a control of tone and emotion, taking the reader from an almost anaesthetized calm to a sudden panic of realizing it was his brother they were burying. This movement from something "out there" to "right here" becomes typical of these war poems.

Several themes and poetic ideas are revealed. One is the "titan." "Girl to a Soldier on Leave" uses this image for the infantry soldier: Romantic love cannot really be sustained in the face of trench experience. Some new mode of tragedy is being forged. In "Soldier: Twentieth Century," Rosenberg makes a political comment for the first time.

The modern soldier is a "great new Titan." In the past, soldiers were fodder to keep tyrants in power. Now it is time that they wake up from sleeping "like Circe's swine" and rebel.

The second theme is a Jewish one: the burning of Solomon's Temple. "Destruction of Jerusalem by the Babylonian Hordes" is too anachronistic to be fully effective. The theme is reworked in "The Burning of the Temple." The poet asks if Solomon is angry at the burning of his glorious temple, to which the answer is, apparently not. If "God" is read for "Solomon" and the human body for the "Temple," then a powerful statement emerges: God's anger can be only ambiguously discerned.

The third theme is humorous. "The Immortals" is mock heroic, leading the reader to believe the soldier is fighting a heroic battle. In fact, he is fighting lice, which are immortal. Similarly, "Louse Hunting" depicts the real enemy in its "supreme littleness." In fact, Rosenberg has very little conception of the "enemy." For example, "Break of Day in the Trenches" shows a poet who strikes no poses, makes no gestures, and retains all his sensitivities after two years of continuous warfare. Others were driven insane. It is a gentle, sad, slightly ironic poem that shows Rosenberg as a human being rather than as a soldier. In fact, death on the battlefields is described as "murder," hardly a military perception.

The poem is an address to a rat, which like lice, were all too common in the trenches. However, the rat is not treated as vermin here. Rosenberg apostrophizes it for making no distinction between friend and foe, crossing indiscriminately between the two sides. The rat is "sardonic"; it "inwardly grins" as it sees fine young men from both sides being killed randomly and haphazardly, "sprawled in the bowels of the earth."

"DEAD MAN'S DUMP"

Among the best war poems ever written are two by Rosenberg, "Returning We Hear the Larks," with its sense of precarious joy still possible for the human spirit, and "Dead Man's Dump." This poem is about the quintessential war dilemma: seeing individuals, living and worthy of life, even if on the point of dying, as against seeing the mass of impersonal lifeless corpses that are fit only for throwing into the ground and burying. Rosenberg seems to be on some sort of burial fatigue, jolting along in a mule-drawn cart somewhere in no-man's-land. All around "The air is loud with death," and corpses of friend and foe alike lie scattered around. Sometimes the cart jolts over them, crushing their bones. They approach a dying man who must have heard them coming, as he tried to cry aloud. However, by the time the cart gets to him, he is dead, and "our wheels grazed his dead face."

The poet writes as a human being: There is pity but no sentimentality. Rosenberg's visual imagination is most clearly seen in his images of the corpses, their former strength and spirit seen against their present contorted lifelessness, especially in relationship to the earth, which is sensed as a living entity, to whose embrace the living return in a haphazard, random way. His imagination is also engaged in motion and motionlessness. Verbs are particularly vivid: "lurched," "sprawled," "crunched," "huddled," "go crying," and "breaking," "crying," "torturing," "break," "broke," "quivering," "rushing" in the climactic ending. These verbs are so violent they push away the poet's natural inclination to pity: "The drowning soul was sunk too deep/ For human tenderness." He writes of a soldier whose "brains splattered on/A stretcher-bearer's face."

This is a much more sustained poem than many of the other war poems. It is in free verse, divided into irregular stanzas, twelve in all, with occasional rhymes and half-rhymes. It is modern in its versification, unlike that of fellow war poets Brooke, Owen, and Sassoon, who tried, not always successfully, to adapt forms of the gentle, restrained Georgian versification to the horrendous scenes and emotions they were describing. Rosenberg's images and rhythmic structures create drama and movement much more fluidly, and the climax of the poem is as powerful as anything else in World War I poetry. Clearly, Rosenberg could have become a great poet had he lived. The very control of the poem, written in conditions of chaos and horror, suggests the triumph of the human spirit.

OTHER MAJOR WORKS

MISCELLANEOUS: *The Collected Works of Isaac Rosenberg: Poetry, Prose, Letters, and Some Drawings*, 1937 (Gordon Bottomley and Denys Harding, editors); *The Collected Works of Isaac Rosenberg: Poetry, Prose, Letters, Paintings, and Drawings*, 1979 (Ian Parsons, editor); *The Poems and Plays of Isaac Rosenberg*, 2004 (Vivien Noakes, editor); *Poetry Out of My Head and Heart: Unpublished Letters and Poem Versions*, 2007.

BIBLIOGRAPHY

Bloom, Harold, ed. *Poets of WWI: Wilfred Owen and Isaac Rosenberg*. Broomall, Pa.: Chelsea House, 2002. A collection of essays about the war poets Wilfred Owen and Rosenberg. Contains a biography of Rosenberg and five essays on his works.

Cohen, Joseph. *Journey to the Trenches: The Life of Isaac Rosenberg, 1890-1918*. London: Robson, 1975. Three biographies of Rosenberg were published in 1975, their combined effect being to bring him to public notice as a significant war poet. Cohen's account is the most sympathetic to his Jewish roots and background.

Desmond, Graham. *The Truth of War: Owen, Blunden, Rosenberg*. Manchester, England: Carcanet Press, 1984. A thoughtful approach to three contrasting World War I poets. A good bibliography with good commentaries on all of Rosenberg's trench poems.

Giddings, Robert. *The War Poets: The Lives and Writings of the 1914-18 War Poets*. London: Bloomsbury, 1988. A popular biographical approach, enacting Rosenberg's life and experience in the context of his contemporaries.

Liddiard, Jean. *Isaac Rosenberg: The Half-Used Life*. London: Gollancz, 1975. The second of the 1975 biographies, and probably the most straightforward one. A good approach to the poems.

Maccoby, Deborah. *God Made Blind: Isaac Rosenberg, His Life and Poetry*. Chicago: Science Reviews, 1999. This biography and critical analysis examines how Rosenberg's Jewish faith played a role in his life and writings.

Quinn, Patrick, ed. *British Poets of the Great War: Brooke, Rosenberg, Thomas—A Documentary Volume*. Detroit: Gale Group, 2000. Looks at Rupert Brooke, Edward Thomas, and Rosenberg and compares and contrasts their work.

Roberts, David. *Essential Poetry of the First World War in Context*. Burgess Hill, England: Saxon, 1996. Several critical books have tried to bring a historicist approach to Rosenberg and the other war poets, trying to reconstruct the overall social and political context out of which the poetry was generated. Roberts deals more with the poetic material than some others. Full bibliography.

Wilson, Jean Moorcroft. *Isaac Rosenberg, Poet and Painter: A Biography*. London: Cecil Woolf, 1975. The third of the 1975 biographies, this time tracing the growth of Rosenberg's artistic ideas and the interplay between poetry and painting.

_____. *Isaac Rosenberg: The Making of a Great War Poet—A New Life*. Evanston, Ill.: Northwestern University Press, 2009. This biography of the war poet, whose brief life produced some memorable poems, expands on Wilson's earlier work.

David Barratt

MURIEL RUKEYSER

Born: New York, New York; December 15, 1913
Died: New York, New York; February 12, 1980

OTHER LITERARY FORMS

In addition to her own poetry, Muriel Rukeyser (ROOK-iz-ur) published several volumes of translations (including work by the poets Octavio Paz and Gunnar Ekelöf), three biographies, two volumes of literary criticism, a number of book reviews, a novel, five juvenile books, and a play. She also worked on several documentary film scripts. The translations were exercises in writing during dry spells; the biographies, like her poetic sequence "Lives," combine her interests in the arts and sciences. The two volumes of literary criticism (along with her uncollected book reviews) are central to understanding her views concerning poetry and life.

ACHIEVEMENTS

With the publication of *Theory of Flight* in the Yale Series of Younger Poets in 1935, Muriel Rukeyser began a long and productive career as a poet and author. Her work earned for her the first Harriet Monroe Poetry Award (1941), a National Institute of the Arts and Letters Award (1942), a Guggenheim Fellowship (1943), the Levinson Prize from *Poetry* magazine (1947), the Shelley Memorial Award (1977), the Copernicus Award (1977), a grant from the Eric Mathieu King Fund (1996), an honorary D.Litt. from Rutgers, and membership in the National Institute of Arts and Letters. She won the Swedish Academy Translation Award (1967) and the Anglo-Swedish Literary Foundation Award (1978) for her translations.

BIOGRAPHY

Muriel Rukeyser was born on December 15, 1913, in New York City, the daughter of Lawrence B. Rukeyser, a cofounder of Colonial Sand and Stone, and Myra Lyons, a former bookkeeper. Her childhood was a quiet one, her protected, affluent life a source of her insistence on experience and communication in her poetry. In *The Life of Poetry* (1949), she tells of recognizing the sheltered nature of her life: "A teacher asks: 'How many of you know any other road in the city except the road between home and school?' I do not put up my hand. These are moments at which one begins to see."

Rukeyser's adult life was as eventful as her childhood was sheltered. In 1933, at age nineteen, she was arrested and caught typhoid fever while attending the Scottsboro trials in Alabama; three years later, she investigated at firsthand the mining tragedy at Gauley Bridge, West Virginia; and in 1936, she was sent by *Life and Letters Today* to cover the Anti-Fascist Olympics in Barcelona as the Spanish Civil War broke out around her. These crusades dramatize her intense conviction on the sanctity of human life and her desire to experience life actively, and they all served as inspiration for her poetry, fulfilling her declaration in "Poem out of Childhood" to "Breathe-in experience, breathe-out poetry."

Throughout the remainder of a life filled with traveling and speaking for causes in which she intensely believed, Rukeyser never stopped learning, teaching, and writing; she declared that she would never protest without making something in the process. The wide range of knowledge in her poetry and criticism and the large volume of poetry and prose she published testify to this fact. She attended the Ethical Culture School and Fieldston School, Vassar College, Columbia University, and the Roosevelt School of Aviation in New York City, and she learned film editing with Helen Van Dongen. Besides conducting poetry workshops at a number of different institutions, she taught at the California Labor School and Sarah Lawrence College and later served as a member of the board of directors of the Teachers-Writers Collaborative in New York.

Rukeyser made her home in New York City, except for the nine years she spent in California and the time she was traveling. She moved to California in 1945 and shortly

Muriel Rukeyser
(Library of Congress)

afterward married painter Glynn Collins (although the marriage was soon annulled). Three years later, she had an illegitimate son and was disowned by her family, experiences that figure prominently in her poetry after this date. She moved back to New York in 1954 to teach at Sarah Lawrence College.

Rukeyser left Sarah Lawrence College in 1967. Although in failing health, she continued to write and protest. For the Committee for Solidarity, she flew to Hanoi in 1972 to demonstrate for peace, and later that year, she was jailed in Washington, D.C., for protesting the Vietnam War on the steps of the Capitol. In 1974, as president of the American center for PEN, a society that supports the rights of writers throughout the world, she flew to Korea to plead for the life of imprisoned poet Kim Chi-Ha. Rukeyser died in New York City on February 12, 1980.

ANALYSIS

While Muriel Rukeyser has been linked to W. H. Auden, Stephen Spender, and other political poets, her work more clearly evolves from that of Ralph Waldo Emerson, Herman Melville, and Walt Whitman. From Emerson and the Transcendental tradition, she developed her organic theory of poetry, from Melville, her poetry of outrage. From Whitman, however, she obtained perhaps her most distinguishing characteristics: her belief in possibility; her long, rhythmic lines; her need to embrace humanity; and her expression of the power and beauty of sexuality. Her feminist views link her with Denise Levertov and Adrienne Rich, while her experimentation with the poetic line and the visual appearance of the poem on the page remind one at times of May Swenson. Both the quality and quantity of her work and the integrity of her feminist and mythic vision suggest that she will come to be seen as a significant figure in modern American poetry.

THEORY OF FLIGHT

"Look! Be: leap," Rukeyser writes in the preamble to the title poem of her first collection, *Theory of Flight*. These imperatives identify her emphasis on vision, her insistence on primary experience, and her belief in human potential. Focusing on this dictum, Rukeyser presents to her readers "the truths of outrage and the truths of possibility" in the world. To Rukeyser, poetry is a way to learn more about oneself and one's relations with others and to live more fully in an imperfect world.

The publication of *Theory of Flight* immediately marked Rukeyser as, in Stephen Vincent Benét's words, "a Left Winger and a revolutionary," an epithet she could never quite shake, although the Marxists never fully accepted her for not becoming a Communist and for writing poems that tried to do more than simply support their cause. Indeed, Rukeyser did much more than write Marxist poems. She was a poet of liberty, recording "the truths of outrage" she saw around her, and a poet of love, writing "the truths of possibility" in intimate human relationships. With the conviction of Akiba (a Jewish teacher and martyr who fought to include the Song of Songs in the Bible and from whom, according to family tradition, Rukeyser's mother was descended), Rukeyser wrote with equal fervor about social and humane issues such as miners dying of silicosis, the rights of minorities, the lives of women and imprisoned poets, and about universals such as the need for love and communication among people and the sheer physical and emotional joy of loving.

U.S. 1

Unlike many political poets, Rukeyser tried to do more than simply espouse: to protect, but also to build and to create. For Rukeyser, poetry's purpose is to sustain and heal, and the poet's responsibility is to recognize life as it is and encourage all people to their greatest potential through poetry.

Refusing to accept the negation of T. S. Eliot's *The Waste Land* (1922), Rukeyser uses images of technology and energy extensively in her early volumes to find, in a positive way, a place for the self in modern technological society, thus identifying herself with Hart Crane and with the poets of the Dynamo school. "Theory of Flight" centers on the airplane and the gyroscope. The dam and the power plant become the predominant symbols in "The Book of the Dead" in *U.S. 1*, her next collection.

U.S. 1 also contains a series of shorter, more lyrical poems titled "Night-Music." While these poems are still strongly social in content, they are more personal and are based on what Rukeyser refers to as "unverifiable fact" (as opposed to the documentary evidence in "Theory of Flight" and "The Book of the Dead"). This change foreshadows the shifting emphasis throughout her career on the sources of power about which she writes—from machinery to poetry to the self. It is this change in conception that allowed Rukeyser to grow poetically, to use fewer of the abstractions for which many critics have faulted her, and to use instead more personal and concrete images on which to anchor her message.

A TURNING WIND

This movement is evident in *A Turning Wind*. She begins to see the power and the accompanying fear of poetry, and her poetic voice becomes increasingly personal, increasingly founded in personal experience. Poetry becomes the means, the language, and the result of looking for connections or, in Jungian terms, a kind of collective unconscious. Rukeyser notices, however, that poetry is feared precisely because of its power: "They fear it. They turn away, hand up palm out/ fending off moment of proof, the straight look, poem." The fear of poetry is a fear of disclosure to oneself of what is inside, and this fear is "an indication that we are cut off from our own reality." Therefore, Rukeyser continually urges her readers to use poetry to look within themselves for a common ground on which they can stand as human beings.

"LIVES"

The poetic sequence "Lives" (which extends through subsequent volumes as well as *A Turning Wind*) identifies another of Rukeyser's growing interests—"ways of getting past impossibilities by changing phase." Poetry thus becomes a meeting place of different ideas and disciplines. It is a place where the self meets the self, diving to confront unchallenged emotions in the search for truth, and a place where the self can face the world with newly discovered self-knowledge. Using the resources they discover both inside and outside themselves, people can grow to understand themselves and the world better. The subjects of the "Lives" exemplify values and traditions Rukeyser believes are important to the search.

Rukeyser's growth as a person and as a poet, then, has been a growth of the self, realizing her capabilities and her potential and, in turn, the capabilities and potential of those around her. She becomes increasingly open in her later poems, discussing her failed marriage, her illegitimate son and subsequent disinheritance, her son's exile in Canada during the Vietnam War, and her feelings about age and death. Although these poems may seem confessional, she is not a confessional poet such as Robert Lowell or W. D. Snodgrass. The details of her life, she tells the reader, are events she must consider from various angles as she dives within herself, looking for the essence of being. "The universe of poetry is the universe of emotional truth." Rukeyser writes in her critical work *The Life of Poetry*, and it is the "breaking open" of her preconceived emotions to discover emotional truth that allows her to become closer to the humanity around her. "One writes in order to feel," she continues. "That is the fundamental mover."

"Ajanta"

In "Ajanta," Rukeyser makes perhaps her first statement of inner emotional truth, according to poet-critic Virginia R. Terris. In this mythic journey within the self, Rukeyser realizes that self-knowledge is the prerequisite for all other kinds of knowledge. Yet behind her search for self-knowledge and expansion of the self into the world is her belief in the necessity of communication. The silence she experienced at home as a child had a profound effect on her, and in many early poems, such as "Effort at Speech Between Two People," communication is ultimately impossible. This same silence appears to be at the root of many of the world's problems, and Rukeyser's open outrage and inner searching are attempts to right the problem, to achieve communication. By the time she wrote "Ajanta," silence had become a positive force, allowing her the opportunity to concentrate on her journey within.

Artist and audience

Rukeyser has at times been criticized for combining disparate images within the same poem, as in "Waterlily Fire," from her collection by the same name, but this seems unjust. Far from being unrelated elements, her images grow, change, and develop throughout a poem and throughout her poetic canon. She puts the responsibility for making connections on the reader; she gives clues but does not take all the work out of the poem: "Both artist and audience create, and both do work on themselves in creating." Rukeyser is not an easy poet, and one cannot read her poetry passively. Yet she is a rewarding poet for those who take the time to look at and listen to what she is doing.

Poetic sequences

Another distinguishing mark of Rukeyser's poetry is the numerous poetic sequences (such as "Lives") which are connected by a common situation, theme, or character. "Waterlily Fire," for example, is a group of five poems about the burning of Claude Monet's *Waterlilies* at the Museum of Modern Art in New York City. "Elegies" is a collection of ten poems extending over three volumes. "Poem out of Childhood" is a cluster of fifteen poems, of which one is also a cluster of three, centered on Rukeyser's childhood—what she learns from it and how she uses it poetically.

Rukeyser's interest in poetic sequences grew from her training as a film editor:

> The work with film is a terribly good exercise for poetry . . . the concept of sequences, the cutting of sequences of varying length, the frame by frame composition, the use of a traveling image, traveling by the way the film is cut, shot, projected at a set speed, a sound track or a silent track, in conjunction with the visual track but can be brought into bad descriptive verbal things and brought into marvelous juxtapositions.

The sequence makes more apparent to readers the necessity of looking for connections among poems—recurring images, phrases, and sounds—than could separate poems.

THE SPEED OF DARKNESS

In *The Speed of Darkness*, Rukeyser returns to her preoccupation with silence, expressing it structurally both in and as a subject. From her earliest poems, she used space within lines (often combined with a proliferation of colons) to act as a new type of punctuation—a metric rest—but in *The Speed of Darkness*, she places greater emphasis on the placement of the poem on the page to achieve this metric rest, for space on the page "can provide roughly for a relationship in emphasis through the eye's discernment of pattern."

MOVING TOWARD SHORTER LINES

Rukeyser's verse has often been characterized as half poetry, half prose because of the long, sweeping, encompassing, Whitmanesque free-verse lines especially noticeable in her early poems. In *The Speed of Darkness* and later poems, however, she moves toward shorter lines and works with smaller units of meaning to compensate for breathing. At times, her arrangement of these poems ("The War Comes into My Room," "Mountain: One from Bryant," and "Rune," for example) approaches Swenson's iconographs in their experimentation with the visual and physical movement of the line.

Perhaps another reason for the new, shorter lines is that they are more suited for the introspective journeys of Rukeyser's later work than are the long, flowing, altruistic lines she used earlier. They also help her to control more effectively her penchant for verbosity and maintain the development of her images. Yet the length and conclusion of the later lines are not without precedent. Many of the most powerful passages in the early poems were journalistic or cinematic passages, not yet matured but still effective in their performance. "The Book of the Dead" is especially noteworthy in this respect, for it contains the seeds of the concrete image and colloquial diction fully realized later.

DICTION

Rukeyser's diction also gives ample reason for labeling her poetry half prose. Yet as startling as it may be to encounter words such as "eugenically," "silicosis," and "cantillations" in her poems, these words make the reader pay attention. She also employs words and even sounds as physical, musical, and thematic ties within and among poems in the same way other poets use rhyme and in the same way she uses image sequences.

With the variety of line length and placement evident in Rukeyser's work, it is not surprising that her canon is characterized by a rich variety of styles. Her experiments with language, line length, and rhythm easily lend themselves to experiments with different verse styles, including but extending beyond elegies, sonnets, odes, rounds, and rondels.

"LETTER, UNPOSTED"

While Rukeyser uses traditional as well as nontraditional verse patterns, she often treats even her most traditional subjects untraditionally. Because of her belief in the community of humankind, she has written many love poems, yet she approaches even the most personal subjects in an unexpected way. A notable example is "Letter, Unposted" from *Theory of Flight*, which is centered on the traditional theme of waiting for a lover. Yet it is distinguished from other such poems by the speaker's refusal to languish in love and to see nature languishing along with her. The letter remains unposted because the speaker cannot write all the traditional sentimental foolishness expected of her. Instead, as in even the bleakest situations about which Rukeyser writes, she sees the positive side: "But summer lives,/ and minds grow, and nerves are sensitized to power .. . and I receive them joyfully and live: but wait for you." The speaker rejoices in life rather than feeling sorry for herself.

FEMINIST OUTLOOK

Although a feminine consciousness is evident in every volume of Rukeyser's poetry, *The Speed of Darkness* also begins a new and more imperative feminist outlook. In the same way that she refused to be simply a Marxist poet, neither is she simply a feminist poet. Rukeyser sees with a feminist point of view, but rather than rejecting the masculine, she retains valuable past information and revisualizes history and myth with female vitality. For example, in "Myth," one learns that Oedipus was not as smart as he thought he was; he did not answer the Sphinx's riddle correctly after all: "'You didn't say anything about woman.'/ 'When you say Man,' said Oedipus, 'you include women/ too. Everyone knows that.' She said, 'That's what/ you think.'" "Ms. Lot" adds another perspective to the biblical story of Lot and his wife, and in "Painters" (*The Gates*) she envisions a woman among the primitive cave painters.

Other poems written throughout her career on more contemporary issues reveal the strength of women while upholding their nurturing role. The mother in "Absalom" ("The Book of the Dead") will "give a mouth to my son" who died of silicosis, and Kim Chi-Ha's mother in "The Gates" is portrayed as a pitchfork, one of Rukeyser's few uses of simile or metaphor. She also refuses to let women take the easy way out as some have been trained to do: "More of a Corpse than a Woman" and "Gradus Ad Parnassum," for example, display the vapidity of the stereotypical passive rich woman.

While women are strong in Rukeyser's verse, they are still human. Sex is one of the driving forces in Rukeyser's work, and she frequently expresses the joys of love and sex, especially in *Breaking Open*. Significant examples are the powerful eroticism of "Looking at Each Other," the honesty of "In Her Burning" and "Rondel," and the power of sexual renewal in "Welcome from War." Giving birth is also a powerful image in many of the poems.

"THE GATES"

"The Gates," a fifteen-poem sequence organized around Rukeyser's trip to Korea to plead for the release of imprisoned poet Kim Chi-Ha, synthesizes her recurring images and messages in a final, powerful poetic statement. Like "Night-Music," this sequence is at once social commentary and personal discovery, but it takes a much stronger stance in demanding freedom of speech and assessing Rukeyser's own development as a poet in the light of Kim Chi-Ha's life.

LEGACY

"Breathe-in experience, breathe-out poetry" begins "Poem out of Childhood," the first poem in Rukeyser's first collection. Muriel Rukeyser wrote a poetry developing organically from personal experience and self-discovery, a poetry bringing the anguish and misfortunes of human beings around the world to her readers' attention, a poetry demonstrating her exhilaration with life and love. Readers cannot hide from reality in her poetry, nor can they hide from themselves. There is always the journey, but possibility always lies at its end: "the green tree perishes and green trees grow." Rukeyser's challenge to the world she left behind is found near the end of "Then" (in "The Gates"): "When I am dead, even then,/ I will still love you, I will wait in these poems . . . I will still be making poems for you/ out of silence." The silence and passivity against which she fought throughout her life will not triumph if her readers are alive to her words and to the world around them.

OTHER MAJOR WORKS

LONG FICTION: *The Orgy*, 1965.

PLAYS: *The Colors of the Day: A Celebration for the Vassar Centennial, June 10, 1961*, pr. 1961; *Houdini*, pr. 1973.

NONFICTION: *Willard Gibbs*, 1942; *The Life of Poetry*, 1949; *One Life*, 1957; *Poetry and the Unverifiable Fact: The Clark Lectures*, 1968; *The Traces of Thomas Hariot*, 1971.

CHILDREN'S LITERATURE: *Come Back, Paul*, 1955; *I Go Out*, 1961; *Bubbles*, 1967; *Mazes*, 1970; *More Night*, 1981.

TRANSLATIONS: *Selected Poems*, 1963 (of Octavio Paz's poems); *Sun Stone*, 1963 (of Paz's poems); *Selected Poems*, 1967 (with Leif Sjöberg; of Gunnar Ekelöf's poems); *Three Poems*, 1967 (of Ekelöf's poems); *Early Poems, 1935-1955*, 1973 (of Paz's poems); *Uncle Eddie's Moustache*, 1974 (of Bertolt Brecht's poems); *A Mölna Elegy*, 1984 (of Ekelöf's poem).

MISCELLANEOUS: *A Muriel Rukeyser Reader*, 1994.

BIBLIOGRAPHY

Dayton, Tim. *Muriel Rukeyser's "The Book of the Dead."* Columbia: University of Missouri Press, 2003. Provides a close look at "The Book of the Dead" and describes its critical reception. A radio interview of Rukeyser by Samuel Sillen is included.

Gardinier, Suzanne. "A World That Will Hold All People: On Muriel Rukeyser." *Kenyon Review* 14 (Summer, 1992): 88-105. An in-depth discussion of Rukeyser's poetry as reflecting her life experiences and her political beliefs. Gardinier states that Rukeyser wrote "the poetry of a believer—in an age of unbelief." Many quotations from Rukeyser's early and later poems.

Goodman, Jenny. "'Presumption' and 'Unlearning': Reading Muriel Rukeyser's 'The Book of the Dead' as a Woman's American Epic." *Tulsa Studies in Women's Literature* 25, no. 2 (Fall, 2006): 267. Goodman argues that Rukeyser uses the epic convention to create a narrative of national redemption centered on women.

Herzog, Anne F., and Janet E. Kaufman, eds. *How Shall We Tell Each Other of the Poet? The Life and Writing of Muriel Rukeyser.* New York: St. Martin's Press, 1999. A collection of tributes and essays regarding Rukeyser by poets and literary scholars. Includes bibliographical references and an index.

Kertesz, Louise. *The Poetic Vision of Muriel Rukeyser.* Baton Rouge: Louisiana State University Press, 1980. Kertesz provides the first book-length critical evaluation of Rukeyser's work. This book is flawed in that much of Kertesz's analysis is abandoned in favor of an angry defense of Rukeyser's work against critics who misunderstood it. However, Kertesz puts Rukeyser in the context of her time and place and so provides a valuable study for all Rukeyser students.

Rich, Adrienne. "Beginners." *Kenyon Review* 15 (Summer, 1993): 12-19. In this beautifully written essay, Rich, a prominent poet herself, discusses Rukeyser, Walt Whitman, and Emily Dickinson, calling them all "beginners . . . openers of new paths . . . who take the first steps . . . and therefore seem strange and 'dreadful.'"

Rukeyser, Muriel. *The Life of Poetry.* Rev. ed. Foreword by Jane Cooper. Williamsburg, Mass.: Paris Press, 1996. Rukeyser's explanation of her conception of the role of the poet in society, drawing on such diverse authorities as English mathematician/philosopher Alfred North Whitehead, Austrian psychoanalyst Sigmund Freud, German philosopher Georg Hegel, and American physicist Willard Gibbs. As the title suggests, Rukeyser believed that poetry should be a way of life.

Thurston, Michael. *Making Something Happen: American Political Poetry Between the World Wars.* Chapel Hill: University of North Carolina Press, 2001. Thurston examines the political poetry of Rukeyser, Edwin Rolfe, Langston Hughes, and Ezra Pound, arguing that it is worth reading for its aesthetic qualities as well as its message.

Ware, Michele S. "Opening *The Gates*: Muriel Rukeyser and the Poetry of Witness." *Women's Studies* 22 (June, 1993): 297-308. An extensive analysis of *The Gates*, the last volume of Rukeyser's new poetry to be published before her death. Praises her oracular characteristics and lyricism while maintaining the integrity of her political and social messages.

Kenneth E. Gadomski

NELLY SACHS

Born: Berlin, Germany; December 10, 1891
Died: Stockholm, Sweden; May 12, 1970

PRINCIPAL POETRY

In den Wohnungen des Todes, 1946
Sternverdunkelung, 1949
Und niemand weiss weiter, 1957
Flucht und Verwandlung, 1959
Fahrt ins Staublose, 1961
Noch feiert Tod das Leben, 1961
Glühende Rätsel, 1964 (parts 1 and 2; 1965, part 3 in *Späte Gedichte*; 1966, part 4
  in the annual *Jahresring*)
Späte Gedichte, 1965
Die Suchende, 1966
O the Chimneys, 1967
The Seeker, and Other Poems, 1970
Teile dich Nacht, 1971

OTHER LITERARY FORMS

Nelly Sachs (saks) published the short play, or "scenic poem," *Eli: Ein Mysteriens-piel vom Leiden Israels* (pb. 1951; *Eli: A Mystery Play of the Sufferings of Israel*, 1967).
Her fiction is collected in *Legenden und Erzählungen* (1921) and her correspondence
with Paul Celan in *Paul Celan, Nelly Sachs: Correspondence* (1995).

ACHIEVEMENTS

Nelly Sachs arrived at her characteristic poetic style late in life. She was heavily influenced by the German Romantic poets and did not consider her lyric poetry of the
years prior to 1943 to be representative of her mature work, excluding those poems from
the collection of 1961. Her first published book, a small volume of legends and tales
published in 1921, was heavily indebted in style and content to the Swedish novelist
Selma Lagerlöf. In the 1920's and 1930's, Sachs published lyric poetry in such respected newspapers and journals as the *Vossische Zeitung* of Berlin, the *Berliner
Tageblatt*, and *Der Morgen*, the journal of the Jewish cultural federation.

Sachs's stylistic breakthrough came with the traumatic experience of her flight from
Germany and exile in Sweden. The play *Eli* was written in 1943 but published privately
in Sweden in 1951. It was first broadcast on Süddeutsche Rundfunk (South German Radio) in 1958 and had its theater premiere in 1962 in Dortmund. Acceptance of her poetry
in West Germany was equally slow, partly because her main theme (Jewish suffering

Nelly Sachs
(©The Nobel Foundation)

during World War II) stirred painful memories. In the late 1950's and 1960's, however, she was hailed as modern Germany's greatest woman poet and received numerous literary prizes. She was accepted for membership in several academies. In 1958, she received the poetry prize of the Swedish broadcasting system and, in 1959, the Kulturpreis der Deutschen Industrie. The town of Meersburg in West Germany awarded her the Annette Droste Prize for female poets in 1960, and the city of Dortmund founded the Nelly Sachs Prize in 1961 and presented her with its first award. In the same year, friends and admirers published the first volume of a Festschrift, followed by the second volume, *Nelly Sachs zu Ehren*, on the occasion of her seventy-fifth birthday in 1966. On October 17, 1965, she received the Peace Prize of the German Book Trade Association, and on December 10, 1966, she was awarded the Nobel Prize in Literature. Berlin, the city where she was born and in which she had lived for nearly half a century, made her an honorary citizen in 1967. The city of Dortmund, Germany, and the Royal Library in Stockholm, Sweden, have valuable collections of her letters and transcriptions of her early poems in their Nelly Sachs Archive.

BIOGRAPHY

Nelly Leonie Sachs was born Leonie Sachs in Berlin on December 10, 1891, the only child of William Sachs, an inventor, technical engineer, and manufacturer, and his wife, Margarete (Karger) Sachs. The family lived in very comfortable financial circumstances, and Nelly Sachs was educated in accordance with the custom for daughters of the upper-middle class. Although both of her parents were of Jewish ancestry, her family had few ties with the Jewish community and did not practice their religion. Sachs attended public schools from 1897 to 1900, but because of poor health, she was removed and received private instruction until 1903. She then attended a private secondary school for daughters of wealthy and titled families and finished her education in 1908 without any formal professional training. In the summer of that year, she fell in love with a man whose name she never revealed. That experience, which ended unhappily, escalated into a crisis, making Sachs consider suicide. The man was later killed in one of Germany's concentration camps.

For the next twenty-five years, even after the death of her father in 1930, Sachs led a sheltered and not particularly noteworthy existence. She produced some poetry, read extensively, and did watercolors, some of which have been preserved in the Nelly Sachs Archive in Stockholm. In 1906, Sachs received Lagerlöf's novel *Gösta Berling* (1891) as a birthday present. Her admiration for the writer resulted in a correspondence between the two, and Sachs sent Lagerlöf many of her own literary experiments. Through the intervention of Lagerlöf and the brother of the reigning Swedish king, Sachs and her mother received permission to emigrate to Sweden in 1939. Shortly after Lagerlöf's death in 1940, Sachs received orders from German authorities to appear for deportation to a work camp. Leaving all their possessions behind, Sachs and her mother fled Germany, arriving in Stockholm on May 16, 1940. They took up residence in a small apartment in the industrial harbor area, where Sachs remained until her death in 1970.

The imagery in Sachs's later lyric poetry draws to a large extent on influences from her youth. Her father's extensive collection of rocks, gems, and fossils was a source of inspiration to her, and she continued his hobby with a collection of her own in Stockholm; not unexpectedly, the use of the stones as a cipher is very prevalent in her work "Chor der Steine" ("Chorus of the Stones"). From her father's library, she was also familiar with the work of Maria Sibylla Merian, a seventeenth century entomologist and graphic artist who specialized in the study of butterflies. Sachs's poem "Schmetterling" ("Butterfly") exemplifies her metaphoric use of this and other insects in her work. In 1959, Sachs wrote that of all childhood influences on her later works, her father's musical talent was paramount. When he played the piano during evenings after work, she frequently danced for hours to the strains of his music. In addition to her early lyric poems, which she characterized as "dance and music poems," the motif of the dance is also important in her later work.

In 1960, Sachs returned to Germany for the first time since her exile to receive the

Annette Droste Prize. Not wishing to spend a night in Germany, she stayed instead in Zurich, traveling the short distance to Meersburg only to accept the honor. Hearing the German language spoken again proved to be so traumatic, however, that she experienced a "memory trip to hell." In Zurich, she met Paul Celan, another exiled poet, who invited her to his home in Paris. The meeting resulted in a continuing correspondence, but Celan was in the midst of a personal crisis as well, and the relationship may have contributed to Sachs's difficulties. After her return to Stockholm, Sachs suffered a mental breakdown and was hospitalized with severe delusions of persecution. Although she worked feverishly during the next decade, she continued to suffer periodic attacks in which she imagined herself persecuted and threatened with death. Her cycle *Noch feiert Tod das Leben* (death still celebrates life) was written while she recovered in the hospital. Celan attempted to aid her recovery through an intensive, supportive correspondence that was also, however, an attempt at self-healing, inasmuch as he suffered from a similar ailment. Their poetry, beginning with Sachs's *Noch feiert Tod das Leben* and Celan's *Die Niemandsrose* (1963), shows their continuing "dialogue in poems." In the spring of 1970, Sachs became mortally ill and thus was not informed when Celan was reported missing early in April of that year. He was later found—an apparent suicide by drowning; his funeral services took place in the Cimetière Parisien near Orly, France, on the same day in May on which Sachs died in a Stockholm hospital.

ANALYSIS

It is difficult to speak of development in Nelly Sachs's poetic works, inasmuch as she was well beyond fifty years old when she produced her first significant poems. It is true that she had published lyric poetry before the 1940's, but this early work has little in common with that of her mature years. Most of the poems from the 1920's and 1930's are thematically quite distinct from the later work, devoted to musicians such as Johann Sebastian Bach, Wolfgang Amadeus Mozart, Jean-Philippe Rameau, and Luigi Boccherini or dealing poetically with certain animals, such as deer, lambs, and nightingales. The Nelly Sachs archives in Dortmund and in Stockholm have copies of a substantial number of these early efforts.

IN DEN WOHNUNGEN DES TODES

In contrast, the work of Sachs's last twenty-five years concerns itself largely with existential problems, particularly with topics related to the Holocaust and rooted in personal experiences of flight, exile, and the death of friends. Her first collection of poems, *In den Wohnungen des Todes* (in the habitations of death), refers in its title to the Nazi death camps and is dedicated to those who perished there. It is a mistake, however, to perceive her work solely in the context of these historical events. Her topic is on a larger scale, the cycle of life itself—birth, death, rebirth—and Sachs develops various metaphors and ciphers to express the agony and the hope of this cycle.

STERNVERDUNKELUNG

Although it is desirable to interpret Sachs's work separately from the context of specific historical events, it is almost impossible to analyze an individual poem without relying on information gained from a broader knowledge of her work. This difficulty is the result of her frequent use of ciphers, poetic images that can be "decoded" only by reference to other poems in which the same images occur. Such a cipher in Sachs's work is the stone. Its properties are chiefly those of inert matter: lack of emotion, or lifelessness. The cipher may depict human callousness, death, or desolation in different contexts, and it is related to similar poetic images such as sand and dust—decayed rock—which signify the mortal human condition.

The poem "Sinai," from the collection *Sternverdunkelung* (eclipse of the stars), contains entirely negative images of the stone. Sachs compares the ancient times of Moses, in which humanity was still in intimate contact with the divine and thus vibrantly alive, with the present state of lifelessness; there are only "petrified eyes of the lovers" with "their putrefied happiness." Recounting Moses's descent from Mount Sinai, Sachs asks: "Where is still a descendent/ from those who trembled? Oh, may he glow/ in the crowd of amnesiacs/ of the petrified!" The eyes of the lovers turned to stone signify the death both of sensibility and of sensuousness, and the inability to re-create or reproduce. It is ultimately a death of humankind. The call is for one perhaps still alive among the multitude of those dead in mind and body.

In "Chassidische Schriften" ("Hasidic Scriptures"), from *Sternverdunkelung*, Sachs writes: "And the heart of stones,/ filled with drifting sand,/ is the place where midnights are stored." "Drifting sand" is sand blown skyward by the wind; thus, while it is inert matter, it has lost this inertia momentarily on the wings of the wind. The dead has come to life. Midnight, on the other hand, represents the end of one day and the dawning of the next, a time of rebirth. Sachs contends that the stone, dead as it is, is imbued with the desire for rebirth and transubstantiation. Another possibility for the stone to attain a semblance of life is offered in "Golem Tod!" ("Golem Death!"), from *Sternverdunkelung*. There, "The stone sleeps itself green with moss." The suggestion that the stone is merely sleeping, not dead, and that it is capable of producing living matter (moss) is also an affirmation of the possibility of renewal of life after death.

"CHORUS OF THE STONES" AND "MELUSINE, IF YOUR WELL HAD NOT"

Scarcely less negative is the stone cipher in the poem "Wenn nicht dein Brunnen, Melusine" ("Melusine, If Your Well Had Not"), from *Und niemand weiss weiter*. If it were not for the possibility of transformation and escape, "we should long have passed away/ in the petrified resurrection/ of an Easter Island." Easter Island's petrified statues are merely reminders of an extinct civilization, not a resurrection from the dead. Still, the poem indicates that transformation is possible (the symbol for it is Melusine). In the poem "Chorus of the Stones," from *In den Wohnungen des Todes*, stones are, like the statues of Easter Island, venerable objects depicting the history of humankind. The stone is symbolic of all that has died, but it carries memories within it and thus is not entirely devoid of life. The last lines of the poem even offer the hope that the stone is only "sleeping," that it may come to life again: "Our conglomeration is transfused by breath./ It solidified in secret/ but may awaken at a kiss."

Three ideas in "Chorus of the Stones" suggest that death is not the final answer to life: The lifeless entity (the stone) contains memories; it is imbued with breath, a necessary element of life; and it may be awakened by an act of love. Transformation, resurrection, and transfiguration are therefore within the realm of possibility. Such a flight from lifelessness to a new beginning is nevertheless fraught with difficulties.

"HALLELUJA"

The most dramatic depiction of the rebirth of the dead is to be found in Sachs's poem "Halleluja" ("Hallelujah"), from the volume *Flucht und Verwandlung* (flight and metamorphosis). The poem describes a mountain rising from the sea by volcanic action. The rock is portrayed as a beloved child, the crowning glory of its mother, the ocean, as it thrusts forth from the womb to the light of day. While still embedded in the sea, the rock showed signs of sustaining life. As in "Golem Death!" with its stone covered with moss, this rock has been nurturing life. For the sea algae, birth of the rock means death, which the "winged longing" of the rock will bring about; although one form of life dies, another takes its place. These poems therefore encompass the cycle of life and death of living and inert matter on Earth.

"BUTTERFLY" AND "FLEEING"

In tracing the cipher of the stone, it is evident that the nihilism of the earlier cycles has given way to a guarded optimism in the later ones. A more traditional image of transfiguration is that of the butterfly. Its life cycle includes the apparent death of the homely caterpillar and its re-emergence from the cocoon as a beautiful winged creature, and thus it is readily adaptable as a symbol of the soul's resurrection after physical death. Sachs uses the image of the butterfly within this tradition. The poem "In der Flucht" ("Fleeing"), from *Flucht und Verwandlung*, compares the flight of the Jews from their persecutors with the never-ending process of transformation, mutation, and metamorphosis. There is no rest and no end (no "Amen") for that which is considered mortal (sand, dust), for it experiences endless metamorphoses. The butterfly, itself a symbol of metamorphosis, will reenter the life-giving element at its death and complete the cycle of life.

In "Butterfly," from *Sternverdunkelung*, the butterfly is depicted as a mortal creature (one made of "dust") which nevertheless mirrors the beauty of a world beyond: "What lovely hereafter/ is painted in your dust." The butterfly is a messenger of hope for those who are dying, because it is aware through its own metamorphosis that death is only sleep. The butterfly is the symbol of farewell, just as it was the symbol of the last greeting before sleep.

"DANCER" AND "SHE DANCES"

More obscure than the image of the butterfly are Sachs's ciphers of music and dance. The dancer appears to be able to defy gravity in graceful and effortless leaps and spins. A new image of man is created in the dance—that of emancipation from earthly limitations and acceptance into the sphere of the incorporeal. On this premise, Sachs bases her depiction of the dancer as a re-creator, savior, and emancipator from material limitations. In the poem "Sie tanzt" ("She Dances"), from *Noch feiert Tod das Leben*, the dancer rescues her lover from the dead. This act of rescue is not meant to save him from physical death, for he is no longer alive; metamorphosis is her aim. This she achieves, paradoxically, by her own death: "Aber plötzlich/ am Genick/ Schlaf beünt Sie hinüber" ("But suddenly/ at the neck/ sleep bends her over"). In German, the word "over" (*hinüber*) signifies "to the other side" and thus clearly suggests death; this connotation is underscored by the image of her bending at the neck (hanging) and by the word "sleep," which Sachs frequently uses as a synonym for physical, but not spiritual, death. In the act of dancing, the dancer has liberated both the dead lover and herself. The metamorphosis has released her from life and has rescued him from death. They are united in the spiritual realm. In *Flucht und Verwandlung*, a somewhat different form of creation is discussed in the poem "Tänzerin" ("Dancer"). Here the dancer becomes the vessel for the hope of the future, and Sachs depicts with physiological clarity the birth canal for a messianic prophecy: "In the branches of your limbs/ the premonitions/ build their twittering nests." The dancer's body becomes the maternal, life-giving promise of the future.

In the poem "She Dances," the beginning and the end of life are shown to coincide at the point of metamorphosis, the dancer being the agent. The medium for transfiguration is music. The poem "O-A-O-A," in *Glühende Rätsel* (glowing enigmas), describes the rhythmic "sea of vowels" as the Alpha and Omega. Music is the means of metamorphosis: "Du aber die Tasten niederdrücktest/ in ihre Gräber aus Musik/ und Tanz die verlorene Sternschnuppe/ einen Flügel erfand für dein Leiden" ("But you pressed down the keys/ into their graves of music/ and dance the lost meteor/ invented a wing for your anguish"). The English word "keys" is ambiguous, but the German *Tasten* refers solely to the keys of a piano in this context. The graves are made of music, the transforming factor, and are being played like the keys of a piano, while dance provides the wings for the flight from the corporeal.

"IN THE BLUE DISTANCE"

Finally, in the poem "In der blauen Ferne" ("In the Blue Distance"), from *Und niemand weiss weiter*, the pregnant last lines combine the ciphers of stone, dust, dance, and music in the depiction of metamorphosis: "the stone transforms its dust/ dancing into music." The lifeless element needs no mediator here but performs the ritual of transubstantiation into music (release from corporeal existence) by "dancing" as "dust"—an action functionally identical to that of the drifting sand in the poem "Hasidic Scriptures."

It has frequently been assumed that Sachs is chiefly a chronicler of Jewish destiny during World War II, a recorder of death and despair. This narrow view does not do justice to her work. Sachs's poetry has many aspects of faith, hope, and love, and need not be relegated to a specific historical event or ethnic orientation. Sachs writes about the concerns of every human being—birth, life, love, spiritual renewal, and the possibility of an existence beyond physical death. To diminish the scope of her appeal is to misunderstand her message and to misinterpret her work.

OTHER MAJOR WORKS

SHORT FICTION: *Legenden und Erzählungen*, 1921.

PLAYS: *Eli: Ein Mysterienspiel vom Leiden Israels*, pb. 1951 (*Eli: A Mystery Play of the Sufferings of Israel*, 1967); *Zeichen im Sand: Die szenischen Dichtungen*, pb. 1962.

NONFICTION: *Paul Celan, Nelly Sachs: Correspondence*, 1995.

BIBLIOGRAPHY

Bahti, Timothy, and Marilyn Sibley Fries, eds. *Jewish Writers, German Literature: The Uneasy Examples of Nelly Sachs and Walter Benjamin*. Ann Arbor: University of Michigan Press, 1995. Biographical and critical essays of Sachs's and Benjamin's lives and works. Includes bibliographical references and an index.

Bosmajian, Hamida. *Metaphors of Evil: Contemporary German Literature and the Shadow of Nazism*. Iowa City: University of Iowa Press, 1979. A historical and critical study of responses to the Holocaust in poetry and prose. Includes bibliographical references and index.

Bower, Kathrin M. *Ethics and Remembrance in the Poetry of Nelly Sachs and Rose Ausländer*. Rochester, N.Y.: Camden House, 2000. Critical interpretation of the works of Sachs and Ausländer with particular attention to their recollections of the Holocaust. Includes bibliographical references and index.

Garloff, Katja. *Words from Abroad: Trauma and Displacement in Postwar German Jewish Writers*. Detroit: Wayne State University Press, 2005. This work on German Jewish writers contains a chapter on Sachs as well as one on her friend Celan.

Langer, Lawrence L. *Versions of Survival: The Holocaust and the Human Spirit*. Albany: State University of New York Press, 1982. Brilliantly illuminates the paradoxes in Sachs's verse.

Roth, John K., ed. *Holocaust Literature*. Pasadena, Calif.: Salem Press, 2008. Contains a chapter that analyzes Sachs's "In the Blue Distance."

Rudnick, Ursula. *Post-Shoa Religious Metaphors: The Image of God in the Poetry of*

Nelly Sachs. New York: Peter Lang, 1995. A biography of the poet and an in-depth interpretation of seven poems. Rudnick traces the biblical and mystical Jewish tradition that grounds Sachs's work. Includes bibliographical references.

Sachs, Nelly. *Paul Celan, Nelly Sachs: Correspondence*. Translated by Christopher Clark. Edited by Barbara Wiedemann. Riverdale-on-Hudson, N.Y.: Sheep Meadow Press, 1995. A collection of letters by two poets living outside Germany and tormented by guilt that they had escaped the Holocaust. Includes bibliographical references and index.

Soltes, Ori Z. *The Ashen Rainbow: Essays on the Arts and the Holocaust*. Washington, D.C.: Eshel Books, 2007. This work on art and the Holocaust contains a chapter that discusses Sachs.

Helene M. Kastinger Riley

SIEGFRIED SASSOON

Born: Brenchley, Kent, England; September 8, 1886
Died: Heytesbury, England; September 1, 1967
Also known as: Saul Kain; Pinchbeck Lyre; Sigmund Sashun

PRINCIPAL POETRY
The Daffodil Murderer, 1913
The Old Huntsman, and Other Poems, 1917
Counter-Attack, and Other Poems, 1918
War Poems, 1919
Picture Show, 1920
Recreations, 1923
Selected Poems, 1925
Satirical Poems, 1926
The Heart's Journey, 1927
Poems of Pinchbeck Lyre, 1931
The Road to Ruin, 1933
Vigils, 1935
Poems Newly Selected, 1916-1935, 1940
Rhymed Ruminations, 1940
Collected Poems, 1947
Common Chords, 1950
Emblems of Experience, 1951
The Tasking, 1954
Sequences, 1956
Lenten Illuminations and Sight Sufficient, 1958
The Path to Peace, 1960
Collected Poems, 1908-1956, 1961
An Octave, 1966

OTHER LITERARY FORMS

Siegfried Sassoon (suh-SEWN) is nearly as well known for his prose works as for his poetry. From 1926 to 1945, he spent most of his time working on the two trilogies that form the bulk of his work in prose. The first of these was the three-volume fictionalized autobiography published in 1937 as *The Memoirs of George Sherston*. It begins in *Memoirs of a Fox-Hunting Man* (1928), by recounting the life of a well-to-do young country squire in Georgian England up to his first experiences as an officer in World War I. The second volume, *Memoirs of an Infantry Officer* (1930), and the third,

Sherston's Progress (1936), describe the young man's war experiences. In the later trilogy, Sassoon discarded the thinly disguised fiction of the Sherston novels and wrote direct autobiography, with a nostalgic look back at his pleasant pastoral life in prewar England in *The Old Century and Seven More Years* (1938) and *The Weald of Youth* (1942). In *Siegfried's Journey, 1916-1920* (1945), Sassoon looks again at his own experiences during and immediately following the war. These autobiographical works are invaluable to the student of Sassoon's poetry because of the context they provide, particularly for the war poems.

Two other significant prose works should be mentioned. The first is Sassoon's *Lecture on Poetry*, delivered at the University of Bristol on March 16, 1939, in which Sassoon delineated what he considered to be the elements of good poetry. The second work is Sassoon's critical biography of the poet George Meredith, titled simply *Meredith* (1948), which also suggests some of Sassoon's views on poetry.

ACHIEVEMENTS

According to Bernard Bergonzi, Siegfried Sassoon was the only soldier-poet to be widely read during the war itself. This gave Sassoon a unique opportunity to influence other war poets, which he did. Though his war poetry has been criticized for being mere description, for appealing to only the senses and not the imagination, and for being uncontrolled emotion without artistic restraint, there can be no doubt than Sassoon's poetry represented a complete break with the war poetry of the past in tone, technique, and subject matter. With uncompromising realism and scathing satire, Sassoon portrayed the sufferings of the front-line soldier and the incompetency of the staff for the express purposes of convincing his readers to protest continuation of the war. His *Counter-Attack, and Other Poems* was nearly suppressed because of poems such as "The General," which broke the prohibition against criticizing those in charge of the war effort.

Unquestionably, Sassoon's realistic subject matter and diction influenced other poets, most notably his friend Wilfred Owen, whose poetry was posthumously published by Sassoon in 1920; but Sassoon failed to influence later poetry because, as John Johnston notes, his war poetry was all negative—he provided no constructive replacement for the myths he had destroyed. Nor did Sassoon influence poetry in the 1930's because, according to Michael Thorpe, he was still a prisoner of war, and through his autobiographies he retreated from the political struggle of W. H. Auden and Stephen Spender and others into his own earlier years.

When in the 1950's Sassoon finally did have something positive to offer, no one was willing to listen. He was no longer well known or critically acknowledged. Certainly his future reputation will rest on the war poems; but in his religious poems of the 1950's, Sassoon did achieve a style of simple expression, compact brevity, and concrete imagery with a universally appealing theme, and this should be noted as a remarkable though largely unrecognized achievement.

BIOGRAPHY

Siegfried Lorraine Sassoon was born in the Kentish weald in 1886, the second of three sons of Alfred Ezra Sassoon and Theresa Georgina Thornycroft. His father was descended from a long line of wealthy Jewish merchants and bankers who, after wandering through Spain, Persia, and India, had come to settle in England. The family was proud of its orthodoxy, and Siegfried's father was the first to marry outside the faith. Siegfried's mother, in contrast, was an artist, the close relative of three well-known sculptors, and a member of the landed gentry. The marriage was a failure, and Alfred Sassoon left when Siegfried was five, leaving the younger Sassoon to be reared by his mother as an Anglican.

Siegfried had no formal schooling as a child, though from the ages of nine to fourteen he learned from private tutors and a German governess. In 1902, he attended Marlborough, and in 1905, he entered Clare College, Cambridge. Sassoon's temperament was not disciplined enough for scholarly pursuits; he began by reading law, switched to history, and ultimately left Cambridge without a degree. He returned to Kent, where, on an inherited income of five hundred pounds a year, he was able to devote his energies to foxhunting, racing, and writing poetry. Sassoon loved the pastoral beauty of the Kentish downs and attempted to portray it in a number of dreamy, sentimental lyrics. Between the ages of nineteen and twenty-six, Sassoon had nine volumes of poetry privately published, before he enjoyed a mild success with *The Daffodil Murderer* in 1913. The poem was chiefly intended as a parody of John Masefield's *The Everlasting Mercy*, but Sassoon's poem had a strong human appeal of its own. By this time, Sassoon had been befriended by Edward Marsh, the editor of *Georgian Poetry*. Marsh encouraged Sassoon's literary endeavors and persuaded him to come to London in May, 1914, where Sassoon began to move in the literary world and to meet such notable authors as Rupert Brooke. Sassoon, however, felt unhappy and lacked a sense of purpose, and when he enlisted in the army on August 3, 1914 (two days before England entered the war), it was to escape a sterile existence.

Sassoon's early life had been extremely sheltered, even pampered, and it was a very immature twenty-eight-year-old who went to war, totally unprepared for what he would find. After convalescence from injuries received in a fall during cavalry training, he accepted a commission and went through training as an infantry officer. Thus, he did not arrive in France until November, 1915, where he became transport officer for the First Battalion of the Royal Welch Fusiliers. Here he met and befriended the poet Robert Graves. In *Goodbye to All That* (1929), Graves describes his first meeting with Sassoon and relates how, when he showed Sassoon his first book of poems, *Over the Brazier* (1916), Sassoon, whose early war poems were idealistic, had frowned and said that war should not be written about in such a realistic way. Graves, who had been in France six months, remarked that Sassoon had not yet been in the trenches.

Graves already knew what Sassoon would soon discover, indeed what all the British troops in France were coming to feel: growing disillusionment at the frustration and the staggering casualties of trench warfare. There were 420,000 British casualties in the Somme offensive beginning on July 1, 1916—an offensive that gained virtually nothing. The Somme was Sassoon's most bitter experience in the trenches; after it, he would never write the old kind of poetry again.

In spite of his pacifist leanings, Sassoon distinguished himself in the war. Called "Mad Jack" by his troops, Sassoon was awarded the Military Cross and recommended for the Distinguished Service Order for his exploits in battle: After a raid at Mametz, he took it upon himself to bring back the wounded; in the Somme in early July, he single-handedly occupied a whole section of an enemy trench, after which he was found in the trench, alone, reading a book of poetry. Ill with gastric fever in late July, he was sent home for three months, where he worked on poems to be included in *The Old Huntsman, and Other Poems*.

While in England, Sassoon met Lady Ottoline Morrell and her liberal husband, Philip, at whose home he spoke with such pacifists as Bertrand Russell, listened to open criticism of the war, and heard of Germany's peace overtures and the impure motives of members of parliament who wanted the war to continue.

Sassoon returned to active service in France in February, 1917, but in April, he was wounded in the Battle of Arras and sent home again. Haunted by nightmares of violence and by what the pacifists were saying, Sassoon resolved to protest the war on a grand scale. In July, in a remarkable move, risking public disgrace and military court-martial, Sassoon refused to return to active duty and wrote a formal declaration of protest to his commanding officer, which was reproduced in the press and which Russell arranged to have mentioned in the House of Commons. In his letter, Sassoon charged that the war was being deliberately prolonged by the politicians for ignoble purposes, even though there was a chance for a negotiated settlement with Germany, thus leading the men at the front line to be slaughtered needlessly. Sassoon hoped to be court-martialed, so that his protest would have propaganda value. To his dismay, however, the official reaction was largely to minimize the letter. In a moment of despair, Sassoon flung his Military Cross into the Mersey River and vowed to continue his protest.

At that point, Graves stepped in. Graves agreed with Sassoon's letter, but considered the gesture futile and feared for Sassoon's personal welfare. Graves arranged to have Sassoon appear before a medical board, and chiefly on Graves's testimony, Sassoon was found to be suffering from shell shock. The incident was closed, and Sassoon was sent to Craiglockhart hospital in Edinburgh, where physician W. H. R. Rivers became his counselor and friend, and where in August he met the brilliant young poet Wilfred Owen. Owen knew and idolized Sassoon as the author of *The Old Huntsman, and Other Poems* (which had appeared in May), and Sassoon's encouragement and insistence on realism had greatly influenced him. At Craiglockhart, during the autumn of 1917, Sassoon composed many of the poems of *Counter-Attack, and Other Poems*, which was published the following year.

Owen returned to active duty in November, and Sassoon, feeling that he was betraying his troops at the front by staying away in comfort, returned to duty a few weeks later. He went first to Ireland, then to Egypt, where he became a captain, then back to France in May. On July 15, 1918, Sassoon, returning from an attack on a German machine gun, was wounded in the head by one of his own sentries. He was sent to a London hospital, where he spent the rest of the war.

After the war, Sassoon retreated from the active life, becoming more and more contemplative (he had always been introspective and solitary) until he acquired a reputation as a virtual hermit. Immediately after the war, he joined the Labor Party and became editor of the literary pages of the *Daily Herald*, where he published satirical pieces with a socialist point of view. His satire of the 1920's, however, was uneasy and awkward, stemming from the fact that the issues of the day were not as clear-cut as the right and wrong about the war had been. Besides, he was not really sure of himself, feeling a need to explore his past life and find some meaning in it. Still, as the 1930's grew darker, Sassoon wrote poems warning of the horror of chemical and biological warfare. No one seemed to want to listen, however, and Sassoon, disillusioned, forsook "political" poetry completely. In part, the autobiographies that he worked on in those years were a rejection of the modern world and an idealization of the past. In part, too, they were an effort to look inside himself, and that same urge characterizes most of his later poetry, which is concerned with his personal spiritual struggle and development.

Thus, the incidents of Sassoon's later life were nearly all spiritual. Only a few isolated events are of interest: In 1933, he finally married; he had a son, George, but Sassoon kept his personal relationships private, never mentioning them in his poetry. During World War II, Sassoon's home was requisitioned for evacuees, and later, fifteen hundred American troops were quartered on his large estate. After the war, Sassoon remained very solitary and appears to have cultivated his image as the "hermit of Heytesbury." When his volumes of poetry appeared in the 1950's, they were largely ignored by critics and public alike. The fiery war poet had outlived his reputation, but he had reached a great personal plateau: On August 14, 1957, Sassoon was received into the Catholic Church at Downside Abbey. His last poems, appearing in a privately published collection, *An Octave*, on his eightieth birthday (a year before his death), display a serene and quiet faith.

ANALYSIS

In 1939, Siegfried Sassoon delineated his views on poetry in a lecture given at Bristol College. While what he said was not profound or revolutionary, it did indicate the kind of poetry Sassoon liked and tried to write, at least at that time. First, Sassoon said, poetry should stem from inspiration, but that inspiration needs to be tempered by control and discipline—by art. Second, the best poetry is simple and direct—Sassoon disliked the tendency toward complexity initiated by T. S. Eliot and Ezra Pound. Third, Sassoon held the Romantic view that poetry should express true feeling and speak the language of the heart. Fourth, poetry should contain strong visual imagery, the best of which is drawn from nature. Finally, the subject matter of the best poetry is not political (again, he was reacting against the avowedly political poetry of Auden and his associates), but rather personal, and this examination of self led Sassoon to write spiritual poetry.

A review of Sassoon's poetry will reveal, however, that even in his best poems he did not always follow all these precepts, and that in his worst poems he seldom followed any. Sassoon's worst poems are most certainly his earliest ones. Sassoon's prewar lyric verses are lush and wordy, in weak imitation of Algernon Charles Swinburne and the Pre-Raphaelites, but full of anachronisms and redundancies. Some, such as "Haunted" and "Goblin Revel," are purely escapist; Lewis Thorpe suggests that Sassoon was looking for escape from his own too-comfortable world. The best thing about these early poems is their interest in nature—an interest that Sassoon never lost and that provided him with concrete images in later pieces. The best poems that Sassoon wrote before the war, *The Daffodil Murderer* and "The Old Huntsman," abandon the poetic diction for a colloquial style, and "The Old Huntsman" reveals a strong kinship with nature.

THE WAR POETRY

Sassoon's early, idealistic war poetry is characterized by an abstract diction and generalized imagery. He was writing in the "happy warrior" style after the manner of Rupert Brooke's famous sonnet sequence and was even able to write of his brother's death early in the war as a "victory" and his ghost's head as "laureled." Perhaps the best example of these early poems is "Absolution," written before Sassoon had actually experienced the war. Sassoon romanticizes war, speaking of the glorious sacrifice of young comrades in arms who go off to battle as "the happy legion," asserting that "fighting for our freedom, we are free." The poem is full of such abstractions, but no concrete images. Its language is often archaic ("Time's but a golden wind"), and it is the sort of thing that Sassoon soon put behind him.

Edward Marsh, after reading some of Sassoon's earlier poetry, had told him to write with his eye directly on the object. As Sassoon began to experience the horrors of trench warfare, he did exactly that. His poems became increasingly concrete, visual, and realistic, his language became increasingly colloquial, and his tone became more and more bitter as the war went on. Early in 1916, he wrote "Golgotha," "The Redeemer," and "A Working Party," in which he tried to present realistically the sufferings of the common soldier. Such realistic depiction of the front lines characterized one of two main types of war poetry that Sassoon was to write in the next few years. The best example of sheer naturalistic description is "Counter-Attack," the title poem of Sassoon's most popular and most scathing volume of poetry. "Counter-Attack" begins with a description of the troops, who, having taken an enemy trench, begin to deepen it with shovels. They uncover a pile of dead bodies and rotting body parts—"naked sodden buttocks, mats of hair,/ Bulged, clotted heads."

"REPRESSION OF WAR EXPERIENCE"

The horror of this description is without parallel, but where Sassoon really excels is in his realistic portrayal of the psychological effects of the war. Perhaps his best poem in this vein is "Repression of War Experience," from *Counter-Attack, and Other Poems*. The poem, in the form of an interior monologue, explores a mind verging on hysteria, trying to distract itself and maintain control while even the simplest, most serene events—a moth fluttering too close to a candle flame—bring nightmarish thoughts of violence into the persona's mind. In the garden, he hears ghosts, and as he sits in the silence, he can hear only the guns. In the end, his control breaks down; he wants to rush out "and screech at them to stop—I'm going crazy;/ I'm going stark, staring mad because of the guns."

"THEY"

Sassoon was not merely presenting realistic details; he was being deliberately didactic, trying to use his poetry to incite a public outcry against the war. When home on leave, he had been appalled by the jingoistic ignorance and complacency on the home front. Sassoon's second main type of war poetry made a satirical attack on these civilians, on those who conducted the war, and on the irresponsible press that spread the lying propaganda. Justly the most famous of these poems is "They" (*The Old Huntsman, and Other Poems*), in which Sassoon demolishes the cherished civilian notion that the war was divinely ordained and that the British were fighting on God's side. Sassoon presents a pompous bishop declaring that, since the "boys" will have fought "Anti-Christ," none will return "the same" as he was. The irony of this statement is made clear when the "boys" return quite changed: blind, legless, and syphilitic. The bishop can only remark, "The ways of God are strange." "They" caused a great outcry in England by ruthlessly attacking the Church for forsaking the moral leadership it should have provided.

"They" also illustrates Sassoon's favorite technique in satire: concentration of his ironic force in the last line of the poem. This kind of "knock-out punch" may be seen most vividly in the poem "The One-Legged Man" (*The Old Huntsman, and Other Poems*), which describes a soldier, discharged from the war, watching the natural beauty of the world in autumn and considering the bright, comfortable years ahead. The poem ends with the man's crushingly ironic thought, "Thank God they had to amputate!"

Certainly there are flaws in Sassoon's war poetry. Some of the verses are nothing more than bitter invectives designed merely to attack a part of his audience, such as "Glory of Women," "Blighters," and "Fight to the Finish." Even the best poems often lack the discipline and order that Sassoon himself later advanced as one main criterion of poetry. Further, Sassoon almost never got beyond his feelings about immediate experiences to form theoretical or profound notions about the broader aspects of the war. Sassoon himself realized this lack in 1920, when he brought out his slain friend Wilfred Owen's war poetry, which converted war experiences into something having universal meaning.

"THE DUG OUT"

The war poetry, however, has a number of virtues as well. It uses simple, direct, and clear expression that comes, as Sassoon advocated, from the heart. Further, it uses vivid pictures to express the inexpressible horror of the trenches. "The Dug Out" (*Picture Show*) is an example of Sassoon's war poetry at its best. In its eight lines, Sassoon draws a clear picture of a youth sleeping in an awkward and unnatural position. The simple, colloquial language focuses on the emotional state of the speaker, and much is suggested by what is left unsaid. The speaker's nerves are such that he can no longer bear the sight of the young sleeper because, as he cries in the final lines, "You are too young to fall asleep for ever;/ And when you sleep you remind me of the dead." Arthur Lane compares such poems, in which the ironic effect is achieved through the dramatic situation more than through imagery, to those in the *Satires of Circumstance* (1914) of Sassoon's idol, Thomas Hardy, suggesting an influence at work.

"EVERYONE SANG"

Perhaps the culmination of Sassoon's attempt to transcend his war experience is the much-admired lyric "Everyone Sang" (*Picture Show*). It is a joyous lyric expressing a mood of relief and exultation, through the imagery of song and of singing birds. Sassoon seems to have been expressing his own relief at having survived: "horror/ Drifted away." Lane calls these lines "pure poetry" of "visionary power," comparing them to poems of William Wordsworth and William Blake. He might have also mentioned Henry Vaughan, Sassoon's other idol, whose path toward poetry of a very personal spirituality Sassoon was soon to follow.

"LINES WRITTEN IN ANTICIPATION . . ."

Unquestionably, it is for his war poetry that Sassoon is chiefly admired. Still, he lived for nearly fifty years after the armistice, and what he wrote in that time cannot be disregarded. He first flirted with socialism after the war; "Everyone Sang" may be intended to laud the coming utopian society. Then he attempted satiric poetry during the 1920's, which must be regarded as a failure. His targets varied from the upper classes to political corruption and newspapers, but the poetry is not from the heart; the satire is too loud and not really convincing. Michael Thorpe points out the wordiness of Sassoon's style in these satires, together with the length of his sentences. One blatant example is

"Lines Written in Anticipation of a London Paper Attaining a Guaranteed Circulation of Ten Million Daily." Even the title is verbose, but note the wordy redundancy of the lines:

> Were it not wiser, were it not more candid,
> More courteous, more consistent with good sense,
> If I were to include all, all who are banded
> Together in achievement so immense?

RELIGIOUS SEARCHING AND SPIRITUALITY

Though he soon abandoned the satiric mode, Sassoon did maintain what Joseph Cohen calls the role of prophet that he had assumed in the war years, by continually warning, through *The Road to Ruin* and *Rhymed Ruminations*, of the coming disaster of World War II. His total despair for the modern world is expressed in "Litany of the Lost" (1945), wherein, with the ominous line "Deliver us from ourselves," Sassoon bid farewell to the poetry of social commentary. By now he was more interested in his spiritual quest.

Next to his war poems, Sassoon's poems of religious searching are his most effective. The quest begins with "The Traveller to His Soul" (1933), in which Sassoon asks, as the "problem which concerns me most," the question "Have I got a soul?" He spends over twenty years trying to answer the question. His work, beginning with *The Heart's Journey* and *Vigils*, is concerned with exploration of self and uncertainty about the self's place in the universe, with increasing questioning about what lies behind creation. With *Rhymed Ruminations*, Sassoon ends the 1930's on a note of uneasiness and uncertainty.

SEQUENCES

The questions are answered in the three volumes *Common Chords*, *Emblems of Experience*, and *The Tasking*, which were combined to make the book *Sequences*. In the poem "Redemption" (*Common Chords*), Sassoon yearns for a vision of the eternal, which he recognizes as existing beyond his senses. Sassoon's lines recall Vaughan's mystical visions when he asks for "O but one ray/ from that all-hallowing and eternal day." In *The Tasking*, Sassoon reached what Thorpe calls a spiritual certainty, and his best poems in that volume succeed more clearly than the war poems in satisfying Sassoon's own poetic criteria as expressed in 1939. In "Another Spring," Sassoon speaks in simple, direct, and compact language about feelings of the heart—an old man's emotions on witnessing what may be his last spring. The natural imagery is concrete and visual as well as auditory, concentrating on "some crinkled primrose leaves" and "a noise of nesting rooks." Though the final three lines of the poem add a hint of didacticism, the poem succeeds by leaving much unsaid about the eternal rebirth of nature and its implications for the old man and the force behind the regenerative cycle of nature. It is a fine poem, like many in *The Tasking*, with a simple, packed style that makes these poems better as art, though doomed to be less familiar than the war poems.

OTHER MAJOR WORKS

LONG FICTION: *The Memoirs of George Sherston*, 1937 (includes *Memoirs of a Fox-Hunting Man*, 1928; *Memoirs of an Infantry Officer*, 1930; and *Sherston's Progress*, 1936).

NONFICTION: *The Old Century and Seven More Years*, 1938; *Lecture on Poetry*, 1939; *The Weald of Youth*, 1942; *Siegfried's Journey, 1916-1920*, 1945; *Meredith*, 1948; *Siegfried Sassoon Diaries, 1920-1922*, 1981; *Siegfried Sassoon Diaries, 1915-1918*, 1983; *Siegfried Sassoon Diaries, 1923-1925*, 1985.

EDITED TEXT: *Poems by Wilfred Owen*, 1920.

BIBLIOGRAPHY

Bloom, Harold, ed. *Poets of World War I: Rupert Brooke and Siegfried Sassoon*. Philadelphia: Chelsea House, 2003. Contains numerous essays on Sassoon, covering topics such as realism, satire, and spirituality in his poetry.

Caesar, Adrian. *Taking It Like a Man: Suffering, Sexuality, and the War Poets: Brooke, Sassoon, Owen, Graves*. New York: Manchester University Press, 1993. Caesar explores how four British poets reconciled their ideologies inherited from Christianity, imperialism, and Romanticism with their experiences of World War I.

Campbell, Patrick. *Siegfried Sassoon: A Study of the War Poetry*. Jefferson, N.C.: McFarland, 1999. Through primary documents and research, Campbell provides critical analyses of Sassoon's war poetry. Includes bibliographical references and an index.

Egremont, Max. *Siegfried Sassoon: A Life*. New York: Farrar, Straus and Giroux, 2005. This biography of Sassoon examines his life, including his relationship with Stephan Tennant, its breakup, and his subsequent marriage.

Fussell, Paul. *The Great War and Modern Memory*. 1975. Reprint. New York: Oxford University Press, 2000. This classic study of the literature arising from the experience of fighting in World War I pays special attention to Sassoon's fiction, autobiography, and poetry. Provides a useful context for Sassoon's work in comparison to other writers of the period.

Hipp, Daniel. *The Poetry of Shell Shock: Wartime Trauma and Healing in Wilfred Owen, Ivor Gurney, and Siegfried Sassoon*. Jefferson, N.C.: McFarland, 2005. Contains chapters examining the lives and works of three war poets: Sassoon, Wilfred Owen, and Ivory Gurney.

Lane, Arthur E. *An Adequate Response: The War Poetry of Wilfred Owen and Siegfried Sassoon*. Detroit: Wayne State University Press, 1972. Lane highlights the use of satire and parody as he analyzes Sassoon's war verse. Contends that Sassoon and others, when faced with the horrors of trench warfare, were charged with creating a new mode of expression since the traditional modes proved inadequate.

Moeyes, Paul. *Siegfried Sassoon: Scorched Glory—A Critical Study*. New York: St. Martin's Press, 1997. Moeyes draws on Sassoon's edited diaries and letters to explore Sassoon's assertion that his poetry was his real autobiography. Includes bibliography and an index.

Wilson, Jean Moorcroft. *Siegfried Sassoon: The Journey from the Trenches—A Biography, 1918-1967*. London: Duckworth, 2003. Describes the later years of Sassoon's life, looking at his life after the war.

_____. *Siegfried Sassoon: The Making of a War Poet—A Biography*. New York: Routledge, 1999. Details Sassoon's early life, covering the years from his birth through 1918, and in doing so, closely examines his struggle to come to terms with being gay.

Jay Ruud

JON SILKIN

Born: London, England; December 2, 1930
Died: Newcastle upon Tyne, England; November 25, 1997

OTHER LITERARY FORMS

In addition to being a noted poet, Jon Silkin (SIHL-kihn) was also an important literary critic, authoring a study of English poetry from World War I, *Out of Battle: The Poetry of the Great War* (1972, 1987), and a study of modern twentieth century poetry, *The Life of Metrical and Free Verse in Twentieth-Century Poetry* (1997). Related to his criticism was his editing of the significant collections *The Penguin Book of First World War Poetry* (1979, 1981), *Wilfred Owen: The Poems* (1985), *The Penguin Book of First World War Prose* (coeditor with Jon Glover; 1989), and *The War Poems of Wilfred Owen* (1994). Silkin also wrote one play, *Gurney*, published in 1985 and produced in London, as *Black Notes*, in 1986.

ACHIEVEMENTS

Jon Silkin was honored with the Geoffrey Faber Memorial Prize (1965) for *Nature with Man* and a C. Day Lewis Fellowship (1976-1977), and he was made a Fellow of the Royal Society of Literature (1986). Just as important is Jon Silkin's inclusion in such prestigious anthologies as *New Poets of England and America* (1957, 1962), *The New Poetry* (2d ed., 1966), *Poems of Our Moment* (1968), *British Poetry Since 1945* (1970), *The Norton Anthology of Modern Poetry* (1973), *The Oxford Book of Twentieth-Cen-*

Jon Silkin

tury English Verse (1973), *The Hutchinson Book of Post-War British Poets* (1989), and *Anthology of Twentieth-Century British and Irish Poetry* (2001). His role as founder and continuing editor of the magazine *Stand*—devoted first to publishing modern poetry and its criticism, and later including modern fiction—also ensures Silkin a lasting place in the history of modern British literature.

BIOGRAPHY

Jon Silkin was the son of Jewish parents, Joseph Silkin, a lawyer, and Dora Rubenstein Silkin. War made a deep impression on Silkin as a child; as a youngster, one of Silkin's most vivid memories, referred to in his poetry, was of being evacuated from London to the countryside during the German bombing during World War II. After National Service in the Education Corps (1948-1950), during which he reached the rank of sergeant, Silkin spent the years between 1950 and 1956 as a manual laborer in London, an experience partly reflected in his first-person poems about cemetery groundskeeping and about workingmen. During this period, he founded the literary periodical *Stand* in 1952 and published his first major poetry collection in 1954.

After working as an English teacher to foreign students in 1956-1958, Silkin was appointed Gregory Fellow in Poetry at the University of Leeds, a position he held from 1958 to 1960. He came relatively late to a formal college education, earning his B.A. from the University of Leeds as a mature student. The degree, awarded in 1962, took him only two years to complete. In 1964, he became founding coeditor of Northern House Publishers in Newcastle upon Tyne and subsequently, as reflected in the locales of his poetry, held a variety of teaching, visiting instructor, and visiting writer-in-residence posts at universities and colleges in England, the United States (in Ohio, Iowa, Idaho, Kentucky, and Washington, D.C.), Australia, Israel, Japan, and Korea.

Married to the writer Lorna Tracy in 1974 and divorced in 1995, Silkin had four children; the death of the first, Adam, and birth of the second, David, had profound impacts on Silkin, manifested in his poetry, which likewise indicates how important love, marriage, children, and parenting remained throughout his life. He died in 1997.

ANALYSIS

A third or more of Jon Silkin's approximately 350 poems deal with or touch on the subject of the natural world and humanity's relation with it, through concord, discord, or symbolic parallels. Animals, such as the persecuted fox of Silkin's antihunting poems, or various caged or free birds; insects, such as the bees, butterflies, moths, ants, and flies, with their interesting symbolism applicable to nature and humanity; plants, such as the various flowers of Silkin's distinctive flower poems; and inanimate nature, especially stones, river, sea, sky, and stars—all pervade Silkin's poetry both as subjects and repositories of imagery and symbolism. The poems most often anthologized have been selections from the fifteen flower poems (so named by Silkin himself) in *Nature with Man*: "A Bluebell," "Crowfoot (in Water)," "A Daisy," "Dandelion," "Goat's Beard and Daisy," "Harebell," "Iris," "Lilies of the Valley," "Milkmaids (Lady's Smock)," "Moss," "Peonies," "Small Celandine," "The Strawberry Plant," "The Violet," and "White Geranium." As Silkin himself explains in "Note on 'Flower' Poems" in *Nature with Man*, the flowers are either wild or cultivated, suggesting certain relationships with humanity, and the garden is "a kind of human bestiary, containing in the several plants earlier developed and anticipatory examples of human types and situations." Silkin goes on in his note to discuss almost every flower poem, explaining for example that "'Dandelion' . . . sees its subject as a seizer of space, and asks for political parallels to be made," including the idea of "nature being a 'preying upon.'" While Silkin's analyses of his own flower poems are perceptive (not always true of writers about their own work), they are not exhaustive: for example, lurking in the background of "Dandelion" is the etymology of the flower's name, from "lion's tooth."

As meritorious as these flower poems but not as well known are the ones from

Silkin's later books: "Snow Drop" (from *Poems, New and Selected*), which suggests the paradoxes of a flower having insect-like qualities and appearing in sunshine, despite its name; "Ajuga" (from *The Ship's Pasture*), which explores the flower's intercontinental intermixture, the paradox of a mineral appearance of a plant, and the powerful psychological effects on the viewer; and "Inside the Gentian" (from *The Lens-Breakers*), which examines the flower's combination of visual art, mystery, magic, violence, and communicativeness.

HUMAN RELATIONSHIPS

A third or more of Silkin's poems deal with romantic love, including marriage and the parent-child relationship, and an even larger proportion of his poems deal with all the varied relationships between human beings individually and in groups, societies, or nations. Romantic love, frequently with marriage implied, is celebrated in physical terms, sometimes quite sexually explicit, in poems such as "Community" and "Processes" (both from *Nature with Man*); "Opened" and "Our Selves" (both from *Amana Grass*); "Untitled Poem: 'The Perfume on Your Body'" (from *The Little Time-Keeper*); "Acids," "Going On," and "Water" (all from *The Psalms with Their Spoils*); "Given a Flower" and "The Lamps of Home" (both from *The Ship's Pasture*); and "Beings," "The Hand's Black Hymns," "Juniper and Forgiveness," and "Psalmists" (all from *The Lens-Breakers*). Such love may sometimes emphasize a triumph of life over death, or reach to the spiritual beyond the physical, an issue that is recurrent in Silkin's poetry, as are the words "flesh," "mind," and "spirit." Such physical love gone wrong is shown in one of Silkin's poetic sequences, "Poems Concerning Salome and Herod" (from *The Ship's Pasture*). Another difficult issue in romantic love includes separation, as in "Absence and Light" and "A Hand" (both from *The Ship's Pasture*) and "A Psalm Concerning Absence" (from *The Lens-Breakers*). Recurrent words in Silkin's poetry are "absence" and "space," which refer to lovers' separation as well as death. Also problematic in love may be constancy or fidelity, as in "Fidelities" (from *The Lens-Breakers*).

For many couples, with love and marriage come children, and Silkin's responses to them range from elegy on their tragically premature death, as in "Death of a Son: Who Died in a Mental Hospital Aged One," to wonder and celebration at their birth, as in "For David Emanuel"—both autobiographical poems from *The Peaceable Kingdom*. "Death of a Son," based on the death of Silkin's son and possibly his best-known poem, ends with these memorable lines:

> He turned over as if he could be sorry for this
> And out of his eyes two great tears rolled, like stones,
> And he died.

A link between children and social criticism is shown in the poetic sequence "The People" (from *The Principle of Water*), in which a couple have difficulties with obtuse governmental authorities about the institutionalization and treatment of their disabled child in a case resembling that in "Death of a Son" and "For a Child: On His Being Pronounced Mentally Defective by a Committee of the LLC" (from *The Re-ordering of the Stones*). Lastly, the other side of the relationship—child to parent, rather than parent to child—is explored in "Fathers" (from *The Lens-Breakers*), in which the speaker deals with his father's death and cremation.

Unlike the passionless poet-critics he censures in "Three Critics" (from *The Re-ordering of the Stones*), Silkin is emotionally and socially engaged, writing poetry with social criticism of a government's or a society's mistreatment of parents and children, as in "For a Child"; of the working poor, as in "And I Turned from the Inner Heart," "Bowl," and "Furnished Lives" (all from *The Two Freedoms*), "Savings" (from *The Re-ordering of the Stones*), and "Killhope Wheel, 1860, County Durham" (from *The Principle of Water*); of whole groups of people, as in "Cherokee" (from *The Lens-Breakers*); or of pollution of the environment, as in "Crossing a River" (from *The Ship's Pasture*) or "The Levels" (from *The Lens-Breakers*). Worst of all, perhaps, is the failure of societies and nations to stop wars, spanning history from ancient times to the future nuclear war complacently lectured about by a government bureaucrat in "Defence" (from *Nature with Man*). The epigraph to *The Peaceable Kingdom*, drawn from the Biblical book of Isaiah about the wolf dwelling with the lamb, and the poem "Isaiah's Thread" (from *The Principle of Water*) show Silkin's continual awareness and criticism of the injuries inflicted in war throughout history: the Romans' war against the Jews in "Footsteps on the Downcast Path" (from *The Ship's Pasture*); the wars of the English against the Irish or Scots, in "Famine" (from *The Lens-Breakers*), "What Can We Mean?" (from *The Principle of Water*), and "Poem: 'At Laggan'" (from *Amana Grass*); the American Civil War, in "Paying for Forgiveness" and "Civil War Grave, Richmond" (both from *The Lens-Breakers*); World War I, in "Mr. Lloyd's Life" (from *The Lens-Breakers*); and World War II, in "We Stock the Deer-Park" (from *The Ship's Pasture*) and numerous poems about the Holocaust.

JEWISH HERITAGE AND HISTORY

Related to Silkin's Jewish heritage are nearly fifty poems referring to the history and culture of the Jewish people from ancient to modern times, scattered throughout all of Silkin's works. In "First It Was Singing" (from *The Peaceable Kingdom*), Silkin equates the outcries of hunted animals and persecuted Jews, which motivate the "singing" of the animals and the Jewish poet. The suffering of Jews and the guilt of Christian societies involved in their massacre and oppression in medieval England is the subject of "Astringencies No. 1: The Coldness" (from *The Re-ordering of the Stones*), "The Malabestia" (from *The Principle of Water*), and "Resting Place" (from *The Psalms with Their Spoils*). The Holocaust of World War II is a focus of "Culpabilities" (from *The Re-ordering of the Stones*), "Jaffa, and Other Places" (from *Amana Grass*), "The People,"

"The Plum-Tree" (from *The Little Time-Keeper*), "Footsteps on the Downcast Path," and "Fidelities" and "Trying to Hide Treblinka" (both from *The Lens-Breakers*). An eight-poem section of *Amana Grass* ("A Word About Freedom and Identity in Tel-Aviv," "Reclaimed Area," "Jaffa, and Other Places," "What are the lights, in dark," "Conditions," "Ayalon," "Bull-God," "Divisions") is devoted to Israel, and in these poems, as well as "Communal" and "Climbing to Jerusalem" (both from *The Ship's Pasture*) and "Jews Without Arabs" (from *The Lens-Breakers*), Silkin considers how, from ancient through modern times, Jews have confronted the issues of struggling with the natural world to make the land more habitable or living in harmony with non-Jewish fellow inhabitants.

METAPOETICS, LANGUAGE, AND COMMUNICATION

More than fifty of Silkin's poems deal with the topics of metapoetics (poetry about the nature, effects, or creation of literature or art), language, and communication. In *The Peaceable Kingdom*, Silkin suggests that the suffering and persecution of animals and Jews create their "singing." In "Prologue" and "Epilogue," the poems that open and close the book, he says that his poetry may function as a kind of Noah's ark to save the animals from injury by human beings as well as, perhaps, to unite all in enlightened, considered, and considerate harmony. In "From . . . the Animal Dark" (from *The Two Freedoms*), each of whose two sections is a partly disguised sonnet, appropriate to love poetry, the poet-speaker suggests that language charged by the poem may help create light, enlightenment, and the reunion of lovers. Likewise, in "Amber" (from *The Lens-Breakers*), the poem is equated to an amber pendant, a combination of art, nature, and preserver, whose beauty, warmth, electrical charge, and electrical attraction may touch the beloved both literally and metaphorically.

In contrast with the power of literature and language to enrich or unite, or to communicate with the divine, are the thwarting of this potential in sterility and divisiveness. "Three Critics," with implied ironic tautology, criticizes poet-critics who, following theory and social class, separate intellect from feeling and thus drain their verse of emotion, warmth, and conviction. "The Uses of Man and the Uses of Poetry" (from *The Psalms with Their Spoils*), with similar social criticism, laments the prison inmate who learns lyric and then satiric poetry but is rewarded with beating by the "warders" (guards). In "Crowfoot (in Water)," one of Silkin's celebrated flower poems, details suggest that the flower is "articulate" and has a capacity for communication, but this communication is "smutched" in the mouths and throats of hungry cattle that devour it. Also, in "Douglas of Sorbie and the Adder" (from *The Lens-Breakers*), based on a folktale, a mother is horrified by the realization that her young son and an adder are not only sharing food but also communicating. She orders the farm's day laborers to kill the snake, hoping for the child's success in Georgian London, but in an example of Silkin's ironic social criticism, she causes the death of her son through his grief over the death of the snake.

OTHER MAJOR WORKS

PLAY: *Gurney*, pb. 1985 (pr. 1986 as *Black Notes*).

NONFICTION: *Out of Battle: The Poetry of the Great War*, 1972, 1987; *The Life of Metrical and Free Verse in Twentieth-Century Poetry*, 1997.

TRANSLATION: *Against Parting*, 1968 (of Nathan Zach).

EDITED TEXTS: *Poetry of the Committed Individual: A "Stand" Anthology of Poetry*, 1973; *The Penguin Book of First World War Poetry*, 1979, 1981; *Wilfred Owen: The Poems*, 1985; *The Penguin Book of First World War Prose*, 1989 (with Jon Glover); *The War Poems of Wilfred Owen*, 1994.

BIBLIOGRAPHY

Bell, Arthur, Donald Heiney, and Lenthiel Downs. *English Literature: 1900 to the Present*. 2d ed. New York: Barron's, 1994. A section in chapter 12, "Varieties of Experimental Verse," gives a brief overview of Silkin's career through 1986, with comments on "Death of a Son" and the flower poems.

Brown, Merle. *Double Lyric: Divisiveness and Communal Creativity in Recent English Poetry*. New York: Columbia University Press, 1980. Chapter 6, "Stress in Silkin's Poetry and the Healing Emptiness of America," is a thirty-three-page survey of Silkin's work up to 1979 from the perspective of the "stress between imaginative realization and ideological commitment" by Silkin's most appreciative critic. Brown's brief "Afterword" is included in the 1975 edition of *The Peaceable Kingdom*, indicating themes of that book. Silkin composed an elegiac poem about Brown, "Wildness Makes a Form: In Memoriam the Critic Merle Brown."

Cluysenaar, Anne. "Alone in a Mine of Reality: A Matrix in the Poetry of Jon Silkin." In *British Poetry Since 1960*, edited by Michael Schmidt and Grevel Lindop. Oxford, England: Carcanet Press, 1972. A seven-page survey of Silkin's poetry books from 1954 to 1971 stresses Silkin's awareness in his poetry of the interconnectedness of things.

Forbes, Peter, ed. *Scanning the Century: The Penguin Book of the Twentieth Century in Poetry*. New York: Penguin, 2000. This anthology covering the poets of the twentieth century chronologically and by theme contains poems by Silkin in its "Lost Tribes" section. Some analysis included.

Huk, Romana. "Poetry of the Committed Individual: Jon Silkin, Tony Harrison, Geoffrey Hill, and the Poets of Postwar Leeds." In *Contemporary British Poetry: Essays in Theory and Criticism*, edited by James Acheson and Romana Huk. Albany: State University of New York Press, 1996. Taking her title from the title of Silkin's anthology from *Stand* magazine, Huk analyzes the poetry from the perspective of political engagement.

Schmidt, Michael. *An Introduction to Fifty Modern Poets*. 1979. London: Pan Books, 1982. A five-page survey of Silkin's poetry books from 1954 to 1974 stresses the progression from book to book, as well as the worth of the poetry because of what it attempts despite the "unfinished" quality of individual poems.

Wheatley, David. "Grief and Women." Review of *Making a Republic*. *Irish Times*, August 31, 2002, p. 59. Wheatley notes that although this book is about Silkin's finding love late in life, instead of being celebratory, it is filled with the theme of British Jewish inheritance.

Norman Prinsky

LOUIS UNTERMEYER

Born: New York, New York; October 1, 1885
Died: Newtown, Connecticut; December 18, 1977

OTHER LITERARY FORMS

The poetry of Louis Untermeyer (UHN-tuhr-mi-uhr) represents only a fraction of his total work. He put his name on well over a hundred books, ranging from *The Kitten Who Barked* (1962, a children's story) to *A Treasury of Ribaldry* (1956), and from his historical novel *Moses* (1928) to *A Century of Candymaking, 1837-1947* (1947). Most of his effort, however, went into four areas: anthologies of poetry, criticism, biography, and children's literature. Some of the most important works that he edited were *Modern American Poetry* (1919), *Modern British Poetry* (1920), and *A Treasury of Great Poems* (1942, 1955). He broke new ground in criticism with *The New Era in American Poetry* (1919, 1971) and provided a useful literary reappraisal in *American Poetry from the Beginning to Whitman* (1931), which he edited. His early textbook *Poetry: Its Understanding and Enjoyment* (1934, with Carter Davidson) paved the way for *Understanding Poetry: An Anthology for College Students* (1938), edited by Cleanth Brooks and Robert Penn Warren, and a host of other works. Although Untermeyer published one massive analytical biography, *Heinrich Heine: Paradox and Poet* (1937), he was better known for the biographical essays in *Makers of the Modern World* (1955) and *Lives of the Poets* (1959). Untermeyer's contributions to children's literature include collections of poetry such as *This Singing World* (1923-1926) and *Stars to Steer By* (1941), as well as many stories and collections of stories—among them, *Chip: My Life and Times* (1933), *The Donkey of God* (1932; winner of the 1932 Italian Enit Award for a book on Italy by a non-Italian), *The Last Pirate: Tales from the Gilbert and Sullivan Operas* (1934), and *The Golden Treasury of Children's Literature* (1959, with Byrna Unter-meyer).

Achievements

Louis Untermeyer exerted a shaping influence on modern American poetry. That in-fluence, however, did not derive from his own voluminous verse. Indeed, Untermeyer has not been greatly honored as a poet. His verse has escaped the scrutiny of modern scholars, and his work was never awarded a Pulitzer Prize, although he did serve as con-sultant in poetry (poet laureate) to the Library of Congress from 1961 to 1963. More-over, Untermeyer seemed to regret his poetic profligacy and lamented that "too many facile lines of praise and protest" had filled his volumes. In *Long Feud*, he trimmed the canon of poems he cared to preserve to a spartan 118 pages.

If Untermeyer's impact as a poet was limited, his impact as a critic, critical biogra-pher, and anthologist was almost limitless. He has been described as Robert Frost's Boswell, but he really ought to be seen as a twentieth century version of James Boswell and Samuel Johnson combined. Through appreciative reviews, loving editorial labors, and reverent selections in his anthologies, Untermeyer was able to do more for Frost than Boswell ever did for Johnson. Moreover, Untermeyer's engaging *Lives of the Po-ets* is a worthy sequel to Johnson's biographical sketches and is massively supple-mented by the scientific, political, and literary biographies in his *Makers of the Modern World*.

Although Untermeyer modestly understated his contribution to Frost's success, Frost himself was quick to acknowledge it, saying publicly, "Sometimes I think I am a figment of Louis' imagination." Indeed, in an article for the Chicago *Evening Post* on April 23, 1915, Untermeyer became the first reviewer in the United States to praise Frost's *North of Boston* (1914). He was the second scholar to praise Frost's poetry in a book, *The New Era in American Poetry*, and he was among the first to include Frost in an anthology.

As the friendship between the two poets strengthened, Untermeyer's advocacy con-tinued. Every new edition of *Modern American Poetry* included more poems by Frost, who wrote appreciatively to his friend in 1941, "I look on [the anthology] as having done more to spread my poetry than any one other thing." Untermeyer continued to write warm reviews of Frost's poetry. He became Frost's earliest biographer and pub-lished the first volume of Frost's letters and conversations. In 1943, Untermeyer made himself "somewhat unpleasant" with his fellow judges on the Pulitzer poetry jury by insisting in a minority report that the year's prize should be awarded to *A Witness Tree*, making Frost the only author ever to win four Pulitzer Prizes.

What Untermeyer did massively for Frost, he did less passionately but just as selflessly for many other poets. *The New Era in American Poetry* devoted whole chapters to Vachel Lindsay, Carl Sandburg, Edwin Arlington Robinson, Amy Lowell, Edgar Lee Masters, and Ezra Pound, while also giving prominence to Sara Teasdale, H. D., Stephen Vincent Benét, and William Rose Benét. His ten editions of *Modern American Poetry* and nine editions of *Modern British Poetry* helped to win recognition and popularity for three generations of young poets. His service for nearly a quarter century as chairman of the Pulitzer poetry jury allowed him to assist the careers of Mark Van Doren, both Benéts, Karl Shapiro, Robert Lowell, W. H. Auden, Peter Viereck, Gwendolyn Brooks, Carl Sandburg, Marianne Moore, Archibald MacLeish, Theodore Roethke, Wallace Stevens, Elizabeth Bishop, Richard Wilbur, Robert Penn Warren, Stanley Kunitz, W. D. Snodgrass, Phyllis McGinley, and William Carlos Williams. He served as Merrill Moore's literary adviser during Moore's life, and he was a faithful literary executor after Moore's death.

In brief, through poems, lectures, reviews, anthologies, and personal services, Untermeyer did more than any of his contemporaries to win a popular audience for modern poetry.

BIOGRAPHY

Louis Untermeyer was born in 1885 into a well-to-do family of German-Jewish jewelers. His formal education ended at fifteen when he refused to return to high school and discovered that Columbia University would not admit him without passing marks in algebra and geometry. He then worked in the family jewelry business while establishing his career as a poet and literary jack-of-all-trades. His literary successes allowed him to devote less and less time to the jewelry business until he formally resigned at the age of thirty-seven.

Untermeyer eventually moved away from New York City and bought Stony Water, a 160-acre farm in the Adirondacks that became the setting for some of his finest lyrics. Although he continued to earn his living through writing and lecturing, he made a brief stab at commercial farming, raising Hampshire pigs and Jersey cows, tapping maples, harvesting apples, and marketing Stony Water preserves. In his autobiography *Bygones: The Recollections of Louis Untermeyer* (1965), Untermeyer compared his situation with that of the gentleman farmer who celebrated the first anniversary of his venture into dairy farming by proposing a toast: "Friends," he said, "you will notice that there are two shaped bottles on the table. One shape contains champagne; the other contains milk. Help yourself to them carefully; they cost the same per quart."

The outbreak of World War II brought Untermeyer back to the city. He joined the

Office of War Information, where he worked with Howard Fast, Santha Rama Rau, and the film director John Houseman. Later, as editor of the Armed Services Editions, Untermeyer oversaw the republication of forty works of literature a month. By the end of the war, he had helped to deliver some 122 million books into the hands of American servicemen.

When the war ended, Untermeyer wished to remain in a salaried position for a variety of reasons, not the least of which was the expense associated with his growing contingent of former wives. He accepted a position with Decca Records directing its efforts to sell recordings of plays and poetry. In 1950, he became a celebrity as one of the original panelists on CBS-TV's *What's My Line?* McCarthyism was, however, frothing and unfettered in the early 1950's, and Untermeyer became its victim, not because of communist sympathies on his part, but because nearly forty years earlier he had published a book titled *Challenge* (criticized at the time for too lavish praise of democracy) and worked on a liberal magazine called *The Masses.* The baseless hostility of the self-appointed censors was sufficiently rabid that Untermeyer was forced from the show and even from public life.

He retreated to the Connecticut countryside, where he soon became intimate with Arthur Miller, Van Wyck Brooks, Robert Penn Warren, Malcolm Cowley, and actress Margaret Sullavan. Untermeyer's complete repatriation did not come until 1961, when he was honored by being chosen consultant in poetry to the Library of Congress. During the next two years, he was twice asked by the State Department to serve as a literary ambassador, giving lectures in India and Japan. In 1963, Untermeyer returned to his home in Connecticut, where he wrote his memoirs, published books for children, and continued to update his anthologies until his death on December 18, 1977.

The love of poetry demonstrated in Untermeyer's anthologies was in large part a love of passion, and for him a life of emotion was not a vicarious ideal only. In life, particularly in married life, Untermeyer experienced every variation of happiness, heartache, and humorous complexity. In all, he was married six times and divorced five times by a total of four women. In 1907, he married his first wife, the respected poet Jean Starr; he divorced her sixteen years later in Mexico and remarried her shortly thereafter in New Jersey (*not* New York, since state law there held that he had always remained married to Jean). These complications led Louis to wonder "which state was the state of matrimony" and whether he "might be committing bigamy by illegally marrying the same wife twice." Virginia, his second wife, married Louis in Mexico in 1923, became pregnant in Switzerland, delivered a baby in London, and divorced Louis (who had returned to Jean) in Missouri—all within a period of two years. Esther, the third wife and a lawyer, helped Louis obtain a second Mexican divorce from Jean—this time by mail. Esther then married Louis in 1933 in a ceremony performed, appropriately, by a professional comedian. Louis and Esther lived together in contentment for a number of years before they gradually drifted apart. At the age of sixty-two, Untermeyer divorced Esther in Mexico to marry his fourth wife, Byrna. When Esther learned of the divorce, she sued, alleging that Louis's Mexican divorce from Jean had been valid, while his Mexican divorce from her was not. The somewhat bemused judge ruled that Untermeyer had never been married to Esther or Virginia, was not married to Byrna, and remained legally tied to Jean from whom he had been separated for more than twenty years. Untermeyer subsequently persuaded Jean to divorce him in Nevada (their third divorce) so that he could marry Byrna a second time and live legally with the woman he loved.

Despite his fondness for children, Untermeyer was generally too busy to take much part in rearing his own sons. Richard, his son by his first wife, hanged himself at the age of nineteen. His second son, John, was reared by Virginia, who rarely allowed Louis to see the child. His adopted sons, Lawrence and Joseph, were reared less by Untermeyer than by his caretakers at Stony Water.

ANALYSIS

The qualities of mind and temperament that made Louis Untermeyer such a superb anthologist kept him from attaining the same level of excellence in his poetry. He was too appreciative of the moods, approaches, and words of others—too prone to imitation and parody. He was rarely able to find his own voice; or rather, his own voice was often the mockingbird's, wryly reproducing the songs of others. Moreover, the virtues of his impressionistic criticism—directness and clarity—were poetic vices in a period of Empsonian ambiguity.

Untermeyer's poems fall into five broad categories: parodies; modern re-creations of religious or mythological events; adaptations of another poet's spirit, tone, or verse form; idealistic exhortations concerning social consciousness; and a few entirely new creations. Thus, Untermeyer's poems range from the overtly imitative to the mildly innovative. They vary widely in subject and style but are unified by romanticism undercut with irony. This romanticism was a fundamental part of Untermeyer's personality. It guided him as he exuberantly collected belongings, friends, experiences, passions, and poems.

The instincts of a romantic collector were evident throughout Untermeyer's life. His earliest memories were of the "colorful mélange" of assorted portraits, porcelains, and petit-point cushions that littered his parent's home. During reveries before a Dutch landscape or a jeweled bird, Untermeyer's mind turned to fantasy, while his taste was tutored by delight in the diversity of the family's collections. His love of fantasy led him to read, as he put it, "a hodge-podge of everything I could lay my mind on": *Alf laya wa-laya* (fifteenth century; *The Arabian Nights' Entertainments*, 1706-1708), books from Edward Stratemeyers's Rover Boys series, Alexandre Dumas, père's *Les Trois Mousquetaires* (1844; *The Three Musketeers*, 1846), Samuel Taylor Coleridge's *The Rime of the Ancient Mariner* (1798), Jean de La Fontaine's *Fables choisies, mises en vers* (1668-1694; *Fables Written in Verse*, 1735), Alfred, Lord Tennyson's *Idylls of the*

King (1859-1885), Dante's *Inferno* (in *La divina commedia*, c. 1320; *The Divine Comedy*, 1802), and so on. This eclectic but diverting reading in bed by night naturally reduced Untermeyer to mediocrity in school by day. He found the classroom too limiting and controlled in its approach to life and learning.

Thus, at the age of seventeen, Untermeyer entered the family jewelry business—the first in what was to become the startlingly diverse collection of his occupations. Yet, even the jewelry business was too mundane for Louis. He devoted long afternoons to the unfinished verses he kept concealed in his desk beneath production reports and packets of gemstones. In the evenings, he wrote poems and reviews, for which he found a ready market. His first collection of poems, *First Love*, was a vanity press edition subsidized by his father, but its sales quickly offset the cost of publication. His next volume, *Challenge*, was picked up by the Century Company, and Untermeyer's poetic career was launched.

The dual careers of poet and businessman were insufficient to quench Untermeyer's romantic thirst for experience. He used his contacts in the literary world to help him to his third career as a magazine editor. He first obtained a position as a contributing editor to *The Masses*, where he made friends of such prominent left-wing personalities as Max Eastman and John Reed. He then became one of the founding editors of *The Seven Arts*, a short-lived (1916-1917) literary magazine that published pieces by Sherwood Anderson, D. H. Lawrence, Carl Sandburg, Robert Frost, Eugene O'Neill, Vachel Lindsay, and John Dewey. From 1918 to 1924, he was a contributing editor to the *Liberator*; from 1934 to 1937, he was poetry editor of the *American Mercury*; and for many years, he wrote a weekly column for the *Saturday Review* (known as *Saturday Review of Literature* until 1952).

In 1919, Untermeyer collected and revised a number of his impressionistic reviews and published them in *The New Era in American Poetry*. When Alfred Harcourt decided to bring out an anthology of modern American poetry, Untermeyer was the logical editor. *Modern American Poetry* was followed in the next year by *Modern British Poetry*. Thus, Untermeyer, who had already been a success as a jeweler, poet, and magazine editor, now assumed the role of anthologist. It was the right task for a man who, by his own confession, had "the mind of a magpie" and who collected stamps, flowers, pictures of actresses in cigarette packs, cats (both living and artificial), careers, and wives. This multiplicity of interests continued to shape Untermeyer's life. In subsequent years, he became a gentleman farmer, publisher, record producer, and television celebrity. Despite these varied careers, Untermeyer always felt most at home at his desk. There, he wrote, "I am doing what I am supposed to do: fulfilling my function whether I write in the role of biographer, storyteller, editor of anthologies, impressionistic critic, or, occasionally, poet." The order of those activities says much about Untermeyer's own priorities and poetic self-image.

WORKS OF PARODY

For a collector who wished to be a poet, parody was the natural literary mode. Indeed, Untermeyer's first booklet, *The Younger Quire*, was a parody of *The Younger Choir*, an anthology of youthful poets (including Untermeyer) that was introduced and lavishly praised by Edwin Markham. Untermeyer's parody came to exactly twenty-four pages (one quire) and included a series of "back-of-the-hand tributes" combining "simulated innocence and real malice." He continued to write burlesques throughout his long career, publishing them in... *and Other Poets, Including Horace, Collected Parodies*, and *Selected Poems and Parodies*.

RELIGIOUS THEMES

Parody is, however, parasitic, and Untermeyer was too thoughtful and creative to remain locked into such a limited style. In another large group of poems, the penchant for parody is reined in as Untermeyer re-creates a religious, mythological, or literary event from a modern perspective. In "Eve Speaks," for example, Eve asks God to pause before judging her. She argues that Eden was a place for child's play and angelic calm but not a place for Adam who, being neither child nor angel, was formed to struggle and create. Untermeyer implies that eating the fruit of the tree of knowledge was essential to human fulfillment and that God had been wrong to forbid it. Thus, the poem is a typical statement of Untermeyer's philosophy of life. He implies that the Judeo-Christian religions have distorted the old myths in an effort to impose order and morality. For Untermeyer, the romantic collector, life is truly lived only through struggle, passion, sexuality, creation, and experience. All these were to be gained only through knowledge, the forbidden fruit.

Untermeyer's romantic sensuality led him to fill his poems with descriptions of almost Keatsian opulence and vividness. The terrors of Judgment Day, for example, are suggested by phenomena: "trampling winds," "stark and cowering skies," "the red flame" of God's anger licking up worlds, the stars falling "in a golden rain." Here, the pathetic fallacy, which often mars other descriptions by Untermeyer, becomes an effective indication of God's fearful power; before his wrath, the elements, too, cringe and flee. By standing unterrified amid such fury, Eve immediately wins the reader's respect, just as her boldness in questioning God's judgment had piqued the reader's interest. As she begins to explain herself, her description of Paradise is traditional except for the contemptuousness of the occasional reference to its "drowsy luxury" and "glittering hours." Such descriptive phrases prepare the reader to see Eden as Eve saw it, a place where Man and Woman are treated like children, "swaddled with ease" and "lulled with . . . softest dreams." The circling night-bird "out beyond the wood," the "broadening stream," and the distant hills become symbols of freedom, symbols of the unknown. Eve learns that individuality can be obtained only through rebellion, that knowledge must be reached through uncertainty, and that creation grows out of struggle. She eats of the fruit of sensual knowledge, as Untermeyer would have all men and women do.

Untermeyer makes other particularly interesting attempts to modernize religious mythology in "Sic Semper," "God's Youth," and "Burning Bush." The first of these looks at the myth of the Fall from another perspective. In "Eve Speaks," Untermeyer had made no mention of Satan; Eve's revolt grew out of her understanding of Adam's human needs. In "Sic Semper," Untermeyer brilliantly and economically overturns the traditional view of Satan. The fallen angel becomes "the Light-Bringer, Fire-Scatterer"—humankind's benefactor and not its foe. Lucifer and Prometheus become one, bringing light to minds in darkness. Then, in a horrifying betrayal, man—knowing too well the future costs of truth, wisdom, and love—puts Lucifer in hell.

Similarly, "God's Youth" is a delightful reconception of deity. The God of the Old Testament is himself old—bored by the unchanging march of years and the "yawning seasons." During the Creation, Untermeyer insists, "God was young and blithe and whimsical," letting loose his desires and filling the earth with "fancies, wild and frank." During the Creation, then, the child-god lived as Untermeyer would have the man-child continue to live.

"Burning Bush" is by far the most sacrilegious of Untermeyer's biblical re-creations. The poem's title is an allusion to Exodus 3:2 in which the angel of the Lord appears to Moses in the form of a burning bush. Through imagery that is intentionally indirect and metaphoric, Untermeyer transforms the burning bush into a sexual symbol. In the still of the night "runners of the flame" fill the "narrowest veins," and in "an agony of Love" bodies burn but are not consumed. The biblical voice of God becomes the ecstatic cries of the lovers that later give way to "the still, small voice" of contentment in the postcoital quiet. The sexual act, which is itself "knowledge," passion, creation, and experience, becomes a metaphor for the presence of God, who still speaks to humankind through the burning bush. Through this metaphor, the poem becomes a twelve-line exposition of Untermeyer's temperament and philosophy of life.

EMULATION OF ROMANTIC THEMES

The poems in the third category of Untermeyer's verse all involve emulation. Many of them reflect the spirit and sometimes the words of the favorite poets of Untermeyer's youth: Robert Herrick, Heinrich Heine, A. E. Housman, Thomas Hardy, and Horace. They tend to be witty, ironic, and sensuous. They frequently deal with the traditional subject matter of romantic poetry—love, spring, snow, dawn, sunset, birdsongs, the moon, and the stars—but Untermeyer is well aware that these poetic topics can often become substitutes for real passions. The romanticism of many of these poems is, therefore, undercut by irony; in others—"Georgian Anthology" and "Portrait of a Poet," for example—Untermeyer is openly scornful of formalized, passionless romanticism. For this reason, Untermeyer classified himself (along with John Crowe Ransom, Robert Lowell, and Richard Wilbur) as a romantic ironist, but given his devotion to passion, struggle, and creativity, one can question the sincerity of much of the irony. One feels that Untermeyer's scorn of the romantic posturing of others is itself a form of romantic posturing.

On the whole, these are Untermeyer's least successful poems. Untermeyer was a romantic and therefore became a romantic ironist only with difficulty. Moreover, most of the poems give one the impression of having been written before and better by others. A typical example is "Fairmount Cemetery," a poem in Housman's style. The speaker looks back on the cemetery, his first trysting spot, and remembers his extravagant claims that "love is all that saves"; meanwhile, the dead men lie "Chuckling in their graves." The cemetery setting is too obviously a contrivance, the claims of the lover are overblown and unrealistic, and the concluding commentary of the dead injects a crude blatancy. The only part of Untermeyer's personality that shows up in "Fairmount Cemetery" is the collector's love of varied poetic styles.

INFLUENCE OF ROBERT FROST

A smaller, but far better, group of poems was written in imitation of Frost's understated style. As in Frost's best lyrics, an understanding of life's tragic possibilities emerges through the speaker's recollection of an occurrence in nature. "Nightmare by Day," for example, begins with a setting and even a verse form that are nearly identical to Frost's in "Dust of Snow." In search of peace, the speaker has walked alone far into the woods until there are no more tracks in the snow. Something in front of him, glimpsed but not yet recognized, makes his "pulses freeze," and, as he watches, a trail of blood begins to grow, spreading as it melts the snow. The mystery of this image of death in a place of peaceful isolation disturbs the speaker so that ever after he himself awaits the sudden blow and the red droplets on the snow.

The impact of this terrifying incident is augmented by the plain diction and the stark imagery. In the poem, 98 of the 110 words are monosyllables; the average sentence contains only 9 words; the only colors are white, black, and red; and the only objects are the snow, the speaker, the trees, the trail of blood, and one "chuckling crow." However, upon reflection, the incident itself is both mysterious and premonitory, just as the simple, unforced verse reveals, upon reflection, the technical difficulty of densely rhymed iambic dimeter.

If the poem has a weakness, it is in the improbability of the events described. At its best, Frost's lyric poetry grows out of an ordinary occurrence. That is not the case in "Nightmare by Day." Here, the ultimate situation is extraordinary. The blood is very fresh, but there has been no sign of a bleeding animal or of a hunter, and no sound of gunfire. These are not insuperable difficulties, of course; hawks and owls, for example, hunt silently and leave no trail. Untermeyer is, however, less interested in the incident as a natural phenomenon than as a symbol of sudden, unpredictable violence and impending death. Hence, he makes no effort to explain the ominous scene. Nevertheless, the odd congruence of events, the dreamlike improbability, demands recognition, and

Untermeyer does recognize it, calling the entire incident a "dream" in the final stanza. The poem's title, however, "Nightmare by Day," emphasizes that the events have been real, and the nightmarish reality of this waking dream contributes largely to its impact.

An equally good imitation of Frost's style is found in "The Scraping of the Scythe." The poem grows out of the contrasts between two sounds: the song of the bluebird and the screech of the sharpening scythe. The one is a song of leisure, the other a sound of labor; the one pleasurable, the other painful; the one the call of summer, the other the call of fall. As the speaker notes, when the two fill the air at once, one need not hear the words, "To know what had transpired." The sharpening of the scythe is an omen of colder weather to come and a symbol of inevitable death. Thus, in order not to hear that sound, the speaker never allows his own fields to be cut, but the reader knows that nothing can postpone the fall—and the speaker does, too.

The success of these poems arises at least in part from the fact that they are compatible with Untermeyer's outlook on life. If death is unavoidable and unpredictable, then it makes all the more sense to live fully, freely, and passionately. As much as Untermeyer admired Frost and Frost's poetry, he could not wholly endorse the somber pessimism embodied in Frost's style or the conservatism of Frost's personality. For a more compatible political and emotional outlook, Untermeyer occasionally turned to William Blake, whose radical politics and unconventional piety were much closer to his own views. Hence, Untermeyer's religious re-creations make many of the same points that Blake did in his poems objecting to those who would bind "with briars [his] joys and desires."

INFLUENCE OF WILLIAM BLAKE

Sometimes Blake's influence on Untermeyer gives rise to weak imitation, as in "Envy," a poem in the manner of Blake's "The Clod and the Pebble," which pits the rooted willow against the meandering brook in a debate about lifestyles; a poem such as "Glad Day (After a Color Print by Blake)," however, grows out of inspiration more than out of imitation. This paean to daylight is pure Untermeyer—lover of generosity, confidence, sensuality, clarity, and joy. Like "Eve Speaks," this poem excels in its descriptions, particularly in the personification of day, which becomes a naked body, free, outgiving, and rejoicing. Hence, as before, the pathetic fallacy is made tolerable because it is a "given," a part of Blake's drawing that Untermeyer must accept and explain.

Thus, Untermeyer's parodies, re-creations, and imitations derive from, and play upon, his strengths as a collector and a romantic, appreciative reader. The two final groupings are more original. One group of poems is largely hortatory. They include some of Untermeyer's most widely known pieces—"Caliban in the Coal Mines," "Prayer," and "On the Birth of a Child." They are light verse suitable for communicating their overt moral and political messages, but too blatantly propagandizing to qualify as significant poems. The best that can be said is that in them Untermeyer remains true to himself. Particularly in "Prayer," he speaks from the heart as he asks to remain "ever insurgent," "more daring than devout," "filled with a buoyant doubt," and wide-eyed and sensual while cognizant of others' misery. His final prayer, that of a thoroughgoing romantic, is to remain at the end of life "still unsatisfied."

INFLUENCE OF WALT WHITMAN

If the last group of Untermeyer's poems is derivative at all, it owes its inspiration to Walt Whitman. In a style all his own, Untermeyer attempts to describe common aspects of the contemporary world, often striving to see mundane things with a childlike wonder and a romantic imagination. The poems' titles identify their unconventional subjects: "In the Subway," "To a Vine-Clad Telegraph Pole," "A Side Street," "Boy and Tadpoles," "Food and Drink," "Hairdressing," "Hands," "Portrait of a Child," "Portrait of a Dead Horse," "Portrait of a Machine," and so on. In these poems, Untermeyer eschews both the subject matter of romantic poetry and the introspective approach of most modern verse. The poem "Still Life" is both an example of Untermeyer's approach and an explanation of it. Like Untermeyer's poems, a still-life painting portrays things, "A bowl of fruit upon a piece of silk," but it also conveys emotions through the choice of color and form. The still life contains no direct autobiography, but the artist's "voice so full of vehement life" can still be "heard." In the same way, Untermeyer's poems about modern life convey his perspective without descending into private symbolism, autobiographical digressions, or Freudian associations.

"Coal Fire" is a good example of what can be achieved through such verse. The poem explains to a child why fire comes out of coal. In doing so, it uses poetic devices that particularly appeal to children, yet it uses those devices with a mastery that should delight adults. The actual content of the poem is, however, entirely mundane; coal is the remnant of ancient trees. To interest the child, Untermeyer personifies parts of these trees, putting them in situations with which a child could empathize. Like children, each leaf must be "taught the right/ Way to drink light." Each twig must "learn/ How to catch flame and yet not burn." Each branch must grow strong on this "diet of heat." Simultaneously, Untermeyer develops a series of delightful paradoxes. The dead black coal was once a living green net. Before there was any running thing to ensnare, this net snared the sun. Paradoxically, the leaves "drink light," catch flame without burning, and eat heat. Finally, the poem's heavy alliteration and frequent rhyme heighten the delight, especially since the alliteration and the rhyme so frequently emphasize key words: "these . . . were trees," "to learn . . . not burn," "branch and . . . bough began," "to eat . . . of heat," and so on. More important, however, this lucid examination of coal fire subtly describes the burning coal as though the light within it were passion imprisoned. The intensity of the verse increases as the fire fingers the air, grows bolder, twists free, consumes the imprisoning coal, "leaps, is done,/ And goes back to the sun." There is nothing allegorical in the poem, but a reader would have to be curiously insensitive not to recognize in it Untermeyer's love of freedom, light, and passion.

"A DISPLACED ORPHEUS"

In 1955, when Untermeyer had already lived his biblically allotted three score years and ten, he was selected Phi Beta Kappa poet by Harvard University. For a man who had virtually ceased composing poetry twenty years earlier, it was a rare opportunity to pronounce dispassionate judgment upon his long and extraordinarily varied career. The poem he wrote, "A Displaced Orpheus," did just that. In it, Orpheus awakens after a long silence to discover that he has lost the knack of moving mountains and assuaging lions. He attends a series of universities to relearn the lost art and produces sterile stanzas in the manner of W. H. Auden, T. S. Eliot, and William Empson. Although Untermeyer intended these parodies to illustrate the deficiencies of much modern poetry, they also illustrate the limitations of his own imitative approach to composition. Thus, Orpheus's situation becomes Untermeyer's. Time has stripped him of his reputation, and his failures have cost him the woman he loves. All that remains is the desire to struggle, the urge to create. Only when he retrieves his "still unbroken lute" and sings for "that last listener, himself" does he rediscover his power. The birds and beasts gather about him, the trees bow down, and his woman looks upon him with "rediscovering eyes."

One could wish that Untermeyer had taken Orpheus's lesson more truly to heart and that he had sung for himself more often, but perhaps then the passionate collector would only have delighted himself with more parodies. Songs coming out of the soul often have a hard and bitter birth. All but a few are stillborn. In "Eve Speaks," "Nightmare by Day," "Coal Fire," "A Displaced Orpheus," and a handful of others, Untermeyer produced more healthy offspring than most poets do. Posterity should be grateful.

OTHER MAJOR WORKS

LONG FICTION: *Moses*, 1928; *The Wonderful Adventures of Paul Bunyan*, 1945.

NONFICTION: *The New Era in American Poetry*, 1919, 1971; *Poetry: Its Understanding and Enjoyment*, 1934 (with Carter Davidson); *Heinrich Heine: Paradox and Poet*, 1937; *From Another World*, 1939; *A Century of Candymaking, 1837-1947*, 1947; *Makers of the Modern World*, 1955; *Lives of the Poets*, 1959; *The Letters of Robert Frost and Louis Untermeyer*, 1963; *Bygones: The Recollections of Louis Untermeyer*, 1965.

CHILDREN'S LITERATURE: *This Singing World*, 1923-1926 (3 volumes); *The Donkey of God*, 1932; *Chip: My Life and Times*, 1933; *The Last Pirate: Tales from the Gilbert and Sullivan Operas*, 1934; *Stars to Steer By*, 1941; *The Golden Treasury of Children's Literature*, 1959 (with Byrna Untermeyer); *The Kitten Who Barked*, 1962.

EDITED TEXTS: *Modern American Poetry*, 1919; *Modern British Poetry*, 1920; *American Poetry from the Beginning to Whitman*, 1931; *A Treasury of Great Poems*, 1942, 1955.

MISCELLANEOUS: *A Treasury of Ribaldry*, 1956.

BIBLIOGRAPHY

Frost, Robert, and Louis Untermeyer. *The Letters of Robert Frost to Louis Untermeyer.* New York: Holt, Rinehart and Winston, 1963. The most valuable collection of Frost's letters to Untermeyer in a correspondence that lasted almost fifty years. The letters are remarkably edited.

Harcourt, Brace. *Sixteen Authors: Brief Histories, Together with Lists of Their Respective Works.* New York: Author, 1926. Offers short histories of sixteen authors and their works, including Sinclair Lewis, Carl Sandburg, Virginia Woolf, and Untermeyer. The entry on Untermeyer provides a fine assessment of his poetry and poetic development. Contains illustrations and a bibliography.

Lowell, Amy. "A Poet of the Present." Review of *These Times. Poetry* 11 (December, 1917): 157-164. This review of Untermeyer's early verse volume, *These Times*, turns out to be a lovely appreciation of the young poet.

Pound, Ezra. *EP to LU: Nine Letters Written to Louis Untermeyer by Ezra Pound.* Edited by J. A. Robbins. Bloomington: Indiana University Press, 1963. A fine collection of letters written by Pound to Untermeyer. Useful as a source of information on Pound's perception of Untermeyer.

Untermeyer, Louis. *From Another World: The Autobiography of Louis Untermeyer.* New York: Harcourt, Brace, 1939. Untermeyer's first attempt at autobiography is devoted to anecdotes and comments on the author's friends and acquaintances among the literary community. Untermeyer passes judgments, comments on works and relationships, and tells stories and jokes. In general he deals only with the surfaces of events and encounters and does not explore any issue in great depth. His style and energy are as vivid as the range of his acquaintances is impressive.

_____. *Bygones: The Recollections of Louis Untermeyer.* New York: Harcourt, Brace & World, 1965. The second of Untermeyer's reminiscences, in which the eighty-year-old looks back on his life. Where the earlier (1939) "autobiography" was about other people, this one is primarily, and self-consciously so, about the author. It is a very personal volume focusing on the highlights of Untermeyer's career, including excellent chapters on the McCarthy years, his tenure at the Library of Congress, and his travels.

Jeffrey D. Hoeper

LOUIS ZUKOFSKY

Born: New York, New York; January 23, 1904
Died: Port Jefferson, New York; May 12, 1978

OTHER LITERARY FORMS

Louis Zukofsky (zew-KAHF-skee) was as much respected for his criticism as he was for his poetry. His volumes of criticism include *Le Style Apollinaire* (1934, with René Taupin), *A Test of Poetry* (1948), *Prepositions: The Collected Critical Essays of Louis Zukofsky* (1968, 1981), and *Bottom: On Shakespeare* (1963). In 1932, he edited *An "Objectivists" Anthology*. A play, *Arise, Arise*, was published in 1962; a novel, *Ferdinand, Including "It Was"* in 1968.

ACHIEVEMENTS

Louis Zukofsky was, in many ways, a poet's poet, who won the admiration of such contemporaries as Ezra Pound and William Carlos Williams for his innovative use of language, for his stretching of the boundaries of poetic form, and for his perceptive readings of their works. With George Oppen and Charles Reznikoff, he became known as an Objectivist, a term he chose to distinguish these poets from Amy Lowell's Imagists and the French Symbolists. Objectivists were concerned with the precise use of language, honesty and sincerity in their communication with their audience, and the creation of a poem that in itself would be an object, part of the reader's reality.

Zukofsky's voice was that of an urban American Jew, tied to the Yiddish tradition of his immigrant parents, yet Americanized into twentieth century New York. He was conscious of living in what he called the "age of gears," where machines and technology dominated everyday life, and he was sensitive to social problems and movements—socialism, communism, Marxism, the Depression, urban unrest. His epic _"A"_ provides an idiosyncratic autobiography of one poet's life from 1922 to 1976.

Throughout his life, Zukofsky taught at universities and colleges and, with reluctance, read his poetry in public. He was awarded the Lola Ridge Memorial Award of the Poetry Society of America (1949); the Longview Foundation Award (1961); the Union League Civic and Arts Poetry Prize (1964) and the Oscar Blumenthal/Charles Leviton Prize, both from _Poetry_ magazine (1966); the National Endowment for the Arts and American Literary Anthology awards (1967 and 1968); and an Academy Award in Literature from the American Academy and Institute of Arts and Letters (1976). He was nominated for a National Book Award in Poetry in 1968.

Biography

Louis Zukofsky was the son of Russian-Jewish immigrants and was reared on the lower East Side of New York City. His father, a religious and deeply sensitive man, was a presser in a clothing factory; his mother was a gaunt, quiet, introspective woman. Zukofsky's first introduction to literature was through the Yiddish poems and stories read in his home, together with the plays produced at the renowned Thalia theater. In particular, he was attracted to the work of Solomon Bloomgarten, who wrote under the pen name Yehoash (an acronym of the initials of his Hebrew name) and earned much admiration for both his own poetry and for his Yiddish translations of major English and American poems. Zukofsky first read untranslated English literature in the public schools of New York. He began to write poetry in high school, then at Columbia University, where he was encouraged to continue by his professor, Mark Van Doren. Zukofsky received an M.A. degree from Columbia in 1924.

Zukofsky's first submission to _Poetry_ was a translation of Yehoash, which was not published. His own work ("Of Dying Beauty") first appeared in the journal in January, 1924, and he published _Poem Beginning "The"_ in _Exile_, a journal edited by Ezra Pound, who saw in the young poet a literary heir. Pound dedicated his own _Guide to Kulchur_ (1938) to Zukofsky (along with the English poet Basil Bunting), promoted his work in _Exile_, and persuaded Harriet Monroe to turn over an issue of _Poetry_ to him as guest editor. It was this issue, appearing in February, 1931, which made Zukofsky's work visible to his contemporaries and established several poets—Oppen, Reznikoff, Bunting, and Zukofsky himself—as Objectivists, a term conceived by Zukofsky but apparently approved by all. The Objectivists established their own press, To Publishers, a short-lived venture.

Zukofsky found only a small audience for his work, supporting his wife, Celia (a composer, whom he married in 1939), and his son Paul (who became a virtuoso violinist) by teaching technical writing and literature at Brooklyn Polytechnic Institute between 1947 and 1966. He also taught English and comparative literature at the University of Wisconsin, 1930-1931; Shakespeare and Renaissance literature at Colgate University in 1947; creative writing at Queens College, 1947-1948; and in the summer of 1958 was poet-in-residence at San Francisco State College.

Zukofsky preferred to write at night, never going to bed before one or two in the morning, and he revised continually. His epic poem *"A"* was the product of several decades of work, though sections were published at intervals. As his reputation waned, some friends believed he became bitter toward readers who would not take the time and effort to understand him, and the inaccessibility of his later poems seems to reflect his antagonism toward his audience. The 1960's, however, brought renewed interest in the Objectivists, and Zukofsky has been warmly praised by such critics as Hugh Kenner and Guy Davenport.

"A" was going to press and Zukofsky was working on *Eighty Flowers* when, in 1978, he died at the age of seventy-four.

ANALYSIS

Under pressure from Monroe to declare himself part of a new "movement" in poetry, Louis Zukofsky coined the term "Objectivist." Later, he admitted that the term was unfortunate; at the very least, it has been confusing to readers and critics who interpret objectivity as an indication that reality will be rendered undistorted by the poet's personality. Zukofsky did aim at such objective honesty or "care for the detail," as he put it, but he emphasized that being an Objectivist meant that the poet created a poem as an object, in much the same way that a builder constructs a house or a carpenter, a cabinet. These two aims—an objective rendering of reality and the creation of the poem as object—give Zukofsky's poetry its distinction.

The prevailing metaphor throughout Zukofsky's work is the correspondence between the ego and the sense of sight: "I" equals "eye" in his poetry and the terms are often playfully interchanged, as in the poems "I's (pronounced *eyes*)" or "After I's." Similarly, "see" becomes "sea" or even the letter *c* and "sight" is transformed into "cite." Like Benedictus de Spinoza (who figures in his works along with Ludwig Wittgenstein and Aristotle), Zukofsky was a lens-grinder; but Zukofsky's lenses were organic and his method of sharpening them was an ever closer examination of objects. Just as the objective lens of a microscope is the one in closest proximity to the object being studied, so Zukofsky as Objectivist attempted to apprehend objects directly and report on his findings.

Zukofsky believed that an object must be examined for its "qualities," and once these qualities are recognized, the observer can go no further in his understanding of the object. The object exists in itself and is not dependent on the observer for its existence. It is not the observer's function to postulate theories about the object, to explain, embellish, or comment on it. He merely bears witness to its reality. Only by placing the object in the context of the poem can the poet use the object to communicate something of his own reality. In a poem, juxtapositions imply connections, transitions, and relationships between objects. The poet does not editorialize. "Writing presents the finished matter, *it does not comment,*" Zukofsky wrote in *A Test of Poetry.*

In his concern for precise language to express visual perception and to render faithfully the qualities of an object, Zukofsky follows Pound's statements about Imagism: "Direct treatment of the 'thing'" using "no word that does not contribute to the presentation" (*Poetry,* 1912). Zukofsky, however, shared Williams's concern that Imagism, in the years since Pound first promoted the movement, had deteriorated into impressionistic free verse, lacking form. "The Objectivist theory was this," Williams explained in his *The Autobiography of William Carlos Williams* (1951), "We had had 'Imagism' . . . which ran quickly out. That, though it had been useful in ridding the field of verbiage, had no formal necessity implicit in it." The poem, he went on, "is an object, an object that in itself formally presents its case and its meaning by the very form it assumes."

Zukofsky also believed that the poem's form was one with its meaning. The objects, or elements, of the composition should take their meaning from their placement in the structure. The poet should not intrude his personality into the poem with what Zukofsky called predatory intent: the use of decorative adjectives or adverbs, and especially the use of transitional passages or devices which might explain a poem's interior logic. In *Poem Beginning "The,"* for example, each line is numbered, but the numbers do not imply sequence. "Poetry convinces not by argument," Zukofsky wrote, "but by the *form* it creates to carry its content."

"Hi, Kuh"

Reporting about an object, Zukofsky's initial perception undergoes transformation into poetry. "Hi, Kuh" was Zukofsky's response to the billboard advertisement for Elsie, the Borden dairy company's cow. The advertisement showed "gold'n bees" which appeared to the eyes of the poet as eyes, and then when the astigmatic and myopic Zukofsky removed his glasses, they appeared as the shimmering windows of a skyscraper. "Hi, Kuh" also reminds the reader that the poet's "I" was moved to think of a haiku, with the last unexpected word elevating the meaning of the poem beyond that of a bystander commenting on a billboard. Zukofsky does not explain the thought process that led from Elsie the cow to the towering emblem of the city; he presents, flatly, objects that are assembled to reveal his meaning.

"Mantis"

"Mantis" gives a more elaborate example of Zukofsky's method. The poem begins with a vivid description of a praying mantis encountered in a subway car. Gradually, the incongruity of the object in its surroundings, and its obvious helplessness, leads the poet to thoughts of a similar incongruity: the poor, who are helpless, alone, segregated from society, and as terrified as the mantis of an environment over which they have no control. "Mantis" was written as a sestina, a form Zukofsky rarely used, and one he knew was considered obsolete and archaic by many of his contemporaries. To defend his use of that form, he followed the piece by "'Mantis,' An Interpretation," written, he said, "as an argument against people who are dogmatic" about the use of old metered forms for modern poems.

Zukofsky maintained that both the form and language he used were suited to the experience of finding a mantis lost in the subway, so frightened that it flew against the poet's chest as if to communicate its despair. That experience was "only an incident," Zukofsky said, *compelling any writing.*" The mantis was the object that proved seminal for the poet's analysis of his own reality: "The mantis *can start/* History," Zukofsky wrote; and he was moved to think not only of the urban poor but also of Provençal and Melanesian myths, all alluded to in the poem. He was not interested in explaining how the incident led him to think of other things but tried to build a poem that, in its structure, echoed the experience. The poem's ungainliness reflects the lanky body of the insect; "'the lines' winding around themselves" reflect the contorted emotions of the poet as he experienced the encounter with the mantis; "the repeated end words" show his obsessive return to the same themes.

Zukofsky emphasized in his interpretation that the mantis experience engendered thoughts that were felt immediately, spontaneously, and apparently simultaneously. They were not, as William Wordsworth would have had it, recollected in tranquillity. The poet had no time for analysis or reflection. In the poem, then, Zukofsky tried to create what Gertrude Stein called the "continuous present," an ahistorical interval of time that is not caused by the past and which does not affect the future. By omitting transitions and relying, instead, on juxtaposition, Zukofsky forces the reader to experience an encounter with an object, in this case a mantis, with the same immediacy felt by the poet.

POEM BEGINNING "THE"

Much more complex, but with the same underlying intentions, is Zukofsky's *Poem Beginning "The,"* which he wrote in 1926. The poem begins with a brief preface acknowledging its sources. These include Johann Sebastian Bach, Ludwig van Beethoven, Yehoash, T. S. Eliot, Benito Mussolini, and Pound. Zukofsky had, of course, read Pound's *Hugh Selwyn Mauberley* (1920) and Eliot's *The Waste Land* (1922) which allude to literary sources, and intended, like Pound and Eliot, to challenge the reader to work in order to understand the poem.

The structure is deceptively straightforward: six "movements" (anticipating the sections of *"A,"* the poem which seems to have grown directly from "The") and 330 lines, each numbered to remind the reader to stop before going on to the next line. "The," being a definite article, suggests that the poem might be less amorphous than *"A,"* but it is not easily accessible in its entirety. The first movement, titled "And out of olde bokes, in good feith," asks a series of questions about the meaning of some well-known literary works—among them, James Joyce's *A Portrait of the Artist as a Young Man* (1916) and *Ulysses* (1922), Eliot's *The Waste Land*, E. E. Cummings's *Is Five* (1926), and Virginia Woolf's *Mrs. Dalloway* (1925). Allusions to these works follow one another in a disjointed monologue until, at lines 52 and 53, the poet admits that his "dream" is over and he is awake. After a pause, he decides that men have not lived "by art" or "by letters," though it is never clear why the poet remains unsatisfied by the literary works about which he, apparently, dreamt.

The second movement, "International Episode," deals, for the most part, with a deeply personal incident: the suicide of Richard Chambers, the younger brother of Zukofsky's college friend Whittaker Chambers. This "Ricky" section sensitively portrays the sadness of a young man's death for the poet who grieves. Following the elegy, Zukofsky translates lines from Yehoash that encapsulate the theme of the elegy and transform it to myth. In the Yehoash section, a young Bedouin can only reign in his kingdom at night because he is threatened by the sun, and the "Desert-Night" takes on magical, ethereal qualities; Ricky, in the realm of the dead, also reigns in shadow and darkness "with the stars."

The "Ricky" section is a quiet, reflective core of a movement otherwise raucous and irreverent. The poet is walking on Broadway with an oddly named companion, "Peter Out," whose name suggests sexual puns. While they are trying to decide which show to see, the poet, in a kind of reverie, thinks of Ricky. Suddenly, however, Peter breaks in and the two engage in a vaudevillian dialogue with their exchanges placed in quotation marks as if they were titles of plays.

The fifth movement, "Autobiography," returns to some of the themes already set forth by Zukofsky. There is another translation from Yehoash, a neo-folk song that again, as in the "Ricky" section, lifts the themes of the movement to a mythical level. Here, Zukofsky deals with the immigration of Russian Jews to a place where there are "gastanks, ruts,/ cemetery-tenements" and where their children will be assimilated and will take as their culture Bach, William Shakespeare, Samuel Taylor Coleridge, and John Donne. The poet promises not to forget his heritage, carrying that theme further in "Finale, and After," the final movement, which begins with a Jewish folk song that may well have been sung to him as a child. He ends with a last translation from Yehoash, its inclusion itself a demonstration that his parents' heritage has not been lost; the lines celebrate the ability of the poet to "sing" and endure under any hardship—even that of coming to artistic maturity in a country where few poets are lauded.

In *Poem Beginning "The,"* Zukofsky omits all transitions that would help the reader understand the connection between Ricky and Yehoash, for example, or between Christopher Marlowe and Woolf. Because the poem is relatively short, however, with some accessible sections, it is not as difficult as the poem it most resembles, the epic *"A."*

"A"

"A" begins at a performance of Bach's St. Matthew's Passion in Carnegie Hall on Thursday evening, April 5, 1928, during Passover. As in "Mantis," this incident starts the poet's thoughts spiraling, this time on history, economics, art, Jews, physics, music, his family, Karl Marx, Henry Adams, Mickey Mouse, Hamlet, Walt Whitman, and Wittgenstein. The concert also indicates the poem's form, which consists of long "musical" movements and ideas which develop and interweave as fugues.

"A" is the autobiography of a poet in twentieth century America and may be approached as if it were an archaeological site. From an accumulation of objects, the reader might piece together the reality that existed at the site, but Zukofsky is careful to reveal the objects in precise juxtaposition. The cumulative effect of the objects, then, is more than the sum of the parts. Zukofsky likened a poem to beads on an Egyptian necklace: Each bead might be an interesting artifact, but only when strung in precise order do they form a distinct artistic object.

Each section of *"A"* reveals Zukofsky's care for detail and his effort to structure those details. In "A"-12, for example, the themes of the poet's heritage and his relationship to American culture that were presented in the final sections of *Poem Beginning "The"* are expanded and developed, with Zukofsky's father, Pinchos (anglicized as Paul), and his son, Paul, appearing throughout. The culture that Pinchos brought from Russia is depicted in several vignettes, and Paul's childhood is evoked by the boy's remarks, including even a reproduction of one of his valentines to his father. By interweaving details, Zukofsky reveals the transition from Paul, who fled the czar with his mournful songs, to Paul who has two balloons named Plato and Aristotle and is quickly becoming a prodigy on the violin, playing not his grandfather's Russian melodies but Bach.

"All who achieve constructions apart from themselves, move in effect toward poetry," Zukofsky wrote in *Prepositions*. *"A"* is Zukofsky's most elaborate structure, a report of a witness to modern reality who did not care to comment, only to build.

OTHER MAJOR WORKS

LONG FICTION: *Ferdinand, Including "It Was,"* 1968; *Little, for Careenagers*, 1970; *Collected Fiction*, 1990.

PLAY: *Arise, Arise*, pb. 1962.

NONFICTION: *Le Style Apollinaire*, 1934 (with René Taupin); *A Test of Poetry*, 1948; *Five Statements for Poetry*, 1958; *Bottom: On Shakespeare*, 1963, 1987; *Prepositions: The Collected Critical Essays of Louis Zukofsky*, 1967, 1981 (revised as *Prepositions +: The Collected Critical Essays*, 2000); *Autobiography*, 1970 (text, with poems set to music by Celia Zukofsky); *Pound/Zukofsky: Selected Letters of Ezra Pound and Louis Zukofsky*, 1987 (Barry Ahearn, editor).

TRANSLATION: *Catullus*, 1969 (with Celia Zukofsky; of Gaius Valerius Catullus).

EDITED TEXT: *An "Objectivists" Anthology*, 1932.

BIBLIOGRAPHY

Ahearn, Barry. *Zukofsky's "A": An Introduction.* Berkeley: University of California Press, 1983. Zukofsky once said that a poet writes only one poem for his whole life. He began the eight-hundred-page poem *"A"* in 1928, when he was twenty-four years old, and did not finish it until 1974. Ahearn gives the student a framework to understand Zukofsky's magnum opus. Includes bibliographical references and indexes.

Leggott, Michele J. *Reading Zukofsky's "Eighty Flowers."* Baltimore: The Johns Hopkins University Press, 1989. Leggott attempts to explain Zukofsky's rare work, written the last four years of his life. Zukofsky wanted to condense the sense of his lifetime of poetry into a last book. Leggott offers a plausible interpretation for *Eighty Flowers* and thus explains the entire philosophy of Zukofsky's writing.

Maerhofer, John W. *Rethinking the Vanguard: Aesthetic and Political Positions in the Modernist Debate, 1917-1962.* Newcastle upon Tyne, England: Cambridge Scholars, 2009. Contains a chapter on Zukofsky that sees him as moving toward a "revolutionary formalism." Looks at his position among the modernists.

Pound, Ezra. *Pound/Zukofsky: Selected Letters of Ezra Pound and Louis Zukofsky.* Edited by Barry Ahearn. New York: New Directions, 1987. Zukofsky considered Pound to be the greatest twentieth century poet writing in English. Therefore, he wrote to Pound more than he wrote to anyone else, in part to glean some words of literary wisdom. The two men met only three times, yet Zukofsky considered Pound to be his literary father.

Quartermain, Peter. *Disjunctive Poetics: From Gertrude Stein and Louis Zukofsky to Susan Howe.* 1992. Reprint. New York: Cambridge University Press, 2009. Examines the poetic style of Zukofsky, Stein, and Howe, who are known for writing less accessible poetry.

Rothenberg, Jerome, and Steven Clay, eds. *Poetics and Polemics, 1980-2005.* Tuscaloosa: University of Alabama Press, 2008. Contains a reminiscence of Zukofsky that looks at his poetics.

Schuster, Joshua. "Looking at Louis Zukofsky's Poetics Through Spinozist Glasses." In *Radical Poetics and Secular Jewish Culture*, edited by Stephen Paul Miller and Daniel Morris. Tuscaloosa: University of Alabama Press, 2010. An analysis of Zukofsky's poetry through the philosophy of Baruch Spinoza.

Scroggins, Mark. *The Poem of a Life: A Biography of Louis Zukofsky.* Emeryville, Calif.: Shoemaker & Hoard, 2007. Biography of Zukofsky examines his life and his long poem *"A."*

Stanley, Sandra Kumamoto. *Louis Zukofsky and the Transformation of a Modern American Poetics.* Berkeley: University of California Press, 1994. Stanley argues that Zukofky's works serve as a crucial link between American modernism and postmodernism. Stanley explains how Zukofsky emphasized the materiality of language and describes his legacy to contemporary poets.

Terrell, Carroll Franklin. *Louis Zukofsky: Man and Poet.* Orono: National Poetry Foundation, University of Maine, 1979. Zukofsky essentially lived the history of twentieth century American poetry. This is the essential Zukofsky biography. It was written shortly after the poet's death in 1978, at the age of seventy-four. Contains a bibliography and an index.

Linda Simon

CHECKLIST FOR EXPLICATING A POEM

I. THE INITIAL READINGS

A. Before reading the poem, the reader should:
1. Notice its form and length.
2. Consider the title, determining, if possible, whether it might function as an allusion, symbol, or poetic image.
3. Notice the date of composition or publication, and identify the general era of the poet.

B. The poem should be read intuitively and emotionally and be allowed to "happen" as much as possible.

C. In order to establish the rhythmic flow, the poem should be reread. A note should be made as to where the irregular spots (if any) are located.

II. EXPLICATING THE POEM

A. *Dramatic situation.* Studying the poem line by line helps the reader discover the dramatic situation. All elements of the dramatic situation are interrelated and should be viewed as reflecting and affecting one another. The dramatic situation serves a particular function in the poem, adding realism, surrealism, or absurdity; drawing attention to certain parts of the poem; and changing to reinforce other aspects of the poem. All points should be considered. The following questions are particularly helpful to ask in determining dramatic situation:
1. What, if any, is the narrative action in the poem?
2. How many personae appear in the poem? What part do they take in the action?
3. What is the relationship between characters?
4. What is the setting (time and location) of the poem?

B. *Point of view.* An understanding of the poem's point of view is a major step toward comprehending the poet's intended meaning. The reader should ask:
1. Who is the speaker? Is he or she addressing someone else or the reader?
2. Is the narrator able to understand or see everything happening to him or her, or does the reader know things that the narrator does not?
3. Is the narrator reliable?
4. Do point of view and dramatic situation seem consistent? If not, the inconsistencies may provide clues to the poem's meaning.

C. *Images and metaphors*. Images and metaphors are often the most intricately crafted vehicles of the poem for relaying the poet's message. Realizing that the images and metaphors work in harmony with the dramatic situation and point of view will help the reader to see the poem as a whole, rather than as disassociated elements.

1. The reader should identify the concrete images (that is, those that are formed from objects that can be touched, smelled, seen, felt, or tasted). Is the image projected by the poet consistent with the physical object?
2. If the image is abstract, or so different from natural imagery that it cannot be associated with a real object, then what are the properties of the image?
3. To what extent is the reader asked to form his or her own images?
4. Is any image repeated in the poem? If so, how has it been changed? Is there a controlling image?
5. Are any images compared to each other? Do they reinforce one another?
6. Is there any difference between the way the reader perceives the image and the way the narrator sees it?
7. What seems to be the narrator's or persona's attitude toward the image?

D. *Words*. Every substantial word in a poem may have more than one intended meaning, as used by the author. Because of this, the reader should look up many of these words in the dictionary and:

1. Note all definitions that have the slightest connection with the poem.
2. Note any changes in syntactical patterns in the poem.
3. In particular, note those words that could possibly function as symbols or allusions, and refer to any appropriate sources for further information.

E. *Meter, rhyme, structure, and tone*. In scanning the poem, all elements of prosody should be noted by the reader. These elements are often used by a poet to manipulate the reader's emotions, and therefore they should be examined closely to arrive at the poet's specific intention.

1. Does the basic meter follow a traditional pattern such as those found in nursery rhymes or folk songs?
2. Are there any variations in the base meter? Such changes or substitutions are important thematically and should be identified.
3. Are the rhyme schemes traditional or innovative, and what might their form mean to the poem?
4. What devices has the poet used to create sound patterns (such as assonance and alliteration)?
5. Is the stanza form a traditional or innovative one?
6. If the poem is composed of verse paragraphs rather than stanzas, how do they affect the progression of the poem?

7. After examining the above elements, is the resultant tone of the poem casual or formal, pleasant, harsh, emotional, authoritative?

F. *Historical context.* The reader should attempt to place the poem into historical context, checking on events at the time of composition. Archaic language, expressions, images, or symbols should also be looked up.

G. *Themes and motifs.* By seeing the poem as a composite of emotion, intellect, craftsmanship, and tradition, the reader should be able to determine the themes and motifs (smaller recurring ideas) presented in the work. He or she should ask the following questions to help pinpoint these main ideas:
1. Is the poet trying to advocate social, moral, or religious change?
2. Does the poet seem sure of his or her position?
3. Does the poem appeal primarily to the emotions, to the intellect, or to both?
4. Is the poem relying on any particular devices for effect (such as imagery, allusion, paradox, hyperbole, or irony)?

BIBLIOGRAPHY

GENERAL REFERENCE SOURCES

BIOGRAPHICAL SOURCES

Colby, Vineta, ed. *World Authors, 1975-1980*. Wilson Authors Series. New York: H. W. Wilson, 1985.

_____. *World Authors, 1980-1985*. Wilson Authors Series. New York: H. W. Wilson, 1991.

_____. *World Authors, 1985-1990*. Wilson Authors Series. New York: H. W. Wilson, 1995.

Cyclopedia of World Authors. 4th rev. ed. 5 vols. Pasadena, Calif.: Salem Press, 2003.

Dictionary of Literary Biography. 254 vols. Detroit: Gale Research, 1978-   .

International Who's Who in Poetry and Poets' Encyclopaedia. Cambridge, England: International Biographical Centre, 1993.

Seymour-Smith, Martin, and Andrew C. Kimmens, eds. *World Authors, 1900-1950*. Wilson Authors Series. 4 vols. New York: H. W. Wilson, 1996.

Thompson, Clifford, ed. *World Authors, 1990-1995*. Wilson Authors Series. New York: H. W. Wilson, 1999.

Wakeman, John, ed. *World Authors, 1950-1970*. New York: H. W. Wilson, 1975.

_____. *World Authors, 1970-1975*. Wilson Authors Series. New York: H. W. Wilson, 1991.

Willhardt, Mark, and Alan Michael Parker, eds. *Who's Who in Twentieth Century World Poetry*. New York: Routledge, 2000.

CRITICISM

Brooks, Cleanth, and Robert Penn Warren. *Understanding Poetry*. 4th ed. Reprint. Fort Worth, Tex.: Heinle & Heinle, 2003.

Classical and Medieval Literature Criticism. Detroit: Gale Research, 1988-   .

Contemporary Literary Criticism. Detroit: Gale Research, 1973-   .

Day, Gary. *Literary Criticism: A New History*. Edinburgh, Scotland: Edinburgh University Press, 2008.

Draper, James P., ed. *World Literature Criticism 1500 to the Present: A Selection of Major Authors from Gale's Literary Criticism Series*. 6 vols. Detroit: Gale Research, 1992.

Habib, M. A. R. *A History of Literary Criticism: From Plato to the Present*. Malden, Mass.: Wiley-Blackwell, 2005.

Jason, Philip K., ed. *Masterplots II: Poetry Series, Revised Edition*. 8 vols. Pasadena, Calif.: Salem Press, 2002.

Lodge, David, and Nigel Wood. *Modern Criticism and Theory.* 3d ed. New York: Longman, 2008.

Magill, Frank N., ed. *Magill's Bibliography of Literary Criticism.* 4 vols. Englewood Cliffs, N.J.: Salem Press, 1979.

MLA International Bibliography. New York: Modern Language Association of America, 1922-   .

Nineteenth-Century Literature Criticism. Detroit: Gale Research, 1981-   .

Twentieth-Century Literary Criticism. Detroit: Gale Research, 1978-   .

Vedder, Polly, ed. *World Literature Criticism Supplement: A Selection of Major Authors from Gale's Literary Criticism Series.* 2 vols. Detroit: Gale Research, 1997.

Young, Robyn V., ed. *Poetry Criticism: Excerpts from Criticism of the Works of the Most Significant and Widely Studied Poets of World Literature.* 29 vols. Detroit: Gale Research, 1991.

POETRY DICTIONARIES AND HANDBOOKS

Carey, Gary, and Mary Ellen Snodgrass. *A Multicultural Dictionary of Literary Terms.* Jefferson, N.C.: McFarland, 1999.

Deutsch, Babette. *Poetry Handbook: A Dictionary of Terms.* 4th ed. New York: Funk & Wagnalls, 1974.

Drury, John. *The Poetry Dictionary.* Cincinnati, Ohio: Story Press, 1995.

Kinzie, Mary. *A Poet's Guide to Poetry.* Chicago: University of Chicago Press, 1999.

Lennard, John. *The Poetry Handbook: A Guide to Reading Poetry for Pleasure and Practical Criticism.* New York: Oxford University Press, 1996.

Matterson, Stephen, and Darryl Jones. *Studying Poetry.* New York: Oxford University Press, 2000.

Packard, William. *The Poet's Dictionary: A Handbook of Prosody and Poetic Devices.* New York: Harper & Row, 1989.

Preminger, Alex, et al., eds. *The New Princeton Encyclopedia of Poetry and Poetics.* 3d rev. ed. Princeton, N.J.: Princeton University Press, 1993.

Shipley, Joseph Twadell, ed. *Dictionary of World Literary Terms, Forms, Technique, Criticism.* Rev. ed. Boston: George Allen and Unwin, 1979.

INDEXES OF PRIMARY WORKS

Frankovich, Nicholas, ed. *The Columbia Granger's Index to Poetry in Anthologies.* 11th ed. New York: Columbia University Press, 1997.

_____. *The Columbia Granger's Index to Poetry in Collected and Selected Works.* New York: Columbia University Press, 1997.

Guy, Patricia. *A Women's Poetry Index.* Phoenix, Ariz.: Oryx Press, 1985.

Hazen, Edith P., ed. *Columbia Granger's Index to Poetry.* 10th ed. New York: Columbia University Press, 1994.

Hoffman, Herbert H., and Rita Ludwig Hoffman, comps. *International Index to Recorded Poetry*. New York: H. W. Wilson, 1983.

Kline, Victoria. *Last Lines: An Index to the Last Lines of Poetry*. 2 vols. Vol. 1, *Last Line Index, Title Index*; Vol. 2, *Author Index, Keyword Index*. New York: Facts On File, 1991.

Marcan, Peter. *Poetry Themes: A Bibliographical Index to Subject Anthologies and Related Criticisms in the English Language, 1875-1975*. Hamden, Conn.: Linnet Books, 1977.

Poem Finder. Great Neck, N.Y.: Roth, 2000.

POETICS, POETIC FORMS, AND GENRES

Attridge, Derek. *Poetic Rhythm: An Introduction*. New York: Cambridge University Press, 1995.

Brogan, T. V. F. *Verseform: A Comparative Bibliography*. Baltimore: Johns Hopkins University Press, 1989.

Fussell, Paul. *Poetic Meter and Poetic Form*. Rev. ed. New York: McGraw-Hill, 1979.

Hollander, John. *Rhyme's Reason*. 3d ed. New Haven, Conn.: Yale University Press, 2001.

Jackson, Guida M. *Traditional Epics: A Literary Companion*. New York: Oxford University Press, 1995.

Padgett, Ron, ed. *The Teachers and Writers Handbook of Poetic Forms*. 2d ed. New York: Teachers & Writers Collaborative, 2000.

Pinsky, Robert. *The Sounds of Poetry: A Brief Guide*. New York: Farrar, Straus and Giroux, 1998.

Preminger, Alex, and T. V. F. Brogan, eds. *New Princeton Encyclopedia of Poetry and Poetics*. 3d ed. Princeton, N.J.: Princeton University Press, 1993.

Spiller, Michael R. G. *The Sonnet Sequence: A Study of Its Strategies*. Studies in Literary Themes and Genres 13. New York: Twayne, 1997.

Turco, Lewis. *The New Book of Forms: A Handbook of Poetics*. Hanover, N.H.: University Press of New England, 1986.

Williams, Miller. *Patterns of Poetry: An Encyclopedia of Forms*. Baton Rouge: Louisiana State University Press, 1986.

POETRY OF JEWISH CULTURES

Alonso Schokel, Luis. *A Manual of Hebrew Poetics*. Subsidia Biblica 11. Rome: Editrice Pontificio Istituto Biblico, 1988.

Alter, Robert. *The Art of Biblical Poetry*. New York: Basic Books, 1985.

Burnshaw, Stanley, T. Carmi, and Ezra Spicehandler, eds. *The Modern Hebrew Poem Itself: From the Beginnings to the Present, Sixty-nine Poems in a New Presentation*. With new afterword, "Hebrew Poetry from 1965 to 1988." Cambridge, Mass.: Harvard University Press, 1989.

Gevirtz, Stanley. *Patterns in the Early Poetry of Israel*. Chicago: University of Chicago Press, 1963.

Kugel, James L. *The Great Poems of the Bible: A Reader's Companion with New Translations*. New York: Free Press, 1999.

Liptzin, Solomon. *A History of Yiddish Literature*. Middle Village, N.Y.: Jonathan David, 1985.

Madison, Charles Allan. *Yiddish Literature: Its Scope and Major Writers*. New York: F. Ungar, 1968.

O'Connor, M. *Hebrew Verse Structure*. Winona Lake, Ind.: Eisenbrauns, 1980.

Pagis, Dan. *Hebrew Poetry of the Middle Ages and the Renaissance*. Berkeley: University of California Press, 1991.

Petersen, David L., and Kent Harold Richards. *Interpreting Hebrew Poetry*. Minneapolis: Fortress Press, 1992.

Suleiman, Susan Rubin, and Éva Forgács, eds. *Contemporary Jewish Writing in Hungary: An Anthology*. Lincoln: University of Nebraska Press, 2003.

Watson, Wilfred G. E. *Classical Hebrew Poetry: A Guide to Its Techniques*. 2d ed. Sheffield, England: JSOT Press, 1986.

Wiener, Leo. *The History of Yiddish Literature in the Nineteenth Century*. 2d ed. New York: Hermon Press, 1972.

Zinberg, Israel. *Old Yiddish Literature from Its Origins to the Haskalah Period*. Translated and edited by Bernard Martin. Cincinnati: Hebrew Union College Press, 1975.

Maura Ives
Updated by Tracy Irons-Georges

GUIDE TO ONLINE RESOURCES

Web Sites

The following sites were visited by the editors of Salem Press in 2010. Because URLs frequently change, the accuracy of these addresses cannot be guaranteed; however, long-standing sites, such as those of colleges and universities, national organizations, and government agencies, generally maintain links when their sites are moved.

Academy of American Poets
http://www.poets.org
The mission of the Academy of American Poets is to "support American poets at all stages of their careers and to foster the appreciation of contemporary poetry." The academy's comprehensive Web site features information on poetic schools and movements; a Poetic Forms Database; an Online Poetry Classroom, with educator and teaching resources; an index of poets and poems; essays and interviews; general Web resources; links for further study; and more.

Contemporary British Writers
http://www.contemporarywriters.com/authors
Created by the British Council, this site offers profiles of living writers of the United Kingdom, the Republic of Ireland, and the Commonwealth. Information includes biographies, bibliographies, critical reviews, and news about literary prizes. Photographs are also featured. Users can search the site by author, genre, nationality, gender, publisher, book title, date of publication, and prize name and date.

LiteraryHistory.com
http://www.literaryhistory.com
This site is an excellent source of academic, scholarly, and critical literature about eighteenth, nineteenth, and twentieth century American and English writers. It provides individual pages for twentieth century literature and alphabetical lists of authors that link to articles, reviews, overviews, excerpts of works, teaching guides, podcasts, and other materials.

Literary Resources on the Net
http://andromeda.rutgers.edu/~jlynch/Lit
Jack Lynch of Rutgers University maintains this extensive collection of links to Web sites that are useful to researchers, including numerous sites about American and English literature. This collection is a good place to begin online research about poetry, as it

links to other sites with broad ranges of literary topics. The site is organized chronologically, with separate pages about twentieth century British and Irish literature. It also has
separate pages providing links to Web sites about American literature and to women's
literature and feminism.

LitWeb
http://litweb.net

LitWeb provides biographies of hundreds of world authors throughout history that
can be accessed through an alphabetical listing. The pages about each writer contain a
list of his or her works, suggestions for further reading, and illustrations. The site also
offers information about past and present winners of major literary prizes.

The Modern Word: Authors of the Libyrinth
http://www.themodernword.com/authors.html

The Modern Word site, although somewhat haphazard in its organization, provides a
great deal of critical information about writers. The "Authors of the Libyrinth" page is
very useful, linking author names to essays about them and other resources. The section
of the page headed "The Scriptorium" presents "an index of pages featuring writers who
have pushed the edges of their medium, combining literary talent with a sense of experimentation to produce some remarkable works of modern literature."

Outline of American Literature
http://www.america.gov/publications/books/outline-of-american-literature.html

This page of the America.gov site provides access to an electronic version of the ten-
chapter volume *Outline of American Literature*, a historical overview of poetry and
prose from colonial times to the present published by the Bureau of International Information Programs of the U.S. Department of State.

Poetry Foundation
http://www.poetryfoundation.org

The Poetry Foundation, publisher of *Poetry* magazine, is an independent literary organization. Its Web site offers links to essays; news; events; online poetry resources,
such as blogs, organizations, publications, and references and research; a glossary of literary terms; and a Learning Lab that includes poem guides and essays on poetics.

Poet's Corner
http://theotherpages.org/poems

The Poet's Corner, one of the oldest text resources on the Web, provides access to
about seven thousand works of poetry by several hundred different poets from around
the world. Indexes are arranged and searchable by title, name of poet, or subject. The

site also offers its own resources, including "Faces of the Poets"—a gallery of portraits—and "Lives of the Poets"—a growing collection of biographies.

Representative Poetry Online
http://rpo.library.utoronto.ca

This award-winning resource site, maintained by Ian Lancashire of the Department of English at the University of Toronto in Canada, has several thousand English-language poems by hundreds of poets. The collection is searchable by poet's name, title of work, first line of a poem, and keyword. The site also includes a time line, a glossary, essays, an extensive bibliography, and countless links organized by country and by subject.

Voice of the Shuttle
http://vos.ucsb.edu

One of the most complete and authoritative places for online information about literature, Voice of the Shuttle is maintained by professors and students in the English Department at the University of California, Santa Barbara. The site provides countless links to electronic books, academic journals, literary association Web sites, sites created by university professors, and many other resources.

Voices from the Gaps
http://voices.cla.umn.edu/

Voices from the Gaps is a site of the English Department at the University of Minnesota, dedicated to providing resources on the study of women artists of color, including writers. The site features a comprehensive index searchable by name, and it provides biographical information on each writer or artist and other resources for further study.

ELECTRONIC DATABASES

Electronic databases usually do not have their own URLs. Instead, public, college, and university libraries subscribe to these databases, provide links to them on their Web sites, and make them available to library card holders or other specified patrons. Readers can visit library Web sites or ask reference librarians to check on availability.

Canadian Literary Centre

Produced by EBSCO, the Canadian Literary Centre database contains full-text content from ECW Press, a Toronto-based publisher, including the titles in the publisher's Canadian fiction studies, Canadian biography, and Canadian writers and their works series; *ECW's Biographical Guide to Canadian Novelists*; and *George Woodcock's Introduction to Canadian Fiction*. Author biographies, essays and literary criticism, and book reviews are among the database's offerings.

Literary Reference Center

EBSCO's Literary Reference Center (LRC) is a comprehensive full-text database designed primarily to help high school and undergraduate students in English and the humanities with homework and research assignments about literature. The database contains massive amounts of information from reference works, books, literary journals, and other materials, including more than 31,000 plot summaries, synopses, and overviews of literary works; almost 100,000 essays and articles of literary criticism; about 140,000 author biographies; more than 605,000 book reviews; and more than 5,200 author interviews. It contains the entire contents of Salem Press's MagillOnLiterature Plus. Users can retrieve information by browsing a list of authors' names or titles of literary works; they can also use an advanced search engine to access information by numerous categories, including author name, gender, cultural identity, national identity, and the years in which he or she lived, or by literary title, character, locale, genre, and publication date. The Literary Reference Center also features a literary-historical time line, an encyclopedia of literature, and a glossary of literary terms.

MagillOnLiterature Plus

MagillOnLiterature Plus is a comprehensive, integrated literature database produced by Salem Press and available on the EBSCOhost platform. The database contains the full text of essays in Salem's many literature-related reference works, including *Masterplots*, *Cyclopedia of World Authors*, *Cyclopedia of Literary Characters*, *Cyclopedia of Literary Places*, *Critical Survey of Poetry*, *Critical Survey of Long Fiction*, *Critical Survey of Short Fiction*, *World Philosophers and Their Works*, *Magill's Literary Annual*, and *Magill's Book Reviews*. Among its contents are articles on more than 35,000 literary works and more than 8,500 poets, writers, dramatists, essayists, and philosophers; more than 1,000 images; and a glossary of more than 1,300 literary terms. The biographical essays include lists of authors' works and secondary bibliographies, and hundreds of overview essays examine and discuss literary genres, time periods, and national literatures.

Rebecca Kuzins
Updated by Desiree Dreeuws

GEOGRAPHICAL INDEX

CATEGORY INDEX

SUBJECT INDEX